North Carolina's Experience during the First World War

North Carolina's Experience during the First World War

Edited by
Shepherd W. McKinley
and
Steven Sabol

The University of Tennessee Press / Knoxville

All photographs are courtesy of the State Archives of North Carolina.

Library of Congress Cataloging-in-Publication Data
Names: McKinley, Shepherd W., editor. ⏐ Sabol, Steven, editor.
Title: North Carolina's experience during the First World War / edited by Shepherd
W. McKinley and Steven Sabol.
Description: First edition. ⏐ Knoxville: The University of Tennessee Press, [2018] ⏐
Includes bibliographical references and index. ⏐
Identifiers: LCCN 2018021892 (print) ⏐ LCCN 2018022240 (ebook) ⏐
ISBN 9781621904151 (pdf) ⏐ ISBN 9781621904144 (hardcover)
Subjects: LCSH: World War, 1914–1918—North Carolina. ⏐
North Carolina—History—20th century.
Classification: LCC D570.85.N8 (ebook) ⏐ LCC D570.85.N8 N67 2018 (print) ⏐
DDC 940.3/756—dc23
LC record available at https://lccn.loc.gov/2018021892

CONTENTS

Part 3: Memory

Part 4: Homefront

Part 5: Business and Labor

ILLUSTRATIONS

Photographs

Figures

Tables

ACKNOWLEDGMENTS

When we started this project in 2012, it is fair to say that we underestimated its complexities. Organizing an edited book means coordinating between multiple individuals and institutions. Too often, it can become a frustrating process, but that was not the case with this book. As editors, we benefitted from a truly cooperative group of scholars, all keen to produce a work that chronicles this important era in North Carolina's rich history. Indeed, the opportunity to work with so many talented scholars proved thoroughly enjoyable, and we believe it is evident throughout this collection.

Every book is a process, from conception to publication. Numerous people contributed their time, energy, enthusiasm, and labor to see it to fruition. We want to express our gratitude to our colleagues in the Department of History at the University of North Carolina at Charlotte, but in particular Dr. John David Smith, an early enthusiast for this project and one who consistently offered advice and encouragement. We also want to thank Jeff Crow, former Director of the North Carolina Office of Archives and History, for his willingness to write the introduction to this book.

During the development of this project, we joined several contributors to this volume in their participation at various conferences, including the American Historical Association and the North Carolina Historical Society. In 2017–2018, the Charlotte Mecklenburg Library sponsored several First World War related events at the Charlotte Museum of History in which some of our authors participated. These events, as well as others, greatly assisted the conceptual framing of this book, and we are sincerely indebted.

Special thanks go to Angela Robbins and her colleagues at Meredith College for hosting the 2017 Symposium on WWI, which featured many of our authors. In particular, we greatly appreciated the work of Provost Matthew Poslusny, Greg Vitarbo, Jackie Law, and the faculty and students of Meredith's Department of History; Veronique Machelidon and the faculty and students of the Department of Foreign Languages; and Carlyle Campbell Library, Media Services, Meredith Archives, Meredith Events, and Meredith Marketing.

We also want to express our tremendous gratitude to the staff at the North Carolina Department of Natural and Cultural Resources, especially the support provided by Kim Anderson and Matthew Peek.

Finally, but certainly not least, we greatly appreciate the faith and patience that our editors at the University of Tennessee Press exhibited as this book slowly evolved. Thomas Wells and Jon Boggs guided us through the process with consummate skill and professionalism, for which we will always be grateful. To anyone we failed to mention here, please know that your support and efforts are truly appreciated. Any shortcomings rest on our shoulders, not those of our contributors or editors.

INTRODUCTION

Jeffrey J. Crow

For the past century, North Carolina's role in the First World War has not been the subject of intense scholarly interest. To be sure, a number of excellent articles have appeared in the *North Carolina Historical Review* and other journals. The Office of Archives and History in the North Carolina Department of Natural and Cultural Resources has published three studies of the war that provide a general introduction to North Carolina's participation; compelling first-hand accounts by Tar Heel doughboys; and a visual cornucopia of images, artifacts, and documents commemorating the centennial of the Great War. Political figures who played prominent parts in the war have also received due attention. Josephus Daniels, publisher and editor of the *News and Observer* (Raleigh), helped elect Woodrow Wilson president in 1912 and then became Wilson's secretary of the navy. Walter Hines Page, a prominent journalist and publisher, served as ambassador to the Court of St. James under Wilson. Page, a noted Anglophile, made no pretense of neutrality despite Wilson's purported policy of evenhandedness toward the warring powers in Europe. Senator Furnifold M. Simmons provided critical support for Wilson's reforms in Congress, and Senator Lee S. Overman introduced and passed legislation giving Wilson extraordinary powers to coordinate the activities of various government agencies during wartime. Representative Claude Kitchin, who initially opposed the United States' entry into the war, served as majority leader of the House of Representatives.[1] Wilson himself had lived in the Tar Heel state, making the Presbyterian manse where his father pastored in Wilmington his home from 1874 to 1882. Wilson also attended Davidson College outside Charlotte in 1873.

Despite the important roles of North Carolinians in the Wilson administration and in prosecuting the war effort, the state itself was ill prepared for war. Its political, economic, educational, and social systems remained largely undeveloped compared with much of the rest of the nation. Race, class, and gender sharply defined those systems. When the First World War began, the state was less than two decades past the White Supremacy campaigns of 1898 and 1900. Those elections had engrafted on the state Democratic Party hegemony, disfranchisement of black and poor white voters, and de jure segregation. The war might well have become an agent of change; instead, the state's political system went largely unchallenged until the Civil Rights movement of the 1960s.

The war could potentially have had a greater impact on the economic and social life of the state than on the polity. Nominally, North Carolina appeared to be buoyed by the Progressive movement that inspired the nation and the region. But as historian C. Vann Woodward memorably stated, Progressivism was "for whites only." The African American community remained largely excluded from reforms and services benefiting the white community. After 1900 North Carolina greatly expanded education and built hundreds of new schools, but black education languished and remained decidedly separate and unequal.[2] The state did adopt prohibition in 1908, regarded as a Progressive reform, more than a decade before the Eighteenth Amendment was ratified, and North Carolina took steps to limit if not end child labor. But before the war, other reforms in health care and public services remained tenuous and unfulfilled.

The essays in this striking collection, skillfully edited by Shepherd W. McKinley and Steven Sabol, provide much greater texture and granularity to the interpretation of North Carolina's experience in the First World War. One theme woven through several essays addresses the increasing development of the modern state and the inexorable growth of bureaucracies to manage complex political, social, and economic arrangements in both the public and private sectors. As Lauren A. Austin and William P. Brandon point out, bureaucracy necessarily followed the expansion of public health care. Before the war the state's public health care system was rudimentary at best. The influenza pandemic of 1918–1919 and presence of military camps spurred public health efforts. Austin and Brandon highlight the role of Watson Smith Rankin in the extension of health care services to rural areas. After the war, the Duke Endowment and federal assistance ensured the expansion of hospitals across the state.

In a complementary essay, Pamela C. Edwards argues that health care for veterans brought North Carolina into a closer relationship with the federal government. The low educational attainment of both black and white soldiers shocked military officials. In 1900 North Carolina led the nation in illiteracy rates for both races. One in five whites and one in two blacks could not read or write. Regardless, the rigors of war and camp life had a profound effect on the overall health of Tar Heel doughboys. The flu pandemic spread quickly in military camps. The most common reasons for discharging soldiers, says Edwards, were tuberculosis and Post Traumatic Stress Disorder, although this term did not emerge to describe its symptoms until well after World War II. It is clear that the needs of such veterans did not disappear with the end of the war.

James S. Bissett analyzes how the North Carolina Council of Defense and its subsidiaries attempted to mobilize the state's economy for war. Largely unsuccessful in that effort, the council proved more successful in organizing draft registration and dealing with deserters and draft dodgers. The council, Bissett contends, also tried to enforce "one hundred percent Americanism" by stifling dissent and reporting "disloyal" comments by those opposed to the United States' entry into the war.

Elaborating on the theme of disloyalty, Gary R. Freeze offers the unknown story of disaffection among German descendants in the Piedmont. Surprisingly, although they were many generations removed from colonial settlement, German descendants often felt a strong affinity for Germany and German *Kultur*. In rural areas that had studiously avoided the single-crop agriculture that characterized much of southern farming, at German-based colleges, and in Lutheran and German Reformed churches, pockets of disaffected people opposed the draft. Not coincidentally, in Freeze's judgment, some of those areas, especially Davidson County, had harbored deserters and anti-Confederate groups such as the Heroes of America during the Civil War.[3] As the novelist William Faulkner said, the past is not dead; it is not even past.

Traditionally, African Americans and women have been left out of the state's grand narrative. Several essayists pointedly remind us of what those groups contributed to the war effort. Jerra Jenrette's essay follows more than two hundred North Carolina women to Europe where they served as nurses during the war. On the home front, Angela Robbins discusses women's organizations such as the North Carolina Federation of Women's Clubs that took the lead in local councils of defense and Liberty Loan drives. Yet women's roles remained limited. They practiced "social housekeeping" and focused on social welfare and reform. Strictly segregated, African American women nonetheless supported the war effort despite the decision of the North Carolina Council of Defense not to create a "Negro" council. The North Carolina College for Women in Greensboro and Meredith College in Raleigh, Robbins demonstrates, became hotbeds of agitation for woman's suffrage. The Nineteenth Amendment, ratified in 1920 shortly after the war ended, became a lasting legacy of the First World War despite North Carolina's abject failure to ratify it. Governor Thomas Walter Bickett and US Senators Furnifold Simmons and Lee Overman opposed woman's suffrage. With an opportunity to deliver the thirty-sixth and final state for ratification in 1920, the North Carolina General Assembly rejected the amendment. That honor went to Tennessee, and North Carolina did not ratify the amendment until 1971.

The economic effect of the First World War on North Carolina could be measured in two ways: domestic spending that briefly stimulated the textile and tobacco industries and military spending that established three training camps in the state, two temporary and one permanent. The two seemingly disparate economic developments were actually related. The First World War fueled a textile boom in North Carolina. As Annette Cox notes, it ranked third in textile production, trailing only Massachusetts and South Carolina. The military was the chief customer, but the textile market also expanded into Latin America. However, the boom was short lived. Higher wages and labor shortages, Cox argues, ended in the 1920s. Overproduction, reduced wages, and labor unrest resulted in mill owners' moving to scientific management.

Similarly, tobacco farmers and manufacturers enjoyed widespread expansion during the war. Evan P. Bennett documents the surge in demand for tobacco, tripling production to 48 billion cigarettes between 1914 and 1920. Farmers switched from cotton to tobacco as Durham and Winston-Salem, the chief centers for production of cigarettes, accounted for 29 percent of the state's production. Just as in the textile industry, however, the tobacco boom collapsed with the end of the war. Reforms in managing overproduction of tobacco, Bennett posits, would have to await the New Deal in the 1930s.

To overcome labor shortages during the war, mill owners began to hire black workers who traditionally had been excluded from textile mills. Such potentially revolutionary change did not last. As Pamela C. Edwards cogently remarks, the First World War was less a turning point for labor in North Carolina than a missed opportunity. Organized labor and collective bargaining could not overcome racial caste and rigid class distinctions. Edwards details the distrust that existed between middle class whites and the laboring classes, both black and white. Laborers were less likely to receive deferments or honorable discharges for hardships. They were expected to work full time in the mills or go into the draft. Towns issued "work or fight" ordinances to discourage "slackers" and "vagrants." When the war ended, only child labor experienced improvements (although limited) by raising the minimum age for employment to fourteen. For other workers, not much had changed.

In agriculture the same rigid racial divisions remained uninterrupted. Hugh MacRae, an agricultural reformer, wanted to bring scientific efficiency to farming. He had participated in the Wilmington Race Riot of 1898, a coup d'état that forced from office Republicans and African Americans. As J. Vincent Lowery observes, MacRae regarded African Americans as incapable of adopting such scientific practices. He wanted to marginalize black labor by bringing in European immigrants or creating farm settlements for returning white veterans. MacRae's ambitious plans persisted into the New Deal era. But his racial attitudes reflected white society at large. They echoed those of Clarence Poe, editor of the *Progressive Farmer* (Raleigh). Between 1913 and 1915, on the eve of the First World War, Poe had led a crusade to establish rural seg-regation throughout the South.[4]

The military's impact on North Carolina—economically, politically, and socially—proved the most permanent outcome of the war. Lee A. Craig, Josephus Daniels's biographer, examines the Raleigh newspaperman's tenure as secretary of the navy and Wilson's close adviser. Jonathan F. Phillips ex-plains how Fort Bragg in Fayetteville became an artillery training center that would outlast the war. Civic boosters in the town had long sought a military installation, and military planners determined that the Sandhills handsomely met their criteria. Camp Greene in Charlotte, however, proved temporary. Kurt D. Geske describes how the racial makeup of the training camp changed between 1917 and 1919. In September 1918, African Americans composed nearly one-half of the camp. By the time the camp closed in 1919, African Americans, ravaged by the flu pandemic, comprised the overwhelming ma-jority. After eagerly wooing the training camp to Charlotte, the white commu-nity voiced little opposition to its closure. Camp Polk in Raleigh, never fully completed for tank training, also closed after the war.

In a remarkable feat of research and analysis, Janet G. Hudson explores the military service of the 20,000 Tar Heel blacks that donned uniforms during the First World War. Using the World War I Service Card file in the North Caro-lina State Archives, she compiled a database of all soldiers labeled "colored." From that database, she made a random selection of 1,500 soldiers. About 10 percent of the African Americans saw combat, but all who served faced discrimination.

Politically, Karl E. Campbell posits, the First World War shaped two gen-erations of politicians: those who came to power in the first quarter of the twentieth century, and those who ruled from the Great Depression to the 1950s. Governor Bickett (1917–1921) earned a reputation as a Progressive. A veteran of the White Supremacy campaigns of 1898 and 1900, Bickett espoused the racial dogmas of the day. But under his administration, Campbell argues, business progressivism began. It would reach a zenith during the 1920s with the expansion of government services, good roads, and educational reforms. Campbell, biographer of Senator Sam Ervin, also includes a poignant de-scription of Ervin's combat experience. Other North Carolina politicians who served in the war, such as governors Gregg Cherry and Luther Hodges, would play prominent roles in post-World War II politics. In a sense, they tracked the political career of another World War I veteran—Harry S. Truman.

Two essays explore the war's impact on the cultural life of the state. Shannon Bontrager deconstructs the World War I collection in the North Carolina State Archives. He finds a collection that reflected whites' cultural memory and valorized white elites who upheld the ideals of the Lost Cause. In particular he emphasizes the work of Robert B. House, who, having served in the war, decided what got collected and who collected it. Efforts to recruit local African Americans to document what their community did in the war proved largely unsuccessful. Bontrager believes the collection reflects a segregated society and the influence of such prominent cultural leaders and educators as D. H. Hill Jr., Robert D. W. Connor, and House. Interestingly, a number of essays in this anthology rely heavily on the Archives' World War I collection for sources and evidence.

Melissa Edmundson takes an intimate look at the literary output of North Carolina soldiers, including memoirs, letters, books, articles, and plays. She finds that works more contemporaneous with the war displayed greater patriotic fervor and even sympathy for the hated Huns. The farther removed writers became from the war, however, more anti-war, more bitter, and even pacifist the writings became. Paul Green, who won the 1927 Pulitzer Prize for his play *In Abraham's Bosom*, knew combat. For him it held no illusions of honor and glory. His 1936 Broadway play *Johnny Johnson* epitomized the interwar years' cynicism about war and a rising anti-war sentiment that preceded the Second World War.

So collectively what does this excellent collection tell us about North Carolina's experience in the First World War? As Pamela C. Edwards suggests in her essay on labor, it was more a lost opportunity than a transformative moment. Race, and more particularly white supremacy, was the irreducible element that affected all parts of society. Class and gender, too, defined social and economic relationships. North Carolina was a poor state and would continue to be so until long after the Second World War. War sometimes disrupts such regimes, but despite the First World War not much changed in the Tar Heel state. Race relations remained precarious. Riots broke out in Winston-Salem and Fayetteville near the end of the war. Agriculture still relied on small producers, including a phalanx of tenants and sharecroppers. The tobacco, furniture, and textile industries brought jobs and dollars to North Carolina's increasingly prosperous towns and cities, but workers earned relatively low wages, depended on mill owners' paternalism, and failed to challenge the economic hierarchy until the labor unrest of 1929–1934 brought on by the Great Depression.

What did change was the relationship between business and government. Government became an increasingly important part of the fabric of society and the economy. A century later, Fort Bragg remains the largest military base in the United States. Business progressivism during the 1920s promoted economic growth with better education, good roads, increased public services, cheap non-union labor, and segregation. The Progressive Plutocracy that political scientist V. O. Key Jr. identified in 1949 had its origins in the First World War.[5] Beginning with Thomas Walter Bickett, North Carolina established a pattern of electing governors from a class of moderately conservative lawyers and businessmen, friendly to business and willing to assist commerce and agriculture with the powers of government. With only a few exceptions, that pattern would persist for the next century. As the essays in this anthology make clear, wars provide the opportunity for unsettling the *ancien régime*. Yet old ways die hard. Unlike the Civil War and Second World War, the First World War would have relatively little effect on North Carolina's race relations, class arrangements, women's roles, economic order, and political leadership. But for those men and women who served in the war or families that lost loved ones, the "war to end all wars" would not be forgotten.

Notes

1. Sarah McCulloh Lemmon and Nancy Smith Midgette, *North Carolina and the Two World Wars* (Raleigh: Department of Cultural Resources, 2013); R. Jackson Marshall III, *Memories of World War I: North Carolina Doughboys on the Western Front* (Raleigh: Department of Cultural Resources, 1998); Jessica A. Bandel, *North Carolina in the Great War, 1914–1918* (Raleigh: Department of Natural and Cultural Resources, distributed by the University of North Carolina Press, 2017); Lee Craig, *Josephus Daniels: His Life and Times* (Chapel Hill: University of North Carolina Press, 2013); John Milton Cooper Jr., *Walter Hines Page: The Southerner as American* (Chapel Hill: University of North Carolina Press, 1977); Richard L. Watson Jr., "A Testing Time for Southern Congressional Leadership: The War Crisis of 1917–1918," *Journal of Southern History* 44 (February 1978): 3–40.

2. J. Morgan Kousser, "Progressivism—For Middle-Class Whites Only: North Carolina Education, 1880–1910," *Journal of Southern History* 46 (May 1980): 169–194.

3. William T. Auman, *Civil War in the North Carolina Quaker Belt: The Confederate Campaign against Peace Agitators, Deserters, and Draft Dodgers* (Jefferson, NC: McFarland, 2014); Paul D. Escott and Jeffrey J. Crow, "The Social Order and Violent Disorder: An Analysis of North Carolina in the Revolution and Civil War," *Journal of Southern History* 52 (August 1986): 373–402.

4. David S. Cecelski and Timothy B. Tyson, eds., *Democracy Betrayed: The Wilmington Race Riot of 1898 and Its Legacy* (Chapel Hill: University of North Carolina Press, 1998); LeRae S. Umfleet, *A Day of Blood: The 1898 Wilmington Race Riot* (Raleigh: Department of Cultural Resources, 2009); Jeffrey J. Crow, "An Apartheid for the South: Clarence Poe's Crusade for Rural Segregation," in *Race, Class, and Politics in Southern History: Essays in Honor of Robert F. Durden*, ed. Jeffrey J. Crow, Paul D. Escott, and Charles L. Flynn Jr. (Baton Rouge: Louisiana State University, 1989), 216–259; Jeffrey J. Crow, Paul D. Escott, and Flora J. Hatley, *A History of African Americans in North Carolina* (Raleigh: Department of Cultural Resources, 1992), 122.

5. V. O. Key Jr., *Southern Politics in State and Nation* (New York: Knopf, 1949).

North Carolina's Experience during the First World War

PART ONE

Military

"Now It Is All Good and Better"

Fayetteville and the Origins of Fort Bragg

Jonathan F. Phillips

In 1919, if a reporter had asked the US Army's chief of field artillery and the president of the Fayetteville Chamber of Commerce how and why Fort Bragg was established in 1918, its intended purpose, and why it was located in the Sandhills of North Carolina, the two would have replied with very different answers despite their similar motives and goals. Both men, as well as the institutions they represented, desperately wanted the post to be established; both men had worked for years, even decades, for such an installation; both men wanted Fort Bragg to call the Sandhills home; and both men had sound reasons and a substantial body of knowledge to call upon in support of their answer. Nevertheless, these men had entirely different notions of the process of and reasons for the creation of the army post. Thus, there are really *two* histories of the origins of Fort Bragg, one based on military operational requirements (i.e., the military view) and the other the result of a long-term campaign to promote Fayetteville as a New South city on the rise (i.e., the booster view).

The creation of Fort Bragg and the other "superbases" of 1918 (Forts Benning and Knox, in Georgia and Kentucky, respectively) transformed vast portions of the American landscape and signaled the beginning of a militarized homefront that became a permanent feature of American life in the twentieth century, especially in the South. Unlike the training camps established immediately after the United States formally entered hostilities in 1917, the superbases created in the summer of 1918 were designed and constructed to be permanent. The continued existence of wartime training installations *after the conclusion of hostilities* was something new in the nation and certainly a surprise to residents of the upper Cape Fear region of North Carolina. Due to the boom and bust nature of land force mobilization and demobilization in all of America's wars to this point, civilians in 1918 did not foresee a permanent change to the nation's landscape, even though communities such as Fayetteville had long pursued economic development strategies designed to attract permanent military installations as well as other national government projects.

Military leaders, of course, had urged the government to build the super-bases of 1918. Senior American field artillerists and military thinkers such as Chief of Field Artillery William J. Snow had spent the previous two decades seeking to establish permanent training reservations for the testing of new weapons and doctrine as a result of what was dubbed the "artillery revolution" and to transmit "lessons learned" from recent wars in the quest to prepare American field artillery units for modern warfare. The exigencies of the Great War provided the US Army's Field Artillery Branch with the opportunity in 1918 to create the training facilities it had long desired, and North Carolina Sandhills offered the appropriate terrain, soil, and transportation routes that the artillerists needed. For General Snow, the reasons for building Fort Bragg were obvious: the new installation matched the military requirements of a great power in the modern era and the associated mission and doctrine of field artillery.

Fayetteville's boosters *also* had spent twenty years working towards a goal; local leaders sought to create an "upper Cape Fear Metropolis," as they called it, supported in large part by national government funding. Chamber President William Sutton and his predecessors, in their quest to secure some type of defense-related facility for their town, had pushed for a new arsenal in 1896 on the grounds of an 1830s arsenal, and had tried but failed to secure an encampment during the War of 1898, an armor plate plant in 1916, a national army cantonment and a national guard camp in the summer of 1917 (as well as an artillery range), and a military depot in early January 1918.[1] Thus, it is hardly surprising that many locals believed that their long-term efforts to convey the merits of their community as a host for the military had been decisive in the War Department's decision to establish a field artillery camp near the town in the summer of 1918.[2] As this essay will demonstrate, military necessity—and not local boosterism—created Fort Bragg.

In the summer of 1917, William J. Snow, then a Colonel, reported to Fort Sill, Oklahoma, and took command of stateside artillery training. He soon developed plans for establishing additional training facilities. In September, he was transferred to Columbia, South Carolina, to command a brigade of artillery at recently established Camp Jackson. On February 10, 1918, Snow was promoted into a new position created by the War Department, chief of field artillery, and immediately reported to Washington, DC. He soon began a search for firing ranges east of the Mississippi.[3] Snow first considered land he knew well. Since 1903, army units posted near Louisville, Kentucky, had leased several thousand acres twenty-five miles to the south at West Point, known as Camp Young, for maneuvers. Snow arranged to meet local decision makers and, with surprising ease, the army secured much of the land in a very short time.[4] In addition to the West Point site, now known as Fort Knox, Snow created firing ranges at three existing facilities: Camp Doniphan, Oklahoma; Camp Jackson, South Carolina; and Camp McClellan, Alabama. McClellan's size, a mere 16,000 acres, was insufficient for modern artillery ranges.[5]

Snow then began his search for a firing ground to replace McClellan. Due to railroad traffic and seaport congestion in the North, Army Chief of Staff General Peyton C. March ordered Snow to limit his search to the South. In June 1918, Snow directed Colonel Edward P. King Jr. to head south from Washington, DC, to find a suitable location.[6] Dr. T. Wayland Vaughan, a geologist, accompanied the colonel. Vaughan instructed Colonel King to follow a route south and west, over the sandy ridges at the western extremity of the Coastal Plain. As King would testify in the early 1920s, his top priority was finding a large parcel of land that was not used extensively for agriculture, was not bisected by a major railroad, had few natural obstacles such as streams or creeks that would limit the movement of troops and equipment, and had the varied terrain preferred for artillery training. Eventually, King and Vaughan reached a large area, approximately twelve by twenty-five miles, of largely cut-over turpentine land to the northwest of Fayetteville. With support from locals, they concluded that this parcel fulfilled the artillery's requirements. Snow then toured the property and agreed with his search team's assessment.[7] On July 1, 1918, General Snow formally submitted his request to General March to make this plot a site for a field artillery cantonment.[8]

He had, however, one more obstacle. When Snow submitted his report, General March replied that he supported the decision but noted that the Infantry Board was interested in the parcel as well. As Snow recounted in his memoirs, he had forgotten about the Infantry's parallel search. Snow then learned that the Infantry Board preferred a site (now Fort Benning) near Columbus, Georgia. His staff examined the Georgia site and found it adequate but inferior to the North Carolina location; Snow would have taken either site. The Infantry Board remained undecided, so Snow took the initiative and secured the North Carolina location for field artillery training.[9] On August 21, 1918, the War Department issued General Order 77 establishing the field artillery site near Fayetteville and naming it for North Carolina native Braxton Bragg, a captain of artillery in the Mexican War who distinguished himself at the Battle of Buena Vista.[10]

In 1916, Fayetteville's boosters did not overly concern themselves with the national and international implications of America's possible involvement in the Great War.[11] The capital of the upper Cape Fear looked at the war as a chance to make up for lost time and to succeed after countless missed opportunities in its quest for greater economic development. Certainly, if the decidedly pro-booster *Fayetteville* (North Carolina) *Observer*'s account can be accepted, the town was truly a New South city on the rise by 1916. The *Observer* trumpeted Fayetteville as "one of the most progressive cities in the state," the site of a "great revival . . . [and] increase in business, home to a new flour mill and a building and loan association, and a revived department store."[12] The *Observer*'s editors wrote optimistically of the soon-to-be completed and federally funded Cape Fear canal project and expected a "wave of prosperity" that would result in the creation of a "metropolis" in the upper Cape Fear region.[13] "Nature formerly gave certain countries and cities peculiar commercial advantages," argued the *Observer* in May 1916, "but the peoples and communities that expect to maintain their position because of the nearness to a given point or port, soon find their natural superiority challenged and frequently discounted by rivals. . . . [T]owns can no longer lie back and wait for commerce to put in an appearance."[14] *Observer* writers presented Fayetteville and environs as a veritable Garden of Eden with a modern transportation network and good schools. But as much as anything, Fayetteville's strength rested upon its "moral, law-abiding and hospitable" citizenship, unsurpassed in any city, South or North.[15]

The *Observer* read much like a booster pamphlet. Dreaming big, the small newspaper even had an office in New York.[16] The *Observer*'s mission was the "Selling of the South," to borrow historian James Cobb's phrase, or at least the selling of a small part of the South. This phenomenon happened throughout the South as "state frantically sought to out do state, town to out do town," as writer W.J. Cash noted, "at once to further the great common enterprise and to get the lion's share of the new industry and commerce for themselves. . . ."[17]

But Fayetteville needed more than starry rhetoric and enthusiasm to prevail. Success *also* required *preparedness* on the part of the citizenry. The *Observer* urged its readers to prepare themselves both mentally and physically for the rigors of the business world, "something most have not been doing very well."[18] Of course, Fayettevillians read and heard the term preparedness employed most often by the Wilson administration and in the context of the World War. And, although the most vilified enemy in 1916 was Mexican raider Pancho Villa and not the Kaiser, the war in Europe dominated headlines.[19] *Observer* editors argued that the United States should entangle itself in a war among European powers only as the last option, but the sense of inevitability was palpable. "The die has been cast," noted an April 1916 editorial, "and Uncle Sam is getting ready, whether such a step is wise or unwise." Reinforcing its ambivalence to the approaching crisis, the *Observer* wrote cheerful accounts of martial activities of local residents while it sympathetically described the symbol of an anti-preparedness group—"Jingo," an imitation dinosaur, about to embark on a nationwide tour. Jingo, according to the report, represented "too much armor."[20] For many Americans, the industrialists who manufactured armor plate and munitions were largely responsible for the war in Europe. The *Observer* never reported the arrival of Jingo in Fayetteville during the summer of 1916. Certainly by September, the dinosaur, or anyone who shared its views, would most likely not have been welcome in the upper Cape Fear city. In an odd twist of history, the city that became one of America's best-known army towns mentally prepared itself for that eventual result by working desperately to secure a large *naval* armor plate factory.

How did a southern town with anti-munitions inclinations come to embrace Big Steel? Fayetteville, like much of the South, seems not to have been as staunchly opposed to a armor plate plant if it was government owned. Since the navy had created a bona fide steel fleet, southern leaders had accused the producers of price fixing. Democratic Senator Benjamin "Pitchfork" Tillman of South Carolina had railed against the armor trust for almost twenty years, always suspecting collusion among steel manufacturers and acceptance of this behavior by Republican administrators.[21] With the election of Democrat Woodrow Wilson in 1912, Republicans lost their stranglehold on the procurement process, and anti-trust activists hoped that, for once, the government would conduct an investigation of armor plate bidding.[22]

The new secretary of the navy, North Carolinian Josephus Daniels, embraced the investigation of steel companies. As editor and owner of the *News & Observer* (Raleigh, NC), Daniels had been an outspoken critic of trusts of all kinds. As secretary, he soon had the manufacturers' collusion strategy explained to him in correspondence from an unlikely source. In April 1913, Daniels received a letter from Eugene Grace, the president of the Bethlehem Steel Corporation. Grace claimed that it had long been the policy of the navy department to divvy up large orders among multiple firms with the expectation that these companies would enhance their manufacturing capability. Grace added that the bidders also worked together on pricing; high bidders would reduce their price to that submitted by the lowest. If Grace had stopped here, Daniels might well have considered this policy to be reasonable even if it did not adhere to the letter of the law. Grace, however, further explained that "in view of [this] practice, it has come to be understood that the naming of the lower figure by him [the low bidder] would merely lower the price that he and each one of his competitors would receive for part of the order." Therefore, the armor plate manufacturers colluded on the low bid, making sure that it was not low at all.[23] As a result of Grace's letter, Secretary Daniels concluded that the solution might well be a government-owned armor plate and projectile plant.[24]

By 1916, the battle between public and private interests had intensified. Many opposed the armor trust but also feared excessive federal power and unnecessary spending, or "pork." North Carolinian Arthur Page, editor of the monthly magazine *World's Work* and son of Walter Hines Page, ambassador to the Court of Saint James, wrote in January, "Every district that thought it might have a dockyard or an arsenal would send its representative to Congress pledged to produce armament in that district." Eventually, he concluded, "the production of armament would take its place with the work on rivers and harbors, with the granting of special pensions, with the erection of unnecessary public buildings, with the maintenance of useless army posts—it would take first rank in the pork barrel."[25] Page's list of "pork projects" mirrored Fayetteville's wish list. Boosters hoped that their city would achieve "first rank."

Ultimately, the anti-government, anti-preparedness ideology expressed by Page could not compete in practical terms with opportunities for economic advancement.[26] Like most southerners, Fayetteville's leaders proved quite selective in their denunciation of the expansion of federal power. Where federal programs threatened the social, political, or economic hierarchy, such as in the realm of race relations, elections, and labor laws, local power brokers responded with customary southern white intransigence.[27] Boosters were far less critical of programs such as the armor plate and projectile plant because it did not challenge the existing social and economic order.

National public opinion turned in favor of the government-owned plant when the steel trust threatened to raise the price of armor by $200 a ton.[28] The Baltimore *Manufacturers' Record*, an influential business journal in the South, considered the armor trust's announcement to be "one of the most unfortunate statements ever issued in this country by any great business organization dealing with the government."[29] The *Fayetteville Observer* reacted like many newspapers nationwide, declaring that " . . . the plate manufacturers, evidently regarding themselves as separate and distinct from the people, threaten to do all in their power to retard preparedness if they are not allowed to grow richer by having a monopoly of armor plate."[30]

After the passage of a naval bill authorizing purchase or construction of an armor plate and projectile plant was reported in the *Observer* on June 7, 1916, the Fayetteville Chamber of Commerce dispatched a flurry of letters to Secretary Daniels. He responded by directing the chamber to submit its brief to the General Naval Board before September 13, 1916. In the first few weeks of September 1916, the General Board received briefs from towns and cities nationwide. In addition, many jurisdictions, including Fayetteville, sent delegations to Washington, DC.[31]

Local residents did not have to travel far to see how wartime could transform a regional economy. In 1916, Fayetteville's boosters looked admiringly at a boom town near Petersburg, Virginia, optimistically named Hopewell. In just eighteen months, the hamlet beside a small gunpowder factory at the confluence of the James and Appomattox Rivers transformed itself into a beehive of activity, growing its population to nearly 25,000. The reason for Hopewell's "explosion" was the extraordinary expansion of that factory into the massive DuPont powder mills.[32] For the *Observer*, this was "proof of the saying that 'labor follows capital,' and is an object lesson of the South to bid for capital first" and then watch as the value of local real estate rises.[33] Boosters gave little thought to the ephemeral nature of the munitions industry, which often caused wartime boom towns to bust in peacetime.

Although inspired by the federal government's need for munitions, the plant at Hopewell was privately owned and operated and located in Hopewell due to the presence of a previously existing facility. Fayetteville's economy was grounded in commerce, textile manufacturing, and agriculture. The town simply did not have a heavy industrial base upon which to build. In addition, industrial development required capital mobilization. "Labor may follow capital," as the *Observer* noted, but Fayetteville could not generate sufficient funds for such private-sector development.[34]

Fortunately, southern port towns provided more relevant models of defense-related economic development. Charleston, South Carolina, and Norfolk, Virginia, evolved from mid-sized seaports into federally funded naval shipbuilding centers in the early twentieth century.[35] Like Fayetteville, Charleston and Norfolk had no substantial industrial base. In fact, if either town had had a substantial private-sector industrial base, it could not have challenged the supremacy of existing industry by luring a publicly financed facility.[36] What each city did have was a prominent Democratic senator—Benjamin Tillman of South Carolina and Claude Swanson of Virginia—serving as its spokesman and advocate in Washington. Charleston's example proved particularly instructive. Like Fayetteville's boosters, Charlestonians' experience in securing river and harbor improvements had prepared them well for a public relations effort to attract naval facilities.[37] Yet Fayetteville's effort differed from the seaport campaign in that it was led by local boosters, not politicians of national stature.

Fayetteville was well suited for the government's armor plate plant. After several years of ongoing improvements at the federal government's expense, the Cape Fear River had become far more reliable as a transportation route. Three major railroads passed through or near the city. Coal and iron ore were located nearby. The city enjoyed an abundant labor supply and inexpensive river front land. In addition, Fayetteville's Chamber of Commerce enjoyed widespread support of the project in both the region and the state. The town's elder residents, although a little unsure about the long-term effect of such an undertaking, favored the plant as well, perhaps as a step toward a better future but also as a return to the glory years. "We do not know what the Old Market House and the FILI [the Fayetteville Independent Light Infantry, a local militia unit started in the 1790s] Majors . . . think of an invasion of steel workers in overalls on [downtown] Hay Street," commented the Raleigh *Times*, "but the old Fayetteville has managed so well against adversity that it could never be smothered in a new one."[38] And perhaps the Navy, with its armor plate plant, could make amends for the Union Army's destruction of the town's beloved arsenal in 1865, as one letter writer from the Fayetteville suburb of Hope Mills suggested.[39]

Considering North Carolina's geographic layout, Fayetteville's statewide support was not really surprising. Charlotte, Raleigh, and Durham did not have access to adequate water transportation. Wilmington, the state's only port city accessible to major shipping, was located too far from the Chatham coal fields and iron ore deposits of the Piedmont. In addition, although the navy preferred coastal sites for convenience and most port towns were known quantities to mariners, many civilian officials desired an inland site less vulnerable to enemy attack. Fayetteville also had history on its side as the home of an antebellum federal arsenal. Lastly, in some circles in North Carolina, people sensed that Fayetteville was due. "In spite of abundant water power, in spite of an energetic spirit," commented the Raleigh *Times*, "it has been left, with its natural advantages of position and resources, somewhat aside from the march of development. An armor plant . . . would give it the added impetus necessary to realize the hope that it has been working out for itself."[40]

Regardless of Fayetteville's "natural advantages" or the feeling that the city was somehow due, the Chamber of Commerce embarked upon an aggressive promotional campaign with a two-fold purpose. The primary goal was, of course, to convince the Navy Department to select the Fayetteville area for location of its new armor plate and projectile plant. If this effort at public-sector development came to fruition, then private-sector development, they believed, would follow. Fayetteville's second purpose was to promote the upper Cape Fear area by riding the wave of media attention created as a result of the armor plate debate in Congress. If Fayetteville was mentioned in the same breath, or listed in the same newspaper column, with New York, Birmingham, Baltimore, Cincinnati, and Petersburg, the promotional campaign would prove successful, and industry might be attracted to the upper Cape Fear valley even if the armor plate plant was constructed elsewhere.[41]

Fayetteville solicited and received the support of the entire North Carolina congressional delegation.[42] The town's congressional representative, Hannibal Lafayette Godwin of Dunn, worked tirelessly as did Congressman John Humphrey Small of Washington, North Carolina, Chairman of the Rivers and Harbors Committee in the House of Representatives and the elected official most responsible for the Cape Fear River improvements.[43] Most notably, Congressmen Claude Kitchin of Scotland Neck, House Majority Leader and outspoken "anti-militarist" and opponent of just about any navy or army project, endorsed the project.[44] Senator Furnifold M. Simmons, a member of both the Commerce and Finance committees, also threw his considerable weight behind Fayetteville's booster effort.[45]

Over the course of just a few days, Secretary Daniels' General Naval Board heard presentations by countless cities and towns and reviewed proposals from across the nation. Even with statewide support, Fayetteville competed against several other Tar Heel towns.[46] The *Army and Navy Register*, a Washington, DC-based weekly journal devoted to military issues, dismissed the hearings as little more than "an opportunity for local 'boosting' committees to come up to Washington [for] . . . speech-making that went from one extreme to the other. . . ."[47] "All the 'boosting' in which local committees have indulged," commented the October 7th *Register*, "counts for nothing and cannot be expected to influence those with whom the responsibility of the selection of a site finally rests."[48] The *Register*'s views influenced national newspapers such as the *New York Times*, which quoted the journal extensively and considered the proceedings "a waste of time."[49] Optimistic early accounts considered Fayetteville to be one of the leading candidates for the plant, but others suggested the town would likely lose out to an existing maritime facility such as the Philadelphia Naval Yard, or to a location like long-time frontrunner Birmingham, Alabama, where the industrial infrastructure was already in place.[50]

In December 1916, Fayetteville learned that it lost the competition for the plant because the Army War College principle of September 11, 1915, stated that the facility could not be within two hundred miles of a coast or border.[51] Why the War College principle became part of the evaluation criteria after the September hearings is open to conjecture. Although the timing suggested conspiracy, it may well have been that the General Board had overlooked that criteria early on. After all, according to the *Register*, the principle originated at the Army War College and not the navy's school in Newport, Rhode Island. The use of the principle did eliminate all port towns from contention, thus weakening the uniformed officers' hold on the process.

Those who predicted that the plant would never be constructed proved incorrect, as the boosters of Charleston, West Virginia, learned in April 1917.[52] The plant eventually employed a few thousand civilians and a small contingent of uniformed personnel. By the late 1920s, however, little more than the skeleton of the once-mighty Naval Plant and Projectile Factory remained.[53] Fayetteville never realized its dream of becoming another Hopewell,[54] but, fortunately, the upper Cape Fear city was saved from becoming another Charleston, West Virginia.

In the early months of 1917, the Chamber of Commerce and the *Observer* tried to put a positive spin on the failed campaign by emphasizing the awareness gained for the region.[55] Although the primary goal had not been achieved, Fayetteville was now recognized as a New South town worthy of greater investment.[56] As the nation moved ever closer to armed conflict in Europe, more and better opportunities might arise. The advantage lay with those who were prepared. Boosters who had their promotional plans at the ready might well win out over less- organized towns.

Compared to Fayetteville's economic expectations for the armor plate factory, the predictions for a local army post in 1917 reached new heights of hyperbole. "If Fayetteville [with a population of 12,000] should be so fortunate as to get an army camp," contended an *Observer* editorial, "the town's . . . monthly payroll would be equal to that of a city of about 230,000 inhabitants."[57] The *Observer* commented, "When a military camp was placed in Tampa, Florida, during the Spanish–American War, the little town began to grow, and today it is the second largest and wealthiest city in Florida." El Paso, by virtue of proximity to the Mexican border and the campaign to capture Pancho Villa, also gained the attention of the *Observer*'s editorial writers.[58]

Bad news arrived quickly. The city soon learned that it had been passed over for one of many national Army cantonments sited in 1917.[59] But all was not yet lost, as the *Observer* noted a week later that the upper Cape Fear city still stood a chance of winning one of the national guard camps. "Except for the fact that there would be no tremendous outlay for lumber and other material and demand for workmen to construct buildings," concluded the *Observer,* "a National Guard camp would be as desirable as a [army] cantonment, as the soldiers draw the same pay and spend it just as freely as the 'war army' men."[60] The retail-oriented Fayetteville Chamber of Commerce considered the purchasing power of encamped soldiers to be by far the greatest benefit of winning a training camp. Local merchants were less sure about the impact of the post on the local labor supply; businessmen believed that they could ill afford greater competition for labor.[61]

Some Fayettevillians already feared a labor shortage for the summer of 1917 due to selective service and the ever-growing black exodus from the former Confederacy.[62] "I fear there will be a scarcity of laborers . . . so many 'darkies' have gone North," noted one prominent resident in a letter to her son.[63] While cotton prices had risen sharply since 1914, the mercurial nature of the market led many Fayetteville area farmers to believe that they could not compete against the higher wages offered by government construction projects.[64] Fears of a labor shortage were not limited to the upper Cape Fear. "We must have the Negro in the South," stated the *Telegraph,* the leading newspaper in Macon, Georgia, one of Fayetteville's competitors in the base chase of 1917. "It is the only labor we have, it is the best we possibly could have—if we lose it we go bankrupt!"[65]

On Independence Day 1917, Fayetteville learned from reports in the *Charlotte* (North Carolina) *Observer* that it had been selected as the site of a national guard encampment. The *Fayetteville Observer* noted that the announcement was not a surprise, as military authorities in the region had been impressed by the town. Fayetteville's boosters claimed that the town was selected solely on merit.[66] The federal government, it was expected, would pump fifty thousand dollars a day into the local economy.[67] The *Observer* reprinted a glowing report from the *News & Observer* that stated that the camp could approach 4000 acres with a complement of 30,000 men and an annual budget of 10 million dollars.[68]

But euphoria soon changed to frustration. Just two weeks after learning of the "selection," the residents of the upper Cape Fear were stunned to learn that the post had been awarded to another North Carolina city, the seemingly always victorious "Queen City" of the Carolinas. "Charlotte got the Camp," the *Observer*'s July 18th headline stated. Fayetteville lost out, according to press reports, because of questions regarding the area's water supply.[69] Many residents suspected conspiracy on the part of Charlotte and wondered what the boosters from the Queen City did to change the minds of the War Department officials. One report asked, "Why is Greenville, South Carolina, allowed to make special arrangements for water when Fayetteville cannot?" The *Observer* concluded, "Suddenly water was a problem, and sand turned to clay."[70]

Like Fayetteville, Charlotte also considered itself a New South city on the rise, and with justification. Since the turn of the century, its Chamber of Commerce had pursued a variety of booster campaigns, most with the slogan "Watch Charlotte Grow."[71] General Leonard Wood, commander of the Southern District and the man responsible for site selection, received the red carpet treatment during his one-day tour of Charlotte's three proposed sites on July 5, 1917. Pressing business back at his Charleston headquarters necessitated a brief and intensive review. Wood seemed particularly interested in the nature of the soil. He had been led to believe that the Charlotte sites consisted of red clay. However, he was pleasantly surprised to learn that the soil, although partially clay, had the consistency of a sandy loam.[72] Wood noted that the War Department was trying to "make a fair distribution of them [camps], with the view of giving the soldiers good soil, good water, transportation facilities, and the like." Charlotte had sufficient water and excellent overland transportation facilities, the latter far exceeding what Fayetteville could offer. As Wood noted, "All this is for the soldier for personally we do not give a 'hump' who gets a camp, but we must play the game squarely and try to give them the best place possible."[73] After Charlotte had been selected, General Wood visited Fayetteville, inspected two possible sites, and deemed both acceptable.[74] Fayetteville continued to pursue a cantonment for the area and took action on the supposed unavailability of water.[75]

In the next months, Fayetteville's hopes ebbed and flowed. On August 10, 1917, the *Charlotte Observer* reported that Fayetteville would be the site of the artillery range for the division stationed near Charlotte. The town, however, received no confirmation. Fayetteville sent yet another delegation to Washington in late August with the task of securing a camp.[76] In September, the *Fayetteville Observer* announced that a "Big Cantonment and Machine Gun School" would soon be located near Fayetteville. "The city is going to get the biggest cantonment . . . ever established in the United States and perhaps the world," according to the September 12, 1917, *Observer*. Unconfirmed reports indicated that the War Department sought close to 160,000 acres, a tract approaching 30 miles in length and 8 miles in width, sufficient, according to one observer, "to have the entire U. S. Army—from requirements."[77] Considering the typical size of a cantonment or camp in 1917—three to four thousand acres—this comment was not too far off the mark. By early October, the *Observer* was less certain of success and started preparing its readers for yet another campaign failure. "Whichever way the cat may jump," noted the paper, " . . . it is safe to say that Fayetteville is going to keep in the front rank of progress."[78] And *Observer* editorials made it abundantly clear that the prospective installation would be for Fayetteville and not the surrounding Cumberland County. There was little apparent concern regarding the plight of the hundreds or even thousands of rural residents who would be forced to relocate so they would be outside the prospective camp's borders.[79]

In the October 10th *Observer*, Fayetteville's residents learned that the War Department had decided not to establish additional camps. Due to the town's efforts and the favorable report made by General Wood, Secretary of War Newton Baker noted that Fayetteville would receive first consideration if additional training camps were needed in the future.[80] But in January 1918, two episodes revived hopes of Fayetteville landing some type of military installation. First, the town got word that the War Department intended to establish several ordnance depots (i.e., weapon and ammunition storage facilities) throughout the nation, especially in the South. Due to Fayetteville's association with the nineteenth-century arsenal, a depot was especially attractive, and the town lobbied the War Department for one of the prospective facilities. Like the naval armor plate facility, the War Department plant promised to increase Fayetteville's industrial base and be a magnet for other heavy industry. Raleigh, also once the site of an ordnance facility, and Salisbury, lobbied for a depot as well.[81] Someone who approached Fayetteville's boosters hoped to take advantage of towns desperate to secure a post. Fayetteville declined his offer but did send a delegation to Washington, at considerable expense, based upon the man's information, only to find his claims unfounded.[82]

By late February, North Carolina newspapers regularly announced the awarding of contracts for new federal construction projects including camps, ordnance depots, port terminals, and munitions plants. Frustrated by the dissembling of January and early February, the *Fayetteville Observer* struck a haughty and hypocritical tone on February 20. "We venture to suggest that the War Department, in 'giving out' these plants, would do the right thing by letting it be known in the beginning that no congressional delegations or delegations from cities wanting camps need apply at the department. . . ." The editorial concluded that the selection of sites should be made entirely on merit—strange words, indeed, from a booster organ.[83] Soon thereafter, the *Observer* urged Fayetteville's residents to " . . . drop the subject of military camps. . . ."[84] It looked as if the war, or at least the War Department, had passed Fayetteville by. The army had selected locations for army and national guard camps, depots, and ordnance facilities, and Fayetteville had lost out on all accounts.

To a great extent, the South became the nation's boot camp in 1917. Nineteen of thirty-one army and national guard training camps were located in southern states. And most were sited near towns and cities with the same aspirations as Fayetteville.[85] By the fall of 1917, boosters in the upper Cape Fear city could do little else but sit back and read the glowing accounts from base towns—the energy, the enthusiasm, the excitement, and above all else, the economic boost of war camps.[86] In early 1918, Wilmington was awarded a shipyard.[87] Fayetteville was now flanked by booster "success stories," with Charlotte to the west and Wilmington to the east.

There were several reasons why the South became the temporary home to so many recruits. Labor and land were cheap. Unlike the Northeast, railroads and seaports in the former Confederacy were unencumbered by the need to move industrial war production. By 1917, New York and Philadelphia overflowed with materiel awaiting transport to France. But the mild southern climate played as great a role as any in the decision-making process. National guard camps were meant to be temporary affairs, little more than large campgrounds. The winter climate of the Southeast was thought to be sufficiently balmy for tent living.[88]

Fayetteville's boosters had gained some small measure of satisfaction upon learning how slowly camp construction in Charlotte had progressed in the fall of 1917. The Fourth Division, stationed at Camp Greene, squeezed ten and twelve men into tents designed for eight. Soldiers arrived at a work in progress, not a completed camp.[89] A few months later, the Fourth Division men needed all the body heat overcrowding could generate as the troops endured one of the coldest winters ever recorded in the Southeast. Soldiers at Camp Greene burned green pine in an effort to keep warm inside their canvas huts. When temperature rose above freezing, the entire camp turned into a morass of clay mud, a "hogwallow" as one observer later described, completely impassable for motorized vehicles. Lurking beneath the sandy loam soil that so impressed General Wood was Piedmont clay. The experience of the Camp Greene troops was repeated throughout the South.[90]

Irrespective of weather-induced schadenfreude, Fayetteville's promoters knew that an army post would have both real and symbolic meaning for the town. The presence of an installation demonstrated that a town had "arrived," that it had become worthy of having a facility and perhaps most important, was *more worthy than others*. A cantonment was a badge of honor coveted by most New South towns. A town that wanted to be "something" had to have an army post along with a busy rail depot, new textile mills, parks, and a modern physical plant. And if the War Department considered a city worthy of such an honor, competitors took notice. What competitors noticed in this case, of course, was that Fayetteville had been overlooked once again and had lost out to a regional rival.

The size and scale of the carnage on the Western Front would, ultimately, help the town's cause, as the horrific nature and vast scale of industrialized warfare soon came to Fayetteville's rescue. Regardless of soil type or climate, Camp Greene proved inadequate in preparing troops for the Western Front because it was too small. The size and makeup of the training camps established in 1917 differed little from those of the Spanish–American War, but the size and scale of the warfare for which the troops were preparing had undergone a dramatic transformation. Industrialization and technology made warfare more deadly and vast. In the Civil War, hand-held weapons had been responsible for two-thirds of battlefield casualties and artillery just one-third, but in World War I the proportions were reversed. Long-range artillery and automatic weapons fire proved to be the greatest threat to battlefield survival.[91] Modern warfare required large training reservations for maneuvering large units and for employing long-range artillery.

In July 1918, the *Fayetteville Observer* repeated a familiar refrain: "Fayetteville May Land Big Project." According to reports from Washington, DC, Congressman Hannibal Godwin had "definite assurance that Fayetteville will land one of the biggest projects yet established in North Carolina."[92] The citizenry, once bitten and twice shy, waited for confirmation. Few believed that Godwin had actually underestimated the size and scope of the base. The *Observer* reported a week later that the Fayetteville area had been selected as the location of the largest military camp in the United States and a permanent one at that, far exceeding one hundred thousand acres. The nature of the installation was not yet known, but some expected it to be for the artillery branch. Fayetteville would soon be host to a gargantuan artillery training facility.[93] The *Charlotte Observer*, congratulatory in tone, reported that "now it is all good and better [for] . . . the upper Cape Fear Metropolis."[94]

On August 21, 1918, Secretary of War Baker announced that construction would begin immediately on "Camp Bragg, Fayetteville, North Carolina," the post's formal name, a "field artillery cantonment and training center" capable of holding six brigades. Other reports suggested that the camp's complement might exceed sixty thousand soldiers.[95] Estimates of construction costs varied, from $8 million to $15 million, with the latter being the official number.[96] Regardless, for a town the size of Fayetteville, the project's expense far surpassed expectations.

Many locals believed as said above, and with some justification, that their long-term efforts to champion the merits of their community as a host for the military had been integral in the War Department's decision to establish a field artillery installation near the town in 1918. Convinced of their essential role in the siting process, local advocates fell victim to a common fallacy of causation, *post hoc, ergo propter hoc* (after, therefore, because of). Evidence indicates that Fayetteville's boosters played a minor role in the site selection process.[97] But the role of boosterism should not be dismissed, because it prepared the region and its citizenry for hosting (or enduring and tolerating) a military installation that far exceeded what anyone in the upper Cape Fear expected or imagined. In a sense, Fayetteville's boosters got far more than they bargained for—a massive, permanent, and *underutilized* military installation that would prove to have a profound but uneven economic impact on the region in the short term. After all, the war ended just a few months after the post was authorized and long before construction was complete. Fort Bragg eventually became the powerful economic engine that Fayetteville's boosters had envisioned, but the upper Cape Fear region had to wait for a *second* World War to see that vision realized.

Notes

1. Jonathan F. Phillips, "Building a New South Metropolis: Fayetteville, Fort Bragg, and the Sandhills of North Carolina" (PhD diss., University of North Carolina at Chapel Hill, 2003), 101–102, 142–144, 161–168, 288–293.

2. Phillips, "Building a New South Metropolis," 288–293.

3. William J. Snow, *Signposts of Experience: World War Memoirs of Major General William J. Snow, USA-Retired* (Washington, DC: United States Field Artillery Association, 1941), 117, 122–123; William J. Snow, Major General, *Report of the Chief of Field Artillery*, October 14, 1919, House Documents, Vol. 14, No. 426, War Department Reports, 1919, Vol. 1, Part 4, 66th Congress, 2nd session, 1919–1920, 5056–5057; *History of Fort Bragg, 1918–1967* (Fort Bragg, NC: Office, A C of S, G-3, Headquarters, XVIII Airborne Corps, 1967), 21.

4. Snow, *Signposts of Experience*, 115–117; *Retention of Camp and Cantonment Sites for Future Uses, January 3–4, 1919*, US House of Representatives, 65th Congress, 3rd session (Washington, DC: Government Printing Office, 1919), 25–26; W. H. Radcliffe, Major, *Completion Report, Camp Knox, Kentucky*, 1 September 1919, 6–7; Gilbert F. Woods, Report of the Director, Real Estate Service, War Department, November 7, 1919, in *War Department, Annual Reports*, Vol. 1, Part 4, (Washington, DC: Government Printing Office, 1920), 4538, 4541, 4564, 4566.

5. Snow, "Report of the Chief of Field Artillery, 1920," 1939; Major General William J. Snow, "Report of the Chief of Field Artillery, 1919," *War Department Annual Reports, 1919* (Washington, DC: Government Printing Office, 1920), 5159–5160; *Retention of Camp and Cantonment Sites for Future Uses, January 3–4, 1919*, 54–55.

6. *History of Fort Bragg, 1918–1967*, 26.

7. Snow, "Report of the Chief of Field Artillery, 1920," 1939; Snow, *Signposts of Experience*, 117–118; *History of Fort Bragg, 1918–1967*, 26.

8. *History of Fort Bragg, 1918–1967*, 21, 26; Snow, *Signposts of Experience*, 117–118; Gibson Prather, "Lawyer's Speech led to Location of Bragg," *Fayetteville Observer*, 150th Anniversary Edition, September 17, 1967, from Fort Bragg History Files at North Carolina Room, Cumberland County Library, Fayetteville, NC.

9. Snow, *Signposts of Experience*, 123–125.

10. *History of Fort Bragg, 1918–1967*, 26.

11. "The 'booster' perspective of Fort Bragg's creation that follows was drawn from my 2003 dissertation, "Building a New South Metropolis: Fayetteville, Fort Bragg, and the Sandhills of North Carolina," chapters three and four.

12. "Fayetteville's Improvement," *Fayetteville Observer*, February 23, 1916; "Fayetteville's Streets," *Fayetteville Observer*, March 15, 1916; "Fayetteville Moving Forward," *Fayetteville Observer*, March 29, 1916.

13. "Fayetteville Moving Forward," *Fayetteville Observer*, March 29, 1916.

14. "Will Fayetteville Seize the Opportunity?" *Fayetteville Observer*, May 3, 1916.

15. "The Water Supply of Cities," *Fayetteville Observer*, May 10, 1916.

16. Editorial Page, *Fayetteville Observer*, April 12, 1916.

17. James C. Cobb, *The Selling of the South: The Southern Crusade for Industrial Development, 1936–1990*, 2nd ed. (Urbana: University of Illinois Press, 1993); Wilbur Joseph Cash, *The Mind of the South* (New York: Alfred A. Knopf, 1941), 23.

18. "Preparedness for Business," *Fayetteville Observer*, January 5, 1916.

19. "Preparedness for Business," *Fayetteville Observer*, January 5, 1916; "The National Guard," *Fayetteville Observer*, January 19, 1916; "Preparedness is $3.20 per capita," *Fayetteville Observer*, January 26, 1916, from the *Greensboro News*; "President Wilson Warns Country," *Fayetteville Observer*, February 9, 1916; "The Cost of War," *Fayetteville Observer*, April 19, 1916; "The Hardships of War," *Fayetteville Observer*, April 19, 1916.

20. "In the Interest of Peace," *Fayetteville Observer*, April 12, 1916.

21. Benjamin Franklin Cooling, *Gray Steel and Blue Water Navy: The Formative Years of America's Military-Industrial Complex, 1881–1917* (Hamden, CT: Archon Books, 1979), 189.

22. Cooling, *Gray Steel and Blue Water Navy*, 185; Melvin I. Urofsky, "Josephus Daniels and the Armor Trust," *North Carolina Historical Review* 45, no. 3 (July 1968): 238.

23. Urofsky, "Josephus Daniels and the Armor Trust," 239–242.

24. Urofsky, "Josephus Daniels and the Armor Trust," 243; Cooling, *Gray Steel and Blue Water Navy*, 203–204.

25. Arthur W. Page, "Armor Plate Lobby vs. The Pork Barrel," *The World's Work*, 31, no. 3 (January 1916): 244–245.

26. Bion H. Butler, "Patriotism and Plunder," *Moore County News*, August 11, 1921.

27. "States Rights," *Hoke County Journal*, December 25, 1924.

28. Urofsky, "Josephus Daniels and the Armor Trust," 255–256.

29. Quoted in Cooling, *Gray Steel and Blue Water Navy*, 203.

30. "Threat by the Armor Plate Men," *Fayetteville Observer*, February 16, 1916; Cooling, *Gray Steel and Blue Water Navy*, 203.

31. "The Naval Bill," *Fayetteville Observer*, June 7, 1916; "Armor Plant for Cape Fear City," *News & Observer*, September 8, 1916; "Great Government Armor Plate Plant," *Fayetteville Observer*, September 20, 1916.

32. George B. Tindall, *Emergence of the New South, 1913–1945* (Baton Rouge: Louisiana State University Press, 1967), 56–57. See also, Thomas B. Robertson, "Hopewell and City Point in the World War," in Kyle Arthur Davis, ed., *Virginia Communities in War Time: First Series* (Richmond: The Executive Committee, State Capitol, 1926), 215–234.

33. "Hopewell to Celebrate," *Fayetteville Observer*, April 12, 1916.

34. David L. Carlton and Peter Coclanis, "Capital Mobilization and Southern Industry: The Case of the Carolina Piedmont," *Journal of Economic History* 49 (March 1989): 73–94; Wayne K. Durrill, "Producing Poverty: Local Government and Economic Development in a New South County, 1874–1884," *Journal of American History* 71 (March 1985): 764–781; David L. Carlton, *Mill and Town in South Carolina, 1880–1920* (Baton Rouge: Louisiana University Press, 1982), 458.

35. Henry C. Ferrell Jr., "Regional Rivalries, Congress, and the MIC: The Norfolk and Charleston Navy Yards, 1913–1920," in Benjamin Franklin Cooling, ed., *War, Business, and American Society: Historical Perspectives on the Military-Industrial Complex* (Port Washington, NY: Kennikat Press, 1977), 59–60.

36. Ferrell, "Regional Rivalries," 60–62, 71–72.

37. Don H. Doyle, *New Men, New Cities, New South: Atlanta, Nashville, Charleston, and Mobile, 1860–1910* (Chapel Hill: University of North Carolina Press, 1990), 180–181.

38. "Entire State Indorses Fayetteville's Claims for Armor Plate Plant," *Charlotte Observer*, 12 September 1916; *Minutes of the Fayetteville City Council*, 9 October 1916, 22; *City Council Minute Docket H*, City of Fayetteville, August 7, 1916–April 30, 1920; "The Big Plant," *Fayetteville Observer*, October 4, 1916; "That Government Armor Plant," *Cape Fear News*, September 12, 1916, reprinted from the *Raleigh Times*.

39. "Hope Mills Letter—News from our Rural Correspondents," *Fayetteville Observer*, October 4, 1916.

40. Quoted in "That Government Armor Plant," *Fayetteville Observer*, September 12, 1916.

41. "Great Government Armor Plant," *Fayetteville Observer*, September 20, 1916; "Fayetteville on the Map," *Fayetteville Observer*, September 20, 1916.

42. "Entire State Indorses Fayetteville's Claim for Armor Plate Plant," *Charlotte Observer*, September 12, 1916; "Armor Plate Plant," *Fayetteville Observer*, December 20, 1916.

43. Richard L. Watson, "Principle, Party, and Constituency: The North Carolina Congressional Delegation," *North Carolina Historical Review* 65, no. 3 (July 1979); "Armor Plant for Cape Fear City," *News & Observer*, September 8, 1916; "To Waterways Convention," *News & Observer*, September 14, 1916.

44. "The Big Plant," *Fayetteville Observer*, October 4, 1916

45. "Simmons Stands by Fayetteville," *Fayetteville Observer*, October 4, 1916, from September 28, 1916, *News & Observer*; "Senator Simmons for Fayetteville—He Confers with Secretary [Josephus] Daniels Relative to Locating Plant Here," *Fayetteville Observer*, October 4, 1916, from *Greensboro News*.

46. Nixon S. Plummer, "Many So. Cities Seek U.S. Armor Plate Plant," *Charlotte Observer*, September 14, 1916; Want Armor Plant on Breaker Island," *New York Times*, September 14, 1916; "Raleigh Munitions Plant is Bankrupt—Cary K. Durkey and W. F. Harding appointed receivers for Raleigh Iron Works," *Charlotte Observer*, January 1, 1916.

47. "The Armor Plant," *Army and Navy Register* 60, no. 1888 (September 23, 1916), 390.

48. "Erection of Armor Plant," *Army and Navy Register* 60, no. 1890 (October 7, 1916), 459.

49. Quote from editorial, "That Armor Plate Plant," *New York Times*, September 26, 1916.

50. "Two to One on Fayetteville," *Fayetteville Observer*, October 4, 1916; "Fayetteville Has Chance to Get US Armor Plant," *Charlotte Observer*, September 17, 1916; "Armor Plate Hearings Close," *News & Observer*, September 15, 1916; "Fayetteville's Prospects," *News & Observer*, September 16, 1916; "Government Armor Plant," *Army and Navy Register* 60, no. 1884 (August 26, 1916): 266. According to this report in the *Register*, Daniels favored Birmingham, Alabama.

51. "100 Towns Barred for Armor Plant," *New York Times*, 10; "The Armor Plant," *Army and Navy Register* 60, no. 1900 (December 16, 1916), 702–703; "The Armor Plate Plant," *Fayetteville Observer*, December 20, 1916.

52. "New Navy Armor Plant," *Army and Navy Register* 61, no. 1917 (April 14, 1917): 418–419; "Armor Plate Plant," *New York Times*, April 12, 1917.

53. Cooling, *Gray Steel and Blue Water Navy*, 210–212.

54. F. W. Vaughn, "Fayetteville—Its Suitableness for the Location of the Government Armor Plate and Projectile Plant," *Fayetteville Observer*, October 25, 1916. Source of the quote, "NOW I KNOW why they love HOPEWELL!!!"

55. "Fayetteville—Resources that Warrant Location of Plate Mill Warrant Location of Other Industries on the Same Large Scale," *Fayetteville Observer*, January 24, 1917, reprint of January 13, 1917 essay by Bion Butler in *News & Observer*; "Cumnock Mine," *Fayetteville Observer*, June 6, 1917.

56. "Fayetteville Is Being Advertised to Great Advantage," *Fayetteville Observer*, October 18, 1916, from the *York* (Pennsylvania) *Dispatch*, October 10, 1916; "Sec. Daniels Gets 115 Applications—Spokesmen of Many Cities Advance Their Claim," *New York Times*, September 14, 1916.

57. "The Cantonments," *Fayetteville Observer*, June 13, 1917.

58. "The Cantonments," *Fayetteville Observer*, June 13, 1917.

59. "The Last Camp Site Has Been Selected," *Fayetteville Observer*, June 20, 1917.

60. "Military Camps in the South," *Fayetteville Observer*, June 27, 1917.

61. J. W. MacKethan to Alfred MacKethan, May 1, 1917, Edwin R. MacKethan papers (hereafter cited as MacKethan papers), #4928, Southern Historical Collection, University of North Carolina at Chapel Hill (hereafter cited as SHC-UNC).

62. Jack Temple Kirby, "The Southern Exodus, 1910–1960: A Primer for Historians," *Journal of Southern History* 49, no. 4 (November 1983): 585–600, especially 589–590.

63. Mrs. E. R. MacKethan to Alfred MacKethan, 1 May 1917, Folder 245, MacKethan papers, #4298, SHC-UNC.

64. Mrs. E. R. MacKethan to Alfred MacKethan, June 20, 1917, Folder 246, MacKethan papers, #4298, SHC-UNC.

65. Quote in David Kennedy, *Over Here: The First World War and American Society* (New York: Oxford University Press, 1980), 280–281.

66. "Fayetteville and its Military Camp," *Fayetteville Observer*, July 4, 1917.

67. "What It Means," *Fayetteville Observer*, July 4, 1917.

68. *Fayetteville Observer*, July 4, 1917, reprint of June 28, 1917 article from the *News & Observer*.

69. "Charlotte Got the Camp," *Fayetteville Observer*, July 18, 1917.

70. "The Military Camp," *Fayetteville Observer*, July 25, 1917.

71. Miriam Grace Mitchell and Edward Spaulding Perzel, *The Echo of the Bugle Call: Charlotte's Role in World War I* (Charlotte: Dowd House Preservation Committee, Citizens for Preservation, Inc., 1979), 2.

72. Mitchell and Perzel, *The Echo of the Bugle Call*, 3.

73. Mitchell and Perzel, *The Echo if the Bugle Call*, Appendix C, "General Wood's Speech at the Selwyn Hotel," 82–83.

74. "General Woods' Visit to Fayetteville, *Fayetteville Observer*, August 15, 1917.

75. "Board of Aldermen Minutes," *Fayetteville City Council Docket*, August 10, 1917, 133.

76. "Fayetteville to Get Artillery Range," *Fayetteville Observer*, August 15, 1917, reprint from *Charlotte Observer* article; Alfred MacKethan to Lula B. MacKethan, August 30, 1917, MacKethan papers, #4298, SHC-UNC.

77. "Big Cantonment and Machine Gun School," *Fayetteville Observer*, 12 September 1917; Alfred MacKethan to Lula B. MacKethan, September 10, 1917, MacKethan papers, #4298, SHC-UNC.

78. *Retention of Camp and Cantonment Sites for Future Uses, Hearings Before the Committee on Military Affairs, January 3–4, 1919*, U. S. House of Representatives, 65th Congress, 3rd session (Washington, DC: Government Printing Office, 1919), 20; "Observations," *Fayetteville Observer*, October 3, 1917.

79. "Big Cantonment and Machine Gun School," *Fayetteville Observer*, September 12, 1917.

80. "Camp Notes," *Fayetteville Observer*, October 10, 1917; "The Camp Matter," *Fayetteville Observer*, October 10, 1917.

81. "The Camp Matter," *Fayetteville Observer*, January 2, 1918; "No Ordnance Camp for North Carolina," *Fayetteville Observer*, February 13, 1918, reprinted from the *News & Observer*.

82. "Decline to Consider Proposition," *Fayetteville Observer*, February 6, 1918; "Man Would Secure Camp for a Price," *Fayetteville Observer*, February 13, 1918.

83. "The Abandoning of Camp Greene," *Fayetteville Observer*, February 20, 1918.

84. "About Military Camps," *Fayetteville Observer*, March 13, 1918.

85. Tindall, *Emergence of the New South*, 54; Office of the Judge Advocate General, *United States Military Reservations, National Cemeteries, and National Parks*, rev. ed. (Washington, DC: Government Printing Office, 1916), 297–303.

86. Tindall, *Emergence of the New South*, 54.

87. "Profiteering, in the face of Unusual Conditions, Wilmington Sets a Good Example for Fayetteville," *Fayetteville Observer*, July 31, 1918, from the July 23, 1918 *Wilmington Star*.

88. Tindall, *Emergence of the New South*, 54; *Retention of Camp and Cantonment Sites for Future Uses, January 3–4, 1919*, 4, 14–15, 51–54.

89. Edward M. Coffman, *The War to End All Wars: The American Military Experience in World War I* (Lexington: University Press of Kentucky, 1998), 64; "Charlotte's Military Camp," *Fayetteville Observer*, August 8, 1917.

90. Coffman, *The War to End All Wars*, 68; "The Abandoning of Camp Greene," *Fayetteville Observer*, February 20, 1918. "Hogwallow" reference from *Retention of Camp and Cantonment Sites for Future Uses, January 3–4, 1919*, 4.

91. M. W. Ireland, "Report of the Surgeon General of the U. S. Army to the Secretary of War, 1920," *War Department Annual Reports*, 1920 (Washington, DC: Government Printing Office, 1920), 62–65; Benedict Crowell and Robert Forrest Wilson, *Demobilization: Our Industrial and Military Demobilization after the Armistice, 1918–1920* (New Haven, CT: Yale University Press, 1921), 256–257.

92. S. R. Williams, "Fayetteville May Land Big Project," *Fayetteville Observer*, July 17, 1918, reprinted from July 9, 1918, *News & Observer*, Washington, DC, bureau.

93. "Fayetteville Gets Big Military Camp," *Fayetteville Observer*, July 24, 1918.

94. "Good for Fayetteville," *Fayetteville Observer*, August 7, 1918, reprinted from the *Charlotte Observer.*

95. "The Camp," *Fayetteville Observer*, August 7, 1918.

96. Sawyer, *Completion Report*, 1–2.

97. Snow, *Signposts of Experience*, 122.

2

Where Johnnie Got His Gun

Charlotte and Camp Greene

Kurt D. Geske

In 1914, shortly before the First World War began, the entire Regular US Army numbered just under 98,000 men, less than 70 percent the size of the Swiss army.[1] In spite of this modest beginning, in just nineteen months, from April 1917 until November 1918, the United States successfully mobilized and trained over 4 million men.[2] One of the key elements of the mobilization effort was the establishment of thirty-two temporary training camps. During the summer of 1917, more than 200,000 workers built what were essentially 32 small cities, each designed to hold about 40,000 men.[3] Into these camps poured tens of thousands of young men, with "regulars" and national guardsmen joined by the members of the new "National Army," composed of millions of men drafted from the states and territories.[4] Each camp consisted of hundreds of hastily constructed wood frame buildings and vast canvas "tent cities" erected near the ranges and training areas that came to occupy thousands of acres of former farms and woods. Workers also built the many miles of roads; sewers; water lines; and telephone, telegraph, and electrical wires required to support the camps. In essence, within a few weeks of being notified that their location had been selected for a camp, leaders of and civilians in each of the thirty-two selected communities found themselves hosting a nearby "military city."

Camp Greene, located in Charlotte, was one of these temporary camps. Although it functioned as a training base from September 1917 until January 1919 and closed completely in June 1919, the creation and operation of Camp Greene had a significant impact on Charlotte and its neighboring communities. For the duration of the war, Charlotte became an "army town." Between 1917 and 1919, more than thirty million government dollars poured into the city as the War Department paid both the direct costs necessary for the construction and maintenance of the camp and the salaries of thousands of individuals who served or worked there during this period. During the war, Charlotte's pre-war population of about 45,000 more than doubled. In addition to the tens of thousands of young men who mobilized and trained at the camp, a significant number of civilian visitors came to Charlotte during the war; construction workers, entrepreneurs, and vendors (including those who sold liquor, gambling, and sex) were drawn to Camp Greene's financial opportunities, and hundreds of "war camp service workers" came to work at or near the camp.

During the war, Charlotte's retail and service industry businesses experienced unprecedented increases in business as the soldiers and civilians drawn to the city and camp attended theaters, rode streetcars, ate in restaurants, shopped in stores, and generally supported the local economy. Historian Mary Kratt noted that due to Camp Greene, "business proved excellent for banks, restaurants, saloons, amusement parks, churches, stores and prostitutes."[5] State and local leaders upgraded Charlotte's infrastructure by building new roads, sewer and water systems, public parks, streetcar lines, and commercial and residential buildings to accommodate the expanding population of the city. Shortly after the July 1917 announcement that Charlotte had been selected as a camp location, the *Charlotte* (North Carolina) *Observer* accurately reflected the city's wartime mood when it declared that, "Nothing has ever before happened in the history of Charlotte that meant so much to the city as does the locating of an army camp here."[6]

Shortly after hostilities ended on November 11, 1918, the War Department decided that some of the temporary camps should be retained for further use but that most should be deactivated and abandoned as quickly as possible. While some of Charlotte's fellow "host cities" retained their respective camps and remained more or less permanent "army towns," Camp Greene was among those camps chosen for closure. In a matter of months, all operations ceased, the remaining soldiers were discharged or transferred elsewhere, and the physical camp was dismantled and sold for salvage.[7] By the end of summer 1919, the soldiers were gone, and Camp Greene had physically ceased to exist.

After the War Department announced its intention to build the new training camps in 1917, the Charlotte Chamber of Commerce initiated a lobbying campaign and began "using every contact it had" to secure one of the camps for its city.[8] Less than two weeks after the United States declared war on Germany, the Chamber met to establish a committee to "formulate plans for quick action in stating Charlotte's claim [for a camp] including her many military advantages, such as railroad facilities, grounds, etc., before the officials of the War Department."[9] At the committee's first meeting, Chamber leaders debated "the advisability of going after one of the camps" and "decided that Charlotte would make a hard fight."[10] Consequently, following an intensive lobbying effort and much political maneuvering, federal officials designated Charlotte as the site of one of the new training camps.

The construction of Camp Greene began in July 1917, and the camp was substantially complete when the first soldiers arrived in September. It then operated until June 1919. During that time, there were actually several "versions" of Camp Greene. The first was as a national guard mobilization center; this lasted from September to November, when the national guardsmen departed the camp for deployment in France. During these first months, Charlotteans seemed pleased to be hosting the "citizen soldiers" of the national guard and treated them to band concerts, dances, ice cream socials, church suppers, speeches, and invitations to have "Sunday supper" with local families. The guardsmen evidently enjoyed the attention, and both local newspaper accounts and official camp records indicate that there was little trouble involving soldiers during the camp's "national guard period."

This situation changed somewhat in late fall, when troops from two regular army divisions replaced the national guardsmen. From late October 1917 through January 1918, the Third and Fourth Divisions, composed of pre-war "professional soldiers," were mobilized at Camp Greene where they organized and trained before deploying to fight in France. Some of the "baggage" that followed these regular army units to Charlotte was not well received by the civilian community. "Regulars" had the reputation—rightly or wrongly—as being better disciplined, in terms of adapting to army regulations and routine, but more likely than the national guardsmen to become involved with women of ill repute, purveyors of strong drink, and professional gamblers. While Charlotteans still expressed enthusiasm about hosting their soldier-guests, negative news stories about Camp Greene soldiers began spreading, and it seemed as though Charlotteans were realizing that hosting tens of thousands of young men on their way to a war had a potential, unforeseen downside.

With the departure of the regular army divisions in early 1918, Charlotteans debated and speculated about the future of Camp Greene. For a time, it appeared as though military and government officials were going to abandon the camp after the national guard and regular army divisions had shipped out. However, during the early months of 1918, new training units replaced the last of the divisional units. The camp evolved from a mobilization post to a seemingly more permanent training base, which some locals hoped would continue operation long after the war ended.

Several months later, another change further altered the composition of the camp's population. Recognizing at the outset of the war the potential controversy associated with stationing thousands of armed black men in the Jim Crow South, the War Department established a policy of assigning only white soldiers to the southern camps and sending black soldiers to the Northeast and West. However, in August 1918, without prior notice or discussion, officials decided to assign black soldiers to posts in the South, including Camp Greene.[11] Consistent with the legal and social rules of the day, the camp remained segregated; black soldiers were part of separate units led by white officers and remained physically separated from white units on the post. By September 1918, just under half of the enlisted men assigned to Camp Greene were identified as "colored," and their numbers continued to increase dramatically in the next few months.[12] In October, there were 14,336 black soldiers and 13,512 white soldiers at the camp.[13] By the time of the Armistice on November 11, 1918, black troops significantly outnumbered white troops, with 8,012 men assigned to the black units, and only 4,933 white enlisted soldiers in camp.[14] The civilian community was quick to note the changing demographics of the camp; at the end of October, the *Charlotte Observer* noted that Camp Greene's main function was to serve as a "mobilization point" for black labor troops.[15] It seems likely that this perception strongly influenced Charlotte's white leaders and citizens; there was little protest when the camp closed in 1919.

Although the units, functions, and demographics of the camp changed over time, life at Camp Greene was in many ways the same for the various groups of soldiers who occupied the camp between 1917 and 1919. Like all soldiers, the men of Camp Greene trained, complained, discussed rumors and gossiped, speculated about the future, and sought amusement. Some men read their Bibles, attended religious services, went to moral and physical "hygiene" lectures at the YMCA (Young Men's Christian Association), and participated in the wholesome athletic activities designed to amuse and exhaust them. Others chose to pass the time pursuing sporting activities of a different sort, including gambling, drinking, and consorting with prostitutes. Overall, while life at Camp Greene was not always pleasant, it was seldom dull.

The camp was still a "work in progress" when the first national guardsmen arrived in September 1917. Although the key buildings and facilities were in place by the time the camp began full-time operation, inspectors reported that during the first few weeks, many soldiers were "trying to keep comfortable . . . cutting and hauling wood, digging ditches, [and] building up company streets."[16] In addition, soldiers arriving for duty in the "Sunny South" soon learned that it was not always so. Both the weather and the temporary, unfinished nature of Camp Greene conspired to make living conditions there somewhat less than perfect.

One of the principal features of camp life was the presence of mud after periods of heavy rain, which occurred quite frequently. One soldier later recalled that when he arrived, "Camp Greene was a mud hole. I imagine it had rained for forty days and forty nights before we got here."[17] Mud was also very much on the mind of another soldier when he wrote home that "the camp is in a miserable condition there is no doubt of that, the earth being as I have probably said before a slimey red clay which will not absorb the water, thereby causing much inconvenience and they say in the summer would cause a lot of sickness."[18] A writer for the camp newspaper, *Trench and Camp,* agreed that conditions were miserable but cheerfully added "but wait until the sun shines—then, the mud will dry up and the beautiful southern breezes will blow all the mud away—away in your face as dust."[19] Unfortunately, the writer was wrong; spring and summer 1918 brought more sunshine and hotter temperatures, but periodic rains continued to flood the camp. Consequently, the soldiers of Camp Greene discovered how humidity made high temperatures almost unbearable, particularly for men wearing wool uniforms living in canvas tents. In a June 1918 letter to his sweetheart at home, one soldier from New England commented "you say you have had hot weather, believe me girlie, you don't know what hot weather is."[20]

A February 1918 congressional investigation revealed that Camp Greene had open latrines—"filled with 6 or 8 feet of decaying, putrid, festering animal matter"—but no bathing facilities, and latrines and ditches full of kitchen garbage were found to be located near many soldiers' tents.[21] Those tents lacked wooden floors, and they were overcrowded, with eight or nine men sharing a space that was supposed to accommodate five.[22] The soldiers relied on small conical stoves in which they burned green wood that they had to cut themselves, and one man complained that "there is a shortage of even this fuel at the present time."[23] Commenting on Camp Greene's conditions, a congressman noted that "the Government of the United States has no right to ask the boys to die ignominiously like rats in a mud pen," and that he expected an "instant and radical remedy" to these conditions.[24]

Although many Camp Greene soldiers might have thought otherwise, both the War Department and the camp authorities were very concerned about their health, hygiene, and nutrition. The US Public Health Service and camp authorities regularly inspected all sources of food, beverages, animal fodder, and other supplies for the camp, and they were quick to place Charlotte businesses such as creameries, bottling companies, and food vendors "off limits" if they did not comply with standards for cleanliness.[25] In addition, officials established many rules and procedures regarding sanitation, food storage, transportation, and dish washing, and they sent out regular reminders that "Army Regulations require that each man shall wash his hands before each meal and immediately after visiting the latrine."[26]

Some of the rules and regulations at Camp Greene related to "race issues" and "vice." For example, officers ordered soldiers to keep out of the African American districts of segregated Charlotte, although some soldiers ignored those orders. In response to an influx of black vendors and laundresses seeking business at Camp Greene, authorities issued an order prohibiting the sale of food, candy, or other items by civilians on the post, as well as another order that specifically prohibited "negro women from entering the reservation."[27] The latter order, whatever its merits as a method of protecting the health of the men of the camp, had some unexpected consequences; many soldiers were accustomed to "sending their laundry out" to black laundresses, and, when they were barred from the camp, there was an acute shortage of clean underwear on the post.

The food at Camp Greene was plentiful if not of high quality, and the soldiers ate well. Recognizing that soldiers in the new training camps were going to be exceptionally active, the army mandated a daily ration of 4,761 calories.[28] How well cooks prepared that food was, of course, another matter. One soldier, writing to his family, put it rather succinctly: "At 6:00 o'clock we have breakfast. Sometimes we have something good to eat and sometimes we do not."[29] For those who found the mess hall's regular offerings less than palatable, there were other options. In town, owners of restaurants, short-order diners, and soda fountains eagerly courted the "soldier trade," advertising heavily in the camp newspapers. Some soldiers needed alternatives to these relatively high-priced commercial establishments; a $1 dinner was not an inconsequential expense for a private who "took home" perhaps $8 per month. So the YWCA (Young Women's Christian Association) cafeteria and the Red Cross canteen also wooed the men of Camp Greene. The YWCA's prices were more reasonable than restaurants in town, with a "full breakfast" costing only ten cents. The Red Cross offered free sandwiches, coffee, cigarettes, candy, cakes, and other treats to the camp's soldiers and other servicemen who were visiting or passing through Charlotte.[30]

Early in the war, the War Department decided that "diversion by amusements and athletics" was the first line of defense against venereal disease and other problems; as Secretary of War Newton Baker noted, "wholesome recreation [is] the best possible cure for irregularities in conduct which arise from idleness and the baser temptations." [31] Consequently, like its sister camps, Camp Greene offered a full program of team sports and other athletic activities for soldiers. Organizers placed special emphasis on those athletic activities thought to contribute directly to the training of "fighting men." They believed that all sports involving running were valuable because the soldier accustomed to running "goes 'over the top' quickly and isn't winded when he reaches the enemy."[32] Baseball was useful because "the ball player makes good as a grenade thrower."[33] A football player "will be a good man in a mixup," a point one camp publication vividly illustrated with a sketch of a uniformed football player using the butt of his rifle to knock off a German soldier's spiked helmet.[34] Not surprisingly, military and civilian recreation leaders lauded boxing as perhaps the most valuable sport for soldiers because it promoted general physical fitness and skills such as balance, coordination, and endurance and because of its direct usefulness in combat, especially for bayonet warfare.

Perhaps the most exciting sporting event associated with Camp Greene was one that took place in Chicago and New York City: the 1917 World Series. From October 6 through October 15, the Chicago White Sox battled the New

York Giants in a six-game series that ended with a White Sox championship. Thanks to the *Charlotte Observer,* both the men of Camp Greene and the people of Charlotte had "front row seats," of a sort, for each of the games. On an open field at the camp, the newspaper erected what it called its "Great Automatic Baseball Player," a large scoreboard that contained the key information for each game, reported "play by play, balls and strikes, just as soon as they happen."[35] With a direct line to each ballpark, a Western Union telegrapher relayed each new statistic to the five men operating the camp's scoreboard. In addition to runs, hits, errors, and the up-to-the-minute score, the newspaper reported that "the very movement of the ball on the playing field itself is duplicated in the movement of the artificial baseball as it moves around the green playing field of the scoreboard," and that the board also displayed the "movements of the runners on the bases."[36] An estimated 12,000 to 14,000 Camp Greene men and 5000 to 10,000 civilians were able to "attend" the first game of the series, creating "probably . . . the largest crowd ever assembled in Charlotte," as well as "the largest gathering of soldiers many here have ever seen, except probably a few of the Confederate veterans who have doubtless seen much larger gatherings."[37] With a crowd only slightly smaller than the one attending the real game in Comiskey Park, the Camp Greene event was, in the opinion of its sponsor, "by far the greatest sporting event this city has ever known."[38]

The men of Camp Greene had a wide variety of other entertainment options. The YMCA and other organizations brought movies, concerts, theatrical performances, and lectures to camp. In town, theaters offered movies and live entertainment, the latter including concerts, especially by popular jazz bands, and vaudeville shows, which were advertised as "high class" but promised "Girls, Girls, Girls."[39] Charlotte's famous Lakewood Park was a short trolley ride away from Camp Greene. Offering dances, boating, swimming, carnival-type amusements, and a zoo, the park was popular with both soldiers and civilians, including some of the "respectable young ladies" from Charlotte who attended carefully chaperoned dances held by the Daughters of the American Revolution and the United Daughters of the Confederacy. More convenient for soldiers was Liberty Park, a facility built at the camp that included a "Liberty Theater" for films and live performances, food and drink stands, a shooting gallery, and other amusements. Liberty Park's operators advertised their venue as "Your Park—Planned, Built and Operated for the Pleasure of the Soldier," and they assured soldiers that "it is here that you will find high-class amusement and entertainment, courtesy and a spirit of fair treatment that will make the hours that you spend here linger as pleasant memories long after they are gone."[40]

The men of Camp Greene also enjoyed keeping up with the news. They had access to a number of local and national publications through the camp library, but for both "war news" and news of the camp and the civilian community, soldiers generally relied upon two weekly publications—the newspaper

Trench and Camp and the magazine *The Caduceus*. Published under the auspices of the YMCA, issues of *Trench and Camp* were available at each of the nation's thirty-two training camps. The *Charlotte Observer* published the "CAMP GREENE EDITION" of *Trench and Camp*, which generally consisted of eight to fourteen pages. Each edition included "national" stories (i.e., war news, sports, and similar items) and local news (i.e., event calendars, gossip, stories, poems, and cartoons) as well as soldier-oriented advertising from ice cream parlors, department stores, cigar shops, and similar businesses anxious to let soldiers know "We Welcome the Boys of Camp Greene!"[41] Unlike *Trench and Camp, The Caduceus* was a true "soldier publication," written, produced, and distributed by the enlisted men of the Camp Greene Base Hospital and funded by sales (five cents per copy) and paid advertising from local businesses. Several of the men who worked on *The Caduceus* had been newspapermen before the war, and due to its high-quality writing and production, the magazine earned national recognition as "America's Greatest Camp Publication."[42] With an average paid circulation of 10,000 copies and an estimated readership of 50,000 soldiers and civilians, *The Caduceus* was, during its short existence, one of the most widely circulated and best-known publications in the Charlotte area.[43]

Unfortunately, the soldiers of Camp Greene sought out other forms of entertainment of which military and local authorities strongly disapproved. At the outset of the war, the War Department made it clear that it considered prostitution and alcohol to be major threats to military mobilization and readiness. In August 1917, Secretary of War Baker sent a letter to civil authorities in the areas surrounding training camps, explaining the department's position. Titled "Suppression of Prostitution and the Sale of Alcohol to Soldiers," the letter noted that while the Draft Act specifically banned prostitution and alcohol sales within five miles of a camp, the War Department discouraged those activities just outside that range as well. Baker threatened that if the civil authorities near a camp could not control the situation, "it might be easier and cheaper to move the camp to a more desirable locality."[44]

Officially, Charlotte had been a "dry" city for a dozen years before the war, and the Charlotte Chamber had emphasized the community's hostility to "the liquor trade" in its arguments for locating a mobilization and training camp in the area. During the period 1917–1919, the *Charlotte Observer* frequently ran items about the diligence of local authorities in making sure "the soldiers at Camp Greene and citizens of Charlotte are going to be given full protection against the designs of the whiskey-runners."[45] In January 1918, when federal authorities issued a national report about communities selling liquor to soldiers, the *Observer* proudly reported that Camp Greene was not on the "roll call of the camps charged with winking at the moonshine traffic."[46] That same month, however, the newspaper admitted that one-third of all illegal liquor distilleries "seized by government revenue officers during the past government fiscal year in the whole United States were in North Carolina."[47] Furthermore, it noted that the 680 "stills" seized in North Carolina represented "not more than one in five of the distilleries actually operated in the state" and that "North Carolina must have constantly no less than 3,500 of these distilleries in operation from time to time."[48] Since Camp Greene was located near one of the nation's largest bootlegging networks, it seems clear that the moonshine traffic near the camp was still substantial.

Despite the best efforts of the authorities, in Charlotte "there were . . . as there are in all prohibition towns, sundry and various locations where supplies of liquor could be mysteriously obtained."[49] Several speakeasies or "blind tigers" (both colorful terms for illegal bars) operated during the Camp Greene era, and several businesses that identified themselves as "hotels" or "restaurants" offered liquor as well. Indeed, judging from the number of alcohol-related disciplinary incidents involving the camp's soldiers, the first commander of Camp Greene may have been mistaken when, in November 1917, he informed the War Department that there was "no liquor problem" in Charlotte and that "there are no saloons, one has to obtain liquor surreptitiously and look hard for it."[50]

He may also have been in error when he informed the War Department that "I know of no way, after a careful observation, how a man can come in contact with prostitutes in Charlotte without diligently seeking them."[51] Others noted at the end of 1917 after the national guard troops left and regular army troops took their place that "there were an unusually large number of prostitutes in Charlotte," many of whom likely followed the troops from their original posts.[52] The *Charlotte Observer* reported in late November that city, state, and federal authorities were conferring "because they viewed with alarm the influx of women of questionable character into the city within the past ten days."[53] At the request of city officials, federal authorities agreed to prosecute all "lewd women" caught "plying their trade" in federal court, instead of local or state court, because "the fines and other punishment [are] more severe and it was believed conviction more sure."[54] According to the newspaper, the prostitution problem had become something of a major crisis for the city: "While the situation is not considered beyond the control of city officials, things have become decidedly alarming within the last ten days. The city is now in a worse condition than at any other time during the life of Camp Greene."[55] Sufficiently concerned about these reports, the War Department sent a sternly worded memorandum entitled "Moral Conditions at Charlotte, North Carolina" to the Commanding General of Camp Greene, warning that "the military police recently have not been as active as they might in suppressing prostitution and the sale of liquor to soldiers" and that "if prompt and aggressive action is not taken by the Commanding General at Camp Greene, these conditions are likely to become much worse."[56] Camp authorities took steps to remedy the situation and then reported to the War Department that now there was "nothing in the conduct of the soldiers and women on the streets to indicate the presence of prostitutes to the average observer."[57]

The War Department's foremost concern with prostitution was the spread of venereal disease, and the suppression of prostitution was not, in and of itself, sufficient. As one official noted, "we found that venereal disease was coming not from the prostitutes, but from the type known in the military camps as the flapper – that is, the young girls who were not prostitutes, but who probably would be tomorrow, and who were diseased and promiscuous."[58] Although perhaps unfair in their judgments since there is no clear evidence to conclude that local girls were "diseased" before they encountered the young soldiers at the camp, Charlotte authorities viewed the "mill girls" from local textile factories as potential sources of illicit sex and disease. Many of them were young, single, and living apart from their families, having come from rural areas throughout the state in search of work in Charlotte's booming wartime textile industry. Believing that some of these girls were likely to be "too friendly" to Camp Greene's lonely soldiers, authorities at the camp did their best to keep the men of the camp away from them; one commander noted that "the Provost Guard has been instructed to exclude or remove all notorious women, others found violating the ordinary proprieties of conduct will be required to leave."[59] City officials also took steps to keep "loose women" away from the men of Camp Greene. In addition to prosecuting prostitutes, Charlotte's leaders took steps to control the behavior of the mill girls and other young women of potentially questionable morals. These steps included the establishment of a detention home for girls and the appointment of several "matrons" to conduct patrols on the streets to help round up wayward girls found "loitering around . . . where soldiers are stationed."[60]

Although generally positive, relations between Camp Greene and Charlotte were sometimes tenuous. When the War Department began sending significant numbers of black recruits to Camp Greene in the summer of 1918, there were no public protests or increases in race-related incidents, despite reports of racial violence, lynching, and other race-related disturbances elsewhere in the South.[61] However, the decision to send black troops to Camp Greene was not a popular one. Articles in the *Charlotte Observer* indicated that (white) Charlotteans were less than enthusiastic about seeing black men wearing Army uniforms.[62] After the Armistice, the War Department issued Special Orders to the commander of Camp Greene, detailing how to expedite the discharge of "colored troops" while retaining enough of them to dismantle the camp. The lack of protest in Charlotte when Camp Greene closed indicates that the city's white leaders and citizens felt a sense of relief, not a sense of civic loss, when the camp's black soldiers left town. Significantly, there does not appear to have been any significant racial strife related to or arising from the presence of African American soldiers at Camp Greene. Both contemporary media coverage and the camp's official disciplinary records indicate that—unlike some of the other mobilization camps—there were no reported instances of race-related conflict, and there appear to have been fewer military disciplinary actions involving Camp Greene's black soldiers than those involving white ones.

Officially and publicly, the soldiers of Camp Greene were well received by the people of Charlotte. In turn, Army officers invited Charlotteans to attend band concerts and other events at the post. The pages of the *Charlotte Observer*, *Trench and Camp*, and *The Caduceus* fail to dispel the notion that all was well between the camp and the city. Further analysis, however, reveals that the relationship was not always tranquil. Camp Greene's thousands of bored, lonely, and anxious men occasionally were not on their "best behavior" while visiting the civilian community. In some cases, the infractions were relatively minor. During the bitter winter of 1917–1918, Camp Greene soldiers responded to the lack of "official" firewood by commandeering a "midnight requisition" from the camp's civilian neighbors. In June 1918, the camp's commander had to remind his soldiers that they were prohibited from stealing peaches from nearby orchards.[63] For the most part, Charlotte residents ignored these minor incidents.

Sometimes, though, the soldiers engaged in more serious misconduct. There were a number of reported instances of civil authorities arresting Camp Greene men, including some junior officers, for drunken brawling or "consorting with questionable women" in public.[64] Some of the complaints involved soldiers "interfering with" the mill girls. [65] Following one incident, the manager of a nearby mill complained to Camp Greene's commander that on the previous Sunday, 100–150 soldiers had invaded the mill village and that, in addition to "bothering" the mill girls, "they danced on the porches of some of our people, using much vulgarity and profanity, and that they entered some of our houses in the village and tore down the electrical wiring and fixtures."[66] Managers at several of the local mills eventually requested that their premises be made "off limits" to the soldiers and that guards be posted to enforce such orders. Authorities at Camp Greene also received complaints from local law enforcement officials concerning soldiers who were involved in offenses ranging from public drunkenness to robbery, assault, and arson.[67] Exasperated by the conduct of soldiers "on pass" in his town, one local police chief requested that the camp post a Provost Guard in his town on Saturday and Sunday to "stop the practice of soldiers coming here on the hunt for women and liquor."[68]

While the soldiers' misconduct obviously "reflected poorly" on Camp Greene, some civilian behavior affected how soldiers saw their civilian hosts.

The most significant issue of this kind was the perception that Charlotteans were "price gouging" or "profiteering" at the soldiers' expense. While many in the city were naturally enthusiastic about the financial opportunities of hosting a training camp, contemporary observers expressed concern about civilians preying on soldiers. One YMCA official, commenting on the prostitutes, bootleggers, gamblers, gangsters, and con artists attracted to "army towns" like Charlotte, opined that "possibly the most repulsive occurrence in the civilized community in war time is the gathering of the bloodsuckers. Profiteers burr around the honeypot in countless numbers...."[69] "Legitimate" businesses (i.e., those not selling prohibited goods) were not immune to these accusations. The War Department made its position clear when it advised all army commanders that any confirmed incidents involving soldiers being overcharged for goods or services "shall result" in the posting of that business's name on the camp bulletin board and the local Chamber of Commerce being advised that the business had been placed "off limits."[70]

Camp Greene authorities relayed the official position concerning price gouging to Charlotte merchants, who were also reminded, by a number of articles and editorials in the *Charlotte Observer*, that taking advantage of the soldiers was in the long run "bad for business." Furthermore, the soldiers themselves had strong opinions about profiteering. One soldier, a cynical Bostonian named Joseph Matthews, commented that "the Charlotte people are benefitting wonderfully by the soldier presence so they should treat them kindly" but noted that "there's going to be a lot of newly rich people when the time comes for the camp to break."[71] In a letter home written shortly after the Armistice, Matthews expressed surprise that he had recently gotten a ride back to camp in a civilian's automobile and that it was the first time that he had not been asked for money.[72] In another post-war letter, he wrote that he observed a civilian contractor pushing his men to quickly finish a job at the base hospital, "possibly figuring it's the last chance to hook a little graft."[73] Soon after, Matthews commented that Charlotteans "evidently thought it would be shame to have a soldier go away from here with money in his pocket."[74] Clearly, some of those stationed at Camp Greene did not believe all Charlotteans were above taking economic advantage of the camp's soldiers.

The single most significant event that occurred at Camp Greene was one that also profoundly affected the city: the Great Flu Epidemic of 1918–1919. During this pandemic, between fifty million and one hundred million people would die from complications associated with the disease. In the United States alone, an estimated 700,000 people died from the flu and related illnesses.[75] In late September and early October 1918, the influenza pandemic struck the US Army's training camps. Between September 12 and October 18, camps reported 274,745 cases, 46,286 of which developed into pneumonia and 14,616 of which resulted in death.[76] During the peak of the epidemic, official reports listed 621,000 soldiers infected, about one-sixth of the total number who served in the war.[77] Of these, at least 43,000 died.[78] There were an estimated 111,179 American military deaths during World War I, with a little more than half of these (56,532) attributable to disease rather than to battle.[79]

Camp Greene was devastated by the flu epidemic, suffering a far greater incidence of disease and death than the city of Charlotte. With a population of about 45,000, Charlotte in 1918 reported 3,281 cases of influenza and influenza/pneumonia leading to 344 deaths. In 1919, there were only 625 cases of influenza/pneumonia and just ninety-nine deaths.[80] By contrast, in October 1918, Camp Greene had a population of only 28,852 officers and enlisted men,[81] but, by October 16th, the camp had over 3,000 influenza cases, and the epidemic caused 193 deaths between September 29 and October 16.[82] Clearly, the young soldiers of Camp Greene had a far more harrowing experience with the flu than did their host city.[83] As a soldier later recalled, "hundreds, hundreds of boys died from the flu . . . the Southern [Railway] station was full of caskets every morning, going up North."[84] There were so many deaths at Camp Greene that local undertakers were swamped; at one establishment, sixty bodies were stacked awaiting funerals or transportation home. Military funeral processions took place regularly on Trade Street in Charlotte, with many of the dead soldiers being buried in the city's Elmwood Cemetery.[85]

The flu epidemic significantly altered ordinary life at Camp Greene. A quarantine order was put into effect at the start of the outbreak and was not completely lifted until February 1919. Military authorities suspended or placed off limits virtually all forms of recreation during this time. Soldiers could no longer play musical instruments; play cards; or attend movies, lectures, plays, or other gatherings. Officers discouraged them from attending any activities not mandated by the army and encouraged them to wear gauze masks when in public. Denied the pleasures of Charlotte and its surrounding towns, most of the men had "nowhere to go and nothing to do" during the quarantine. As Joseph Matthews wrote in October, "most everything is demoralized around here to some extent."[86] Noting that the epidemic even prevented him from attending church, he later commented that "this old quarantine is getting monotonous."[87] Only in late October did life at the camp begin to return to normal. On October 26, *The Caduceus* reported that camp hospital authorities stated that "the crisis has been passed."[88] Interestingly enough, the end of the epidemic's crisis phase—marked by the raising of the quarantine that had been placed on the camp—coincided with the end of Camp Greene's *raison d'etre*. On the morning of November 11, 1918, the camp commander announced that "the quarantine against Spanish influenza which had been in effect for nearly six weeks at Camp Greene," prohibiting most soldiers from visiting Charlotte and most civilians from visiting the camp, was lifted. That same morning, the camp authorities received word that an armistice had been signed and that the war was effectively over.[89]

After the Armistice, the War Department declined to select Camp Greene to become a permanent post for America's postwar Army. In spite of the obvious financial benefits, the experience of hosting a military base likely dampened Charlotteans' enthusiasm for being an army town; the Charlotte Chamber of Commerce and other civic and business groups were noticeably silent when the War Department announced its decision to close Camp Greene in mid-1919. Instead, the city's leaders focused on dismantling the camp, selling off any equipment or building materials not claimed by the military, and then returning the land that had been occupied by the camp to civilian use. As a result, by the end of 1919, the soldiers were all gone, and the physical camp had essentially disappeared.

In the years after the war, Charlotteans had fond memories of the "Camp Greene boys" and the days when the city played host to the camp. The city, though, essentially returned to normal, with its population returning to near-pre-war levels almost as quickly as the physical camp was dismantled and sold, and census records indicate that the existence of Camp Greene had little appreciable impact on the long-term population growth of the city.[90] Overall though, Charlotte's bank accounts were fatter after the war, and there were certainly new buildings, roads, and other infrastructure in place by 1920. However, there is no evidence that the experience of hosting an Army camp fundamentally changed the character of the city or its people. After World War I, Charlotte remained a business-oriented city, devoted to self-promotion and growth, much as it has been during its pre-war history.

Notes

1. Edward Coffman, *The Regulars: The American Army, 1898–1941* (Cambridge, MA: Harvard University Press, 2004), 203.

2. Ibid., 283.

3. Edward M. Coffman, The *War to End all Wars: The American Military Experience in World War I* (Lexington: University Press of Kentucky, 1968), 30.

4. Ibid., 18.

5. Mary Kratt, *Charlotte, North Carolina: A Brief History* (Charleston: The History Press, 2009), 114.

6. *Charlotte Observer,* July 13, 1917.

7. Nearby examples include Camp (Fort) Bragg in Fayetteville, North Carolina, and Camp (Fort) Jackson in Columbia, South Carolina.

8. Jack Claiborne, *Crown of the Queen City: The Charlotte Chamber From 1870 to 1999* (Charlotte: The Charlotte Chamber, 1999), 46.

9. *Charlotte Observer,* April 19, 1917, 12.

10. *Charlotte Observer,* July 13, 1917, 2.

11. One of the factors behind this decision was the 1918–1919 influenza pandemic. Military medical authorities evidently believed that with cold weather approaching, it would be "healthier" to send men to camps in the South rather than those in the North.

12. "Zone of the Interior: Territorial Departments and Tactical Divisions Organized in 1918 Posts, Camps and Stations," in *Order of Battle of the United States Land Forces in the World War,* Vol. 3, Part 2 (Washington, DC: Center of Military History, 1988), 823–824.

13. Ibid.

14. Ibid.

15. *Charlotte Observer,* October 26, 1918, 2.

16. Jennifer D. Keene, *Doughboys, the Great War, and the Remaking of America* (Baltimore: Johns Hopkins University Press, 2001), 37.

17. J. C. Boyarsky, oral interview transcript, May 22, 1979, Special Collections, J. Murrey Atkins Library, University of North Carolina at Charlotte.

18. Joseph Mathews to Eva La Flamme, February 18, 1918, Joseph B. Mathews Papers, Special Collections, J. Murrey Atkins Library, University of North Carolina at Charlotte.

19. *Trench and Camp,* January 29, 1918.

20. Joseph Mathews to Eva La Flamme, June 5, 1918, Joseph B. Mathews Papers, Special Collections, J. Murrey Atkins Library, University of North Carolina at Charlotte.

21. "Conditions at Camp Greene," speech given by Hon. Sherman E. Burroughs of New Hampshire in the House of Representatives, February 22, 1918 (Washington, DC: Government Printing Office, 1918).

22. Ibid. During the period when the population of the camp peaked (in early 1918), ten to twelve men were sometimes crowded into each tent. Coffman, *The War to End All Wars,* 64.

23. Ibid.

24. Ibid. It would appear that Burroughs' speech—and the confirmation provided by the Surgeon General—prompted both calls for the abandonment of the camp and substantial remedial work that was done to improve the living conditions at Camp Greene.

25. See, for example, the placing of (among other businesses) a prominent local dairy creamery "off limits" in Camp Greene Memorandum No. 206, July 15, 1918, Box 20, Entry 177–1, "Camp Green, NC; General Correspondence, July 1917–March 1919," Record Group 393, Part V. Records of US Army Continental Commands, 1821–1920, National Archives and Record Administration, Washington, DC.

26. Unnumbered Camp Greene Memorandum, November 14, 1917, Box 20, Entry 177–1, "Camp Green, NC; General Correspondence, July 1917–March 1919," Record Group 393, Part V. Records of US Army Continental Commands, 1821–1920, National Archives and Record Administration, Washington, DC.

27. Unnumbered Camp Greene Memorandum dated May 19, 1918, citing earlier memoranda, Nos. 90 and 105, concerning vendors and "negro women," respectively, Box 22, Entry 177–4, "Camp Greene, NC; Memorandums and Bulletins, May 1918–February 1919," Record Group 393, Part V. Records of US Army Continental Commands, 1821–1920, National Archives and Record Administration, Washington, DC.

28. Coffman, *The War to End All Wars,* 65.

29. Paul Eliot Greene to "Buie," August 11, 1917, Paul Eliot Green Papers, Southern Historical Collection, University of North Carolina at Chapel Hill.

30. Mrs. Ralph Van Landingham, *"History of the Charlotte American Red Cross,"* July 1, 1920, Box 3, Van Landingham Family Papers, Special Collections, J. Murrey Atkins Library, University of North Carolina at Charlotte.

31. Quoted in Allan M. Brandt, *No Magic Bullet: A Social History of Venereal Disease in the United States Since 1880* (New York: Oxford University Press, 1987), 58.

32. *Trench and Camp,* October 22, 1917, 10.

33. Ibid.

34. Ibid.

35. *Charlotte Observer,* October 5, 1917, 1.

36. *Charlotte Observer,* October 5, 1917, 9.

37. Ibid.

38. *Charlotte Observer,* October 5, 1917, 4.

39. *The Caduceus,* July 13, 1918, 11, and August 17, 1918, 14.

40. *Trench and Camp,* March 4, 1918, 3.

41. *Trench and Camp,* October 8, 1917, 4.

42. *The Caduceus,* September 28, 1918, 2.

43. *The Caduceus,* August 31, 1918, 2.

44. Memorandum Secretary of War to Civil Authorities, "Subject: Suppression of Prostitution and the Sale of Alcohol to Soldiers," August 10, 1917, Box 4, Entry 177–1, "Camp Greene, NC; General Correspondence, July 1917–March 1919," Record Group 393, Part V. Records of US Army Continental Commands, 1821–1920, National Archives and Record Administration, Washington, DC.

45. *Charlotte Observer,* February 11, 1918, 4. Ironically, one of the "big blockade stills" seized by the authorities during this time period was said to have been run by a George Dry. *Charlotte Observer,* February 14, 1918, 13.

46. *Charlotte Observer,* January 15, 1918, 4.

47. *Charlotte Observer,* January 1, 1918, 7.

48. Ibid.

49. *Charlotte Observer,* November 5, 1917, 4.

50. Memorandum from Commanding General, Camp Greene to Adjutant General's Office, November 4, 1917, Box 1, Entry 177–1, "Camp Greene, NC; General Correspondence, July 1917–March 1919," Record Group 393, Part V. Records of U.S. Army Continental Commands, 1821–1920, National Archives and Record Administration, Washington, DC.

51. Ibid.

52. Memorandum from Major General Dickman [Commanding General, Camp Greene] to Adjutant General's Office, December 24, 1917, Box 3, Entry 177–1, "Camp Greene, NC; General Correspondence, July 1917–March 1919," Record Group 393, Part V. Records of US Army Continental Commands, 1821–1920, National Archives and Record Administration, Washington, DC.

53. *Charlotte Observer,* November 20, 1917, 11.

54. Ibid.

55. Ibid.

56. Memorandum from Adjutant General's Office to Commanding General, Camp Greene, December 18, 1917, Box 3, Entry 177–1, "Camp Greene, NC; General Correspondence, July 1917–March 1919," Record Group 393, Part V. Records of US Army Continental Commands, 1821–1920, National Archives and Record Administration, Washington, DC.

57. Memorandum from Major General Dickman [Commanding General, Camp Greene] to Adjutant General's Office, December 24, 1917, Box 3, Entry 177–1, "Camp Greene, NC; General Correspondence, July 1917–March 1919," Record Group 393, Part V. Records of US Army Continental Commands, 1821–1920, National Archives and Record Administration, Washington, DC.

58. Brandt, *No Magic Bullet,* 81.

59. Letter from Major General Dickman [Commanding General, Camp Greene] to Mrs. A.T. Aummey–Executive Committee on Training Camp Activities, Carnegie Library, Charlotte, December 10, 1917, Box 3, Entry 177–1, "Camp Greene, NC; General Correspondence, July 1917–March 1919," Record Group 393, Part V. Records of US Army Continental Commands, 1821–1920, National Archives and Record Administration, Washington, DC.

60. *Charlotte Observer,* August 23, 1917, 3.

61. Review of the surviving official records from Camp Greene does not reveal any significant racially oriented issue or event. Although "colored" soldiers appear in disciplinary records, they were cited for the same offenses and infractions as white soldiers, and the number of "colored" offenders appears to have been proportionately equal—or less than—the number of white offenders.

62. *Charlotte Observer,* December 1, 1918, 3.

63. Camp Greene Memorandum No. 146, June 11, 1918, Box 1, Entry 177–1, "Camp Greene, NC; General Correspondence, July 1917–March 1919," Record Group 393, Part V. Records of US Army Continental Commands, 1821–1920, National Archives and Record Administration, Washington, DC.

64. Letter from Major W. D. Wercer to Commanding General, Camp Greene, February 28, 1918, Box 1, Entry 177–1, "Camp Greene, NC; General Correspondence, July 1917–March 1919," Record Group 393, Part V. Records of US Army Continental Commands, 1821–1920, National Archives and Record Administration, Washington, DC.

65. Letter from Atherton Mills to Commanding General, Camp Greene, February 20, 1918, Box 4, Entry 177–1, "Camp Greene, NC; General Correspondence, July 1917–March 1919," Record Group 393, Part V. Records of US Army Continental Commands, 1821–1920, National Archives and Record Administration, Washington, DC.

66. Letter from Elizabeth Mills to Commanding General, Camp Greene, January 28, 1918, Box 4, Entry 177–1, "Camp Greene, NC; General Correspondence, July 1917–March 1919," Record Group 393, Part V. Records of U.S. Army Continental Commands, 1821–1920, National Archives and Record Administration, Washington, DC.

67. Letter from Chief of Police of Salisbury, North Carolina, to Commanding General, Camp Greene, January 22, 1918, Box 4, Entry 177–1, "Camp Greene, NC; General Correspondence, July 1917–March 1919," Record Group 393, Part V. Records of US Army Continental Commands, 1821–1920, National Archives and Record Administration, Washington, DC.

68. Ibid.

69. Brandt, *No Magic Bullet,* 71.

70. Memorandum from Chief of Staff General Peyton March to all Commanding Generals referencing the General Order of July 28, 1918, concerning "price gouging," Box 1, Entry 177–1, "Camp Greene, NC; General Correspondence, July 1917–March 1919," Record Group 393, Part V. Records of US Army Continental Commands, 1821–1920, National Archives and Record Administration, Washington, DC.

71. Joseph Mathews to Eva La Flamme, May 18, 1918, Joseph B. Mathews Papers, Special Collections, J. Murrey Atkins Library, University of North Carolina at Charlotte.

72. Joseph Mathews to Eva La Flamme, November 25, 1918, Joseph B. Mathews Papers, Special Collections, J. Murrey Atkins Library, University of North Carolina at Charlotte.

73. Joseph Mathews to Eva La Flamme, November 14, 1918, Joseph B. Mathews Papers, Special Collections, J. Murrey Atkins Library, University of North Carolina at Charlotte.

74. Joseph Mathews to Eva La Flamme, December 5, 1918, Joseph B. Mathews Papers, Special Collections, J. Murrey Atkins Library, University of North Carolina at Charlotte.

75. Alfred Crosby, *America's Forgotten Pandemic: The Influenza of 1918* (Cambridge: Cambridge University Press, 2003), 206.

76. George A. Soper, "The Influenza Pneumonia Pandemic in the American Army Camps during September and October 1918," *Science.* New Series 48, no. 1245 (November 8, 1918): 453.

77. Crosby, *America's Forgotten Pandemic,* 205.

78. Ibid., 206.

79. Dorothy Petit and Janice Bailie, *A Cruel Wind: Pandemic Flu in America, 1918–1920* (Murfreesboro, TN: Timberlane Books, 2008), 174.

80. "The Notifiable Diseases: Prevalence during 1918 in Cities of 10,000 to 100,000," *Public Health Reports* 34, no. 52 (December 2, 1919): 2966–2998, and *Public Health Reports* 36, no. 15 (April 15, 1921): 752–816.

81. "Zone of the Interior: Territorial Departments and Tactical Divisions."

82. *Charlotte Observer,* October 16, 1918.

83. It is generally agreed that following the November 11, 1918, Armistice, it was difficult to calculate or compare Army camp influenza statistics because the rapid demobilization of the Army made the reliability of those figures suspect. Crosby, *America's Forgotten Pandemic,* 206.

84. Boyarsky, oral interview transcript, May 22, 1979.

85. Grace Mitchell and Edward Perzel, *The Echo of the Bugle Call, Charlotte's Role in World War I* (Charlotte: Dowd House Preservation Committee, 1979), 47.

86. Joseph Mathews to Eva La Flamme, September 29, 1918, Joseph B. Mathews Papers, Special Collections, J. Murrey Atkins Library, University of North Carolina at Charlotte.

87. Joseph Mathews to Eva La Flamme, October 13, 1918, Joseph B. Mathews Papers, Special Collections, J. Murrey Atkins Library, University of North Carolina at Charlotte.

88. *The Caduceus,* October 26, 1918, 7–8.

89. *Charlotte Observer,* November 11, 1918, 5.

90. US Bureau of the Census, *Thirteenth Census of the United States, 1910. Vol. 1, Population* (Washington, DC: Government Printing Office, 1913); US Bureau of the Census, *Fourteenth Census of the United States, 1910. Vol. 1, Population* (Washington, DC: Government Printing Office, 1923); U.S. Bureau of the Census, *Fifteenth Census of the United States, 1910. Vol. 1, Population* (Washington, DC: Government Printing Office, 1933); US Bureau of the Census, *Fourteenth Census of the United States, State Compendium, North Carolina: Statistics of Population, Occupations, Agriculture, Drainage, Manufactures, and Mines and Quarries for the State Counties and Cities.* (Washington, DC: Government Printing Office, 1925).

3

Planting Doughboys on the Farm

Hugh MacRae and the Soldier Settlement Movement

J. Vincent Lowery

On the morning of November 11, 1918, Wilmington businessman Hugh MacRae sat in the audience at the Southern Land Congress in Savannah, Georgia, and listened as William B. Stillwell, vice president of the Georgia Land Owners' Association, made an eagerly anticipated announcement: "[T]oday we have had what we believe to be an unconditional surrender of the remaining two [enemies], Germany and Austria." This news underscored the importance of the conference, at which southern businessmen, politicians, and college professors gathered to discuss the South's potential role in Secretary of the Interior Franklin K. Lane's plan to develop farm communities for returning soldiers. Stillwell explained: "[W]e have the future to make for the returning soldiers and sailors in this Coastal Plain region—these broad acres—millions of acres that we wish to put to beneficial use." MacRae, a committed agricultural reformer and a member of the North Carolina delegation, endorsed the soldier settlement proposal when he addressed the convention on its second day, and he lobbied the state government to support the program for the next two years. He imagined Lane's plan transforming rural life in North Carolina and beyond.[1]

MacRae's work on behalf of the soldier settlement movement represents an example of southern Progressives' advocacy of federal interventionist strategies to solve the South's problems. These reformers anticipated a greater degree of political influence and constructive legislation from the southern-born Democratic president Woodrow Wilson. After 1912, southern Progressives became increasingly active in national campaigns for railroad regulations, child labor laws, prohibition, and various agricultural reforms. Historian Dewey Grantham explains that World War I "created new opportunities for social planning and even nourished the Progressive belief that by altering the environment it was possible to reconstruct society." Throughout the war, southern reformers engaged in Progressive initiatives at the local, state, and national level, seeking this transformation through interventionist policies. Hugh MacRae campaigned for Lane's soldier settlement proposal because he believed in its ability to reorganize rural life around truck-farm communities and to promote more efficient farming methods and cooperative marketing techniques.[2]

Profiling MacRae and his rural development vision for *Collier's* in 1922, muckraking journalist Ida M. Tarbell observed that "MacRae seems to have begun life land-minded and always to have had an appreciation of what people call 'dirt farming.'" According to contemporary accounts, MacRae's interest in land development began with childhood conversations with his father about the family's idle lands. Yet he first followed in the footsteps of his grandfather and father, captains of industry in southeastern North Carolina. Young MacRae earned his engineering degree at the Massachusetts Institute of Technology in 1885 and then worked in the mining industry in western North Carolina. He eventually returned to the "Port City," where he took charge of the Wilmington Cotton Mills after his father's death. He also formed an investment firm and promoted the modernization of the city's infrastructure, but he never forgot those long-ago conversations with his father. MacRae increasingly devoted his energy and resources to the development of idle lands surrounding the city. Edwin Bjorkman, the author of a 1935 North Carolina Federal Writers' Project essay on MacRae, explained that the Wilmington businessman believed "he could begin to pour what he had taken out of business into the materialization of that dream."[3]

In the early twentieth century, MacRae and the Carolina Trucking Development Company recruited European farmers for settlements in southeastern North Carolina. He began this work less than a decade after the Wilmington Race Riot of 1898, which overthrew the city's interracial government and concluded the white supremacists' statewide counterrevolution. MacRae, one of the suspected conspirators responsible for the riot, believed that the region must take further steps to resolve the so-called "Negro Problem." Although Democrats ushered in the era of Jim Crow after retaking control of the state, many whites remained unsatisfied by their incomplete dominance over African Americans. Southern whites often presented the South's agricultural woes in racialized terms, and MacRae echoed the sentiments of many white North Carolinians when he blamed black farmers for the South's agricultural shortcomings. He proposed that African Americans were "better adapted to heavy work, say, in an iron foundry or a rolling mill. Negroes do not have the intelligence back of them to make good at scientific farming. They lower the standard of the whole agricultural situation." Seeking to marginalize or even replace African American farmers, the Carolina Trucking Development Company began bringing Dutch, English, German, Greek, Hungarian, Italian, and Polish farmers to the region. In defense of his recruitment of European labor, MacRae declared, "The South has everything to gain, and nothing to lose in this movement, because we would replace the lowest type of labor, that is labor obtained originally from the lowest race on earth, by a type of labor which would be so selected as to represent a standard immeasurably higher than the one we have been accustomed to."[4]

Historian Tycho de Boer argues that "MacRae's vision was a Progressive one—he wanted to place science, diversification, efficiency, legibility, organization, and integration at the heart of the modern farming enterprise." The company directed settlers to employ small-scale, intensive farming methods. A superintendent operated a demonstration farm to teach settlers best practices, and the company provided various farm implements on reasonable terms. The company also built schools and churches to promote cooperation and social satisfaction among the colonists. *Manufacturer's Record* special correspondent George Byrne visited the colonies in 1912, and he marveled at the achievements made by MacRae's settlers. He observed their profitable and diversified pursuits, their cooperative spirit, and their contentment with their own farms and their communities. Byrne proclaimed the project "the most significant enterprise being carried forward in the South," and he expressed hope that other southern developers would follow the example.[5]

Writing to fellow North Carolinian and renowned Progressive publisher Walter Hines Page in 1913, MacRae claimed that the successes of the colonies validated his vision and warranted a broader rural reform campaign based on that model. He no longer touted the racial dimensions of his plan so forcefully, and the election of Woodrow Wilson likely assured him that the federal government would honor the racial impulses of his vision. He continued to present Europeans as the most suitable farmers for his small-scale, intensive, cooperative plan. He also promoted domestic reforms capable of achieving the same results. MacRae predicted that Wilson, supported by a carefully chosen cabinet, would renew the Progressive promise presumably violated by the administration of his predecessor, William Howard Taft. Like Page and other southern Progressives, MacRae believed that federal agencies under the Wilson administration could combat the South's rural woes. By the end of Wilson's first term in office, the Wilmington businessman imagined the federal government, guided by publicly minded people operating as "a great laboratory in which our national problems are first analyzed and then by synthetic process sound policies constructed and enforced. The results would then be returned to the people in a way that would be most beneficial."[6]

MacRae argued that Interior Secretary Lane's soldier settlement program revealed the Progressive potential of the Wilson administration. Lane's plan represented the climax of Progressive rural planning in the early twentieth century. The Bureau of Reclamation had proposed various settlement projects at the turn of the century, but historian Donald J. Pisani explains that "the bureau provided little aid and spent little time planning the communities."

Lane corrected these problems by following the advice of irrigation specialist and rural planer Elwood Mead, who recommended clustered farms in colonies as a means to transform the isolated frontier tradition into a modern, cooperative endeavor. Although Lane promoted farms as proper rewards for doughboys' service—and the means by which to protect the nation against a postwar unemployment surge—the Secretary also believed that veterans represented a potential new class of farmers capable of strengthening the country's agricultural economy. Yet Mead anticipated an even more sweeping transformation. Historian Bill Reid explains that Mead predicted these soldier settlements "would afford an example of the advantages of co-operative marketing and scientific production and might effect [sic] a revolution in American farming." MacRae shared Mead's hope, and he lobbied for a North Carolina soldier settlement.[7]

In September 1918, MacRae and Matthew Hale, vice president of the Wilmington-based Liberty Shipbuilding Company, met with Lane. MacRae, Hale, and Lane discussed the possibility of establishing a soldier settlement in North Carolina. After the meeting, MacRae advised Governor Thomas W. Bickett that "there is an opportunity of initiating things for North Carolina which will do greater good in the way of development than the people have ever dreamed of." He asked the governor to contact Lane and offer the state's assistance. Bickett's Progressive credentials, which included measures to modernize agricultural methods, diversify crops, and eliminate crop liens and unfair interest rates, warranted Bickett's attention to MacRae's request. MacRae believed that the governor should use the power of his office to advance the solider settlement campaign for the state. The governor accepted this mission, and he named the Progressive land developer one of the state's delegates to the Southern Land Congress.[8]

The Southern Settlement and Development Organization (SSDO) organized the conference in Savannah with the Southern Pine Association, the Georgia Land Owners' Association, the Florida Tick Eradication Committee, the North Carolina Land Owners' Association, and the Savannah Board of Trade. Formed in 1912 by a group of southern governors working in conjunction with leading representatives from the railroad industry, the SSDO coordinated economic development programs across the region. Historian George Brown Tindall observes that SSDO vice president Clement S. Ucker shifted the focus of the organization to federal reclamation initiatives for cutover and swamp lands. Ucker imagined the Southern Land Congress assembling private organizations and state and federal officials to discuss the use of southern lands for soldier settlements.[9]

The Department of the Interior co-sponsored the meeting in Savannah. Although Lane planned to attend the conference, he remained in Washington, DC, to participate in cabinet discussions about the upcoming peace talks in Paris. Several officials, including rural planner Mead and Reclamation Bureau consulting engineer H. T. Cory, spoke at the event and appealed for support for Lane's plan. Assigned to investigate conditions in the South, Cory traveled to Wilmington and toured the colonies, MacRae's livestock farm, and the city before the conference convened. When he addressed the convention, he expressed surprise at his discoveries in the region. Cory attributed his lack of awareness to longstanding false assumptions about sectional attitudes, race relations, and environmental conditions. Addressing those misperceptions, Cory proposed that the nation must be made aware that "the Southern people . . . welcome new blood and new capital." He also asserted that "[t]he negro problem in many ways is solving itself" as "the general public sentiment in the South calls for essential economic justice to the negro." Cory claimed that white southerners he spoke with during his tour believed "that the negroes should be segregated and kept to themselves, but the unanimity was absolute as to making full provision for the returned negro soldier and sailor." Cory's reference to race relations stood out in the conference proceedings; no other speaker mentioned African Americans specifically. When other participants talked about soldiers, they surely intended to refer to whites only. Cory also observed that the region had conquered mosquito-borne diseases and that its swamps and cutover lands were ripe for cultivation. He argued that the establishment of a colony in each southern state "would go far toward breaking up" such misperceptions that curtailed the region's development.[10]

Mead attempted to convince the audience that the soldier settlement program, led by the federal government, offered a sound strategy for improving rural life in the South. He cited similar policies in Denmark and Ireland as proof of the Interior Department's ability to end tenant farming and promote "the organization of communities for co-operative buying and selling and to meet social needs." Historian Daniel T. Rodgers explains that rural reformers identified European models as antidotes to American farmers' economic and social problems in the early twentieth century. Mead intended to transplant state-centered European reforms, but he understood that white southerners were suspicious of federal interference in local affairs. He insisted that federal supervision was essential to the program's success and explained that the Reclamation Service possessed the knowledge and skills to direct the initiative. Mead outlined a small role for each state, but he clearly imagined that the federal government would oversee the communities, thus retaining the centralization of power that defined the European models he cited. He concluded, "Those who believe that the strength and stability of this Nation depend on the character of its rural life, and that the great task of the future is to keep the country a reservoir of intelligent patriotism, must make this problem their own."[11]

The Southern Land Congress convened men who shared Mead's belief that the nation must build soldier settlements. Governor Bickett sent one of the largest state delegations, and Bickett, MacRae, and North Carolina Land

Owners Association President F. L. Finkenstaedt delivered speeches. Finkenstaedt, identified by historian Tycho de Boer as one of the lumbermen eager to sell cutover land to the federal government for proposed settlements, declared, "North Carolina wants to join forces with all the South and work shoulder to shoulder in the interest of our common problem. North Carolina asks all the other Southern States to do the same thing." Speaking of the state's desire to contribute to the soldier settlement movement, Bickett declared that North Carolina offered "desirable homesteads for at least half the returning soldiers who will feel inclined to take advantage of the opportunity the Government affords." The governor cited the success of MacRae's settlers as proof of the state's benefits for veterans.[12]

Asked to speak about his colonization work, MacRae instead chose to speak about his philosophy of "human engineering," which he developed through his work with immigrant farmers. This philosophy reflected MacRae's training as an engineer in an era when these professionals believed they were capable of solving society's problems through careful scientific study, analysis, and planning. MacRae proposed, "The efficiency of the individual, the methods of developing this efficiency and the proper rewards for compensating it will be carefully studied and applied. . . . From the scientific standpoint, the contentment and the happiness of the individual will be recognized as contributing to his efficiency and his value to his associates." Although he did not mention the work of Ellen H. Richards when he addressed the Southern Land Congress, her work likely impacted his reform spirit. A leading member of the home economics movement, Richards graduated from the Massachusetts Institute of Technology and joined the faculty as a chemistry instructor two years before MacRae completed his studies. There is no evidence that they crossed paths in Cambridge, although he probably encountered her, either in the classroom or through her husband. Robert Richards taught minerology, the North Carolinian's concentration, and the couple regularly hosted parties for students, faculty, and friends at their home. Moreover, their respective reform philosophies suggest it was likely she influenced MacRae's intellectual development in some manner. In 1904, Richards introduced the term "euthenics" as an alternative to the conventional concept of home economics. She advocated the transformation of the home through the application of scientific research, education, and public policies. Richards and MacRae both anticipated interventionist policies that would engineer environments and consequently individuals.[13]

MacRae also drew inspiration from Gerald Stanley Lee, who gained notoriety for his pre-war writings on the "crowd" and social control. Lee recognized the power of the emerging profession of advertising to shape public opinion and spread these ideas in books such as *The Voice of the Machines* (1906), *Inspired Millionaires* (1908), and *Crowds: A Moving-Picture of Democracy* (1911). As Lee's biographer Gregory W. Bush explains, "Lee told readers of *Crowds* that when people were presented with clearly identifiable choices between good and evil, between the modern way of life and outdated customs, or between efficiency and lethargy, they invariably chose the correct path." MacRae acknowledged Lee as "[t]he genius of human engineering (although possibly he has never thought of the term in connection with his writings)." The Wilmington reformer believed that "human engineering" required the mobilization and control of manpower, minds, and resources in common cause, and he proposed that President Wilson's wartime policies illustrated the potential of this vision.[14]

MacRae identified Wilson as "the greatest 'human engineer' of the present time" who had "placed the world on a threshold of possibilities which are too vast to be fully conceived of." MacRae contrasted the president's policies with those of Germany, arguing that "this new branch of engineering has had no recognition and has not been utilized by the defeated enemy." He asserted that Germany "has perfected herself in practically every branch of engineering which was thought essential to successful warfare," but MacRae explained that German leaders "blindly ignored the human elements." In contrast, American reformers promoted "a *democratic* greatness of organization by means of a science which shall aim, not merely at piling up trade-balances or perfecting industrial methods, but at our people's fuller industry and happiness through the improvement of social conditions, the better adaptation of each part to the general scheme." Wilson's wartime policies imposed government control over various sectors of the US economy, mobilized American manpower through the draft, and shaped the public mind to unify the nation in support of the war. Yet reformers and labor activists also insisted that the war effort required social welfare policies, fair labor standards, adequate housing for war industries workers, and social insurance policies for servicemen and their families. Many Progressives believed that these economic and social measures anticipated more sweeping actions that would irrevocably change the nation and the world for the better. MacRae shared this sentiment, and he cited Lane's proposal as proof of Progressivism on the march.[15]

The economic and philosophical arguments made on behalf of the soldier settlement proposal convinced participants at the Southern Land Congress to unanimously approve three resolutions in favor of Lane's plan. The first resolution called for cooperation with the Secretary of the Interior. The second resolution sought to coordinate organizations and state governments under the guidance of the SSDO. By voting for the third resolution, participants promised "to the President and the Congress steadfast sympathy and assistance as they now address themselves to the difficult task of reconstructing the political, social, economic and industrial life of America and of the world." The convention thus ended with a confirmation of the Progressive spirit of interventionism that inspired Lane's plan.[16]

Although Lane was unable to attend the Southern Land Congress, he toured the South to survey prospective settlement sites three weeks later. MacRae personally escorted the Secretary of the Interior and H. T. Cory from Washington, DC to Wilmington and served as their host in the Port City. Accompanied by Carl Van Leuven, then the president of Hugh MacRae and Company's agricultural development division, and several leading Wilmington businessmen, they visited the colonies of Castle Haynes in New Hanover County and Van Eeden and St. Helena in neighboring Pender County. When Lane spoke at the Royal Theater in Wilmington that evening, he called upon the audience to support the soldier settlement campaign. The Wilmington *Morning Star* summarized Lane's appeal: "This state is not what it can be . . . and never will become what it can be until the people have it burned into their souls that they are going to make North Carolina the greatest, richest state of all the states." He argued that a veterans' community represented an important step toward that prosperous future. One day later, Lane, MacRae, Van Leuven, and Cory continued their tour of southeastern North Carolina. Lane later shared his impressions with North Carolina's US senator Furnifold M. Simmons: "I greatly enjoyed a brief visit recently to Wilmington and the country thereabouts and was much impressed with the advantages of that section as a location for a soldiers' settlement."[17]

Signaling Lane's desire to establish a settlement in the state, Cory advised Governor Bickett to form a committee responsible for reviewing possible sites and proposing one location to the Reclamation Bureau. The governor asked MacRae to serve on this committee, but the Wilmington businessman declined because he worried that his efforts to sell land to the Interior Department might represent a conflict of interest. MacRae's concern was justified; critics of Lane's proposal accused speculators of promoting soldier settlements for their own benefit. Although MacRae did not serve on the committee, he nonetheless played a central role in the state's campaign to develop a veterans' community by approving each of Bickett's appointments.[18]

MacRae, however, did not simply wish to sell his property to the federal government; he wanted to play an active role in the development of a North Carolina soldier settlement. The Department of the Interior welcomed MacRae's assistance. Seeking to capitalize on MacRae's experiences, Lane asked him to submit a report describing his colonization efforts in southeastern North Carolina. MacRae offered more, sharing his own vision for the soldier settlement movement.[19]

In his memorandum, MacRae imagined the communities as cooperative endeavors in which federal involvement was essential. MacRae proclaimed, "The hearty co-operation of all Government Departments, with their experts, would be essential; and the active co-operation of State officials, State experts, and local public bodies would be necessary in order to de-centralize the work and give it local strength." Like Mead, MacRae understood that most white southerners opposed federal interference in local matters. He therefore reserved roles for state and local officials because he believed that they possessed knowledge of environmental conditions critical to the success of the community.[20]

MacRae recommended Letchworth, England, to the Department of the Interior as a model worthy of emulation. According to historian Paul K. Conkin, English progressive and Letchworth visionary Ebenezer Howard "wished to combine the magnetic attractions of both city and country by combining the higher wages, employment opportunities, social advantages, and well-lit streets of the cities with the beauty of nature, fresh air, low rents, bright sunshine, woods, meadows, and forests of the country." Howard anticipated these conditions resolving social problems and fostering cooperative endeavors. Letchworth became the model "garden city," and city planners in Europe and the United States quickly copied it, harnessing its Progressive potential to reshape the economic and social conditions of residents. During the war, planners designed housing for war workers in Connecticut, Pennsylvania, and Virginia based on this English model. MacRae intended to replicate Letchworth in post-war southeastern North Carolina. He offered Lane a thoroughly Progressive vision, shaping the environment in the interest of social engineering. He proposed that the soldier settlement "should . . . be so attractive that there would not be room for the fatal longing of the socially inclined for other communities; and yet the outlying borders should extend into territory crude enough to suit the restless spirit of the man who likes the frontier experience." Adapting his own scheme based on the Letchworth model, MacRae reserved 1000 acres for a "social and industrial city" consisting of "all industries helpful to an agricultural community, and all of the social activities which would prove to be the 'cement' of the project" surrounded by a much larger green belt. Like Howard, MacRae believed that everyone must till the soil.[21]

MacRae's memorandum also featured a list of potential contributors who possessed the necessary skills to deal with "all of the human engineering problems" of settlement. Among the "human engineering" experts were University of North Carolina rural economics professor E. C. Branson, leading Massachusetts Progressive and town planning advocate Charles S. Bird Jr., Gerald Stanley Lee, and Matthew Hale. He also noted the agricultural expertise of South Carolinian David R. Coker, the garden city planning of Bird, and Mead, and the "Rural Experience" of Castle Haynes superintendent H. A. Rau and Dutch colonist Adrianus Ludeke. When MacRae presented these men as prospective contributors, he revealed the advanced stages of his plans for a North Carolina Letchworth, which he intended to build as part of the soldier settlement program.[22]

MacRae imagined the soldier settlement as an important first step in the reorganization and modernization of rural life. He recognized the potential employment crisis that would follow demobilization and believed that the Department of the Interior possessed the resources to prevent this emergency. Writing to Lane less than one month after the Secretary's visit, MacRae urged that the bill being debated in the House of Representatives be amended to grant settlement farms to industrial workers. Yet MacRae also believed that the planned settlement must be replicated on a much wider scale to address the nation's rural woes. To the North Carolina businessman, Letchworth represented the future of rural life in the United States. Progressive rural experts relied on demonstration farms to promote scientific practices and to modernize agriculture. MacRae believed that, like demonstration agents, "[t]he farmer must be considered a scientist in the making." He perceived the soldier settlement as a demonstration community, illustrating not only new farming techniques but also a new rural lifestyle. MacRae proposed that "a 'WORKING MODEL' . . . will serve as a basis from which agricultural communities can be 'fabricated,' bringing a degree of efficiency similar to that realized in building ships." His proposal thus echoed the Progressive principles that had guided his colonization scheme and then reached new ambitions once inspired by Wilsonian Progressivism during World War I. Lane agreed with the spirit of MacRae's idea. When Lane testified before a congressional committee reviewing the Interior Department proposal, he argued, "[W]e must consider seriously going further with the promotion of agriculture than we have, and not merely in agriculture, but in the line of seeing that the people on the land are taught how to handle themselves and the land." Yet the Secretary advised MacRae that Congress had not appropriated the necessary funds, thus limiting the program's potential.[23]

Seeking to promote Lane's plan, MacRae distributed copies of the Interior Department's annual report to North Carolina legislators. Lane hoped that state legislatures would pass resolutions supporting his proposal; he believed that such action would convince members of Congress that the soldier settlement movement enjoyed widespread support. The General Assembly endorsed the proposed soldier settlements in early 1919. It declared that "the people of the State of North Carolina would welcome any opportunity to make provision for the comfort and prosperity of the returned soldiers, sailors and marines, who have taken part in the recent world war." Other states passed similar resolutions or even formed committees, appropriated funds, and pledged to collaborate with the federal government on soldier settlements within their borders. Although North Carolina's legislature took no further steps to support Lane's plan, the Assembly established a State Reconstruction Commission to coordinate various economic development initiatives with federal agencies.[24]

MacRae believed that he had taken sufficient action to secure a soldier settlement in North Carolina, but the program never obtained congressional approval. Historian Bill Reid attributes this failure to opposition by established farmers who feared "overproduction and low prices" and from those who believed Lane's plan was a "speculator's plot." Reid also identifies resistance by Department of Agriculture officials who doubted soldiers' chances of success on reclaimed cutover lands or swamps. Other critics questioned the necessity of the Reclamation Bureau's plans to bring more land into cultivation instead of utilizing available farms. The decline of Progressive zeal and the embrace of individualistic, laissez faire "normalcy" also surely contributed to the demise of the soldier settlement program. In the face of such opposition, no bill could receive the necessary votes to become law. MacRae acknowledged defeat in a letter to journalist Ida M. Tarbell, when he observed "that very little was done for [soldiers] along practical lines." MacRae explained, "We worked a great deal on the proposition with the net result that one soldier established at the St. Helena Colony."[25]

MacRae, however, remained committed to the planned community idea. Perhaps disheartened by Lane's struggles to secure congressional support for a soldier settlement program and the shift away from interventionist reforms, MacRae began corresponding with planners and rural reformers in 1920, many of whom he had originally identified as advisors to the soldier settlement project. They organized the Farm Cities Corporation of America (FCCA) and attempted to build a model farm community on MacRae's land in Pender County in the early 1920s. MacRae's soldier settlement memorandum provided the foundation for the association's planned "farm city." The FCCA failed to build the settlement, but MacRae continued to promote the idea. In 1933, he successfully translated his plan into a subsistence homestead under the supervision of the Department of the Interior. World War I had impressed upon MacRae the obligation and power of the federal government to implement reforms. He stubbornly pursued a revolution from above, refusing to admit Progressivism had died as he lobbied the federal government to establish model farm communities. Unwilling to accept defeat after the failure of Lane's proposal, MacRae attempted to bridge the divide between the Progressive Era and the New Deal, relentlessly lobbying for government action to initiate his rural revolution in North Carolina and across the South.[26]

Notes

The University of Wisconsin–Green Bay Research Council generously supported research for this essay. Marene S. Baker (National Archives and Records Administration, Rocky Mountain Region Archival Operations) and Elizabeth Bartels (University of Colorado–Boulder) provided invaluable research assistance. Beverly Tetterton, Jennifer Daughtery, Joseph Sheppard, and the staff of the New Hanover County Public Library generously answered questions and examined their holdings to help clarify aspects of local history. Mitchell Scott (University of Wisconsin–Green Bay) located every hard-to-find document and filled requests with amazing speed. Tycho de Boer, Margaret M. Mulrooney, and Tom Okie offered insightful comments on an earlier draft of this essay.

1. *Soldier Settlements in the South, Being the Full and Complete Report of the Southern Land Congress* (n.p., 1918): 9, 98; Michael McGerr, *A Fierce Discontent: The Rise and Fall of the Progressive Movement in America, 1870–1920* (New York: Oxford University Press, 2003): 279–313; Robert H. Zieger, *America's Great War: World War I and the American Experience* (Lanham, MD: Rowman and Littlefield Publishers, 2000): 203–215.

2. Dewey W. Grantham, *Southern Progressivism: The Reconciliation of Progress and Tradition* (Knoxville: University of Tennessee Press, 1983): 351–409.

3. Ida M. Tarbell, "Will Your Home Be Happy as Theirs?," *Collier's*, July 15, 1920, 5; *The Morning Star* (Wilmington, NC), April 28, 1868; *Wilmington* (North Carolina) *Messenger*, September 16, 1892, and *Wilmington Messenger*, September 21, 1892, in "The MacRae Family–Misc. History," Bill Reaves Collection Family History Series I, 1997, 4, 19–20, New Hanover County Public Library, Wilmington, North Carolina; James Sprunt, *Chronicles of the Cape Fear River, 1660–1916* (1916; reprint, Wilmington: Broadfoot Publishing Company, 1992), 675–677; Edwin Bjorkman, "Hugh MacRae: Builder of Human Happiness: A Study in Agricultural Engineering," Federal Writers' Project Papers, #3709, Southern Historical Collection, Wilson Library, University of North Carolina at Chapel Hill; John Faris Corey, "The Colonization and Contributions of Emigrants Brought to Southeastern North Carolina by Hugh MacRae," (master's thesis, Appalachian State Teacher's College, 1957), 5–9, 17–18; "Hugh MacRae," in Christopher Crittenden, William S. Powell, and Robert H. Woody, eds., *100 Years, 100 Men, 1871–1971* (Raleigh: Edwards and Broughton Company, 1971), 235–237; Stanley Tebbs Prewitt, "Hugh MacRae's Agricultural Project: An Example of the Tensions between the Jeffersonian Ideal and the Planners' Ethic" (honors thesis, University of North Carolina at Chapel Hill, 1974), 9–11; Jack Riley, "MacRae, Hugh," in *Dictionary of North Carolina Biography, vol. 4, L-O*, ed. William S. Powell (Chapel Hill: University of North Carolina Press, 1991), 191–192; Hugh MacRae, "Vitalizing the Nation and Conserving Human Units Through the Development of Agricultural Communities," *Annals of the American Academy of Political and Social Science* (January 1916): 280; "The MacRae Colonies in North Carolina," *World Agriculture* 1, no. 4 (1921): 79.

4. "Hugh MacRae's Letter to Editor Daniels," *Twin City Daily Sentinel* (Winston-Salem, NC), February 12, 1907, 5; Hugh MacRae, *Bringing Immigrants to the South: Address Delivered Before the North Carolina Society of New York, December 7, 1908* (n.p., 1908), microfilm, North Carolina Collection, Wilson Library, University of North Carolina at Chapel Hill; *Hearings Before the Committee on Immigration and Naturalization, House of Representatives, Sixty-Ninth Congress, First Session, December 17 and 18, 1925* (Washington, DC: Government Printing Office, 1926), 8; Corey, "Colonization and Contributions," 19–25; Prewitt, "Hugh MacRae's Agricultural Project," 11–14, 20–24; Marcia G. Synnott, "Replacing 'Sambo': Could White Immigrants Solve the Labor Problem in the Carolinas?," *Proceedings of the South Carolina Historical Association* (1982): 77, 82–84; W. Frank Ainsley, "'Own a Home in North Carolina': Image and Reality in Ethnic European Communities," *Journal of Cultural Geography* 5 (1985): 61; W. Frank Ainsley, "Pulsating Patterns of Land Occupancy: The Impacts of Farm Colonization Experiments on the Rural South," *Pioneer America Society Transactions* 10 (1987): 43–44; Erin Elizabeth Clune, "Emancipation to Empire: Race, Labor, and Ideology in the New South" (PhD diss., New York University, 2002), 200–201; Tycho de Boer, *Nature, Business, and Community in North Carolina's Green Swamp* (Gainesville: University Press of Florida, 2008), 132–139; Lauren H. Braun, "Italians, the Labor Problem, and the Project in Agricultural Colonization in the New South, 1884–1934" (PhD diss., University of Illinois–Chicago, 2010), 173–174, 178–179, 187–197; Thomas Luke Manget, "Hugh MacRae and the Idea of Farm City: Race, Class, and Conservation in the New South, 1905–1935" (master's thesis, Western Carolina University, 2012), 6-13, 30-58;; Timothy B. Tyson and David S. Cecelski, "Hugh MacRae at Invershiel," http://www.lib.unc.edu/blogs/morton/index.php/essays

/hugh-macrae-at-inversheil, accessed April 24, 2013; J. Vincent Lowery, "The Transatlantic Dreams of the Port City Prophet: The Rural Reform Campaign of Hugh MacRae," *North Carolina Historical Review* 90 (July 2013): 294–297. On agriculture and Progressive reforms, see William L. Bowers, *The Country Life Movement in America, 1900–1920* (Port Washington, NY: Kennikat Press, 1974); Grantham, *Southern Progressivism*, 320–348; Natalie J. Ring, *The Problem South: Region, Empire, and the New Liberal State, 1880–1930* (Athens: University of Georgia Press, 2012), 120–134; and Manget, "Hugh MacRae."

5. de Boer, *Nature, Business, and Community*, 132–139, 145–146; MacRae, *Bringing Immigrants to the South*; "Plans Are Made Public," *Sunday Wilmington Messenger*, September 22, 1905, Bill Reaves Collection, New Hanover County Public Library, Wilmington, North Carolina; "The Way to Handle Immigrants," *News and Courier* (Charleston, SC), September 9, 1907, 8; George Byrne, "Hugh MacRae's Practical Application of Common Sense in Colonization," *Manufacturer's Record*, May 30, 1912, 49–53; Corey, "Colonization and Contributions," 17–83; Conkin, *Tomorrow a New Deal*, 278–279; Prewitt, "Hugh MacRae's Agricultural Project," 11–28; Synnott, "Replacing 'Sambo,'" 80–84; Ainsley, "'Own a Home,'" 61–69; Ainsley, "Pulsating Patterns," 43–52; Clune, "Emancipation to Empire," 200–201; Braun, "Italians," 168–197; Manget, "Hugh MacRae," 28–58; Tyson and Cecelski, "Hugh MacRae at Invershiel"; Lowery, "Transatlantic Dreams," 290, 293–303.

6. Grantham, *Southern Progressivism*, 351–352, 359; Hugh MacRae to Walter Hines Page, May 4, 1912, November 18, 1912, December 28, 1912, and January 14, 1913, Walter Hines Page Papers, MS Am 1090.2–1090.13, Houghton Library, Harvard University, Cambridge, Massachusetts; MacRae, "Vitalizing the Nation," 285; Ring, *The Problem South*, 120. On the Wilson administration and segregation, see Eric S. Yellin, *Racism in the Nation's Service: Government Workers and the Color Line in Woodrow Wilson's America* (Chapel Hill: University of North Carolina Press, 2013). Conkin, Prewitt, and Manget argue that MacRae accepted government assistance reluctantly and begrudgingly. Synnott contends that he "realized that no private individual had the resources to prevent the South from 'degenerating into an agricultural slum.'" These scholars, however, identify MacRae's first engagement with the government in the 1920s. A closer examination of his speech at the Southern Land Congress and his actions during and immediately following World War I reveals that he was guided by his Progressive philosophy and spurred by Wilson's wartime policies and Lane's soldier settlement plan. See Conkin, *Tomorrow a New World*, 282; Prewitt, "Hugh MacRae's Agricultural Project," 46–50; Manget, "Hugh MacRae and the Idea of the Farm City," 100–101; Synnott, "Hugh MacRae, Penderlea, and the Model Farm Communities Movement," 54; Synnott, "Replacing 'Sambo,'" 83; Lowery, "Transatlantic Dreams," 303–312.

7. Donald J. Pisani, "Reclamation and Social Engineering in the Progressive Era," *Agricultural History* 57 (January 1983): 46–63; Paul Conkin, *Tomorrow a New Deal: The New Deal Community Program* (1959; reprint, New York: Da Capo Press, 1976), 42–54; Paul Conkin, "The Vision of Elwood Mead," *Agricultural History* 34 (April 1960): 88–97; Bill G. Reid, "Proposed American Plans for Soldier Settlement During the World War I Period" (PhD diss., University of Oklahoma, 1963), 25–61; Bill G. Reid, "Franklin K. Lane's Idea for Veterans' Colonization, 1918–1921," *Pacific Historical Review* 33 (November 1964): 447–461; Bill G. Reid, "Agrarian Opposition to Franklin K. Lane's Proposal for Soldier Settlement, 1918–1921," *Agricultural History* 41 (April 1967): 167–180; Keith W. Olson, *Biography of a Progressive: Franklin K. Lane, 1864–1921* (Westport, CT: Greenwood Press, 1979), 149–156; James R. Kluger, *Turning on Water with a Shovel: The Career of Elwood Mead* (Albuquerque: University of New Mexico Press, 1992), 74–101; Thomas Luke Manget, "Hugh MacRae and the Idea of Farm City: Race, Class, and Conservation in the New South, 1905–1935" (master's thesis, Western Carolina University, 2012), 6-13, 30-58; Lowery, "Transatlantic Dreams," 303–307.

8. Hugh MacRae to Thomas W. Bickett, September 23, 1918, MacRae to Bickett, October 22, 1918, and Bickett to MacRae, October 23, 1918, Box 376, Governor's Papers, North Carolina Department of Cultural Resources, Raleigh (hereafter cited as Governor's Papers); "Lane Urges Speed in Land Scheme," *Morning Star*, January 11, 1919, 6; Sandra Sue Horton, "The Political Career of Thomas Walter Bickett" (master's thesis, University of North Carolina at Chapel Hill,

1965), 46–47, 50–56, 110–140; "Thomas W. Bickett," in Crittenden et al., *100 Years, 100 Men*, 27–29; Nathaniel F. MacGruder, "Bickett, Thomas Walter," in *Dictionary of North Carolina Biography, vol. 1, A-C*, ed. William S. Powell (Chapel Hill: University of North Carolina Press, 1979), 149–151; Reid, "Franklin K. Lane's Idea," 452; Manget, "Hugh MacRae and the Idea of Farm City," 83–85.

9. Reid, "Proposed American Plans," 64–69; George Brown Tindall, *The Emergence of the New South, 1913–1945* (1967; reprint, Baton Rouge: Louisiana State University Press, 1999), 128–129; *Southern Settlement and Development Organization: Its Program, the Proceedings of the Meeting, Charter, and Maryland's Appropriation* (Baltimore: Munder-Thomsen Press, 1912); *Soldier Settlements in the South*, 34–37; *The Dawn of a New Constructive Era: Proceedings of the Cut-Over Land Conference of the South* (n.p., 1917), accessed May 20, 2015, http://www.biodiversitylibrary.org/item/114795#page/1/mode/1up; Clement S. Ucker to Alex K. Sessoms, July 2, 1918, Box 1713, Central Classified File, 1907–1936, Department of the Interior Office of the Secretary, Entry A1–749, Record Group 48, US National Archives and Records Administration, College Park, MD (hereafter cited as RG 48).

10. *Soldier Settlements in the South*, 105, 117–128; "South Place for Returned Soldier," *Morning Star*, December 8, 1919, 8; H. T. Cory, "The Nation's Greatest Opportunity for Colonization and for Returning Soldiers Wanting Farms," *Manufacturer's Record*, November 21, 1918, 69–70; "The Colonization of Southern Lands of National Importance as Viewed by a Great Western Engineer," *Manufacturer's Record*, November 21, 1918, 61; Manget, "Hugh MacRae and the Idea of Farm City," 94; F. L. Finkenstaedt to H. T. Cory, November 2, 1918, and Hugh MacRae to Cory, November 5, 1918, Folder 1253–A1, Box 341, General Administrative and Project Records, Entry 3, Record Group 115, Rocky Mountain Region Archival Operations, National Archives and Records Administration, Denver, Colorado (hereafter cited as RG 115).

11. *Soldiers Settlements in the South*, 23–28, 33; Rodgers, *Atlantic Crossings*, 1–7, 318–366.

12. "Large Delegation to Land Congress," *Wilmington Morning Star*, November 8, 1918, 5; *Soldier Settlements in the South*, 19–20, 88–90; de Boer, *Nature, Business, and Community*, 144.

13. *Soldier Settlements in the South*, 97–101; Corey, "Colonization and Contributions," 21–22; Prewitt, "Hugh MacRae's Agricultural Project," 15–22; de Boer, *Nature, Business, and Community*, 139; Manget, "Hugh MacRae and the Idea of the Farm City," 32–37; Lowery, "Transatlantic Dreams," 293–294; Ellen H. Richards, *Euthenics: The Science of Controllable Environment* (1910; reprint, New York: Arno Press, 1977); Caroline L. Hunt, *The Life of Ellen H. Richards* (1912; reprint, Boston: Whitcomb and Barrows, 1918); Robert Clarke, *Ellen Swallow: The Woman who Founded Ecology* (Chicago: Follett Publishing Company, 1973), 24–65, 40–41, 62–63, 208–238; Sarah Stage, "Ellen Richards and the Social Significance of the Home Economics Movement," in *Rethinking Home Economics: Women and the History of a Profession*, ed. Sarah Stage and Virginia B. Vincenti (Ithaca, NY: Cornell University Press, 1997), 17–33; Kristen R. Egan, "Conservation and Cleanliness: Racial and Environmental Purity in Ellen Richards and Charlotte Perkins Gilman," *Women Studies Quarterly* 39 (Fall/Winter 2011): 77–92; Helen Zoe Veit, *Modern Food, Moral Food: Self-Control, Science, and the Rise of Modern American Eating in the Early Twentieth Century* (Chapel Hill: University of North Carolina Press, 2015), 101–122.

14. *Soldier Settlements in the South*, 99–101; Gregory W. Bush, *Lord of Attention: Gerald Stanley Lee and Crowd Metaphor in Industrializing America* (Amherst: University of Massachusetts Press, 1991), 116–117.

15. *Soldier Settlements in the South*, 97–99; Melville Chater, "Making People into Folks," *The Red Cross Magazine*, December 1919, 68; MacRae, "Vitalizing the Nation," 284–285; de Boer, *Nature, Business, and Community*, 139; McGerr, *A Fierce Discontent*, 279–313; David M. Kennedy, *Over Here: The First World War and American Society* (New York: Oxford University Press, 1980); Ronald Schaffer, *America in the Great War: The Rise of the War Welfare State* (New York: Oxford University Press, 1991), 3–74; Rodgers, *Atlantic Crossings*, 302; Lowery, "Transatlantic Dreams," 303, 305.

16. *Soldier Settlements in the South*, 88–90.

17. "Sec. Franklin K. Lane to Arrive in the City Today–Speaks Tonight," *Morning Star,* December 9, 1918, 5, 6; "Secretary Lane Here Today," *Morning Star,* December 9, 1918, 4; "Secretary Lane Talks of Homes for Soldier Boys," *Morning Star,* December 10, 1918, 1, 8; "Sec. Lane Visits Nearby Farm Lands," *Morning Star,* December 10, 1918, 8; "Secretary Lane at Bolton Yesterday," *Morning Star,* December 11, 1918, 5; "Secretary Lane Surprised," *Morning Star,* December 11, 1918, 4; "Landowners' Here to Attend Meeting," *Morning Star,* January 17, 1919, 5, 6; "Landowners Have Perfected Plans," *Morning Star,* January 18, 1919, 5, 6; "Hugh MacRae to Thomas W. Bickett, December 12, 1918, Box 377, Governor's Papers; Franklin K. Lane to Furnifold Simmons, December 27, 1918, Box 1713, Central Classified File, 1907–1936, Records of the Office of the Secretary of the Interior, Entry A1–749, RG 48.

18. Hugh MacRae to Thomas Bickett, December 12, 1918, and December 17, 1918, Box 377, Governor's Papers; Franklin K. Lane to Thomas Bickett, December 31, 1918, Box 1713, Central Classified File, 1907–1936, Records of the Office of the Secretary of the Interior, Entry A1–749, RG 48; E. D. Vincent to A. D. Ward, February 17, 1919, Folder 1253–A1, Box 341, General Administrative Files, 1902–1919, Entry 3, RG 115; Reid, "Franklin K. Lane's Idea," 459.

19. Carl Van Leuven to E. D. Vincent, January 15, 1919, and E. D. Vincent to Carl Van Leuven, January 20, 1919, Folder 1253–A1, Box 341, General Administrative Files, 1902–1919, Entry 3, RG 115; Hugh MacRae, "Farm Communities for Returning Soldiers," Folder 2, Box 344, General Administrative Files, 1902–1919, Entry 3, RG 115; Reid, "Franklin K. Lane's Idea," 452; Manget, "Hugh MacRae and the Idea of Farm City," 83–85; Lowery, "Transatlantic Dreams," 307.

20. MacRae, "Farm Communities for Returning Soldiers."

21. Ibid.; Conkin, *Tomorrow a New World,* 61–72; Stanley Buder, *Visionaries and Planners: The Garden City Movement and the Modern Community* (New York: Oxford University Press, 1990), 64–95; Rodgers, *Atlantic Crossings,* 179–180, 287–290.

22. MacRae, "Farm Communities for Returning Soldiers." On Charles S. Bird Jr., see Richard B. Sherman, "Charles Sumner Bird and the Progressive Party in Massachusetts," *New England Quarterly* 33 (September 1960): 325–340.

23. MacRae, "Farm Communities for Returning Soldiers"; Ring, *The Problem South,* 122–134; *Soldier Settlements in the South,* 100; Chater, "Making People into Folks," 68; Hugh MacRae to Franklin K. Lane, January 9, 1919, Lane to MacRae, January 13, 1919, and MacRae to Lane, January 14, 1919, Box 191, Records Relating to Legislation, 1907–53, Records of the Office of the Secretary of the Interior, Entry A1–753, RG 48; *Work and Homes for Returning Soldiers: Hearings Before the Committee on Irrigation of Arid Lands, House of Representatives, Sixty-fifth Congress, Third Session, January 10, 1919,* 65th Cong. 6 (Statement of Hon. Franklin K. Lane, Secretary of the Interior).

24. *Journal of the Senate of the General Assembly of the State of North Carolina, Session 1919* (Raleigh: Commercial Printing Company, 1919), 224, 229; *Journal of the House of Representatives of the General Assembly of the State of North Carolina, Session 1919* (Raleigh: Edwards and Broughton Printing Company, 1919), 267, 279, 331; S. R. 619, General Assembly Session Records, January–August 1919, Box 17, North Carolina Department of Cultural Resources, Raleigh, NC; "State Action on Soldier-Settlement Plan," Box 191, Records Relating to Legislation, 1907–53, Records of the Office of the Secretary of the Interior, Entry A1–753, RG 48; R. M. Sheppard to E. D. Vincent, January 15, 1919, and Vincent to Sheppard, January 20, 1919, Folder 1253–A1, Box 341, General Administrative Files, 1902–1919, Entry 3, RG 115; "State Action on Soldier-Settlement Plan of the Department of the Interior," Folder 1, Box 368, General Correspondence regarding Soldier Settlement Plans and Methods, General Administrative and Project Records, 1919–1929, Entry 7, RG 115.

25. Hugh MacRae to John Nolen, June 3, 1920, Folder 2, Box 69, John T. Nolen Papers #2903, Division of Rare and Manuscript Collections, Cornell University Library, Ithaca, New York; Reid, "Franklin K. Lane's Idea," 459–461; Reid, "Agrarian Opposition," 167–180; Reid, "Lane's Idea," 93–146; Kluger, *Turning on Water with a Shovel,* 82–83; McGerr, *A Fierce Discontent,* 312, 315; Ida

M. Tarbell, "Will Your Home Be Happy as Theirs?," 5–6, 20, 22; Hugh MacRae to Ida M. Tarbell, May 10, 1926, General Correspondence, Ida M. Tarbell Collection, Special Collections, Allegheny College, Meadville, Pennsylvania, accessed September 26, 2014, http://library.allegheny.edu/content.php?pid=57261&sid=419389; Manget, "Hugh MacRae and the Idea of Farm City," 85–86.

26. Conkin, *Tomorrow a New World*, 277–293; Prewitt, "Hugh MacRae's Agricultural Project," 44–48; Marcia G. Synnott, "Hugh MacRae, Penderlea, and the Model Farm Communities Movement," *Proceedings of the South Carolina Historical Association* (1988): 53–65; Ann Southerland Cottle, *The Roots of Penderlea: A Memory of a New Deal Homestead Community* (Wilmington: The Publishing Laboratory, Department of Creative Writing, University of North Carolina at Wilmington, 2007); Braun, "Italians," 199–205; Manget, "Hugh MacRae and the Idea of Farm City," 59–160; Lowery, "Transatlantic Dreams," 309–324.

4

"Bringing Home to the Trenches"

North Carolina Women on the Warfront During the Great War

Jerra Jenrette[1]

North Carolina's women have a history of being on the forefront of activism in times of crisis. Much like their predecessors, female North Carolinians in the pre–World War I era believed it was necessary to be actively involved in the war effort. "Molly's Daughters" came from the mountains, the Piedmont, and from coastal towns on the Atlantic and "enlisted" to serve their nation.[2] This chapter examines contributions of the Tar Heel state's women, such as Drs. Anna Gove and Emily Lapham, and nurses Irene Brewster, Ione Branch Bain, and May Greenfield Watson, who left the comfort of home and hearth to serve near Europe's frontlines.[3] While societal attitudes have always relegated women to the domestic arena, many believed they had a moral and patriotic responsibility to do what they could to help the nation. If women were aware of the challenges they faced in the hospitals and Red Cross and YMCA Huts, driving ambulances, serving food, reading and writing letters for soldiers, and providing entertainment, they did not show it as they enlisted, volunteered, and trained for service abroad. In addition to helping the military wounded and refugees, they also had to confront the overarching sexism that permeated American culture. This often blatant and persistent sexism did not prevent women like physicians Gove and Lapham—who were forced at times to work as nurses—from becoming fully engaged in helping refugees and soldiers from both sides of the conflict.[4] This essay tells part of their story.

When President Woodrow Wilson finally led the nation into the European conflagration on April 6, 1917, North Carolinians rallied to the national cause as some 86,000 men joined various branches of the military.[5] Within days, the American Women's Hospitals (AWH) began looking for ways to support the military's efforts in Europe and other places. The AWH offered the services of medical women, including physicians, to the government and the Red Cross. More than one hundred female physicians were sent to Europe in 1917 as were significant numbers of nurses, aides, and technicians, all of whom had trained in the AWH. This group of female physicians was referred to as the Battalion of Life. Working closely with the American Red Cross, they contributed significantly to the war effort in France, so much so that six members were recognized by the French government. The AWH established hospitals at Luzancy, Ferté-Milon, Blois, and Levallois in France along with hospitals in Monastir, Serbia, and Aleppo, Turkey.[6] These hospitals ranged in size from 150 beds to just a few. Most of the larger ones also had operating rooms and dispensaries in which thousands of patients were treated; some, including the one at Blois, began as clinics to serve children displaced by the war.[7]

One of wartime's pressing issues was the availability of sufficient numbers of medical personnel, yet the military, Red Cross, and YMCA units did not permit female physicians to work as doctors—only as nurses. According to historian Kimberly Jensen, female physicians faced considerable discrimination even during this time of crisis. She points out that federal regulations, military codes, and societal expectations hindered the progress of women in wartime.[8] The United States Army Medical Department refused to give women physicians the same recognition and authority that male doctors enjoyed.[9] The Army Reorganization Act of 1918 excluded appointments for female physicians, permitted only female nurses to enlist in the US Army Nurse Corps, and raised their base pay to sixty dollars a month. Despite this increase, nurses received half the pay of male soldiers of equivalent military rank with the same responsibilities.[10] North Carolina's women faced these attitudes and ensuing obstacles with determination to serve.

Tar Heel women looked for ways to serve and took advantage of the ways in which the Great War opened new doors for women's involvement in the broader public sphere. Women enlisted in organizations that were already available including the nursing corps of the military, the Red Cross, and the YMCA. Some 200 women from North Carolina served in the military as nurses both domestically and abroad. Others volunteered for service through the Red Cross, the YMCA, and the Smith College Relief Unit (SCRU).[11] The state even contributed at least one Native American female officer, Lula Owl Gloyne, an army nurse. Entering service as a first lieutenant in the medical corps, Gloyne was the only Eastern Cherokee officer in the war.[12]

From the experiences of May Greenfield Watson and Irene Brewster, it was evident that organizers tried to give women the best training possible. Watson recalled that her training began in the local hospital in Winston-Salem and continued in Newburgh, New York.[13] Some nurses, like Brewster, were sent to Fort McPherson, Georgia, where the men of Base Hospital #65, authorized in March 1918 by the Surgeon General of the United States, were already training. Dr. John Wesley Long of Greensboro organized Base Hospital #65 with "32 medical men, 203 enlisted men and 100 nurses; 90 per cent [sic] of the nurses were from North Carolina."[14] A core group of physicians of Base

Hospital #65 hailed from North Carolina with recruits from other regions filling in the gaps by May 1918. The recruits spent two weeks working with the staff at the Army General Hospital #6 in Georgia and then were sent to Camp Upton in New York State.[15]

Part of the training for Brewster, Watson, and other women at Fort McPherson included being issued appropriate attire along with shoes and a hat. Nurses wore a navy-blue suit with a white blouse and a hat; this was considered their "outdoor" uniform. They also wore pins with USA emblazoned along with the Medical Department emblem, the staff of Mercury. Brewster did not think the uniforms were particularly becoming for the women, but women wore them with pride. Nurses also received French lessons to help them communicate with the French population.[16] Some of the women visited New York City, picked out books from the New York Public Library, went to the theater, and attended church. When off duty, the nurses went to Hoboken, New Jersey, to get their passports. They also attended lectures on various topics while waiting for their uniforms to be made.[17] Daily drills were part of their training; yet these only lasted for about an hour, which did not seem to Brewster to be enough to sufficiently prepare women for battlefront situations. Brewster wrote, "I believe we would not have been a credit to the Lieutenant or the Sergeant who worked so diligently to make us a perfect military unit. Maybe our drilling could not be called a success, but the spirit of 65 had been born and would carry on."[18]

Ione Branch Bain of Winston-Salem recalled similar experiences as she answered the call to national duty in 1918. Initially, she was sent to Waynesboro on March 31, 1918, where she and other nurses greeted trainloads of soldiers back from the European front. Bain was one of twenty-five nurses at this location. Her first responsibility was to serve as the dietitian, but she was also attentive to other nonmilitary needs. For example, after a maid mentioned that her invalid daughter was living in squalor, Bain visited the young girl and was appalled to discover that the twelve-year old was paralyzed and her mother could barely move her. Bain immediately went to the commanding officer, a Major Davis, to ask for assistance. "He listened patiently until I had finished and then in a harsh voice said, 'well what do you want me to do?'" Bain responded with, "I want a rolling chair for this child." Major Davis gave her an incredulous look but eventually relented.[19]

Bain was quite content with her work stateside; however, she received orders in July 1918 to prepare to travel to New York City for ensuing departure for France. Like the other women from the state, she experienced intense, albeit brief, training. Bain recalled that she had mixed feelings ranging from excitement and anticipation to outright fear.[20] During the war, seemingly all of New York City honored the women's patriotism by providing complimentary passes to various activities and events in the city. They attended plays, took boat rides in the rivers, and attended church. When Bain and the rest of

Base Hospital #65 were preparing for departure for France and were among some twenty units assembled in the city, they signaled their arrival with the following cheer:

Rah! Rah! Rah! Sixty-five
Happy, brave and alive
Tar Heel born and Tar Heel bred
But now we are after the Kiser's [sic] head.
Carolina'. Carolina'. U.S.A.[21]

Within a month, various units were fully organized, trained, and properly suited; they were ready to leave for France. Each woman's steamer trunk, packed with many personal belongings including numerous books, had already been shipped to France. On the day of departure, they gathered in the lobby of the hotel, ready to depart with a woolen blanket, sleeping bag, overcoat, rubber boots, and shoes.[22]

Units also participated in flag dedications at the Old Trinity Church. Bain recalled that the service occurred on the day prior to departure. "The chaplain made an impressive talk ending with an earnest prayer, and as we filed out singing softly 'keep the home fires burning' there was not a dry eye present."[23] Like so many thousands of others in wartime, the women and men who enlisted or volunteered did not know if they would ever return to the United States. Security guidelines prohibited the women from telling anyone the time of departure. Bain recalled, "We marched down to our ship all alone, leaving behind all we loved . . . a note to be sent to our family after three days."[24]

Members of Base Hospital #65 sailed together on the *Baltic*, one of the White Star Line fleet made famous by the *Titanic*; they departed from New York City harbor on September 1, 1918.[25] The excitement of being in New York City soon passed as the women faced the realization of the important, patriotic decision they had made to enlist or volunteer. Bain remembered that her unit sailed around 3:00 p.m., and she waved at the Statue of Liberty. So many of the women realized as the city's skyline disappeared from view that life was going to change. The thrill of seeing New York City and all of its trappings faded, and "then, I think, for the first time, I realized what a grave step I had taken."[26] Bain spent part of that first day thinking about the future with some sadness because she did not know what was going to happen when her unit arrived in Europe. She said, ". . . for a few hours I fought back tears, but with such a fine bunch of girls one couldn't be sad long."[27] To combat depression and homesickness the chief nurse, Miss Bree S. Kelly, called all the nurses to top deck to sing patriotic verse including the unit song.[28] North Carolinian Elizabeth Herbert Smith Taylor danced on the deck on her first day on the transatlantic trip.[29]

The convoy that carried members of Base Hospital #65 encountered an enemy submarine around 3:00 a.m., which prompted a reaction from the battleship and destroyers.[30] Bain recalled, "A suppressed excitement prevailed everywhere as we spoke in whispers, huddled together in groups awaiting . . . we knew not what . . . until faithful old Sol arose like a giant balloon straight up out of the water, and as the heavens glowed with pink our spirits soared.[31] According to Dorothy and Carl J. Schneider, vessels that departed from England faced the constant threat of attack.[32] Brewster recounted that nighttime travel was challenging as the women and others experienced conditions similar to what they had left in the United States. Blackout rules applied throughout the duration of the trip. Windows, doors, and portholes were covered with black curtains to avoid any light being detected by enemy vessels. Nurses were not permitted to spend time on deck after 9:00 p.m.; their evenings were filled with various activities including playing cards or having conversations with each other.[33]

Members of Base Hospital #65 traveled from New York City to Liverpool, Southampton, Paris, and Brest.[34] Even before the Americans arrived in war-torn France, they witnessed the impact of war firsthand with the encounters they had in Southampton. Faced with poorly clothed and starving children, members of the unit readily gave their food and money away. One little boy pleaded, "Please lady, give me your lunch box so that my daddy will have food to take with him to work tomorrow."[35] Brewster recalled that the stop in England illustrated the harsh conditions under which the British people were living.

Members of Base Hospital #65 crossed the English Channel in a South American vessel, the *Essequibo*. Upon arrival on the French coast, the tide prevented their disembarkation for a full twenty-four hours at Le Havre. Eventually, they landed and boarded trucks that took them to a train. The women were given two-day rations consisting of bread, baked beans, canned tomatoes, corn willy (corned beef), canned salmon, and jam. Due to shortages, only three can openers were available for the entire unit to use. They then boarded a train that traveled through Rouen and Paris and onto their final destination in Brest. Regardless of the unit or organization, North Carolina women who traveled to France witnessed the effects of war-torn communities, villages, and towns.[36] The majority of women were involved in the war effort through the American Red Cross, particularly those who served in France because it was the main battlefield in Europe.

In Paris, they quickly learned the extent to which the city had suffered from the German war machine. The unit spent the night at the Continental Hotel where they expected warm baths, but this was not to be the case. Brewster recalled that the water was icy cold and the rooms were not well heated. They arrived around 10:00 p.m., and Brewster "stood at the open window to watch the flashes of lights flickering against the sky. Was that rumbling sound I heard the muffled roar of guns or the hum of the city streets below?"[37] The women also realized upon arrival that their language training had been inadequate. Also from North Carolina, Dr. Mary Emily Lapham recorded in her journal that she needed to learn how to weigh and measure in French to be more effective in dispensing medicine. She planned to devise her own dictionary of commonly used words.[38]

Brest was the home site for Base Hospital #65 for the duration of the war and was the point of treatment, recovery, or departure back to the United States for the wounded. When the unit reached their destination in mid-September, they faced many unexpected difficulties and challenges. Upon arrival in Brest, they immediately went to work despite ongoing hospital construction and a lack of proper supplies including beds, linens, and food. For hospital serving dishes, the kitchen supervisor requisitioned mess kits of the deceased solders. The members of the unit had to be creative and worked long hours to get the hospital operational. Wards were quickly set up with beds that soon were filled with the wounded.[39] The Surgeon General reported that some 2000 patients were treated at the Brest site within 10 days of the hospital being opened.[40] The women of North Carolina and others quickly learned that they had volunteered or enlisted to serve in a time of great crisis. During the unit's time in Brest, more than 40,000 patients were treated at the hospital. The doctors and nurses assisted the wounded without proper lighting, often using "oil hand lanterns and flashlights."[41]

The American Red Cross, often the first medical assistance, helped the civilian population through the Children's Bureau in Toul, 160 miles east of Paris, to take care of children under 7 years of age who had been moved some 10 kilometers from the warfront. The displacement was due to concerns about enemy forces using gas bombs; young children could not wear gas masks effectively.[42] The situation of women and children so close to the lines presented a painful image for all involved.[43] Sisters Hettie and Louise Reinhardt of Black Mountain, North Carolina, went to Toul where they worked at Base Hospital #87; Hattie G. Lowry of Wilmington and Mattie McNeil of Fayetteville also worked at Toul, Château-Thierry, and Verdun.[44] Started in 1912, the Children's Bureau was the first federal agency created to address the needs of children and was vital to aid displaced children during World War I.[45] North Carolina women like the Reinhardt sisters, Lowry, and McNeil were just some of many who worked in Toul to aid children and other residents.

North Carolina women realized that the Red Cross provided many opportunities to assist in war relief. While the Red Cross did establish "Huts" in several European nations including England, Italy, and Belgium, France was easily recognized as the place that was in most need of assistance. More than any other country, France suffered from the war as it fought to hold back the German invasion.[46] No family was left untouched by the fighting, death, and subsequent displacement of millions of survivors. Dr. Anna Gove, of the SCRU, and hundreds of Red Cross workers not only had to deal with the French refugees but also with those from Belgium who fled as the Germans invaded. By the end of February 1918, the United States had appropriated more than $57,000,000 for war work in France. Another $38,000,000 had been shipped in the form of relief supplies, bringing the total contribution to $95,000,000 for 20 months of work in France.[47] Between July 1917 and February 1919, the Red Cross staffed 551 stations through the country and operated 24 hospitals to assist the US Army medical staff.[48] According to Red Cross reports, German bombing raids compelled people to remain inside their homes unless they had been destroyed. As North Carolina nurses soon learned, some villages were completely wiped out with very few people surviving.[49] Gove's letters indicate that this left a gap that needed to be filled; in fact, children, more than any other group, struggled in the aftermath of war.[50] Basic necessities were scarce, which prompted Gove to advise women to "bring plenty of comfortable shoes, bring plenty of gloves and hose because it is expensive or not worth buying, the coffee is over-roasted and mixed with chicory, 'war bread' is ok to eat so long as you don't have filled teeth because it will break them and there is not the luxury of a good dentist."[51]

Bain began her work at Brest serving in the meningitis unit, where she helped the physician with spinal punctures and treating those with meningitis. She later recalled that she experienced some of her saddest moments in this hospital, remembering one particular situation above all others. After going on duty early one morning, she noticed that many new patients had arrived during the night, all of whom were very ill. One young man who was twenty-one years old was quite sick, so Bain tried to comfort him. When she asked if she could do anything for him, he replied, "Yes, please write my mother and tell her I love her and that I don't mind dying. I only regret that I have to die here and not on the battlefield where it could count."[52] When faced with these emotional encounters, nurses sometimes struggled to deal with death. Bain said, "I was so overcome. . . . "[53] Bain and her sisters from the Tar Heel state experienced situations like this frequently. The number of medical personnel was simply not enough to serve those in need. Bain wrote, "Imagine the appalling situation of a unit of 55 officers, 100 nurses, and 210 enlisted men to care for 4,000 patients, arriving simultaneously."[54]

France was in a state of disarray. In addition to the devastation caused by the war, the weather was also challenging. Several individuals recalled that it rained daily for almost two months. The ground became rain soaked and muddy; people walked around in raincoats and boots for the duration. These conditions made the situation much worse and did not promote a clean and healthy environment in which to heal. Cold temperatures and constant dampness caused considerable sickness among the medical staff.[55] However, the sheer determination and commitment of the women from North Carolina proved to be highly positive, as they maintained morale, never gave up, and found ingenious ways to help the wounded.

Nurses found that the Germans were not the deadliest enemy; indeed, disease and infection caused many deaths. When Bain first arrived at the hospital camp, she "found utter confusion everywhere, as the great influenza epidemic" had arrived.[56] More than forty influenza patients were in her care on her first day of duty. The only person assisting her was wardmaster James Wright, a tailor by trade. He knew little about caring for the sick, but he was dedicated and exhibited a willingness to work hard.[57] Bain was convinced that she had been given the worst assignment in the unit until she chatted with her roommate about *her* day. Her roommate replied with, "Why, child, I have 40 boys with pneumonia."[58] Within three days, thirty-seven of those men had died.[59] Each day for the nurses was like the one before, caring for men brought in sick with some disease or suffering from war wounds. According to Bain, "the boys were dying so fast that they had to take them to the cemetery in coffins and bring the coffins back."[60]

Supplies were low; there was not even one bed sheet for the staff to use. The water was so full of chemicals that it caused nausea for the sick soldiers and even those who were well could barely drink it. In addition to physical wounds, many of the soldiers suffered from psychological issues—what we know today as post-traumatic stress. Bain wrote, "Such a scene could scarcely be imagined, as the patients ranged from irrational to wildly delirious and a few unconscious. While holding one in bed I looked to see another one climbing out the window. Running to him and pulling him back, I spied two had fallen out of bed. Some were singing, others moaning, while many were too sick to make a sound."[61] It is likely that many more would have died from disease and infection had it not been for the development of the Carrel-Dakin method, which included a germicide to counter the ravages of disease. Bain recalled, "I can still see those boys as they were admitted with suppurating wounds literally dying as infection sapped every ounce of their vitality."[62] According to Bain, the Carrel-Dakin method proved to be very effective in treating the diseased. Surgeons operated and "applied tubes which sprayed this solution around the wounds. The tubes were connected with an apparatus which furnished the solution continuously. In some wards, almost every bed was occupied by a boy receiving the Carrel-Dakin treatment."[63]

Heartbreak was also a daily battle for the medical staff. Bain recalled several patients who had been wounded, and infection had developed. The staff tried multiple treatments on one soldier yet nothing seemed to work. After three months of declining health, he pleaded with the medical team to send him home so his mother could tend to his needs. Eventually, the staff complied, but he died in the harbor before the ship sailed.[64] Trains were constantly delivering the wounded from the front; the 4400 bed hospital was always full. Soldiers' wounds ranged from minor cuts caused by shrapnel to mangled bodies; nurses often saw soldiers whose extremities had been shot or blown off. Bain said, "The worst to come through our hospital was a lad devoid of legs or arms and still able to be sent back to America." [65] Members of the medical staff were always impressed by the sheer courage and commitment of the soldiers despite the conditions and the horrible losses they had suffered.

North Carolina provided female physicians as well, but limited opportunities and overt sexism ruled the day. Smith College, located in Northampton, Massachusetts, founded the SCRU to provide aid to war torn France. This organization was quickly supported by the institution's alumnae.[66] Consequently, physicians from around the country signed up with the SCRU because it gave them another venue through which to aid U.S. troops in France. Gove and other female physicians realized that working through the SCRU and the AWH gave them more freedom to actually operate as doctors than did the American Red Cross. Consequently, she signed up with the SCRU so her skills as a physician would be better utilized.[67]

Gove's experience in France was yet another example of how North Carolina's women willingly served in the war effort. As she tried to provide information to North Carolinians in her letters back home, Gove acknowledged that obtaining accurate news about the progress of the war was difficult. Even though she was stationed not far from the battle lines, she could not guarantee that her information was reliable.[68] Because of intense fighting and casualties, nurses were moved closer to the frontlines. Gove wrote, "I guess there is no one of the women here who does not hope to be transferred to the military department for immediate service, whatever may be her duty along civil lines later." [69] The wounded were being brought in daily as war caused millions of deaths, displaced civilian populations, and led to disease and destruction. Gove lamented, "With all this frightful struggle going on this city seems a place remote and unmoved by the fortunes of the contest except as the war has brought fortunes to the lucky trader and six-fold higher living prices to everyone."[70] While refugees streamed into Red Cross hospitals in towns across France, Gove noted some people capitalized on the hardships of others and raised rents to make more money.[71]

Gove was sent to Marseilles for a good deal of her wartime service. In June 1918, the clinic was serving twenty-five to forty patients daily with Saturday always being a busy day. Gove usually saw patients between 2:30 and 6:00 p.m., and the clinic staff was always greeted by what Gove described as a "small mob" who did not have appointments. These individuals were waiting, hoping they could be seen by a physician if someone did not meet their appointment. Gove and her colleague, a Dr. Bonness, treated only those who were physically able to travel to the clinic. [72] Others who could not go to the clinic were referred to hospitals or other doctors who made house calls. Nurses were sent out to treat some of the sicker children who were not able to travel to the clinic; however, unsafe districts were off limits.[73]

In March 1918, Dr. Emily Lapham, though not stationed near the frontlines of the fighting, was sent by the American Red Cross to La Rochelle, on the western coast of France, where she would take the lead in establishing dispensaries and hospitals for war refugees.[74] Far from home and combat, she had opportunities to see, firsthand (like others) the impact of the war on remote areas. La Rochelle was home to more than 14,000 refugees, many of whom were in dire need of medical attention.[75] It was not uncommon for Red Cross workers to observe refugees living in wagons on the streets and washing in unclean water. Lapham recalled seeing a little girl in a "wagon train with her face covered in filth."[76] One can certainly deduce here that some Red Cross workers had less than a favorable view of refugees. She concluded that the living conditions of the refugees led to illnesses including bronchitis. Children were more often than not "fatherless" as the men were away at war, had been killed in combat, or had died from infectious diseases.[77] Lapham was so touched by the hunger of the children that she wanted to provide food, though she was prohibited from doing so by her supervisor, a Miss Evans, so she decided to use her own money to buy food for refugees.[78] It is not clear from her journal if she actually did so; however, it does indicate the commitment North Carolina's female physicians had to helping in the war effort. This single deed demonstrates the impact the war was having on Lapham, that she considered using her own money to help buy necessities for her patients. It is worth noting that unlike some other female physicians and nurses, Lapham was somewhat protected. Her appointment was on the west coast of France, an area that did not experience the devastation found in the east and north. She readily admitted that she was "living with devastated people."[79] Lapham soon realized that one dispensary in La Rochelle was not sufficient, as both military and civilian people were coming in from surrounding areas. Developing plans to open two new dispensaries in nearby towns enabled her to serve others while providing care for more than 150 patients in La Rochelle. While making about forty calls a day, she also worked in a laboratory.[80]

Lapham's experiences, like those of so many others, undoubtedly shaped her worldview and life for years to come as she described the horrors of war but also noted that people were surprised to see a woman in uniform. She recalled that people were accustomed to not seeing men around. "The absence of men is taken for granted—no one asks where the husband is—he is either in the war—or dead—or a prisoner."[81] Perhaps one of the most poignant recollections comes from her acknowledgment that she and other hospital staff actually went out looking for refugees.[82] As the fighting concluded in 1918, she noted in her journal that things were in disarray and people, who had been at war for so long, almost did not know what to do with peace.[83] Of concern to her was the lack of care of "the common people for the refugees."[84] While she does not specifically say that the war changed her, it is clear from her journal musings that it did. Early on she expressed great impatience regarding the lack of necessities she found in La Rochelle, yet as the war progressed, her ingenuity served the city and its refugees well.[85] Lapham must have wondered what her life was going to be like once she returned to the United States, where undoubtedly she would not have the opportunities the war had opened up.

Meanwhile, Gove's team was working on installing army barracks to use as a baby hospital. She remained simultaneously concerned about the lack of proper materials and optimistic about her ability to provide service to babies in need.[86] She was also working with a group of refugees and repatriates who, although they "looked plump" because of their fatty diet, were not healthy due to the lack of nutrition available in wartime France. It was clear to Gove that the refugees would have fared even worse had it not been for the presence of the Red Cross.[87] Gove recalled that "the directors of the public buildings do not care for the children and have even shut the gas off preventing her from preparing food for the babies."[88] North Carolina female physicians, nurses, and other workers faced daily dangers on the battle lines. Even stations located far away from the fighting were not completely safe because German prisoners of war were often incarcerated in these locales, and the possibility of their escape existed. However, Lapham recalled that German prisoners assisted with moving heavy objects in the dispensaries and hospitals.[89]

North Carolina's women who served on the warfront in Europe found that constantly fearing enemy attacks, seeing the war wounded, dealing with disease and infections, and helping refugees cope built up the need for some outlet for their worries. When time and work permitted, the state's war workers in Europe attended dances and the theater, went sightseeing, biked, rode horses, played tennis, and traveled throughout the country.[90] The American Red Cross, the YMCA, and the YWCA all worked to provide soldiers and civilians a place to relax and socialize in war-torn Europe by establishing Huts. The military also realized that religious comfort was a necessity and assigned chaplains to units. Bain remembered that the chaplain assigned to Base Hospital #65 was of high moral fiber who was always ready to listen and comfort those in need. "He was the finest one in France. . . . [H]e went about doing good."[91] Sunday morning church services were always full.

The Huts, or canteens, served recreational and social needs for the troops and civilians as well. Military and government speakers and entertainers frequented the Huts. On occasion, they welcomed visitors from North Carolina. Entertainment was not as organized as it would be during World War II because the United Service Organizations (USO) did not exist during the Great War. Elizabeth E. Jones of Asheville, North Carolina, who served as a nurse with the American Red Cross, wrote of her experiences at Eagle Hut located in London. On October 4, 1917, *The Asheville Times* published a letter to her family in which she wrote,

> I have just come from Eagle Hut. . . . I have met many of our medical men—
> most of whom volunteered only a few months ago—some from Texas . . .
> New England . . . and a great many from New York. I adore the work and I
> wish I could go every day. I go on Saturdays and Sundays. One poor fellow in
> the flying corps came in and asked for a ticket for a cup of tea and a slice of
> bread. It was the dinner hour, and I knew no soldier could be happy on a cup

of tea and a slice of bread for his dinner, but I made out the ticket, then I took another look at him and tore up the ticket, and wrote him out another one for a good square meal and handed it to him. He turned crimson and said, "I only have two pence and cannot get that meal." I said, "that's all right, this place is for the soldiers, and if you can't pay it does not matter at all, I will see that you get it." And he got it, too. Two or three times this has happened.[92]

Eagle Hut served over 6000 men daily. Amenities included ice cream, griddlecakes, a boot-blacking stand, pie, hash, a bubbling fountain, baked beans, chewing gum, loans, money exchange, chocolate, magazines, Bible classes, and of course, "American English." Eagle Hut was the largest Hut in the war zone with an area of 35,000 square feet and included a canteen, a kit room, a lounge, a quiet room, a billiard and concert hall, four dormitories, lavatories, shower baths, a barber shop, and business offices. The canteen could accommodate 245 people; the number of beds was 279. Religious services combined with concerts were held several times a week with an average attendance of 344. In fact, Eagle Hut had some 800 volunteer workers with a YMCA staff of nine men.[93] The mission of Eagle Hut, like the other Huts across Europe, was to make it a "home away from home where the boys will find friends, the American accent, and the American way of doing things, and to which they will come for help and advice as well as for comforts."[94] Volunteers like Jones helped make Eagle Hut successful.

When the armistice was signed on November 11, 1918, 21,480 US army nurses were on active duty, and more than 10,000 of them were serving abroad in France, England, Belgium, Italy, Serbia, the Philippines, Hawaii, and Puerto Rico. With the influenza epidemic raging in the United States and throughout the world in 1918, two hundred army nurses died, though none from war wounds.[95] North Carolina lost one nurse on the warfront during World War I. Anne Dade Reveley of Greensboro died of pneumonia while serving in France in 1918.[96]

Most Americans realize that millions of women served during World War II, but they fail to acknowledge women's contributions during the Great War. The historiographic record is especially weak regarding North Carolina women in World War I. Few people know that some 200 women from the state gave up the comfort of the homefront and traveled to Europe to directly participate in the war effort. Close to the actual fighting, they faced typhus, malaria, typhoid, the influenza epidemic, refugee populations, economic deprivation and poverty, homelessness, and war. Tar Heel women, like their sisters across the nation, were committed to the cause and did what they could. Dorothy Hayden Conyers of Greensboro served on French and German battlefields, and Ruby Gordon of Biltmore worked between thirty-six and forty hours without stopping at Verdun as head of the operating rooms.[97] North Carolina's women engaged in activities above and beyond the call of duty, and Suzanne B.

Hoskins of Summerfield best illustrates their commitment, lying about her age to enlist for foreign duty with the Red Cross.[98]

North Carolina's women stepped out of the roles society prescribed for them while facing sexism even on the warfront. However, they were not dissuaded from their cause. Women like Gove, Lapham, Jones, Brewster, and Bain were devoted to making a difficult situation tolerable for the military and civilian populations they served in Europe. What more can be said about these "ancestors" of the "greatest generation"? Dr. Frank K. Boland, a major in the Medical Corps, captured the essence of their contributions when he wrote, "If there is such a thing as bringing the home to the trenches, the camp and the hospital, the Red Cross has done it."[99] Moreover, General John J. Pershing, the Commander in Chief of the Armed Forces summed up women's contributions during World War I when he wrote, "Your efforts deserve the highest praise. You have added new laurels to the already splendid record of American womanhood. It is a privilege to testify that your glorious accomplishments in the war have given you a new place in the hearts of officers and men of the Army, and have earned for you the admiration of a grateful nation.[100]

Indeed, North Carolina's female "veterans" of World War I "brought home to the trenches" through their service in the American Red Cross, the Army Nursing Corps, and the SCRU, even taking low-level positions for which they were overqualified. Female physicians worked as nurses, and still others established dispensaries, hospitals, and served both military and civilian populations in war-torn Europe. These women, and their sisters, have never been truly recognized or acknowledged for their bravery, fortitude, diligence, compassion, passion, and absolute commitment to the nation. This work demonstrates that so much is left to be done; documents exist to keep students, scholars, and the public alike busy for years to come. Hopefully, others will find these women interesting enough to engage in further research that could lead to books documenting their lives and contributions, thereby bringing the sacrifices of these brave women to the public consciousness.

Notes

1. I would like to acknowledge the work of four former undergraduate students, Roger Stedina, Amber Manson, Hae Seon Lee, and Hannah Schneider, who served as researchers over the course of two years. Stedina and Manson initially helped identify the various collections in North Carolina and built preliminary bibliographies, while Lee and Schneider read through all the documents. Their work identifying and highlighting key contributions of these women added greatly to this work. To them, I am grateful. Many thanks also to my colleagues and friends, Martha Donkor, Associate Professor of History at West Chester University, and Joseph Laythe (deceased), Professor of History at Edinboro University, who read versions of this chapter.

2. My use of "Molly's Daughters" connects these women to the Molly Pitcher of the American Revolution, who replaced her husband on the battlefield.

3. It is important to note that more women from North Carolina served as nurses, volunteers, and in other capacities that are not covered in this brief chapter. Other than a few

sources on nursing, few secondary sources on the role of North Carolina's women on the warfront during World War I exist. Much more research needs to be done to fill in the gaps regarding these brave women.

4. It must be noted that both Gove and Lapham were successful prior to the war in their respective roles in Greensboro and Highlands, North Carolina. Gove had a long-term stint as the physician at the women's college in Greensboro, taking several leaves of absence including one for the war, and Lapham opened a sanatorium in Highlands before the war. Much more work should be done on their contributions, for both left lengthy journals. Very little is known about Lapham after the war ended, though Elena Branca notes she died in Florida in 1936; cf. Elena Branca, "Inspirational Women of World War I," accessed February 15, 2017, http://inspirational womenofww1.blogspot.com/2016/06/dr-mary-lapham-1860–1936–american-ww1.html.

5. William A. Link, *North Carolina: Change and Tradition in a Southern State* (Wheeling, IL: Harlan Davidson, Inc., 2009), 316.

6. *American Women Physicians, Their War and Peace Work in France, Serbia, Armenia, Syria, the Near East* (Boston: American Women's Hospitals, n.d.), located in the State Archives, World War I Collection, Raleigh, North Carolina, n.p.

7. *American Women Physicians*, n.p.

8. Kimberly Jensen, *Mobilizing Minerva: American Women in the First World War* (Urbana: University of Illinois Press, 2008), 77–97.

9. Lettie Gavin, *American Women in World War I: They Also Served* (Boulder: University of Colorado Press, 1997), 157.

10. *The Work of the American Red Cross During The War: A Statement of Finances and Accomplishments for the period July 1, 1917 to February 28, 1919* (Washington, DC, October 1919), n.p., located in the State Archives, World War I Collection, Raleigh, North Carolina; Evelyn M. Monahan and Rosemary Neidel-Greenlee, *A Few Good Women: America's Military Women from World War to the Wars in Iraq and Afghanistan* (New York: Random House, 2010), 12–13, http://www.history.army.mil/books/anc-highlights/chrono.htm.

11. The Smith College Relief Unit and Dr. Gove will be addressed later in the paper.

12. Lula Owl Gloyne Interview, Oral History Collection, Appalachian State University, Boone, North Carolina, http://archive.org/details/LulaOwlGloyne, hereafter cited as Gloyne Interview; John R. Finger, *Cherokee Americans: The Eastern Band of Cherokees in the Twentieth Century* (Lincoln: University of Nebraska Press, 1991), 36.

13. May Greenfield Watson, "Army Nurse" unpublished statement, Military Collection-World War I, State Archives, Raleigh, North Carolina, n.d.

14. Mary Lewis Wyche, *History of Nursing in North Carolina* (Chapel Hill: University of North Carolina Press, 1977), 23.

15. "Report of the Surgeon General, U.S. Army to the Secretary of War, 1919, vol. II (Washington, DC: Government Printing Office, 1919), 1979–1980, Military Collection—World War I, State Archives, Raleigh, North Carolina.

16. Irene Brewster, "The Nurses' Side of It: Being a Story of Their Contribution to the Achievements of Base Hospital #65 Stationed at Kerhuon, France During the World War," Military Collection—World War I, State Archives, Raleigh, North Carolina, n.d.

17. Ibid.

18. Ibid.

19. Ione Branch Bain, "Mission Accomplished: Experiences in World War One," unpublished, Ione Branch Bain Papers, Military Collection—World War I, State Archives of North Carolina (hereafter cited as Bain Papers).

20. Ibid.

21. Ibid.

22. Ibid.

23. Ibid.

24. Ibid.

25. Brewster, "The Nurses' Side of It."

26. Bain Papers.

27. Ibid.

28. Ibid.

29. Elizabeth Herbert Smith Taylor Diaries (#4994), September 8, 1918–May 10, 1919, transcript of the manuscript, "Documenting the American South," University of North Carolina at Chapel Hill, Southern Historical Collection, accessed September 11, 2013, http://docsouth.unc.edu/wwi/taylordiary/summary.html.

30. Brewster, "The Nurses' Side of It."

31. Bain Papers.

32. Dorothy and Carl J. Schneider, *Into the Breach: American Women Overseas in World War I* (Lincoln, NE: toExcel Press, 2001), 25.

33. Brewster, "The Nurses' Side of It."

34. Bain Papers.

35. Ibid.

36. Watson, "Army Nurse"; Brewster, "The Nurses' Side of It"; Bain Papers.

37. Brewster, "The Nurses' Side of It."

38. Mary Emily Lapham Journal, Mary Emily Lapham Collection, The Betty H. Carter Women Veterans Historical Project, University of North Carolina at Greensboro Archives (hereafter cited as Lapham Journal).

39. Watson, "Army Nurse"; Brewster, "The Nurses' Side of It."

40. Report of the Surgeon General, U.S. Army to the Secretary of War, 1919, Vol. II (Washington, DC: Government Printing Office, 1919), 1980.

41. Wyche, *History of Nursing*, 23–24.

42. William Palmer Lewis, "Work of the Children's Bureau, Department of Civil Affairs, American Red Cross, France," *Journal of the American Medical Association* 71.5 (August 3, 1918): 395–365, accessed February 15, 2017, http://guides.library.harvard.edu/-schlesinger_WWI.

43. Summary of the Work of the Children's Bureau, Department of Civil Affairs, from August 12, 1917, to February 6, 1918, Dr. Anna Gove Collection, The Betty H. Carter Women Veterans Historical Project, University of North Carolina at Greensboro (hereafter cited as Children's Bureau, Gove Collection).

44. Wyche, *History of Nursing*, 24.

45. "The Story of the Children's Bureau," https://cb100.acf.hhs.gov/Cb_ebrochure, accessed February 8, 2017.

46. *The Work of the American Red Cross During the War: A Statement of Finances and Accomplishments for the period, July 1, 1917 to February 28, 1919* (Washington, DC: American Red Cross, 1919), 49, Military Collection, World War I Papers, American Red Cross 1917–1923, State Archives of North Carolina, Raleigh, North Carolina.

47. Ibid.

48. "Map of France, 551 Stations from Which the Red Cross Rendered Service in France," *The Work of the American Red Cross During the War: A Statement of Finances and Accomplishments for the period, July 1, 1917 to February 28, 1919* (Washington, DC: American Red Cross, 1919), 50.

49. Children's Bureau, Gove Collection.

50. Dr. Anna Gove Journal, June 2, 1918, University of North Carolina at Greensboro Archives (hereafter cited as Gove Journal, Gove Collection).

51. Ibid.

52. Bain Papers.

53. Ibid.

54. Ibid.

55. Brewster, "The Nurses' Side of It."

56. Bain Papers.

57. Ibid.

58. Ibid.

59. Ibid.

60. Ibid.

61. Ibid.

62. Ibid.

63. Ibid.; Obit. *Not. Fell. R. Soc.*, vol. 8, no. 21, November 1, 1952, 128–148. (Assistance on medical issues provided by Dr. Lenore Barbian, who is a member of the Disaster Mortuary Operational Response Team (DMORT), a professor of Anthropology, and a fellow of the Forensic Sciences Institute at Edinboro University. Barbian's expertise is in forensic/physical anthropology).

64. Bain Papers.

65. Ibid.

66. SCRU Records, 1917–1997, https://asteria.fivecolleges.edu/findaids/smitharchives /manosca95.html, accessed February 8, 2017. From the introduction to the website: "Harriet Boyd Hawes (1892) to bring relief to those areas of France that were most devastated during the first World War. Hawes already had significant experience of relief work when she proposed, at a Boston Smith Club meeting in 1917, to form the SCRU. She had served as a relief nurse in both the Greco–Turkish war of 1897 and the Spanish–American war, and then later in France, when World War I began. Having seen first-hand the effects of the war in Europe, Hawes was dismayed at the apathy expressed towards it by Americans when she returned to the United States. When the United States finally did join the war, Hawes quickly announced her intentions of starting a relief unit, which she hoped to staff with other Smith graduates."

67. Gove Journal, Gove Collection.

68. Ibid.

69. Ibid.

70. Ibid.

71. Ibid.

72. I could not find the first name of this physician. Gove Journal, Gove Collection.

73. Ibid.

74. Lapham Journal.

75. Ibid.

76. Ibid.

77. Ibid.

78. Ibid.

79. Ibid.

80. Ibid.

81. Lapham Journal.

82. Lapham Journal.

83. Lapham Journal.

84. Lapham Journal.

85. Lapham Journal.

86. Gove Journal, Gove Collection.

87. Ibid.

88. Ibid.

89. Lapham Journal.

90. Lapham Journal; Gove Journal, Gove Collection; Bain Papers; Anne Huheey Collection; Glory Hancock Collection; May Jones Collection; University of North Carolina at Greensboro Archives.

91. Bain Papers.

92. Jones, "Experiences at American Canteen."

93. "Souvenir of the Eagle Hut, American Y.M.C.A.," Aldwych-Strand, London, n.d., State Archives of North Carolina, Raleigh, NC (hereafter cited as Jones/Eagle Hut). No date is listed, but this document is clearly from World War I and was included in the Elizabeth E. Jones Papers.

94. Ibid.

95. *The Work of the American Red Cross During the War: A Statement of Finances and Accomplishments for the period July 1, 1917 to February 28, 1919.*

96. Wyche, *History of Nursing,* 25.

97. Ibid.

98. Paula S. Jordan and Kathy W. Manning, *Women of Guilford County, North Carolina: A Study of Women's Contributions, 1740–1979* (Greensboro: Women of Guilford, 1979), 99.

99. Frank K. Boland to Eugene R. Black, "What the Medical Corps Thinks of the Red Cross," printed in *Red Cross Briefs, Southern Division American Red Cross,* Vol. 2 No. 7, November 1, 1918, Military Collection, World War I Papers, American Red Cross 1917–1923, State Archives of North Carolina, Raleigh, North Carolina.

100. John J. Pershing memorandum to the Women Members of the A.E.F., April 30, 1919, Military Collection, World War I Papers, American Red Cross 1917–1923, State Archives of North Carolina, Raleigh, NC.

5

Black North Carolinians as Soldiers in the First World War

The First, the Proud, the Brave

Janet G. Hudson

For 21,609 young African American men who called North Carolina home, the First World War meant leaving families and familiar Tar Heel communities. For more than half of them, the Great War also meant sailing the Atlantic to serve in France. The military service and sacrifice of those tens of thousands of black North Carolinians, however, are not well known among historians or the public. Their contributions, individually and collectively, have been generally ignored, simplistically rendered, represented by only a few, hidden away in disparate and scattered sources, or carried to the grave without articulation or preservation. The war's centennial offers an opportunity to examine that void and to highlight the collective service black North Carolinians rendered—service that included fighting on the frontlines, preparing the French ports, repairing dangerous supply lines, commanding soldiers, cooking food, felling trees, and digging graves. Despite the multifaceted and broad spectrum of individual experiences, which were as varied as any group of soldiers in the war, the label "colored," marked in the corner of their service cards, strongly determined all black soldiers' wartime experiences. Racial categorizing shaped their military experience, just as race prejudice has shaped the telling and remembering of their contribution.[1]

While mobilizing the nation for war in 1917, Woodrow Wilson's administration had no intention of violating the existing plethora of segregation laws in southern states. Nor did the newly reelected Democratic president, a southerner sympathetic to white supremacy, advocate altering the existing policy and practice of segregated military units. Although mobilizing, training, and deploying several million young men for war with effectiveness and speed was incompatible with maintaining racial subordination in the ranks, the US military continually honored the latter, which posed an extraordinary organizational challenge.[2]

National political and military leaders juggled wartime necessities with the assumptions of African Americans' racial inferiority, yielding contorted decisions that defined the boundaries and shaped the contours of the collective story of North Carolina's African American soldiers who served in the First World War.[3] For black North Carolinians, the War Department's plans determined that: (1) ninety percent of black North Carolinians served in the military as laboring soldiers; (2) the ten percent who faced combat served in segregated units with woefully compromised training; (3) the size of the black officer corps nationally and in North Carolina was as small as possible; (4) black volunteers and draftees, unlike their white counterparts, trained in camps across the country and were disbursed to hundreds of different units, rather than to only a few, in order to appease segregationist concerns; and (5) their draft was postponed from October 1917 until March 1918 due to complications that arose while accommodating segregationist demands. Yet even within these extensive limitations, black North Carolinians made their mark. They were among the first American combat soldiers, black or white, to arrive in Europe, among the early stevedore volunteers, among the recipients of military awards and honors, and among the last returning soldiers who performed the arduous task of restoring the killing fields of France for human habitation.

Of course, relegating ninety percent of African Americans to carrying shovels rather than guns and prizing their physical strength above all else testifies most obviously to military leaders' deeply held beliefs in racial inferiority. While accepting that some African Americans would make effective combat soldiers, architects of the war reasoned that most were "best suited" to contribute their manual labor as "laboring soldiers."[4] While this label crudely characterized army men without combat soldier roles, the umbrella term "laboring soldier" served as a civilian simplification that obscures a host of diverse military units and responsibilities. Of the ninety percent who became laboring soldiers, half served overseas, and half remained in the United States.

While ninety percent of all black soldiers from North Carolina served as laborers rather than combat soldiers, half of those laboring soldiers journeyed to France and served in four variations of overseas labor units—quartermaster labor battalions, pioneer infantry regiments, stevedore regiments, and engineering service battalions. In fall 1917, black North Carolinians were among the thousands of first-arriving African American stevedore regiments who rebuilt the waterfront of the French ports, from Brest at the entrance of the English Channel south to the Mediterranean port of Marseilles, including Bordeaux, St. Nazaire, and Marseilles. They performed the intense labor of rapidly loading and unloading all the ships in port that carried construction materials and eventually soldiers and weapons. Further illustrating the variety of laboring soldiers abroad, black North Carolinians served in black pioneer infantry regiments, unique units that trained with and carried weapons as reserve combat units. Subjected to the same hardships as combat soldiers and in range of the same deadly weapons on the frontline, pioneer infantry soldiers repaired heavily rutted and rain-washed supply line roads. Engineer service battalions also built and repaired roads and other structures that took them within shelling range of the battle lines. At least 5000 black North Carolinians served in quartermaster labor battalions, units that did the most difficult and thankless general labor including loading and unloading trucks, cutting wood, hauling rocks for road repair, and digging graves.[5]

The other half of black laboring soldiers from North Carolina spent their entire service to Uncle Sam in the United States, where they had widely varying experiences as well. Some troops remained in their original depot unit, others served as replacement training units preparing to replace fallen soldiers abroad should they receive the call, and still others served in a host of special domestic units. For example, approximately one hundred North Carolinians worked in construction units that built the runways and hangers at Langley Air Field in Virginia, as part of the new Army Aviation Signal Corp, forerunner to the modern United States Air Force. Several hundred black North Carolinians served in hospitals, infirmaries, sanitary corps, medical detachments, and schools for bakers and cooks. At least seven North Carolinians served in the Chemical Warfare Division in Maryland, created to research and manufacture chemical weapons in response to Germany's use of them. More than 130 participated in the War Department's short-lived initiative with institutions of higher education, known as the Students' Army Training Corps, preparing soldiers in historically black colleges in and outside of North Carolina.[6]

Nearly twenty percent of the young men who served stateside had some of the most negative and demeaning experiences of the war. Assigned to reserve labor battalions, units created primarily after July 1918 when the draft expanded to include men ages 18 to 45, these men performed primarily menial and often hard labor in and around the camps with no pretext for military preparation and sometimes without military uniforms or adequate food. White officers, often unsuccessful elsewhere or deemed incapable of serving overseas, commanded these units and addressed the men as "niggers," employed abusive language, and physically assaulted them. The majority of African Americans drafted later not only ended up disproportionally in domestic units with experiences that differed dramatically from those men taken earlier, but they also trained closer to home. Camp Greene near Charlotte hosted numerous reserve labor battalions filled with black North Carolinians, who reported very negative experiences. Major W. H. Loving, who reported on training camp morale issues, criticized Camp Greene for inadequate facilities to meet the needs of black soldiers.[7]

African American combat soldiers also suffered discrimination. For the ten percent of North Carolina's African American soldiers who served their country in combat, military policymakers crafted every detail of these troops' training and assignments to appease racial fears and assuage the demands of segregationists. In late October 1917, Secretary Newton Baker ordered the creation of an all-black combat division and ordered the nineteen different units of this segregated 92nd Division to train in seven different, nonsouthern National Army cantonments located in New York, New Jersey, Ohio, Illinois, Iowa, Kansas, and Maryland. Predetermining that black combat units would never train together as a division, stateside or in France, was the compromise of military principles that Secretary Baker made to create an all-black combat division that many had opposed. His decision enabled African Americans to serve as combat soldiers while appeasing segregationist demands that they not be trained in the South and that a 3:1 white-to-black racial troop ratio exist in all training camps to assuage concerns of concentrating black troops.[8]

The 92nd Division, composed primarily though not exclusively of drafted African Americans from the South, was one of the two segregated combat divisions that served in the First World War. In November 1917, Secretary Baker created the second and only other segregated combat division, the 93rd Division, after months of uncertainty about what to do with two groups: (1) the black National Guard units that came primarily from northern states and had run afoul of local Jim Crow mores in the deep South camps where they trained, setting off a firestorm of opposition, and (2) the one regiment of drafted soldiers that began training at Camp Jackson, South Carolina, before the original plan had been altered to train all black combat units outside the South. From these units Baker created four infantry regiments—the 369th, 370th, 371st, and 372nd—but no other support units, thus the 93rd Division never became a true division and never trained or served together. Greatly compromising military priorities, Baker stopped the training of these four regiments and sent them abroad, ahead of all American combat soldiers— white and black—to ease racial tension in the communities surrounding their training camps near Houston, Texas; Montgomery, Alabama; and Spartanburg, South Carolina. Making the division even more unique, Baker sent all four regiments to serve directly with the French Army, outfitted them with French uniforms and weapons, and placed each of the four regiments with different French units.[9]

Black North Carolinians served in both of these segregated combat divisions—approximately 1700 in the 92nd Division and 500 or more in the 93rd Division—representing 10 percent of all black troops who served and roughly 20 percent of black North Carolinians who served overseas. These men served in all nineteen combat units of the 92nd Division, units that eventually fought on the battlefields of France in the St. Die des Vosges and Meuse-Argonne campaigns. The great majority of North Carolinians who served in the 92nd Division trained at Camp Grant near Rockford, Illinois, ninety miles west of

Chicago. More than one thousand became members of the 365th and 366th, two of the division's four combat infantry regiments, and the 350th, one of only two machine gun battalions composed completely of African American troops.[10] Although in significantly smaller numbers, some black North Carolinians trained at the other six camps—Dix (New Jersey), Upton (New York), Sherman (Ohio), Funston (Kansas), Dodge (Iowa), and Meade (Maryland)— that hosted the support units of the 92nd Division. While all higher-ranking officers in the 92nd Division were white, African Americans, including North Carolinians, served as first and second lieutenants and captains.[11]

The 92nd Division included one field artillery brigade composed of three field artillery regiments (349th, 350th, 351st) and one trench mortar battery. White military leaders had great doubt that enough black soldiers could be found to perform effectively in this very technical unit that required men with education and skills to read scales, manipulate fractions, and interpret technical details. Several dozen North Carolinians served in this highly praised brigade that became the first all-black field artillery. Men such as James Davis of Raleigh and Henry Bryant of Rockfish tested into the 349th regiment initially and sailed with the unit to France in June 1918. Ernest McKissick (349th) of Asheville, Roby Farmer (350th) of Fayetteville, and Burt Stevenson (349th) of Charlotte, among others, transferred in to join the regiments already in France after officials recognized their abilities during the aggressive canvas to identify qualified men. McKissick reflected decades later that you "really [had] to know your stuff" to become a member of the field artillery unit. He credited his success to his education from Livingstone College in Salisbury.[12]

Black North Carolinians served in all four regiments of the 93rd Division. Two hundred or more men served in the 371st Infantry, the regiment that originated at Camp Jackson and was composed primarily of drafted South Carolinians. While the majority of North Carolinians in the 93rd Division were in the 371st, they also served in each of the other three regiments, the core of each composed of National Guard soldiers. Some of these men enlisted early, serving as full members of the regiment from the beginning. For example, Evander Lee and William Jones of Charlotte, Clifton Jones of Winston-Salem, and Mark Knight of Pittsboro all volunteered in 1917 and served in combat with the New York National Guard soldiers as members of the famed 369th "Harlem Hellfighters," famed for its battlefield exploits as well as bringing jazz to Europe. Most, however, transferred into the infantry regiments as replacements for battlefield casualties.[13]

In the long list of apprehensions white Americans expressed concerning African Americans' service in the First World War, the question of training and commissioning black officers proved a major source of political tension. The eventual compromise led to one class of officers trained far from the South, in Iowa. At the segregated officer training camp at Ft. Des Moines,

1000 newly volunteered civilians and 250 experienced soldiers trained from June to October 1917, and 639 African Americans earned their commission on October 15.[14] Consistent with the national success rates at Ft. Des Moines, at least twenty-seven black North Carolinians became officers in October, just over half of the forty-nine men identified for officer training. Fourteen North Carolinians were commissioned 2nd lieutenants, the lowest rank; eight as 1st lieutenants; and five as captains, the highest rank for black soldiers. Sixteen of twenty-seven men commissioned entered Ft. Des Moines from civilian life, and the other eleven underwent officer training as experienced soldiers. Secretary Baker assigned these officers to infantry, artillery, and engineering units of the newly created 92nd Division, and he assured military and civilian leaders that all commissioned black officers would be in the nonsouthern camps.[15]

These officers were among North Carolina's most distinguished African American soldiers, and many became accomplished men after the war. Commissioned officers from civilian life included Second Lieutenant Robert Smalls Bampfield of Wilmington, the grandson of Robert Smalls, famed Civil War hero and Reconstruction era politician from Beaufort, South Carolina. Educated at Johnson C. Smith University in Charlotte, Bampfield also served in World War II, lived much of his civilian life in Washington, DC, and is buried in Arlington National Cemetery. Another Johnson C. Smith alumnus, Second Lieutenant Gurney E. Nelson of Greensboro, became a career educator after pursuing graduate education at the University of Chicago and Ohio State University. Second Lieutenant Lovelace B. Capehart Jr. of Raleigh became a pharmacist and physician after the war. Second Lieutenant Russell C. Atkins of Winston-Salem was educated at Hampton Normal and Agricultural Institute in Virginia and worked before and after the war in agricultural education at Tuskegee Normal and Industrial Institute in Alabama. His father had been president of State Teachers College in Winston-Salem. Lieutenant Bravid W. Harris Jr. of Warrenton became an Episcopal priest, bishop, and eventually a missionary to Liberia. Most black North Carolina officers led men of the 365th Infantry, the regiment with which most black North Carolina infantrymen served. Unfortunately for the state, many of these talented and educated native sons sought opportunities outside of North Carolina when they returned from the war.[16]

Those commissioned officers from North Carolina with prior military experience included, among others, captains Moody Staten of Lincoln County, Herbert Avery of Morganton, and Samuel Reid of Concord, and lieutenants James W. Alston of Raleigh and Thomas Bullock of Henderson. Except for Staten, these men were in their forties at the time of commissioning. Their ages and military experiences set them apart from the other officers and nearly all the enlisted men. Alston, a veteran of the Spanish–American War, had an atypical experience for black soldiers. He was one of the few North

Carolinians who served as an officer in the 93rd Division, rather than the 92nd, leading men in the 372nd Infantry Regiment. He also corresponded during the war with a white employer, Herbert H. Brimley, curator of the State Museum, sharing his experiences and perspective. In his correspondence, Alston continually expressed optimism and conveyed his patriotic, anti-German determination to defeat the enemy. "Fritz can fight like the very devil when he is under cover and has the most men, but can't stand the Yankee steel and these Yanks, white & black sure love to use the bayonet whenever they can get near enough to him."[17]

Another of the seasoned soldiers, Bullock led men in the 367th Infantry. With far more military experience than most North Carolinians, he also had been a veteran of the Spanish–American War and had served three years in the Philippines with the 25th Infantry, one of the US Army's four all-black regular army units. In addition to his military experience, he was college educated. A graduate of Lincoln University, the Pennsylvania alma mater of Thurgood Marshall, Bullock also taught at Williston Industrial School in Wilmington. In 1916 when the 15th Infantry Regiment of the New York National Guard organized, he was among the first to volunteer. William Hayward, commanding officer of the New York regiment, readily identified him as an ideal candidate for officer training, so Bullock left the regiment that later became the 369th "Harlem Fighters" to lead men in the 92nd Division.[18]

While Ft. Des Moines only commissioned one class of African American officers, the army had a few other opportunities for black soldiers to become commissioned officers. African Americans from North Carolina also became commissioned as physicians. Similar to most of their national counterparts, medical officers from North Carolina who treated the wounded in combat were recent medical school graduates. Two of those men, Lieutenant Egbert Theophilus Scott of Wilmington and Lieutenant Max Constuart King of Franklinton, attended Leonard Medical College at Shaw University in Raleigh. King finished his studies and graduated from Meharry Medical School in Nashville. Although born in North Carolina and educated at Biddle University (name changed to Johnson C. Smith in 1923) and Shaw University, Scott left his home state after the war for opportunities in Pennsylvania, where he practiced medicine for fifty years. North Carolinians were also among the commissioned black officers in the chaplaincy. For example, Lieutenant Alexander Huntington Hatwood, pastor of the Grace A.M.E. Church of Salisbury, served as a Methodist chaplain at Camp Taylor in Louisville, Kentucky.[19]

Military decision making repeatedly contorted itself to satisfy contemporary racial expectations and shaped the wartime experiences of black North Carolinians. For example, in the summer 1917 the War Department abandoned its original plan to train solders close to home for the late-developing alternative, a national soldier-shuffle. While the vast majority of white North

Carolinians trained in two neighboring South Carolina camps—Camp Sevier, home of the 30th Division, and Camp Jackson, home of the 81st Division, black North Carolinians had a very different experience. Secretary Baker's revised plan, finalized in October, scattered them across the country to train in thirteen of the sixteen National Army camps and dispersed them into over 300 different units. Thus, Washington's plan, designed to avoid concentrating black troops in the South and to ensure all camps maintained a 3:1 white-to-black ratio, systematically relegated black North Carolinians as outsiders and small minorities in most units.[20]

In early spring 1918, Washington launched the national soldier-shuffle plan. Approximately 5000 black North Carolinians headed to Camp Grant while the majority found themselves dispersed elsewhere in much smaller numbers. An additional 5000 went to five other camps: Taylor, Dix, Sherman, Meade, and Lee (Virginia), approximately 1800 traveled to nearby Camp Jackson, and another 5000 trained in still smaller numbers at other camps throughout the country.[21] By late summer 1918, the army decided to save transportation costs and keep most black inductees closer to home. Local whites endorsed this change, accepting that minimally trained men assigned to menial labor posed negligible threats to surrounding communities. Consequently, approximately 5000 black soldiers drafted late in the war trained in North Carolina at Camp Greene; some of these men served overseas, but the majority did not.[22]

The politically driven soldier-shuffle plan also delayed the large-scale induction of the state's African Americans. As officials originally designed the draft, black soldiers were to be inducted in October 1917, but the revised plan delayed the "black draft" until March 1918 because workers needed to construct extra, segregated quarters in the nonsouthern camps. While black soldiers had been enlisting and serving since the summer of 1917 in scattered numbers, it was not until Holy Week 1918 that thousands of North Carolina's African American families gathered to say good-bye to the first concentrated groups of young men boarding trains for Camp Grant. Three weeks later, more African Americans left the state for the same location, thereby fulfilling the War Department's initial request that North Carolina send its first sizeable quota of black soldiers (5000) to this nonsouthern military training camp. The induction of black North Carolinians that began in early spring continued until the final week of the war, but the majority—nearly 80 percent—began training between Easter and Labor Day 1918.[23]

In the course of that five-month span, the timing of a black man's draft call significantly influenced where he trained, the type of unit with which he served, and his probability of service abroad. Those drafted earliest were most likely to be combat soldiers, train outside the South, and serve overseas. Conversely, those drafted in August or later were far more likely to have trained in North Carolina, remained stateside, and served in a reserve labor battalion. For example, most black North Carolinians selected for combat duty were among the first 5000 men sent to Camp Grant. Approximately 55 percent of all African American soldiers from North Carolina served overseas, and the proportion sent to France steadily declined from 80 percent of the first peak draft week to only about 20 percent of those drafted in late August.[24]

While the vocal and persistent political opposition from white southerners to the War Department's original plans for black soldiers led to months of hand wringing in Washington and delays in announcing the black draft, the military's urgent need for soldiers did not lessen. As many as one thousand black North Carolinians became soldiers before the black draft began, and most were volunteers. These men volunteered for stevedore units that heavily recruited black volunteers, for National Guard units in other states since African Americans were not allowed to volunteer for combat duty with the Regular Army, or for the segregated officer training corps. Others among the first 1000 were already in the Regular Army, serving in one of its four segregated regiments—24th and 25th Infantry, 9th and 10th Cavalry.[25] Numerous draftees were also among those inducted early, despite the War Department's official delay on drafting African Americans in North Carolina. This irregularity demonstrates that altering the draft system in midstream was an imperfect process, leading numerous early draftees to become members of the 371st Infantry.[26]

Since the United States entered the war late, Americans, regardless of race, participated only in the final months of the fighting, primarily in the summer and fall of 1918. African Americans in the four infantry regiments of the 93rd, who fought directly with the French, were the exception. They arrived earlier, engaged the enemy sooner, and fought longer than all other Americans, black and white. Black North Carolinians engaged in frontline combat primarily between September 26 and November 11 in various engagements of the famed Meuse-Argonne offensive, the largest American-led campaign and the Allies' final one.

North Carolinians in the 371st Infantry served in the Champagne campaign that was part of the first phase of the Allied assault in the Meuse-Argonne. At least four black North Carolinians from the unit were killed in the same campaign that took the life of South Carolinian Freddie Stowers, the only African American Medal of Honor recipient in the First World War. The four young North Carolinians—Arthur Deshazo (Woodsdale), George McEachin (Hasty), Fred Reed (Goldsboro), and Robert Thompson (Wilmington)—died September 29 and 30 in the fight for Côte 188, a hill heavily defended by the Germans. Nearly fifty others from the state were wounded in this same fight that left 40 percent of the unit dead or wounded. At least two North Carolinians who survived the three-day battle for Côte 188 received awards. Private Junius Diggs (Lilesville) earned the Distinguished Service Cross for "extraordinary heroism in action" near Ardeuil on September 30. When his company withdrew under heavy fire, Diggs advanced to "rescue wounded comrades, working persistently until all of them had been carried to shelter." Sergeant Lee R. McClelland of Asheville, with the medical detachment, received the same citation the same day in the same battle. The citation noted that while Sgt. McClelland administered "first-aid treatment to wounded soldiers on the field, he received a painful wound on the leg, but without mentioning his injury he remained on duty, caring for the wounded under shell fire, until the regiment was relieved."[27]

Along with the 371st, the 372nd Infantry, imbedded with the "Red Hand" French 157th, also participated in the first phase of the Meuse-Argonne campaign. Lieutenant Alston, a black officer in the unit, described the front "just as General Sherman [had] 'Hell.'" In the bloody but successful initial assault against the Germans in late September, Alston suffered a severe battlefield injury, a machine gun hit to his right shoulder. Recovering in the hospital from the bullet wound, Alston wrote his white boss in Raleigh that he suffered another injury: the isolation he experienced as the lone black officer in the hospital for American officers. Had Alton been an enlisted man, he would have been with other African Americans. The North Carolinian reflected, "I was hungry as a dog the first night that I was here but walking in the dinning [sic] room seeing about one hundred white officers and no colored officers I lost my appetite." Alston complained of no bad treatment but emphasized to Brimley that as the only black officer "you know I am lonesome."[28]

The 92nd Division saw its first combat in August 1918 but fought primarily in the Meuse-Argonne campaign, participating in the St. Die des Vosges sector, the mountainous area near the German border, and in the Marbache sector located in the heart of Lorraine. Many 92nd Division units had been in the "quiet" Marbache sector during the early phase of the Meuse-Argonne offensive, supporting, patrolling, and experiencing occasional action. Low morale became a problem. An officer noted that morale had deteriorated due to excessive "marching at night, exposure to rain and cold, irregularity of supply, insufficient clothing," and minimal supervision. Alston also noted the problem of inadequate food; his men had to make do with half rations when the regiment ran ahead of supplies. As the division's aggressive raids awakened the enemy in November, however, the fight for basic survival quickly replaced low morale concerns.[29]

In the drive toward German-controlled Metz, North Carolinians who fought with the 92nd Division experienced frontline fighting in the last engagement of the war, known as the Woevre Plain operation. Major General Charles C. Ballou, who commanded the division, praised the men for their participation in the last battle with "creditable success, continually pressing the attack against highly organized defensive works." Ballou noted that on the first day of the battle, November 10, the soldiers advanced successfully on the Germans, reaching their objectives of controlling particular geographical areas and capturing prisoners. All of this, he noted, took place "in the face of determined opposition of an alert enemy, and against rift, machine gun and artillery fire." Many North Carolinians were wounded in this short battle, and six of the sixteen soldiers from the 365th Infantry who were killed in action while fighting during the two-day battle were North Carolinians.[30] Russell Atkins, Second Lieutenant from North Carolina, received the Silver Star for rescuing a wounded soldier while under fire in this battle. North Carolina physicians Lieutenant Egbert Scott and Lieutenant Max King treated the horrific wounds from that engagement, wounds caused primarily by artillery and machine gun fire. Lieutenant Bravid W. Harris Jr. received an official commendation for "meritorious conduct" in that same battle. Three privates, James Hill of Faison (365th), Reid Lyons of Winston-Salem (365th), and Walter Mason of Chapel Hill (366th), died on November 11, the day of the ceasefire. French military authorities awarded the *Croix de Guerre* to portions of the 367th infantry, considered the most successful regiment in the division, commending them for "bravery and fine service" during the battle. Second Lieutenant Lorenzo Chambers White of Winston-Salem led his men as part of this decorated unit in the Meuse-Argonne. Moreover, the French awarded the *Croix de Guerre* to elements of the 369th, 371st, and 372nd of the 93rd Division for their outstanding service in other battles.[31]

While the November 11 armistice promptly ended the fighting, it did not immediately conclude soldiers' obligations, and many continued their military service well into 1919. Most black North Carolinians in combat units returned home between February and April 1919. Those abroad in service units generally stayed longer because they had as much work to do after the war as during it. Just as African American stevedore troops arrived first to prepare the way for all others, black labor battalions, engineering service battalions, and pioneer infantry regiments were among the last to return in the summer and fall of 1919. They remained in France performing the battlefield salvage and cleanup work as well as transforming the temporary, makeshift graves into permanent cemeteries by recovering and reburying decomposed bodies and body parts.[32]

Of course, not everyone survived or returned home physically whole, and those buried in France never would. Officially, 575 black North Carolinians died during the war—twenty-one in combat and the rest from accidents and a host of diseases. Most black North Carolinians killed in action fought with the 365th Infantry, a few with the 366th, and one officer, Lieutenant Bullock, in the 367th. On September 2, 1918, Bullock died while in St. Die des Vosges, then a "quiet" sector. Yet Bullock's death revealed that real dangers flared at unexpected times and places. Official reports record that 333 African Americans from North Carolina suffered battle wounds, and many of these included injuries from the Germans' use of chemical weapons. Most of the wounded fought with the 365th, 366th, and 371st infantry regiments. But North Carolinians in other infantry regiments, the machine gun battalions, field artillery, ammunition trains, and supply trains also suffered combat casualties.[33]

Many of the noncombat war dead were victims of the influenza pandemic of 1918–1919, while others suffered from pneumonia, tuberculosis, meningitis, and other diseases. The 344th labor battalion was especially hard hit. In late September 1918, these men left Camp Greene for France just as an outbreak of influenza hit. Likely carrying the germs with them, nearly 100 soldiers in this one labor battalion died either on the voyage across the Atlantic or within two weeks of their arrival in France. These deaths, within ten days of each other, represented nearly 40 percent of all the deaths from disease among black North Carolinians abroad. Just over half of the deaths from disease were suffered by troops stationed in domestic training camps. Hundreds of additional soldiers returned with some level of disability.[34]

As African Americans came home to their Tar Heel communities throughout 1919, they returned amid tensions and national turmoil. After fighting to make democracy real in Europe, Ernest McKissick reported returning home to find that "democracy wasn't working at all at home 'cause they hadn't done anything for us. We had Jim Crow and all. They tried to put us down in every way." Within a week of the armistice, racial violence erupted in Winston-Salem. This incident proved an early indication of the national epidemic of racial and political violence that characterized the postwar years. Throughout 1919, African American soldiers were admonished by white leaders to come home without a haughty attitude, to forget expectations of democratic transformation, and above all else to accept, rather than resist, the well-structured system of white supremacy already in place. As the postwar record of North Carolina's officers demonstrates, many educated soldiers responded to this condescending rhetoric and the obstacles segregation placed in the way of their future success by leaving their home state and crafting successful professional careers outside of North Carolina.[35]

What contribution did black North Carolinians make to the First World War? Lieutenant Alston answered this question by emphasizing their loyalty and wholehearted commitment. "I am glad to know that my people are doing their bit to win the war. They sure make good soldiers," Alston proudly boasted in his private correspondence.[36] Without an examination of all black soldiers from the state, the answer too easily becomes a narrow emphasis on the valor of a few or a generic summation that most were laborers and did not serve in combat. The latter seemingly represents either a paternalist characterization of them as objects of exploitation or a dismissive suggestion they were not "real" soldiers. Notwithstanding the harsh summation, the truth of African Americans' service primarily as laboring soldiers is accurate to an extent. Yet this familiar assertion of oppression conveys only a partial truth, one so powerful and overbearing that it has buried the more familiar American tale of wartime military service as a narrative of pride and sacrifice that Americans have made when their nation called.

For many reasons, African Americans in North Carolina could not easily participate in that patriotic military narrative. Local white journalists did not chronicle their collective experiences, nor celebrate their contributions in the immediate postwar years. Without that early foundation, North Carolinians, during this past century, remained largely uninformed about their state's black soldiers. These men became easy to overlook. They were minorities in every context—a racial minority among soldiers in the state and a Tar Heel minority in every training camp, unit, ship, and military operation. As black men, their participation had been fraught with controversy from the beginning: would they succumb to German spies? Would they support the war effort? Would they be allowed combat service? Were they smart enough and healthy enough? Moreover, their return home was freighted with white fears of insurrection and challenges to white supremacy. Within a few years of the war, their state and region were mired in economic distress. Within a few more years, their nation began to question the wisdom of getting involved in the European war. Consequently, a century of disregard and relative public silence relegated these soldiers' experiences to private reflections and public obscurity.

Yet with a composite rendering of their collective experience, the contributions of 21,609 African American Tar Heels stand as a representative sample of the national experience of African American soldiers in the Great War. Dispersed to train across the nation and scattered to serve in every type of unit organized for African American soldiers at home and abroad, these North Carolinians could not point to any unit with the mark of their native state. But this structural discrimination, exploitation, and restricted opportunity also can be rendered a compelling human drama with nuance, complexity, and great diversity. Black North Carolinians volunteered, submitted to the draft, avoided the draft, participated early, remained to the end, deserted, reenlisted, fought, died, buried the dead, built, repaired, cooked, led, followed, blew bugles, mastered weaponry, cared for the wounded, ministered to the disheartened, dug trenches, won medals, loaded and unloaded ships, carts, and trucks, stayed close to home, and traveled across the nation, the Atlantic Ocean, and France. As Addie Hunton observed in her YMCA work with black laboring soldiers in France: "Throughout the war they wrought as weavers who are given to see only the wrong side of the glorious pattern they are weaving."[37] Her poetic analogy fittingly captures black North Carolinians' military experience. As individual black men, their roles may have seemed limited or insignificant. But the collective view of African American Tar Heel soldiers is comparable to the weaver flipping the completed cloth to reveal an intricately woven pattern that stands complete.

Notes

1. This study draws significantly upon compilation and analysis of the data reported on the Statement of Service Cards created by the War Department, with Congressional authorization, after the First World War and given to each state's adjutant general. North Carolina's are located in the World War I Service Card File, Adjutant General's Records, North Carolina Department of Cultural Resources, Division of Archives and History, Raleigh, North Carolina. With the assistance of many people listed below, and made possible by a Provost's Humanities Grant from the University of South Carolina, I created both a database of all the scanned service cards of North Carolinians identified as "colored" and a random sample from the same scanned service cards. The database included the entire population of 21,883 African American service card scanned images. The scanned images were converted to OCR code and then programmers created a python script to recognize certain patterns in text and remove the data based on these patterns and export that data into a database where further filtering and examination could be done. But due to the inconsistent strength of the original typed characters on the service cards, the OCR was scrambled on many of the cards, leaving too much missing data to make analysis of the whole population reliable. Therefore, I created a random sample of 1500 African American service cards, selected with a randomly generated numbers list corresponding to the entire population of 21,883 African American service card scanned images. These were entered manually into a spreadsheet, thus eliminating the problem of missing and/or unreadable data. Throughout the chapter, estimates of unit size, timing of units' movements, and other details are drawn from the random sample. The database aided in identification of particular soldiers. Hereafter, these are cited as WWIAASC Random Sample and WWIAASC Database. Many thanks to Ashley Yandle and Kelly Eubanks at the State Archives of North Carolina; Kate Boyd, University of South Carolina digital collections librarian; Colin Wilder, W. Wayne Lemasters, and Richard Abercrombie of University of South Carolina Center for Digital Humanities; and Lili E. Kinman, USC undergraduate, who each helped with some aspect of creating the database and/or random sample. Visit http://www.BlackSoldiersMattered.com for a digital rendering of the service data of North Carolina's African American soldiers.

2. On the definition of white supremacy and how it structured the lives of African Americans in this era, see Janet G. Hudson, *Entangled by White Supremacy: Reform in World War I Era South Carolina* (Lexington: University Press of Kentucky, 2009), 40–46.

3. Recent studies that address the national African American experience in the First World War include Chad L. Williams, *Torchbearers of Democracy: African American Soldiers in World War I Era* (Chapel Hill: University of North Carolina Press, 2010); Nina Mjagkij, *Loyalty in Time of Trial: the African American Experience in World War I* (Lanham, MD: Rowman & Littlefield Publishers, 2011); Adriane Lentz-Smith, *Freedom Struggles: African Americans and World War I* (Cambridge, MA: Harvard University Press, 2009); Jennifer Keene, *Doughboys, the Great War, and the Remaking of America* (Baltimore: Johns Hopkins University Press, 2001). Yet none of these studies address the experience of black North Carolinians. Jeffrey J. Crow, Paul D. Escott, and Flora J. Hatley, *A History of African Americans in North Carolina* (Raleigh: Office of Archives and History, North Carolina Department of Cultural Resources, 2002): 123–26, offers cursory treatment of homefront issues. Sarah McCulloh Lemmon, *North Carolina's Role in the First World War* (Raleigh: North Carolina Department of Cultural Resources, Division of Archives and History, 1966) offers a smattering of anecdotes about African Americans but provides primarily the story of white North Carolinians.

4. Memorandum for the Secretary of War, August 24, 1917, File #8142–17, National Archives Microfilm Publication M1024, Correspondence of the War College Division and Related General Staff Officers 1903–1919, Army War College and the War College Division 1900–1948, Records of the War Department General and Special Staffs, Record Group 165 (hereinafter M1024/RG 165), US National Archives and Records Administration, College Park, MD.

5. WWIAASC Random Sample and unit information derived from *Order of the Battle of the United States Land Forces in the World War (1917–19) Zone of the Interior*, vol. 3, Parts 1–2 (Washington, DC: Historical Division Special Staff United States Army, 1949). The type of units and the unit numbers that African American soldiers served in are listed in "Colored Organizations of the United States Army on November 11, 1918," in "Colored Organization of the U.S. Army" Folder, Entry 310/RG 165, US National Archives and Records Administration, College Park, MD. For a discussion of stevedore soldiers see Addie W. Hunton and Kathryn M. Johnson, *Two Colored Women with the American Expeditionary Forces* (1920, reprint, Boston: G.K. Hall & Co., 1997), 98–99. The classic study of African American soldiers in World War I, Arthur E. Barbeau and Florette Henri, *The Unknown Soldiers: African-American Troops in World War I* (1974, reprint, New York: Da Capo Press, 1996), 99–100, 103, 105–06.

6. WWIAASC Random Sample; WWIAASC Database; *Order of the Battle*, Vol. 3, Parts 1–2. More than 130 black North Carolinians participated in the Army's partnership with colleges and universities, Student Army Training Corps (SATC), training young men for military service as part of their collegiate education. They attended SATC programs at schools in North Carolina and other states, but the largest number attended North Carolina A&T State University in Greensboro.

7. Formation and rationale for creating the reserve labor battalions discussed at length in Memorandum for the Chief of Staff, May 16, 1918, File #8142–150, M1024/RG 165, US National Archives and Records Administration, College Park, MD. Reports from various camps with reserve labor battalions document similar problems. Casefile 10218–280: "Reports of the Military Morale Section on conditions Affecting Colored Soldiers, 1918," Reel 21: 105–170, Military Intelligence Division, RG 165, *Federal Surveillance of Afro-Americans 1917–1925*; Memorandum from Major W. H. Loving to Military Morale Section Chief, "Conditions among Negro troops at Camp Greene," October 28, 1918, Reel 21: 120, Military Intelligence Division, RG 165, *Federal Surveillance of Afro-Americans 1917–1925*. Camp Greene was originally designated a Regular Army Cantonment and designed for training only national guard units from New England.

8. Specifics of this debate are evident in Memorandum for the Chairman, Operations Committee of War College Division, July 20, 1917, File #8142–11; Memorandum for the Adjutant General, October 4, 1917, File #8142–27; Memorandum for the Adjutant General, November 1, 1917, File #8142–38. Secretary Baker's orders for all the specific elements of creating the 92nd Division are included in File #8142–34, M1024/RG 165, US National Archives and Records Administration, College Park, MD.

9. Barbeau and Henri, *Unknown Soldiers*, 80–83; Memorandum to the Chief of Staff, November 7, 1917, File #8142–42; Memorandum for the Chief of Staff, November 13, 1917, File # 8142–46, M1042/RG 165, US National Archives and Records Administration, College Park, MD.

10. Originally there were three machine gun battalions but one (349th) was for support only.

11. WWIAASC Random Sample and *Order of the Battle*, Vol. 3, Parts 1–2.

12. The 167th Field Artillery Brigade included 349th, 350th, and 351st Field Artillery Regiments. Memorandum for the Chief of Staff, May 16, 1918, File #8142–152, M1024/RG 165, US National Archives and Records Administration, College Park, MD; NCWWI Service Cards, Adjutant General's Records, North Carolina Department of Archives and History (NCDAH); Transcript of Ernest McKissick Oral History Interview by Dr. Louis Silveri, August 2, 1977, Southern Highlands Research Center, UNC-A, retrieved from http://toto.lib.unca.edu/findingaids/oralhistory /–SHRC/mckissick_ernest.pdf. McKissick's son, Floyd S. McKissick, became the first African American to attend the University of North Carolina Law School.

13. NCWWI Service Cards, Adjutant General's Records, NCDAH. For an overview of the complex formation of the 93rd Division, see Barbeau and Henri, *Unknown Soldiers*, 70–79. At least two dozen North Carolinians served in the 369th and 372nd; see WWIAASC Random Sample and WWIAASC Database.

14. For a thorough examination of African American officers, see Williams, *Torchbearers of Democracy*, 38–51; Barbeau and Henri, *Unknown Soldiers*, 80–83; Emmett J. Scott, *Scott's Official History of the American Negro in the World War*, (1919, reprint, New York: Arno Press, 1969), 82–89.

15. Emmett Scott and William Sweeney list the 639 commissioned officers. State identification is only available for those who came to officer training as civilians and not for those who came from the Regular Army or joined the National Army before attending the school. Sixteen North Carolinians appear in Scott's and/or Sweeney's lists. Eleven others were identified from WWIAASC Database. Lemmon, *North Carolina's Role in the First World War*, 33; *Scott's Official History*, 471–81; William Allison Sweeney, *History of the American Negro in the Great War* (Chicago: G. G. Sapp, 1919), 86–88. Baker ordered the creation of the 92nd Division October 24, 1917, the week following the commissioning of the officer class at Ft. Des Moines.

16. Andrew Billingsley, *Yearning to Breathe Free: Robert Smalls of South Carolina and His Families* (Columbia: University of South Carolina Press, 2010), 197; Omega Psi Phi Fraternity website, 2010, http://www.tq1911.org/Tau_Omega/Gurney_E._Nelson.html; Lovelace Capehart referenced in Nathan Garrett, *A Palette, Not a Portrait: Stories from the Life of Nathan Garrett* (Bloomington, IN: iUniverse, 2010), 19; Russell C. Atkins, Officer Training School in Des Moines, Iowa, http://www.fortdesmoines.org/graduates_a_g.shtml; Lawrence E. London, "Bravid Washington Harris," in William S. Powell, ed. *Dictionary of North Carolina Biography*, vol. 3 (Chapel Hill: University of North Carolina, 1988), 48–49.

17. NCWWI Service Cards, Adjutant General's Records, NCDAH; Sketch of Alston and James W. Alston to H. H. Brimley, November 1, 1918, in James W. Alston Papers Folder, Box 1, VI. Private Collections; World War I Papers, 1903–1933; Military Collection; NCDAH.

18. Cleopatra Bullock to the Secretary, November 13, 1918; Sketch of Bullock, Roll of Honor folder, Thomas J. Bullock, Box 5 "Negroes and the War, VII." Compiled Individual Service Records, World War I Papers, 1903–1933, Military Collection, NCDAH.

Egbert T. Scott Obituary, *Afro-American*, December 16, 1969, http://www.moors-delaware .com/gendat/moors.aspx?Mode=Member&MemberID=S300E1884; Max King started at Leonard. Geraldine Rhoades Beckford, compiler, *Biographical Dictionary of American Physicians of African Ancestry, 1800–1920* (Cherry Hill, NJ: Africana Homestead Legacy Publishers Inc., 2011), 188; Arthur Bunyan Caldwell, ed., *History of the American Negro and His Institutions*, North Carolina, Vol. 4 (Atlanta: A. B. Caldwell Publishing, 1921), 743–44. Foster Burnett of Wilmington was another freshly minted physician from Howard University who was commissioned a medical officer but was discharged within months as "physically disqualified." NCWWI Service Cards, Adjutant General's Records, NCDAH. Hatwood died in 1947 and was buried at the Salisbury National Cemetery. *Charlotte City Directory* (1918) lists his church, and the US National Cemetery Interment Control Forms, 1928–1962 provide his burial information. Both are available at Ancestry.com.

20. WWIAASC Random Sample, *Order of the Battle*, Vol. 3, Parts 1–2. The plan is provided as an attachment to Memorandum for the Adjutant General of the Army from the Chief of Staff, War College Division, August 1, 1917, File #8142–13, M1024/RG 165, US National Archives and Records Administration, College Park, MD.

21. WWIAASC Random Sample and *Order of the Battle*, Vol. 3, Parts 1–2. These other camps included Camps Upton (New York), Dodge (Iowa), Funston (Kansas), and several facilities near Virginia tidewater ports (Newport News, Camps Humphreys, Alexander, and Hill) where African American soldiers were hastily processed and shipped for labor duties to France.

22. See endnote #7 regarding Camp Greene conditions.

23. WWIAASC Random Sample. Uncertainty of when the "black draft" will begin and where the soldiers will train stated in *Charlotte* (North Carolina) *Observer*, February 5, 1918. Estimate of quotas from North Carolina in Memorandum for the Secretary of War, September 7, 1917, File #8142–25, M1024/RG 165, US National Archives and Records Administration, College Park, MD.

Beginning of the large-scale induction reported in *Greenville Daily Record*, March 19, 29, & 31, 1918.

24. Patterns and timing of induction, as well as estimates of overseas service based on analysis of the WWIAASC Random Sample.

25. WWIAASC Random Sample; WWIAASC Database; NCWWI Service Cards, Adjutant General's Records, NCDAH. Two regiments guarded the Mexican border from Arizona—10th Cavalry and the 24th Infantry. The 25th Infantry remained in Hawaii throughout the war, while the 9th Cavalry served in the Philippines (Stotsenburg Camp in Luzon).

26. The policy not to send North Carolinians to Camp Jackson was stated in both of these: Memorandum to the Chief of Staff, October 2, 1917, File #8142–41; Memorandum for the Adjutant General, November 15, 1917, File #8142–49, M1024/RG 165, US National Archives and Records Administration, College Park, MD. The orders to send drafted men to Camp Jackson, *Charlotte Observer*, November 25, 1917; *The State*, December 7, 1917.

27. Chester D. Heywood, *Negro Combat Troops in the World War: The Story of the 371st Infantry* (Commonwealth Press, 1928, reprint, New York: AMS Press, 1969), 162–81. Stowers received the Medal of Honor posthumously in 1991; see Robert J. Dalessandro and Gerald Torrence, *Willing Patriots: Men of Color in the First World War* (Atglen, PA: Schiffer Publishing, Ltd., 2009), 109–110. Junius Diggs citation, "Campbell-Duffy" Folder; Lee E. McClelland citation, "McClelland-Newton" Folder, Box 1 "Citations Awarded to North Carolinians," VII. Compiled Individual Service Records, World War I Papers, 1903–1933, Military Collection, NCDAH.

28. Dalessandro and Torrence, *Willing Patriots*, 110; Alston to Brimley, October 6, 1918, and November 1, 1918, in James W. Alston Papers Folder, NCDAH.

29. WWIAASC Random Sample; Memorandum to Headquarters 92nd Division, A.P.O. 766, October 11, 1918, "92nd Division History" file, Box 1 (Entry NM-91 1241), 92nd Division Historical Decimal File 1.4–22.9, Records of Combat Divisions, 1917–1919, Records of the American Expeditionary Force, RG 120, US National Archives and Records Administration, College Park, MD (hereafter cited as Entry NM-91 1241/RG 120); Alston to Brimley, October 6, 1918, James W. Alston Papers Folder, NCDAH.

30. American Battle Monuments Commission, "92nd Division Summary of Operations in the World War" (Washington, DC: U.S. Government Printing Office, 1944), 26–36, http://www.history.army.mil/topics/afam/92div.htm#6; Memorandum from Chief of Staff that includes Major General Ballou's comments, November 18, 1918, "92nd Division History" file, Entry NM-91 1241/RG 120, US National Archives and Records Administration, College Park, MD.

31. Beckford, *Biographical Dictionary of American Physicians of African Ancestry*, 188; London, "Bravid Washington Harris," in *Dictionary of North Carolina Biography*, Vol. 3, 48–49; Russell C. Atkins, Officer Training School in Des Moines, Iowa, http://www.fortdesmoines.org/–graduates_a_g.shtml; NCWWI Service Cards, Adjutant General's Records, NCDAH; Dalessandro and Torrence, *Willing Patriots*, 106–110.

32. WWIAASC Random Sample. Some postwar responsibilities discussed in Dalessandro and Torrence, *Willing Patriots*, 53–56; Moses N. Thisted, *Pershing's Pioneer Infantry of World War I* (Hemet, CA: Alphabet Printers, 1981), 107; Barbeau and Henri, *Unknown Soldiers*, 65–66.

33. WWIAASC Random Sample and WWIAASC Database. Report of the aggregate data for North Carolina in chart form with data by race and county in "Misc. Records" Folder, Box 84.1, Adjutant General's Records, NCDAH. Sketch of Bullock, Roll of Honor File "Thomas J. Bullock," NCDAH. Bullock's remains were buried in Grave #6, Cemetery #222, in La Chappelle, France.

34. WWIAASC Database. Report of the aggregate data for North Carolina in chart form with data by race and county in "Misc. Records" Folder, Box 84.1, Adjutant General's Records, NCDAH. The 344th shipped out September 25, and the first reported case in Mecklenburg County was three days later on September 28; see "The Doughboys and Camp Greene," http://www.cmstory.org/wwl/greatwar.asp.

35. McKissick interview transcript, 10. For a thorough analysis of the violence in Winston-Salem, see Joanne Glenn, "The Winston-Salem Riot of 1918" (master's thesis, University of North Carolina at Chapel Hill, 1979). See the earlier discussion for the postwar careers of North Carolina officers.

36. Alston to Brimley, September 3, 1918, in James W. Alston Papers Folder, NCDAH.

37. Hunton and Johnson, *Two Colored Women*, 97.

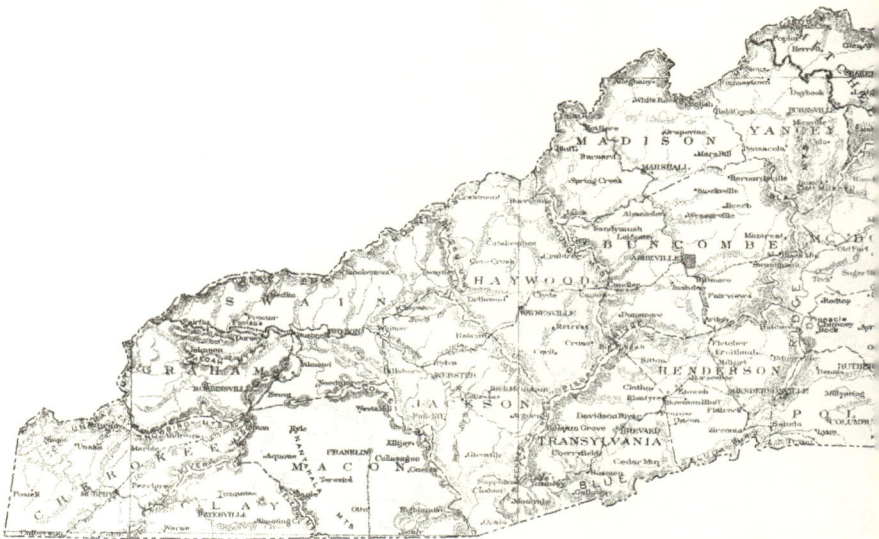

PART TWO

Politics

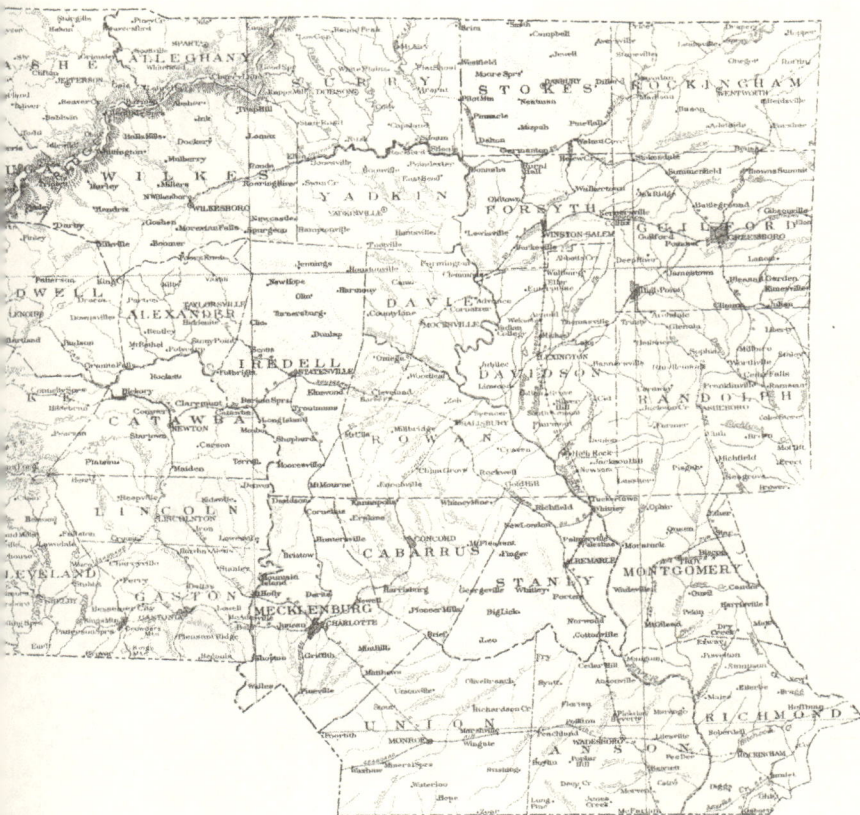

6

War Mobilization and "Purposeful Loyalty"

North Carolina's Council of Defense

James S. Bissett

By the summer of 1916, it was clear to many in the United States that involvement in the European war was inevitable, and federal government officials began to take active steps readying the nation for war. One of the manifestations of these preparations was the creation of the Council of National Defense in August of that year. Consisting of cabinet-level officials associated with the strategically important Departments of War, Navy, Agriculture, Commerce, Labor, and Interior, the Council soon expanded to include representatives of the private sector, with the goal of "harmonizing the American economy, especially relations between business and government."[1] Shortly after the declaration of war, in early May 1917, the Council of National Defense gathered representatives of all of the states in Washington to begin creating state councils to help carry out federal policies.[2] Following that meeting, President Woodrow Wilson asked each of the nation's governors to appoint Councils of Defense in their states, a request to which North Carolina Governor Thomas W. Bickett quickly responded. The North Carolina Council of Defense consisted of fifteen members, including the Governor and the state Adjutant-General as ex-officio members, and its chairman, Dr. Daniel Harvey Hill, President of North Carolina A&M College in Raleigh.[3] The group held its first meeting on May 31.[4] Composed solely of white males—with the exception of one woman, also white, who chaired the committee on "Woman's work"—and drawn largely from academia and the business world, the State Council clearly represented the interests of North Carolina's white male elites.[5]

Given that provenance, it should not be surprising to note that the North Carolina Council of Defense embraced its mission of mobilizing the state for the war. The Council began by conceptualizing how it would successfully complete that mission, listing what it considered to be the fifteen most pressing issues the state faced as it mobilized. Then, the Council created a separate statewide committee made up of prominent North Carolinians to oversee each area of concern.[6] Through this network of fifteen issue-based committees, the North Carolina Council of Defense anticipated that it would play the leading role in war mobilization. It did not turn out that way, however. While ultimately the State Council did prove to be highly effective in mustering patriotism, that contribution came through an organizational structure far different from the issue-based, statewide committees that state leaders thought would be at the center of the war effort. The fifteen statewide committees the Council created as a way of economically mobilizing the state failed in two significant ways to complete that mission.

First, in retrospect, the fifteen issues chosen by the State Council as deserving their own statewide committee did not reflect a particularly prescient analysis of the challenges of war mobilization. While the responsibilities of some of these committees—Public Information, Coordination of Work, Sanitation, Conservation of Resources, Labor, and Transportation, for example—seemed relevant and self-evident, such was not the case for others. The Finance Committee was charged with funding the Council of Defense, not the war effort; and the Committee on Home Defense envisioned organizing a "home guard for the safety of homes and property," a need that never materialized. As a blueprint for organizing the efficient mobilization of an emerging industrial, capitalist, and commercial agricultural economy, then, the fifteen areas identified by the North Carolina Council of Defense left much to be desired. In addition, these committees had no real authority to implement the policies they endorsed. To actually accomplish their mission of mobilizing for the war, these state committees needed to find a way of ensuring that their instructions would be communicated to, and be taken seriously by, those beyond the confines of the capital city.

To their credit, federal officials and State Council members recognized this second weakness and moved quickly to establish a presence at the county and local levels. In North Carolina, the State Council of Defense took up the task of appointing a chairman in each of the state's one hundred counties, asking those county chairmen to create a county-level organization consisting of six additional members.[7] Each county organization, in turn, was expected to form "community councils," expanding the council of defense network exponentially. Indeed, the National Council of Defense was explicit about this, calling for the creation of "an official nation-wide organization reaching into the smallest communities to mobilize and make available the efforts of the whole people for the prosecution of the war." To address this need, it suggested that a separate community council be created in each school district.[8] Historian David Kennedy maintains that the councils, by reaching all the way to the local level in this way, adopted an administrative structure "reminiscent of Thomas Jefferson's system of wards."[9]

Although it is impossible to know just how extensively this system blanketed the cities, towns, and hamlets of North Carolina, the case of Cleveland County is revealing. The stationery of the county's council of defense provided a list of over two hundred people serving on twelve township councils and a variety of other committees associated with the county council. Among the latter were committees responsible for overseeing food and fuel administration, agriculture, manufacturing, public health, and the "Safe Guarding of Moral and Spiritual Forces." The Cleveland County Council also created a "Special Committee for the Ladies," with subcommittees for "Registration and Home Economics." While not every county had nearly as exhaustive a local network as Cleveland County—Randolph County, for instance, had only four additional local committees—the numbers of citizens actively involved in the war effort through the councils of defense were indeed remarkable.[10] According to some estimates, in fact, by war's end, some 184,000 state, county, and local councils of defense existed throughout the nation.[11] This network of county and local volunteers presented state and federal officials with an unprecedented resource, one that they deployed freely throughout the course of the war. In North Carolina, it was this network of county and local councils—not the North Carolina Council of Defense and the fifteen statewide committees it created—that did the real work of implementing war policy.

Even so, some historians point out that, for all its strengths, this network of county and local councils of defense system was in the end something of an anachronism, reflecting the preindustrial world of Thomas Jefferson more than the emerging industrial, capitalist society of the early twentieth century. "Though sound as a principle of political equity, and appropriate to an economically homogenous society," Kennedy argues, the Jeffersonian model followed by federal bureaucrats proved to be "spectacularly irrelevant to the economic character of an industrial nation such as America was in 1917."[12] To be effective in achieving its function of mobilizing the economy for the war effort, Kennedy continues, the Council of Defense system "needed now to run not along geographic lines but along lines of function. Those lines traced the connections among what might be called the new communities of production, distribution, and consumption—communities vertically organized and far flung—that the industrial economy had brought into being."[13] In short, Kennedy and others argue, the Councils of Defense, while demographically impressive, were operationally unsuited for the key task of mobilizing the economy for the war. Interestingly, according to this analysis, the fifteen committees the North Carolina Council created represented the appropriate strategy, had they not been so fatally flawed.

Some county chairmen in North Carolina seemed to sense this critical weakness, expressing frustration at their numerous and varied responsibilities. For example, M. D. Kinsland, the chairman of the Haywood County Council of Defense, wrote a letter to D. H. Hill, chairman of the North Carolina

State Council, in which he expressed in no uncertain terms his frustration over the burdens of his office. "I have neglected my own personal interests to my hurt in order to give to my State and country the best service I could," he wrote. "I have done it freely and willingly without the aid of a dollar from any other source than my own, not even postage, and I am not expecting any thing except perhaps some sweet day I may be permitted to hear the Angels sing."[14] Ed Taylor, Kinsland's counterpart in Brunswick County, expressed a similar sentiment. "People have been worn out with organizing for some special work," he complained to the state chairman, "soon to be replaced with some other new special thing that we preach is the supreme need of the hour."[15] A third county chairman reported that his duties required him to devote over ten hours per day to the war effort. As a result, he reported, "I am almost completely broken down."[16] These were not simply empty complaints; the chairmen of the county councils did yeoman's work in helping North Carolina respond to the challenges presented by the war. Of the 113 men who served as county chairmen during the war years, 82 held another official position, most often that of County Food Administrator. Chairmen's other official responsibilities included helping to promote moral and financial support for the war through leadership positions in their county's Four Minute Men and Liberty Loan efforts, serving on the county draft board, and offering assistance to members of the armed forces through service on their county's Legal Advisory Board and Soldiers' Business Aid Committee.[17]

Even if these men had performed no service other than serving as their county Council of Defense chairmen, their frustration was well founded. In the months between their appointment in June 1917 and the end of the war in November 1918, all of the roughly one hundred men who served as county chairmen received more than sixty letters from the office of the state Council of Defense, each of which made a request that required specific action on their part. At the center of their frustration, no doubt, was the seemingly arbitrary and often unreasonable nature of the State Council's demands. At times, State Council officials were explicit about their expectations, asking county officers to give their "instant attention" or respond "at once," within 24 hours, or "with care but speed" to requests for action or information.[18]

While not all of the appeals included such strict deadlines, responding to others required an inordinate amount of effort on the part of county council chairmen. On two occasions, for example, state officials asked county chairmen to submit typewritten lists of the names and addresses of at least 75 local men to whom the state office could send patriotic literature, a request that must have seemed daunting given the state of office technology in the early twentieth century, not to mention the complete lack of funding for clerical support on the county level.[19] Another request, made twice during the course of the war, asked county chairmen to not only compile a list—this time of deserters in the county—but also to correspond with the deserters' parents to solicit their help in getting their sons to report for military duty.[20] In addition to compiling lists and keeping tabs on their neighbors, county chairmen also spent a significant amount of time organizing patriotic meetings. Each county's Council of Defense was tasked with organizing "simple meetings for patriotic purposes" on the Fourth of July in 1917 and 1918, but such expectations were not limited to this holiday.[21] Additional patriotic meetings, all of which carried significant organizing responsibilities for county chairmen, took place on at least five occasions.[22]

These examples lend credence to Kennedy's charge that the Council of Defense network was anachronistic and largely ineffective. Rather than vertically organized according to the contours of the economy as Kennedy suggests they should have been, the councils in North Carolina were horizontally structured, with each county's council chairman acting as a clearinghouse between the various state committees and the citizens of his county. The State Council's actions related to construction during wartime illustrate this point. When that body decided in fall 1918 that only projects contributing directly to the war effort should be allowed to move forward, it had no relevant statewide committee on which to rely for implementation of construction policy. Lacking a vertically integrated network committed to this issue, the Secretary of the State Council of Defense had to rely on the county chairmen, instructing them to "see to it that no construction work is done in your county except by permit" and, perhaps more significantly, charging those chairmen with the responsibility of approving or rejecting such permits.[23] This instruction became yet another task added to the already extensive list of responsibilities shouldered by county chairmen. Each of them prioritized that task according to his interests and resources—some, no doubt, gave it immediate attention while others treated it with less urgency—and the regulation of construction projects proceeded in a much less rigorous and uniform manner than the State Council of Defense wanted. Not only did this organizational bottleneck limit the efficiency and effectiveness of the Councils of Defense, but it had the added effect of overburdening the county chairmen, contributing directly to their feelings of frustration.

If this weakness made the network of Councils of Defense ill suited for the task of mobilizing North Carolina's economy, such was not the case for the less material aspects of the war, activities that some historians refer to as "the war for the American mind." Indeed, this was a task for which the Jeffersonian organizational vision of the council network was perfectly suited. As Newton D. Baker, President Wilson's Secretary of War and chair of the National Council of Defense, understood, "the elaborate organization of the state councils, which extended to the most remote hamlets in the country, together with their speakers' divisions, their close liaison with the local press, and their publicity activities," made them remarkably valuable, serving as "the guardians of civilian morale in each state; carrying on a work of education and information."[24] The members of the North Carolina Council of Defense recognized this as an important responsibility, asserting that the county and community councils were not merely "channels of communication" between the federal government and local communities. Rather, State Council members envisioned the county and community councils as "the work shops where patriotism would be turned into war action, war protection and war conservation; and thus would be obtained mass action, developed through freely willed team play."[25]

When it came to the war for the American mind, then, the Councils of Defense were not the weak links that some historians portray them to have been. Rather, they were an invaluable resource: a readymade network of thousands of North Carolinians primed to take action when directed and to follow a clearly defined chain of command. Even when they wanted to, federal officials simply could not ignore this resource. On issues related to the war that fell outside of economics, then—conscription, individuals' loyalty to government war aims, and war funding drives, for example—the connection to the local populace that county and local councils brought to the table trumped the preindustrial, anachronistic qualities that weakened them in other areas of war mobilization. Here, the councils played an important, if at times troubling, role.

Perhaps the most significant of these issues was the very real question of whether the American public would be appropriately supportive of the war, especially in light of the recently passed Conscription Act. After all, this was the first time the federal government would draft American men to serve in an overseas war, a precedent made more troubling by the nation's demographic diversity. The questions left unanswered in spring 1917 were deeply troubling. Would the 32 million immigrants or their children with ties to the Central Powers be more loyal to the United States or to their country of birth?[26] Would the nearly five million Irish Americans in the country consent to fighting on the same side as Britain?[27] Could the Wilson administration count on white southerners to support the war since the memory of the "Lost Cause" and resentment toward the federal government remained fresh? These concerns came to the surface as federal officials began to put the Conscription Act into effect. They faced the monumental logistical task of gathering information on all draft-age men to determine who was eligible to serve in the army. To accomplish this, the federal government set aside a single day, June 5, 1917, as "Registration Day," when all men between the ages of 21 and 31 were to report to their voting precinct and register for the draft. As government officials reminded the populace, "Registration is a public duty," and those failing to do so faced possible prison sentences.[28]

Ensuring that all the nation's young men registered was a mammoth job, one for which the Councils of Defense were perfectly suited. Their Jeffersonian organizational structure offered a network of local volunteers who officials could easily contact and mobilize, an attribute made even more valuable by their intimate knowledge of their communities. As Jeanette Keith has pointed out, the lack of even rudimentary record keeping in the South meant that federal officials "had great difficulty seeing into the rural South" during the war.[29] These officials had no way of knowing—beyond census records, which by 1917 were becoming out of date—how many men in a particular community they should reasonably expect to respond on Registration Day, so they found the county and community Councils of Defense to be invaluable. With their community knowledge, members of the county and local councils served as the principal promoters of Registration Day at this level, arranging patriotic meetings and helping to transport young men to the registration sites.[30]

Registration was only the beginning of the conscription process. From the roughly ten million men expected to register on June 5, the federal government hoped to initially draft 687,000 to serve in the army. Of course, not all of the ten million were fit for military service, and almost one-third nationally were disqualified on medical grounds. In addition, all those registering had the option of claiming exemption from military service based on family- or employment-related responsibilities. Just over half of the registrants nationwide and 49 percent in North Carolina made such a claim. Evaluating the legitimacy of these claims required independent verification on a case-by-case basis, an enormous logistical task that fell to locally run "exemption boards." Federal officials estimated that the process of determining which exemption claims were legitimate required the assistance of over 100,000 volunteers serving on some 4,000 local exemption boards.[31]

The War Department initially resisted calling upon state, county, and local Councils of Defense for logistical help, deciding instead to ask each governor to appoint a separate Exemption Board to oversee the conscription process.[32] The strategy of bypassing the councils of defense in favor of governors, however, ultimately proved unsuccessful in light of the enormity of the task at hand. While governors were capable of appointing state-level exemption boards, the real work of evaluating individual exemption claims occurred at the local level. The creation of county exemption boards was a complicated endeavor; each board had to include citizens who were familiar with their communities, commanded the respect of their fellow citizens, and had the necessary time to consider each exemption request. Finding people in every county who satisfied those criteria was not easy, and state officials recognized that the newly created county Councils of Defense could solve this problem. As a result, among the first tasks assigned to the county councils was the creation of county-level exemption boards.[33] That responsibility, it turned out, did not end with the appointment of these boards, and in November 1917 county Council of Defense chairmen recruited additional volunteers to assist with this process. The state chairman estimated that these new volunteers needed to work evenings for two to three weeks to complete the job.[34] Yet another request came the following month, this time to help draftees in their communities fill out their draft questionnaires.[35]

Clearly, federal officials were incapable of carrying out the process of conscription without the assistance of state, county, and community Councils of Defense. After facilitating registration, the councils also had to help deal with the problem of "deserters," men who failed to report on Registration Day or who did not report to the military when ordered. In a letter providing county council chairmen with guidance, the Chairman of the North Carolina Council of Defense first offered a surprisingly nuanced definition of what he meant by deserter, asserting that not all who the federal government categorized as deserters presented a danger to society. Many, he argued, were "young, ignorant, and not fully aware of the serious consequences of their actions." Given this fact, it would be counterproductive for the federal government to simply round up all men who ignored the draft. County and local council members could direct a more targeted effort, encouraging deserters to report and thereby sparing the government the need to prosecute. Hill asked county council members to compile a list of deserters and then to "write a kind letter to the father and mother of these men, assuring them of the friendly interest of their fellow-citizens, and urge them, before it is too late, to save their sons from disgrace and punishment." Those who took this advice, council members guaranteed, would be treated "as leniently as possible."[36] C. M. Vanstory, Chairman of the Guilford County Council of Defense, attested to this method's effectiveness. "We have had a few [deserters] in our county," Vanstory wrote to the state Chairman, "but we have gone to each and every case in person and every man agreed at once to go into service without any trouble whatsoever and we think now that there will not be another man that will fail to answer the call and every man that has been drafted from this county is a good loyal patriotic soldier and anxious and willing to do his part."[37] With their local connections, men like Vanstory and his fellow county council members were uniquely effective in enlisting hesitant draftees with minimal disruption.

After its first year of existence, the state Council of Defense pointed to this nuanced approach as one of its strongest contributions to the war effort. "While we have few alien enemies in our State," the council's first annual report stated, "there were some pacifists and many who were opposed to the draft law." Having acknowledged this, however, the report hastened to add that "in the main, these people were good citizens." As such, council members strove to shield these "good citizens" from the sometimes-harsh federal response: "The Council felt that they ought to be reached in a personal way and either converted or admonished not to allow themselves to come in conflict with the law. The County Councils did excellent work with these people. Quietly they interviewed scores of them and had their friends remonstrate with them and admonish them as to their duty. This work alone would justify the formation of the Council, for it has saved many good people from irretrievable blunders and opened the eyes of many others."[38] The statistics bear out the Council's claims of success in this area. Between July 1, 1917, and July 1, 1918, authorities prosecuted 391 men for failure to register for the draft in 35 counties in eastern North Carolina. Of these, 49 were convicted, a conviction rate of only 13 percent.[39]

In retrospect, then, it seems clear that the councils helped to make the registration process more humane and effective. Not all who came to the attention of authorities, however, did so because of their failure to report for military service. Many Americans, and some North Carolinians, found themselves in trouble because of the vaguer charge of "disloyalty." Indeed, according to some historians, this was one of the most disturbing aspects of America's domestic war effort. The Espionage Act, enacted by the United States Congress shortly after the declaration of war and strengthened the following year with the Sedition Act, provided the federal government with the tools to prosecute those who, in the eyes of authorities, fell into the indistinct category of "opponents of the war." In addition, federal agents associated with the Bureau of Investigation engaged in what one historian refers to as a "systematic campaign to stifle those who objected, resisted, or agitated against" the war effort. [40] These measures contributed to a general sense of *superpatriotism*—often referred to at the time as "one hundred percent Americanism"—that made the war years a time of unprecedented attack on civil liberties.[41] Here, unfortunately, the Councils of Defense in North Carolina played a decidedly less positive role.

Because of its relatively homogenous population and the absence of radical-left insurgent organizations, North Carolina experienced less open opposition to the war than other states and, as a result, escaped most of the worst abuses of "one hundred percent Americanism." Even so, abuses did occur in the Tar Heel state, and the Councils of Defense often played a leading role. Employing rhetoric that laid the groundwork for potential abuse of authority, the state Council of Defense declared that its "chief aim, and perhaps obligation" was "to mould [sic] public thought and sentiment; and to get into the minds of the people" the fact that "WE ARE AT WAR."[42] Getting "into the minds" of North Carolinians involved convincing them of the importance of what the Council called "purposeful loyalty," a term that encompassed "cheerful obedience to law," "prompt conformity to Governmental requests," "honest sacrifice," and, more troubling, "bold dealing with anti-American sentiment."[43] Such purposeful loyalty, the state council informed county council chairmen, resulted in the public becoming "so aroused that Patriotism is driving the Nation at full speed," and "every one of the thousands in your County is doing his most for the Nation."[44]

Purposeful loyalty, then, involved much more than simply choosing not to oppose the war; it required the citizenry to enthusiastically embrace the war effort. The state council was clear on this point, instructing its county chairs to "bring your people into line. Develop your County organization into units so small that their leaders come into personal touch with every resident. According to the plan for community councils take each school district, each township, or each precinct and make it a working member of a Nation fighting for noble cause."[45] In such a cause, "[i]gnorance, carelessness and indifference" were almost as damaging as outright disloyalty.[46] If mere ignorance or indifference could bring one to the attention of the local councils, those who had the temerity to openly oppose the war faced more severe consequences. Thus, when state council Chairman Hill became concerned in spring 1918 about the presence of "German propaganda," his advice to county chairmen was telling: He suggested that "any over-zealous agitators can be reported to your U. S. District Attorney."[47]

While the record indicates that this kind of extralegal behavior was less prevalent in North Carolina than in other places, the network of councils in the state was not above calling in federal officials to deal with local citizens suspected of being disloyal. In its annual report of May 1918, in fact, the state Council of Defense not only acknowledged that it frequently "asked the Department of Justice to send agents to investigate flagrant or suspected disloyalties," but also listed this as one of its most important achievements.[48]

The county chairman in Rockingham County, for example, made such a request regarding several citizens in the county "who [are] so opposed to the Government's policy, that their influence nullifies all efforts to sell Liberty Bonds, Thrift Stamps, or effectively carry out any Food Conservation work." Asking that a "secret Service Man" come to the county, the chairman justified his request by noting that if these people "are not actually talking treason their influence is such as to be noticeable." He predicted that such a visit would have "a wholesome effect" on the county.[49] Another case in Rockingham County involved W. A. Manly, who officials accused of several acts of disloyalty, including criticizing a patriotic speech, opposing the war, advising people not to buy Liberty Bonds, and "cursing and abusing the Government."[50] In response, the County Chairman repeated his request for the "assistance of a Secret Service man for a few days."[51] The case was resolved without prosecution due to the intervention of a member of the Rockingham County Council of Defense, who reported to a local judge that Manly was appropriately contrite: "Mr. Manly called on me this morning and says he may have made statements which may have been misunderstood, in the heat of a political argument . . . that he had no intention of reflecting in any way whatsoever on the Government and that he regrets that if his statements were so construed." The council member suggested to the judge that the matter end there, predicting that Manly would "give all the help possible to us in future, both in word and act."[52]

The chairman of the Lenoir County Council of Defense took his responsibilities to the extreme step of reporting "a very good friend," E. A. Goodman, to federal authorities. In his request, the county chairman reported a conversation that took place during a visit in Goodman's home: "I found that at heart he was disloyal though, under the law at that time, his remarks were not punishable. I reasoned with him at considerable length in an effort to change his views but my efforts were fruitless. I am now advised that he is continuing his disloyal utterances and I feel that the matter should be brought to his attention and he be given to understand that they must be stopped."[53] The request ultimately found its way to a federal agent, who advised the official to write to Goodman "warning him about his utterances." "I thing [sic] it will certainly do good," the agent predicted, "and probably cause him to shut his mouth."[54]

Correspondence between the chairman of the Rockingham County Council of Defense and Rev. S. Brown, accused of "making seditious utterances against the Government of the United States," provides an example of one such written warning. After outlining the charges against the reverend, which, in addition to seditious speech, included attempting to convince his congregants "that the Government was wrong in declaring war," the county chairman warned that, unless the objectionable behavior was ended at once, Brown would be reported to the District Attorney for possible prosecution under the Sedition Act. The letter ended ominously: "You may govern yourself accordingly."[55]

The case of A. A. Martin of Anson County demonstrates just how far the Bureau of Investigation was willing to go to follow up on complaints filed by county council chairmen. In this case, Martin's offense—engaging in "very bitter" criticism of the Wilson administration—occurred prior to the declaration of war. Even so, the Bureau saw fit to dispatch to Anson County an agent who interviewed the chairman and two additional witnesses. While none of the witnesses could document any negative speech following the declaration of war, one of them, the agent reported, "does not believe that Martin has changed his mind and that Martin still is making these kind [sic] of remarks of seditious nature."[56]

In these ways, the county and local Councils of Defense worked aggressively to ensure that North Carolina's citizens appropriately supported the war effort. As the state council noted in a self-evaluation, doing so went well beyond identifying the disloyal and reporting them to federal authorities. "Perhaps the most important of all State Council work though the most difficult to report," the document noted, "was the building of the civilian morale through the community councils by means of 'liberty songs,' financial and other support to four minute speakers, plans for giving honors and memorials to men in military service, and the securing of material for historical records."[57] In doing so, according to one historian's study of the war effort in the South, the councils "served as the primary conduit by which war mobilization propaganda reached the rural South. Local councils helped distribute Committee on Public Information publications, supported the Red Cross, and promoted Liberty loans and War Savings Stamps."[58]

It must be noted that county council chairmen did not always serve simply as conduits, blindly transmitting federal policy to their local comrades. At times, they saw themselves as an ameliorating presence, protecting their local communities from what they saw as overly aggressive or rigid federal intervention. In Nash County, for example, a local citizen contacted the Bureau of Investigation's agent-in-charge about "3 German foreigners" in the county. The federal agent forwarded the tip to Nash County council chairman Joseph B. Ramsey, asking for his advice as to whether further investigation was warranted. Responding that he had not been able to verify the charge, Ramsey advised against additional action.[59] A similar impulse guided council members in New Hanover County, where a "Vigilance Committee," whose duties closely resembled that of the Council of Defense, had formed. The impetus for the committee's formation came from Wilmington's mayor, who also invited the chairman of the county's Council of Defense to its meetings.[60] Confused as to the origin and provenance of the Vigilance Committee, county council Chairman J. G. McCormick wrote to State Council Chair Hill for clarification. Hill's response was illuminating. Reporting that he had "no knowledge whatever of the formation of the Vigilance Committees," Hill made it clear that such committees were not in any way connected to the Councils of Defense and cautioned that "the history of these committees has nearly always been unfortunate. They so frequently degenerate into instruments of violence."[61]

As these final examples suggest, it is difficult to arrive at a single, interpretively coherent conclusion regarding the role played by the Councils of Defense in North Carolina. If those associated with the councils at times victimized their friends and neighbors with the excessive application of one hundred percent Americanism, they also protected their fellow citizens by resisting the temptations of such superpatriotism. While members of the state, county, and local councils represented a demographic that made them disproportionately responsive to the needs of white male elites, they performed yeoman service for the state and nation by faithfully carrying out the myriad tasks assigned to them. If the state council and its fifteen statewide committees proved unsuited for the task of mobilizing the economy for the war, the comprehensive network of county and local councils that emerged during the war turned out to be invaluable nevertheless, representing a crucial interface between local citizens and state and national leaders.

Notes

1. David Kennedy, *Over Here: The First World War and American Society* (New York: Oxford University Press, 1980), 113–115.

2. History of the North Carolina Council of Defense, 13, Box 18, World War I Papers (MARS ID 5757), North Carolina State Archives, Raleigh, North Carolina (hereafter cited as WWI Papers). Although the title, "History of the North Carolina Council of Defense," might suggest that this is a secondary source, such is not the case. This is a collection of documents relevant to the council drawn from the rest of the WWI Papers and organized topically.

3. *The North Carolina Council of Defense: Plan of Organization* (Raleigh: Commercial Printing Co., n.d.), 2, 4.

4. History of the North Carolina Council of Defense, 21, Box 18, WWI Papers. See also William J. Breen, "The North Carolina Council of Defense during World War I, 1917–1918," *North Carolina Historical Review* 50 (1973): 2–3.

5. *The North Carolina Council of Defense: Plan of Organization*, 9. A separate Woman's Committee, formed early in the war, essentially duplicated the activities of the male-dominated councils but had no say in the strategies employed by them. African Americans were even more marginalized, and members of the North Carolina council resisted creating a parallel committee for blacks as it did for women. See History of the North Carolina Council of Defense, 85–86, 100, Box 18, WWI Papers for the Women's Committee; and Hill to County Chairmen, December 17, 1917, History of the North Carolina Council of Defense, 517–518, Box 18, WWI Papers for the correspondence regarding African Americans.

6. The fifteen committees the state council created were Finance, Public Information, Legal, Co-ordination of Work, Sanitation, Conservation of Resources, Industrial Survey, Historical Preservation, Labor, Military, Home Defense, Transportation, Research, Woman's Work, and Soldiers' Business Aid. See *The North Carolina Council of Defense: Plan of Organization*, 5–9.

7. History of the North Carolina Council of Defense, 37–38, Box 18, WWI Papers.

8. National Council of Defense, "The Development of Community Councils," 1918, Box 8, WWI Papers. See also Stephen Vaughn, *Holding Fast the Inner Lines: Democracy, Nationalism, and the Committee on Public Information* (Chapel Hill: University of North Carolina Press, 1980), 112–113.

9. Kennedy, *Over Here*, 116.

10. These documents are available in the "Aliens and alien property" Folder, Box 6, WWI Papers.

11. William J. Breen, *Uncle Sam at Home: Civilian Mobilization, Wartime Federalism, and the Council of National Defense* (Westport, CT: Greenwood Press, 1984), xvi.

12. Kennedy, *Over Here*, 116. Jeanette Keith echoes this argument in *Rich Man's War Poor Man's Fight: Race, Class, and Power in the Rural South during the First World War* (Chapel Hill: University of North Carolina Press, 2004), 137–138.

13. Kennedy, *Over Here*, 116.

14. M. D. Kinsland to D. H. Hill, August 2, 1918, Box 8, WWI Papers.

15. C. Ed. Taylor to D. H. Hill, March 18, 1918, Box 8, WWI Papers.

16. Robert Hairston to Hill, August 3, 1918, Box 8, WWI Papers. Hairston was chair of the Rockingham County Council of Defense and also served as that county's Food Administrator.

17. These insights are drawn from a database of more than two thousand individuals who participated in the war effort, compiled by the author from the WWI Papers.

18. D. H. Hill to County Chairmen, April 9, 1918, History of the North Carolina Council of Defense, 204, Box 18 ("Instant attention"); Hill to County Chairmen, October 25, 1918, History of the North Carolina Council of Defense, 299–300, Box 18 ("at once"); History of the North Carolina Council of Defense, 203, Box 18 ("within 24 hours"); Hill to County Chairmen, September 27, 1917, Box 19 ("with care but speed"); all in WWI Papers.

19. W. S. Wilson to County Chairmen, September 26, 1917, October 3, 1917, Box 19, WWI Papers.

20. Hill to County Chairmen, July 16, 1917, History of the North Carolina Council of Defense, 487–488, Box 18; Hill to County Chairmen, July 16, 1918, Box 18; both in WWI Papers.

21. Hill to County Committees, June 21, 1917, June 14, 1918, Box 19, WWI Papers.

22. Monday, September 3, 1917, was designated Patriotic Day in North Carolina, with celebrations organized by county councils in each county seat. The Monday celebrations were to be preceded by additional weekend activities, also organized by the county councils. Barely a month later, county chairmen received another request to organize local meetings of support for the Liberty Loan. Yet another round of patriotic meetings—with commensurate requests for support on the part of county chairmen—was scheduled for December 14, 1917. A repeat performance, complete with an additional round of meetings at every school in the county, came less than two months later, to coincide with Washington's Birthday (February 22, 1918). In perhaps the final entreaty of the war, the state council asked county chairmen to oversee patriotic speakers at each county fair in the fall of 1918. See Wilson to County Chairmen, August 25, 1917, Box 10; Wilson to County Chairmen, 25, August 28, 1917, Box 19; Hill to County Chairmen, October 8, 1917, Box 19, (first quotation); F. H. Fries to C. F. Harvey, November 27, 1917, History of the North Carolina Council of Defense, 354–356, Box 18 (second and third quotations); Hill to County Chairmen, February 16, 1918, Box 19 (fourth quotation); Hill to County Chairmen, September 26, 1918, History of the North Carolina Council of Defense, 456, Box 18 (fifth quotation); all in WWI Papers.

23. W. S. Wilson to County Chairmen, 14, September 24, 1918, Box 19, WWI Papers.

24. Quoted in Breen, *Uncle Sam at Home*, 49.

25. History of the North Carolina Council of Defense, 71, Box 18, WWI Papers.

26. Kennedy, *Over Here*, 24.

27. John Whiteclay Chambers II, *The Tyranny of Change: America in the Progressive Era, 1890–1920* (New York: St. Martin's Press, 1992), 217. This was not an issue in North Carolina, where only .3% of the population in 1910 was foreign born. See Campbell Gibson and Kay Jung, *Historical Census Statistics on the Foreign-Born Population of the United States: 1850–2000* (Washington, DC: US Census Bureau, 2006), 65.

28. *News & Observer* (Raleigh), May 27, 1917, Box 5, Clippings Folder, WWI Papers.

29. Keith, *Rich Man's War, Poor Man's Fight*, 8–10, 156–160, quote from 9.

30. Hill to County Chairmen, August 28, 1918, Box 19, WWI Papers. It should be noted that the network of county and community Councils of Defense was not fully in place in time to assist with the initial registration day in June 1917.

31. "First Complete Official Record of Draft," *New York Times*, January 20, 1918, 43.

32. Breen, *Uncle Sam at Home*, 24.

33. History of the North Carolina Council of Defense, 37–38, Box 18, WWI Papers. It seems that there was very little overlap between the county councils and the exemption boards. Of the 415 North Carolinians who served on county exemption boards identified in the database, only 27 were also members of their county Council of Defense.

34. Chairman of the state Council of Defense [unnamed in letter] to "Members of the Several Councils of Defense," November 5, 1917, History of the North Carolina Council of Defense, 203, Box 18, WWI Papers.

35. Hill to County Chairmen, December 29, 1917, Box 19, WWI Papers.

36. Hill to County Chairmen, July 16, 1917, History of the North Carolina Council of Defense, 487–488, Box 18, WWI Papers.

37. C. M. Vanstory to D. H. Hill, August 1, 1918, Box 8, WWI Papers.

38. Annual Report of the North Carolina Council of Defense, May 30, 1918, History of the North Carolina Council of Defense, 539, Box 18, WWI Papers.

39. "Prosecutions Under Selective Service and Espionage Acts, Eastern District of North Carolina, July 1, 1917–July 1, 1918," Box 10, WWI Papers. County and local council members offered similar assistance in identifying those who might have falsely claimed an exemption based on employment. Again, there was no substitute for the kind of local intelligence that these council members were able to offer, and they were asked to "report to the Adjutant General the names of all persons within the draft age who are not regularly employed, to the end, that such persons may be called before the draft boards and re-classified and inducted into military service." See Minutes of State Council meeting, June 29, 1918, History of the North Carolina Council of Defense, 545a, Box 18, WWI Papers.

40. William H. Thomas Jr., *Unsafe for Democracy: World War I and the U.S. Justice Department's Covert Campaign to Suppress Dissent* (Madison: University of Wisconsin Press, 2008), 67.

41. See, for example, Christopher Cappozzola, "The Only Badge Needed Is Your Patriotic Fervor: Vigilance, Coercion, and the Law in World War I America," *Journal of American History* 88 (March 2002): 1354–1382; Paul L. Murphy, *World War I and the Origin of Civil Liberties in the United States* (New York: Norton, 1979); Robert K. Murray, *Red Scare: A Study in National Hysteria, 1919–1920* (Minneapolis: University of Minnesota Press, 1955); H. C. Peterson and Gilbert C. Fite, *Opponents of War, 1917–1918* (Madison: University of Wisconsin Press, 1957); William J. Preston, *Aliens and Dissenters: Federal Suppression of Radicals, 1903–1933*, 2nd ed. (Urbana: University of Illinois Press, 1994); Thomas, *Unsafe for Democracy*; Vaughn, *Holding Fast the Inner Lines*; and David Williams, "The Bureau of Investigation and Its Critics, 1919–1921: The Origins of Federal Political Surveillance," *Journal of American History* 68 (December 1981): 560–579.

42. History of the North Carolina Council of Defense, 30, Box 18, WWI Papers. Capitalization in original.

43. History of the North Carolina Council of Defense, 45, Box 18, WWI Papers.

44. History of the North Carolina Council of Defense, 41, Box 18, WWI Papers.

45. History of the North Carolina Council of Defense, 41, Box 18, WWI Papers.

46. History of the North Carolina Council of Defense, 41, Box 18, WWI Papers.

47. Hill to County Chairman, March 30, 1918, Box 19, WWI Papers.

48. Annual Report of the North Carolina Council of Defense, May 30, 1918, History of the North Carolina Council of Defense, 539, Box 18, WWI Papers.

49. Unsigned [Robert Hairston] to D. H. Hill, March 6, 1918, Box 10, WWI Papers.

50. Unsigned [probably Robert Hairston] to Thomas Gregory [US Attorney General], March 12, 1918, Box 10, WWI Papers.

51. Unsigned [Robert Hairston] to W. C. Hammer, US District Attorney, 30 March 1918, WWI Papers, Box 10, WWI Papers.

52. Unsigned to Hon. Charles E. Boyd, April 11, 1918, Box 10, WWI Papers.

53. Unsigned [C. F. Harvey, Lenoir County Council Chair] to E. M. Green, June 17, 1918, Box 10, WWI Papers.

54. Unknown to Ernest M. Green, June 21, 1918, Box 10, WWI Papers.

55. Chairman, Council of Defense for Rockingham County to Rev. S. B. Brown, December 17, 1917, Box 10, WWI Papers.

56. Report, A. A. Nelms, July 23, 1918, Box 10, WWI Papers. There is no record in the archive of the resolution of this case.

57. History of the North Carolina Council of Defense, Box 18, 31, WWI Papers.

58. Keith, *Rich Man's War, Poor Man's Fight*, 138.

59. Dorsey E. Phillips to Joseph B. Ramsey, December 2, 1917; Ramsey to Phillips, December 7, 1917, Box 10, WWI Papers.

60. Parker Quince Moore (Mayor, City of Wilmington) to J. G. McCormick, January 29, 1918, Box 10, WWI Papers.

61. J. G. McCormick to Hill, January 31, 1918; Hill to McCormick, February 2, 1918, Box 10, WWI Papers.

7

"There May Be a Few Obstructionists About"

Mobilization and Resistance in the Germanic Counties of Piedmont North Carolina, 1917–1918

Gary R. Freeze

In 1921 Margaret Little Lippard was so close to her 100th birthday that she confused her wars. Despite the late traumas experienced on the Western Front, the enemy in her mind was more often General Stoneman of the Civil War than Field Marshall von Hindenberg. In 1865 she had entertained Northern raiders intent on ending Confederate resistance in western North Carolina. Margaret's hospitality one morning, she told her children, staved off further destruction to the homestead, and "the Yankees let the family off light." In a similar vein, being "let off light" had been on the minds of her kith and kin since 1917. The Lippards counted themselves among the thousands of North Carolinians who were "of German origin," and during mobilization they had been under scrutiny and suspicion in implicit as well as explicit ways. For that reason, at "Aunt Margaret's 99th birthday party," they talked up their devotion to family, flag, and—somewhat ambiguously—their choice of fatherland to their guests. "This family has a clean, patriotic record," a visitor subsequently reported to the world, "the descendants having followed the flag in three different wars."[1]

Nothing was remarkable in the war stories told that day, given the times, but it was curious that the Lippards took pains to emphasize their "clean patriotic record" in three wars. The Lippards had been among the first Germans to populate the Iredell side of the Catawba River after the Revolution. The sons of the pioneers had marched off to suppress the Red Sticks in 1814. Their sons, in turn, had been reluctant conscripts in 1862 but by and large served faithfully. No Lippard, however, had volunteered for Mexico in 1846, Cuba in 1898, or France in 1917, though several had answered the call in 1918. The tone of the birthday party correspondent, therefore, suggested that an ambivalent message was being conveyed about the most recent war and their involvement in it.

This essay explores a hitherto unexamined aspect of North Carolina history: the idea that substantial numbers of state residents "of German origin" held pro-German sentiments during the First World War. Since Armistice Day, three generations of historians have paid the topic little mind, most likely because no one thought it could be true beyond a few isolated incidents.[2] State historians have assumed that progressive assimilation had superseded ethnocultural identity by the early part of the twentieth century. Since the immigrant waves swept into America in places other than Tobacco Road, the term "North Carolina Germans" verged on the oxymoronic. This essay argues otherwise. What some wartime propagandists disparaged as *Kultur* had lingered in North Carolina, in some parts of the state more than others, and where that was the case, a culturally based resistance played out in public life during mobilization.[3] This essay examines instances of disaffection in the communities where German immigrants had settled in North Carolina.

In 1914 North Carolinians with a Germanic (i.e., a Deutsch or "Dutch") background included descendants of Swiss Protestants who came to New Bern in the late Proprietary period, Moravians who established Wachovia during the Regulation, and a small coterie of Jews who immigrated to Gilded Age towns. These three groups were almost all assimilated and regarded as "100 per cent Americans" during the war—meaning, for purposes here, that they were industrially compliant and sustained mobilization with both body and purse.[4] In contrast, North Carolinians "of German origin" living in the rural areas of the Piedmont settled by their colonial Palatine ancestors—in Cabarrus, Rowan, Davidson, Iredell, Catawba, and Lincoln counties—had over time exhibited a higher likelihood of planting by the signs, a lesser propensity to slaveholding, an ambivalence about revivalist forms of Protestantism, and the continuation of mixed farming defiant of New South norms, which tended to keep them peripheral to some aspects of regional modernization. Most remained devoted to their Lutheran or German Reformed heritages. Those who graduated from their denominational colleges tended to stay within their home communities and carry on in their ways.[5]

Most resistance to mobilization in the state was rooted in economics and ideology, to widespread condemnation by Wilsonian elites. In 1917 University of North Carolina professor Horace W. Williams mimicked Eugene V. Debs when he asserted that "we fight Germany . . . for commercial supremacy." Dr. Hugh Q. Alexander, head of the Farmers Union, was compared with "the Emma Goldman class" for claiming that "we have made a frightful mistake going into a foreign war." Scattered anti-draft meetings were followed by quick measures of ridicule and repression. For example, "Copperheadism had but a brief existence in Union County," a Charlotte eyewitness exulted, when "the undertaking to get up an anti-draft meeting" in Monroe "proved a happy failure." The reference to the Civil War was apt in several of the noted cases of overt resistance. "Every deserter," Governor Thomas Bickett observed in Ashe County, "is the son or grandson of a CSA deserter." In the Uwharrie Mountains, once a hotbed of support for the anti-Confederate Heroes of America, the "Davidson [County] Dozen" collected arms to "fend off an invasion," they said, regardless of who was to do it, and awaited their fate. They, like their compatriots in Ashe, Cleveland, and other counties, were eventually brought in.[6]

There was, as well, evidence that ethnic heritage played a role in division and dissent, at least in the western half of the state. Charlotteans imbued with a mythology rooted in the Mecklenburg Declaration of Independence ethnicized their jingoism in the spring of 1917. "The people of this section of the country will receive with peculiar satisfaction," argued the *Charlotte* (North Carolina) *Observer*, the knowledge that Woodrow Wilson came from "the stock commonly called Scotch-Irish." Americans could depend, as they had in Revolutionary days, on "a fixed and unbending determination" by such people to see the war through. Charlotte tended to be just as virulent about its patriotism in 1917 as it had in the Hornet's Nest in 1780. Right after the American declaration of war, a young girl at South Elementary School refused to salute the flag because, she said, "Her grandfather was a German." Although her parents had been born in the United States, they "were not in sympathy with any patriotic display which intended to idealize the American eagle." The excitement that swept the city was quieted within a day when "the attitude of the refractory unit" had changed.[7]

In a similar vein, individuals mobilizing Charlotte cast a skeptical eye toward the "refractory" units to its north, to the same areas of ethnic diversity that had been mixed in their loyalties in the Revolution and the Civil War. It had been hearing suspicious stories that implicated both citizens and communities since 1914. When Statesville merchant Clarence W. Boshamer, a "strong pro-German," argued that "jealousy, hatred, and aggrandizement" caused the war, with the British more to blame than the Germans, no Statesvillian denounced him publicly. In June 1915, "strong German sympathizer" T. B. Moose argued on the main streets of Newton that "the Germans are going to lick the earth and the fullness thereof before the war is over." The local editor, a former president of the German Reformed Church's Catawba College, concurred that "it begins to look that way." Pressure for these places to be loyal built swiftly once the United States entered the war, and most complied, both individually and institutionally. Frank Fleer, a Philadelphia chewing gum magnate, sold his Davidson County farm because "neighbors resented his defense of the Kaiser." Although the Germanic denominations officially endorsed mobilization and young German American men from urban families, like Wilson L. Warlick of Newton and John W. Wallace of Statesville, quickly enlisted, suspicions remained about folks at the grassroots level.[8]

Proof that more common folks with a German heritage might be sympathetic to the Fatherland played out dramatically in Lincoln County. The local anti-draft meetings in the summer of 1917 only occurred in the Germanic western side of the county and were quickly suppressed. There appeared to be a long-simmering undercurrent of discontent about mobilization, which exploded when men began marching off to war. In June 1918 Lincolnton "spectacle salesman" Silas P. Houser "was taken in hand by a crowd . . . given rather rough treatment and made to kiss the American flag in the public square." He was forced to "publicly acknowledge that he would no longer be the German Kultur professor." The hazers charged that Houser had openly "been making pro-German remarks and gloating over the recent German victories," particularly the actions of U-boats off the New Jersey coast. "A large crowd witnessed the event," and the local editor pronounced victory. "[H]ere was where . . . German sympathizers . . . met their [W]aterloo." Houser was believed to be in league with others; there were "reports circulating of pro-German activities in this county." Still, Houser was "of German descent" and two-thirds of those who signed the petition condemning him were not, suggesting that the strident response had overtones of ethnic tension.[9] Houser's most outspoken critic was a Catawba College history instructor. George C. Warlick, who had left his position to volunteer, affirmed to the public-at-large that the meetings "hinted strongly of disloyalty" and "contain[ed] elements of sedition in the public mind, even of treason." To rally folks, Warlick invoked the memory of Ramsour's Mill, the pivotal battle of the American Revolution fought nearby, which "quelled the spirit of Toryism." What Warlick made implicit, many Lincolnites knew explicitly. Many of the Tories who fought at Ramsour's Mill had been Germans, including a Warlick or two. In an ironic twist to his own heritage, Warlick labeled dissenters "a race of renegades, a sickly bud of a noble stamen" who were shaming the memories of their forebears.[10]

Although "reports" from across Lincoln County "say that the people . . . by overwhelming majority condemn[ed] the anti-draft meeting," the events were so unsettling that Governor Bickett came to a rally designed to show that dissent "was a gross misrepresentation." He spoke at the Rock Springs Camp meeting grounds, in the more non-German side of the county. A military band from Charlotte's Camp Greene was dispatched to arouse patriotic sentiments. Not long after, outsiders purposefully invited themselves to the reunion of the Ramsour family, whose ancestor had built the mill where the battle was fought. "Though this family is of German origin and has well maintained the strong qualities of the race," noted a Greensboro resident, "I have been in no company since the present unpleasantness began where American sentiment and American sympathies were more pronounced." Furthermore, he conjectured, "it would be easy for a man of pro-German sympathies to get the Germans after him in the vicinity of Lincolnton. A million or two German-American families of this type would soon set the Fatherland right."[11]

By comparison, amelioration not animosity characterized the response to resistance in Catawba County. In 1917 some sixty German Americans who lived south of Hickory signed an anti-draft petition under the watchful eye of the sheriff, who was himself a Missouri Synod Lutheran. Still, when a federal agent arrived soon after, he ended up with "quite a lot of information jotted in a note-book." The local response remained conciliatory. "There may be a few obstruc-tionists about," a Hickory editor acknowledged while simultaneously declaring "there is not a section of the county that is not loyal to the cause of the people." But he admitted that this was a new circumstance. "In the summer of 1917," he had observed, the Zimmerman Telegram had "changed sentiments rapidly." Until that revelation, there had been "a large sprinkling of pro-German senti-ment in the community." Since, "the former sympathizers of the German cause" have been warned "that this is a bad time to be expressing sentiments that may be misconstrued as disloyal." In an effort to quell disaffection, Hickory's leading capitalists invited farm families to a town hall meeting to vent their general frustrations about the fundraising and manpower demands of mo-bilization. The rural spokesperson, Maud Yoder Robinson, whose front hall displayed artifacts of local German heritage, criticized urban society's "ap-parent need of waiting on, [and] requiring others to do for them what they could just as easily do for themselves." During the meeting, she and several other farm wives "instruct[ed] Hickory people on their duty in this great world crisis."[12] Although there was no ethnic dimension to Catawbans asking for deferments from the draft, the belief that pro-German citizens walked the streets lingered till the Armistice. As late as the middle of October 1918, "a special agent for the department of justice" was in Hickory because the word was out that "some farmers had been told that where they did not buy bonds, that the government would take the money away from them."

One Catawban was arrested under the Espionage Act. In May 1918, "a sensation was sprung in Newton" when Miles S. Smyre repeated "alleged disloyal remarks . . . after taking quite an interest in the German drive." The hardware store owner was said to have vowed that "when the Kaiser and his army reach[ed] the United States, [he] Mr. Smyre was to join it." The remarks were made during the same weekend that Governor Bickett was in town, and Smyre was turned in by several prominent citizens after word of "loose talk around this city." Smyre later argued he was "jesting when he made the remarks attributed to him, [and] has purchased bonds and War Savings Stamps." He did remain resolute in his opposition to the draft, even before officials. When asked, witnesses agreed about the jesting, but when pressed by authorities, they concurred that, yes, he was out to interfere with mobilization.[13]

The only successful German American effort to thwart the draft occurred in Statesville. The brothers Walter and Hobart Houpe refused to report for duty in 1918 and absconded to Mexico. They made it plain before leaving that their heritage was the motive. Their resistance was rooted in a broader disaffection in the Bethany neighborhood northeast of Statesville. Their uncle J. R. Houpe loudly announced that, though he was both German and English in descent, "if he could do so he would open his veins . . . and let out every particle of English blood in him." A second family member and another member of the Bethany community were later tried under the Espionage Act for claiming that "the moneyed powers" had "foolishly" led America into war. One of the accused, J. D. Gryder, had rendered *Kultur* in the folksiest of idioms, admonishing to all who would listen that "Germans were raised up a smart race of people."[14]

Subtler was the manner of resistance manifested by the rural folks on "Rte. 3 Statesville," the area just to the south of Iredell County's seat. Most Lutherans in this neighborhood were adherents to a culturally conservative form of Lutheranism called Henkelism, which came the closest to a sacerdotal *Kultur* to be found in North Carolina. They were also proud preservers of a more traditional agriculture. These dozen or so interrelated families—including the Lippards, mentioned in the opening to this essay—still took pride in "the hum of binders and the swish of cradles," the phrase one resident used to describe their continuing efforts to avoid one-crop agriculture, sharecropping, and other pitfalls of the New South. As one old farmer of the day observed, "Why do you need banks when you have the Clodfelters?"[15]

The "Rte. 3 Statesville" families revealed their subtle antagonism to mobilization in the neighborhood news reported to the Statesville newspaper. "A pall of gloom hangs over this community," observed Isabelle S. Troutman in April 1917, "since the people realize we are thrust into the thralls of war." Folks in Isabelle's neighborhood admitted to her that they were having nightmares about shooting Germans. Speaking, perhaps, both *to* and *for* her neighbors, the correspondent admonished, "In this struggle we should be loyal to America," and should there be an invasion—intended as a very subtle critique of American overseas intervention— "every man should rally to the flag." In the meanwhile, her people "realize that the life of our country in the present struggle is going to depend materially upon the farmer." So, the farmers of "Rte. 3 Statesville" that summer did what they did best; most stayed home as long as possible and worked harder. That autumn Mrs. Troutman observed, "[E]very man, woman and child are doing their bit for themselves and country, too." So hard were these neighbors working "to plant all they could that 'that even babies are taken to the harvest fields and put into boxes.'" She wanted readers to know that "we are not hysterical or spasmodically economical in this section on account of war conditions, but everyone seems to be raising and conserving all the farm produce they can."[16]

Other events suggested that pro-German sentiment lingered in the neighborhood. Early into mobilization, one resident went to Statesville on business and took dinner at a boarding house. A child present thought he looked so much like the Kaiser that panic spread around the table. In the summer of 1917, resident Cornelius Kesler came forth to make a public confession. As he told *The Landmark* editor, "I sympathized with the Germans until they tried to get Mexico and Japan on us. The reason," he admitted, "was that I am of near German descent." Soon after, two pro-Kaiser men were fired from Statesville post office jobs. One, Albert J. Hoover, came from the "Rte. 3" community. When the Liberty Loan and War Stamp drives were begun in Statesville, the township that included "Rte. 3" was the least likely to contribute, and Iredellians heard about it. In early 1918, operatives in nearby East Monbo, a cotton mill village on the Catawba River, shilled that "the d__d farmers are not giving anything." In contrast, "Baptist people here deserve a complimentary pat on the back . . . They sent their boys to the front." Mrs. Troutman replied that the criticism "may be true to some extent, but the majority of farmers don't handle much ready cash . . . and the seasons govern them." She warned away the urban solicitors who came to rural areas to push folks to buy bonds, which happened in an adjacent neighborhood. "We don't want men of that caliber to dictate to us while financing this war." Still, as the pressures to buy stamps and bonds grew, she and her neighbors went dutifully to hear lectures in town "on the war situation," which "helped to arouse a dormant patriotism." By summer of 1918, she was resigned to draftees leaving and women working "like Trojans" in the fields. "We are in the beginning of a real test of true heroism and character."[17]

The Germanic neighborhoods in Davidson County, to the south of Winston-Salem, endured a more contentious test of ways and will. In the excitement of April 1917, for example, there was the rumor that "a well-known former Lexington man of German proclivities had been arrested in another town for sedition." Soon after, a Thomasville citizen was said to have remarked that "all the powers of the world cannot break the Hindenberg Line." When in June 1917 local elites announced that the process of selective service went well—"there was only one slacker throughout the county"—the assurances proved to be hot air. As the summer lengthened, it was obvious that disaffection had taken on cultural, albeit partisan, tones. Once the first draft had been completed, indignant Lexington elites condemned the "small black-leg, crossroads politicians" in "their seditious work" who had said "it was a Democratic war, fought in the interests of the Democratic Party. People were told that Republicans would be drafted and Democrats left at home." A draft board member claimed that "many of the slackers" were "of the same faith" as the Republican sheriff. Loyalties were scrutinized neighborhood by neighborhood and in some places family by family. "Nearly everyone in the lower part of Davidson County was loyal," said a correspondent from Healing Springs, where few Germans had settled. When the annual reunion of one of the oldest German families was announced, it was declared that "if you are a Sink, *out of jail and Germany,* this is especially for you." In Lexington, the county seat, some folks were known to say that this was a "war so unnecessary, so useless," and others were angry that they were saying it. The Wilsonian editor of the local paper accused such folk of giving in to "ignorance or rank selfishness." The tension was accentuated by news in October that "two Germans" were in the county jail and couldn't go to the army, because they were under indictment for nonrelated crimes. One was a native of nearby Rowan County.[18]

Divisions within Davidson County worsened in 1918, when America went to war in full. In the second draft effort, almost one hundred postcards were returned to the exemption board, "having been unclaimed at the post office where they were sent," a strong statement by those who continued to oppose any further assimilation. "They are deliberately gumming up the machinery whereby the United States is selecting the men," complained an exemption board official. Just as in Iredell, support for mobilization varied by geography. In one school "some of the children were holding their fingers in their ears so they could not hear what their teachers had to say" about buying War Stamps. "They had been instructed to do this by their parents," said one teacher. So recalcitrant were parts of the county that the school superintendent published a diatribe against the disloyalty of those who were in his charge. Local Masons passed a resolution that "the whole county of Davidson as far as possible shall enter into it." In the local push to "enter into it," thirty-seven young men walked into the draft office to volunteer and repair the compromised character of community. They included farm boys from across the county, but only three had well-known German American names.[19]

By summer 1918, the pressure in Davidson County to conform and comply matched that being expressed elsewhere. Resident J. D. Newton recommended "hanging for any man who is expressing his joy at the successes of Germany just now." Elites, including Rev. J. D. Andrew, the German Reformed pastor at the venerated Pilgrim Church, tried to consolidate mobilization support. "Lexington leads the limit club" for maximum investments in War Savings Stamps, it had been announced in March, with the hope expressed in the same essay that farmers in Welcome and Tyro—communities "of German descent"—would soon match the work being done in Linwood, where the "[non-German] farmers are just getting started." (Only two farmers, out of more than 300 in those areas, eventually made the "limit club.") In the late summer, the Lutheran pastor in Thomasville had a sermon that "dispelled the notion that the Kaiser is a Lutheran." Heidelburg Lutheran Church, absolved of such a taint, had a service that dedicated a flag with three stars for the three young men in the congregation who had gone off to war.[20]

The cross currents compromised neighborhoods, with suggestions of feuding. Jesse Leonard, whose German paternal line had been one of the first to settle the area, had "taken to the bushes" in the summer of 1917. In

June of 1918 he was captured by a Reedy Creek neighbor, but then forcefully freed by his father, only to have the neighbor's brother take him back into custody. Then a second brother of the neighbor aimed a shotgun at the pair and freed Leonard for the second time. That second brother, Roy Hill, was the young Leonard's brother-in-law, and the two fled together. Soon after, a third neighbor winged Leonard with bird shot when he was found hiding in a chicken roost. Eventually a twenty-man posse found the pair and brought Jesse to his father, who then delivered him to Camp Greene in Charlotte. The county was riled up again in August when three members of the Samuel Nifong family—whose roots ran to colonial Wachovia—terrorized the Midway neighborhood for several weeks to avoid conscription. "They would," they told the neighbors, "resist to the death," but they were surprised by officials while they dressed at the break of day and surrendered without a shot. So prominent were they in the rural parts of the county—"they live in one of the best farming sections"—that a county commissioner posted the bond for their father, who had abetted their actions. As young men from Davidson County went to Europe to fight, some restoration of order came with the news from France that Jesse Leonard became the first in his company to kill a German. His "successful encounter with the Hun" included collecting souvenirs to bring back home. The *Lexington Dispatch* exulted, "He seems to be making a splendid headway." Leonard was later killed in action.[21]

In contrast to the dissension so rife in Davidson, Iredell, and Catawba counties, Rowan and Cabarrus counties appeared to be more accommodating to the demands of mobilization. This, at least, was the case in the public record, which was dominated in both county seats by Democrats allied with the *Charlotte Observer*. The local newspapers were barren of references to anti-draft activity of any kind in the neighborhoods surrounding the Germanic villages of Faith and Mt. Pleasant. Draft officials in Rowan and Cabarrus beat their breasts almost to death over their induction rates up and down the social stratum and across the ethnic horizon. Lutheran Marvin Trexler, it was noted, was the first Rowan native to die in France. So faithful to the cause were railroad workers in Spencer that Governor Bickett chose that Rowan County locale for his 1918 Labor Day address extolling the virtues of the 107 men serving in the army "who believe in the American flag." Letters home from Lutherans like James M. Waggoner and Hoy L. Fisher vowed not to leave "till we do this thing to a finish [,] then we'll come home." On Armistice Day, Rowan's editors crowed that "no city in the country its size has surpassed Salisbury in glorying over the glorious victory that has come to America."[22]

However, there was clearly some confliction. Carl Hammer grew up in rural southern Rowan County during the war. "In 1917–1918," he wrote decades later, "the antagonistic feeling toward persons of German background made itself evident throughout the land, and Rowan was no different." Yet, "even in the Lutheran congregations . . . divided sentiments prevailed." When the Hammers moved to a new house, "someone" in the new schoolyard "shouted to me . . . 'Hey, ain't your daddy a German?'" Bullied into speaking "in Kraut," he recited a table blessing, "and their curiosity was satisfied." Hammer wryly recalled that his hazers all had German surnames that went back to colonial settlement but didn't seem to know it—an indication, perhaps, that their parents were not talking up heritage.

Only one resident was known to speak out. In the summer of 1918 Silas Overcash, who lived near Kannapolis, was charged with "alleged disloyal talk" and brought before the federal commissioner. There "he talked pretty openly and refused to give bond." Overcash was said to have heard about the war "but did not know it to be a fact," and swore he "would tell President Wilson [personally that] he would not buy loans or stamps, if necessary."[23] Frank R. Brown, Rowan's representative of the American Protective League (APL), reported that his only real problem "[was] the Lutherans."

Brown's report back to the APL was one of the few from the area to survive the war, but comparing his assessment with the experience of nearby APL representatives helps with a final judgment about the pattern of pro-German sentiment. The evidence suggests that acquiescence in resistance, however tacit, went hand in hand with which heritage group controlled the papers and the local power structure. In Hickory, Newton, and Statesville, various German groups were still the core of community; in Salisbury and Concord they were not. In Lexington there seems to have been parity, perhaps an explanation for the low level of overt contention there.[24]

In all these places, mobilization put a strain on cultural and commercial ties that had great impact once the Armistice came. Those in the western Piedmont who were "Dutch" before the First World War had by the start of the Second World War ceased to think much about all the sound and fury of mobilization or what exactly their ethnicity meant. The post-resistance period had been one of casualties and costs. After the war, the German denominational colleges took hits in financial support and enrollment, and almost all of them closed. Lenoir College survived after industrialist Daniel P. Rhyne bought it, intending to move it to Gastonia, then let it remain in Hickory, his name added, making it Lenoir-Rhyne College. Catawba College lost support for its preparatory department when a new high school was opened in Newton, dooming its prospects. It closed for a year and was reopened in Salisbury in 1925. One professor, one piano, a few desks and books, and its annual—*The Swatstika*—were transferred to Rowan County, the yearbook name being changed only after the rise of Nazism in the 1930s. Silas Overcash continued to be "a well-known farmer" for a time and then retired to Kannapolis, where his daughters worked in the mill. M. S. Smyre's twenty-year-old hardware business did not survive the post-war slump. He sold out in 1922, to the second American ever to become a Boy Scout, Claude S. Abernethy, who had served in France. Smyre retired to a farm located not far from the site of the old protest rallies. One of the Houpe brothers was murdered while in exile, and the other came back to Statesville in 1924, eventually served time for his draft dodging, and returned home to live with his family. No one talked about him or seemed to remember what he had done. Isabella Troutman died in the flu epidemic of 1919. One of her sons became a Marine and helped invade Guadalcanal. The process of assimilation picked up pace with the innovations of the New Deal, and news about planting by the signs went the way of the agricultural extension service's brochures. When Catawba County's Weidner Oak—a sort of liberty tree symbol of their heritage and hope for freedom, dating to the colonial generation—was felled in a storm in 1939, it was back page news.[25]

But whiffs of *Kultur* lingered, like smolderings from yesterday's leaf burnings. Even after the Armistice, Isabelle Troutman had remained resilient. "Germany has fallen from the pedestal of honor and fame she has held among other nations, and that blow to her pride will be more galling than the loss of her men through all this warfare." J. C. Leonard, pastor at the Lexington German Reformed Church in the 1920s, put together Davidson County's first local history. In its pages, all the doughboys of 1917 had marched off gladly, prepared to sacrifice themselves for a world made safe for an ethnic-less democracy. No dissent here, and only bravery over there. Yet, when Leonard, whose Palatine forebears had come to North Carolina before the French and Indian War, got to the story of his ancestral neighborhood, he digressed. The German tongue, he admonished, was capable of "expressing shades of meaning that no other language can begin to express" and "eminently" suited for the best in "theology, poetry, and science."[26] The habits of heritage died hard in North Carolina.

Notes

1. *The Landmark* (Statesville, NC), July 23, 1918, 3; undated clippings, Lippard family file, Iredell County Genealogical Society, James Iredell Room, Iredell Public Library.

2. "North Carolina turned its attention from local politics and problems to do its part in this war" appeared in multiple editions of state histories: Albert R. Newsome and Hugh T. Lefler, *North Carolina: The History of a Southern State* (Chapel Hill: University of North Carolina Press, 1954), 583; William S. Powell, *North Carolina Through Four Centuries* (Chapel Hill: University of North Carolina Press, 1989), 459.

3. Tammy M. Proctor, "Patriotic Enemies: Germans in the Americas, 1914–1920," in Panikos Panayi, ed., *Germans as a Minority during the First World War: A Global Comparative Perspective* (Burlington, VT: Ashgate Publishers, 2014), 213–226; Fred K. C. Luebke, *Bonds of Loyalty: German-Americans in World War I* (Dekalb: Northern Illinois University Press, 1974), 100–101.

4. Nothing was found in the records in the Moravian Archives or the Winston-Salem newspapers to suggest inclusion in this study. The author would like to thank former archivist C. Daniel Crews for his assistance. Germans in the eastern half of the state were geographically

left out of the study. Gary R. Freeze, "Roots, Barks, Berries, and Jews: The Herb Trade in Gilded-Age North Carolina," in *Essays in Economic and Business History* (Columbus: The Ohio State University, 1995), 107–127, covers the Jewish presence.

5. Gary R. Freeze, "A Littler Mountain, A Commoner Sage: George M. Yoder, 1824–1920," *Journal of Contemporary History* (Summer 2007): 29–37.

6. D. H. Hill Jr. to F. M. Simmons, February 18, 1918, D. H. Hill Papers, North Carolina State Department of Archives and History (SDAH), Raleigh; *The Landmark*, May 10, September 4, 3, September 18, and November 30, 1917, all 2; *Charlotte Observer*, June 27, 5, July 1 and 3, 1918, 1; Governor Thomas Bickett to Secretary of War Newton D. Baker, July 10, 1918, Governors Papers, SDAH.

7. *Charlotte Observer*, April 4 and 5, 1917, both 1.

8. Boshamer file, Homer Keever Collection, James Iredell Room, Iredell Public Library; Bill Sharpe, *A New Geography of North Carolina*, Vol. IV (Raleigh: Sharpe Publishing Company, 1965), 1798; *The Lutheran Church Visitor* in the Dr. Jacob L. Morgan Papers, James R. Crumley Archives, Lutheran Theological Southern Seminary, Columbia, SC; Jacob C. Leonard, *History of the Southern Synod, Evangelical and Reformed Church* (Raleigh: Edwards & Broughton, 1940).

9. *Lincoln County News*, April 25, 1; June 6, 1918, 1.

10. George C. Warlick, Jr., *What I Know about My Ancestors* (Hickory, NC: n.p., 2000), 87–97.

11. *Lincoln County News*, August 3, 1918, 1, and Joseph R. Nixon, "The German Settlers in Lincoln County and Western North Carolina," *James R. Sprunt Historical Publications of the North Carolina Historical Society*, 11, no. 2 (1912): 54–61, for background on the Ramsours.

12. Gary R. Freeze, *The Catawbans: Pioneers in Progress* (Newton, NC: Catawba County Historical Association, 2002), 166–172, has an expanded version of the debate in the Catawban countryside. In the same vein, see Mrs. E. B. Cline [of Hickory] to James H. Pou, April 4, 1918; James H. Pou Papers, SDAH, "We need you. We are very anxious. . . . Will it be possible for you to come over into Macedonia and help us?"

13. C. H. Mebane, once the Fusionist State Superintendent of Public Instruction, edited the *Catawba County News*. *Hickory Daily Record*, May 4, 6, and 7, 1918, all 1; *Charlotte Observer*, May 6, 1918, 5; *Catawba County News*, May 7 and 10, 1918, 3, covered the Smyre case. "Odum Alexander, a special agent" was profiled in *Hickory Daily Record*, October 16, 1918, 1. Alex Floyd of the Rhodes Local History Room, Catawba County Public Library, assisted with this aspect of the research.

14. Houpe family file, Iredell County Genealogical Society, James Iredell Room, Iredell Public Library. *The Landmark*, July 16 and 19, 1918, 1. The author would like to thank historian Bill Moose of Mitchell Community College for alerting him to this case.

15. William Troutman, ed., "I Remember: An Anthology of Growing Up in North Carolina," memoir of Dessie Troutman Farnsworth (1973), typescript in the Troutman family file, and Harriet R. Schroeder, ed., "The Most Memorable Events of My Life," memoir of Thomas Paul Rumple (2006), typescript in Lippard family file, both in Iredell County Genealogical Society files, Iredell Public Library.

16. *The Landmark* correspondents in Union Grove and Harmony, where there were no Germans, showed far stronger support of mobilization during the same time that the "Rte. 3 Statesville" columns were so cautious. See April 11, 3, August 14, 2, September 25, 3, 1917; February 21, 4; March 22, 2; April 20, 4; May 5, 6; June 12, 4; June 23, 4, 1918.

17. *The Concord Tribune*, August 27, 1917, 3; Kesler family file, McCubbins Collection, Edith Clark History Room, Rowan Public Library, Salisbury. For Hoover's reinstatement by the post office, without comment, see *The Landmark*, November 13, 1917, 2; for hints of ethnic conflict, August 16, 1918, 3. The only two German farmers in the community to buy war bonds were Kesler and W. M. Clodfelter; *The Landmark*, April 16, 1918, 1.

18. *Charlotte Observer*, August 7, 1917, 7; C. E. Godwin to Gov. Bickett, June 28, 1918, Governors Papers, SDAH. *The Lexington Dispatch,* April 11, 3; July 18, 1; August 15, 3; September 5, 6; September 26, 1; October 12, 3; October 12, 4; 1917.

19. *Ibid.,* January 23, 1; February 8, 1; February 30, 1; March 20, 1; March 27, 3, 1918.

20. *Ibid.,* July 24, 2; August 7, 1, 1918.

21. *Ibid.,* May 1, 1; May 8, 1; August 1, 1, and August 28, 1, 1918. According to federal census returns, Jesse Leonard lived in the same neighborhood as the sheriff.

22. *The Literary Digest,* March 30, 1918, 48; George A. Carver to Gov. Bickett, June 17, 1918, Governors Papers; *The Salisbury Post,* September 2, 1, and November 11, 1, 1918.

23. Undated clipping, Carl Hammer file, McCubbins Collection, Rowan Public Library. The *Salisbury Post* covered the Overcash case on July 18, 1918, 1.

24. Jeanette Keith, *Rich Man's War, Poor Man's Fight: Race, Class and Power in the Rural South* (Chapel Hill: University of North Carolina Press, 2004), 172–238, focuses on the class dimension of mobilization. Her research, however, also suggests the APL encountered varying degrees of cultural resistance in the Piedmont. Statesville leaders reported "there was no clash or conflict with the working classes" and did not participate. Lexington and Hickory had APL representatives, but they were not able to quell resistance among German Americans to the extent that Brown was. This suggests that further research on the complexity of mobilization at the grassroots level would be enlightening. See APL Files, Box 10 (North Carolina), US National Archives and Records Administration, College Park, MD.

25. Jacob C. Leonard, *History of Catawba College, Formerly Located in Newton, Now at Salisbury, North Carolina* (Salisbury, NC: Rowan Printing Company, 1927), 187–188, 274–276; Raymond M. Bost and Jeff L. Norris, *All One Body: The Story of the North Carolina Lutheran Synod, 1803–1993* (Salisbury: North Carolina Synod, 1994), 236–237; *Catawba County News,* August 10, 1940, 3; *The Salisbury Post,* September 6, 1940, 17; Houpe family file, Iredell Public Library. Freeze, *Pioneers in Progress,* 374–382, covers the loss of ethnic consciousness.

26. *The Landmark,* November 21, 1918, 4; J. C. Leonard, *A Centennial History of Davidson County* (Raleigh: Edwards & Broughton, 1927), 145. M. Jewel Sink and Mary G. Matthews, *Pathfinders Past and Present* (High Point, NC: Hall Printing, 1972), 100, presented a "united" interpretation: "There was much faith in the righteousness of the cause."

8

Josephus Daniels, "Freedom of the Seas," and North Carolina's Economy during the Great War

Lee A. Craig

Josephus Daniels, a wealthy newspaper publisher and backstage political operator, joined the Democratic National Committee in 1892, and he would remain on the committee for more than twenty years. It was an era during which that body held substantially more power than it does today. Only 30 years old at the time, Daniels subsequently led North Carolina's white supremacy campaigns of 1898 and 1900 that resulted in the disenfranchisement of the state's African American voters. This allowed the Democratic Party, which at the time was overwhelmingly white, to subsequently dominate North Carolina politics. (African Americans did not begin to abandon the Republican Party until the New Deal.) Daniels' wealth and political power allowed him to play an important role in Woodrow Wilson's nomination as the Democratic Party's candidate in the 1912 presidential election, and Daniels served as a member of Wilson's inner circle during the campaign. Out of respect for Daniels' influence in the party and his contributions to the presidential campaign, Wilson resolved to add Daniels to his cabinet and eventually offered him the position of Secretary of the Navy. Understanding that Daniels had no military experience of any kind, Wilson sought a political advisor rather than a military leader in the navy post. However, the outbreak of war in August 1914 compelled Daniels to focus more on the martial aspects of his position than either he or Wilson could have anticipated.

With the onset of the Great War, assuming the belligerents respected international law as it applied to neutral shipping, Daniels argued that neutrality would best serve the United States' and North Carolina's economic interests. Initially, Daniels' tenure at the navy department was primarily impacted by the battle between the British Royal Navy and Imperial Germany's High Seas Fleet for control of the world's sea lanes. That battle ended the "freedom of the seas," which the Royal Navy had ensured over the previous century, and thus it disrupted US trade, the promotion of which was one of the Wilson administration's key policies. In fact, their mutual support for free trade was one of the issues that originally led to the collaboration between Daniels and Wilson. Wilson had campaigned on tariff reform, and Daniels, a lifelong free trader, supported that policy because it was, in his opinion, the most important national policy affecting North Carolina. As the head of the navy, Daniels considered supporting free trade as his most important task in Washington.

At the time Daniels left Raleigh to become Secretary of the Navy, North Carolina was largely an agricultural state.[1] Cotton and tobacco, the two main cash crops of the day, dominated North Carolina's economy. Indeed, despite the prominence of its tobacco processors—most notably James B. Duke's American Tobacco Company—and the emergence of a nascent textile industry, North Carolina farmers grew substantially more cotton and tobacco than the state's industrial sector could process or its citizens could consume. Thus, the state's main agricultural products were largely exported onto the world market where their value was determined, at least partly, by US trade policies. As a businessman, newspaper publisher, and politician, Daniels was for nearly fifty years one of the country's leading advocates of tariff reform, which to Daniels meant simply a reduction in tariff rates. The tariff tended to be disproportionately placed on manufactured goods, and at the time manufacturing activity was disproportionately located in the Northeast and the Midwest. Thus, to Daniels, the tariff protected and further enriched already wealthy northern industrialists while further impoverishing already poor Tar Heel farmers.

For Daniels, then, the tariff proved to be burdensome to North Carolina in two related ways. First, as net purchasers of manufactured goods, the state's farmers and consumers paid a higher price for the goods on which tariffs were placed. Second, as a large exporter of agricultural products, including cotton and tobacco, the state witnessed a decrease in the foreign demand for its output since foreigners' incomes were reduced because they could not sell their wares in the tariff-protected American market. The reduction in foreign demand reduced the prices of cotton and tobacco. The price of these two commodities served as Daniels's leading economic indicators, and he monitored them almost every day of his adult life. In his view, if the prices were up, so was the state's economy; if they were down, the economy went with them. As Daniels summarized the issue, the Republican-dominated Congress "levied high tariff taxes [sic], compelling cotton farmers to buy everything at high prices in a highly protected market, whereas cotton – their only money crop – was sold in the free trade market of the world."[2] Accordingly, southern Democrats referred to the protectionist Republicans in Congress as the "tariff gang,"[3] and the tariff served as a prohibitive federal sales tax disproportionately born by North Carolina farmers. Daniels considered the tariff to be the single most important domestic policy issue of the day. "When I went to

Washington I expected to see tariff reduction made the first and paramount reform undertaken," he wrote.[4]

Thus Daniels interpreted the martial side of his role as navy secretary as, primarily, one of promoting and protecting American trade. To Daniels, the expression "freedom of the seas" was not a meaningless slogan; rather it was an essential extension of the arterial system of his home state's economy. The Great War turned the sea lanes into a battleground, and this put Daniels in the position of having to use the US Navy to keep the sea lanes as open as possible, while simultaneously refraining from actions that would force the country into the war as a belligerent.

In the decades leading up to the Great War, Imperial Germany had been challenging Britain's status as constable of the sea. By rapidly expanding its navy and establishing imperial outposts in Africa and Asia, Germany threatened to disrupt the balance of power that the British had been cultivating since they sent Napoleon to St. Helena nearly a century earlier. Just as Daniels moved into his office in the Navy Building, the Germans threatened to move into the Western Hemisphere. Early in 1913, following the upheaval left in the wake of a contested presidential election, Mexican General Victoriano Huerta staged a coup, after which the recently elected president, Francisco Madero, died under suspicious circumstances. The northern politician Venustiano Carranza took charge of Madero's supporters, and Mexico descended into the chaos of civil war.[5] In the United States, there was strong support, primarily from the right, for direct intervention in Mexico.

The Wilson administration refused to recognize Huerta, adopting a policy of "watchful waiting," but Germany extended recognition. Daniels subsequently received intelligence from Mexico that Germany planned to supply Huerta with arms. German arms and military advisors would grant Huerta the luxury of indifference to whatever position the Wilson administration ultimately took regarding his regime. More troubling to Daniels was what the Germans might seek in return for their support. Among the worst-case scenarios was a naval base in Mexico. Daniels felt that a violation of Wilson's so-called Good Neighbor policy would be less costly than a German naval base in Mexico, which would allow the German navy to threaten the Panama Canal and more generally interdict trade throughout the hemisphere. Therefore, Daniels advised the president to prohibit Germany from making Mexico an imperial outpost.

When word reached Washington that the German steamship *Ypiranga* would arrive in Veracruz early on April 21, 1914, to unload a large shipment of arms, Wilson consulted Daniels, who strongly advised the president to intervene, arguing that the administration could not allow the Germans to arm Huerta, because German control of Mexico would ultimately threaten U.S. trade throughout the region. Wilson concurred. Before dawn on the twenty-first, Daniels wired Admiral Frank Fletcher, the commander of US naval forces in

Mexican waters: "Seize custom house. Do not permit war supplies to be delivered to Huerta government or to any other party."[6] The navy turned back the *Ypiranga* and followed up with the occupation of Veracruz. These actions delayed German meddling in Mexico for another three years.

The Great War began later that summer, following the assassination by Serbian terrorists of Archduke Franz Ferdinand, the presumed heir to the Austro-Hungarian throne, and his wife Sophie. Daniels remained in control of the editorial content of his newspaper, the *News & Observer* (Raleigh, NC), which openly speculated on the subsequent course of the war. The August 2 headline announced that "GERMANY DECLARES WAR ON RUSSIA; FRANCE ANSWERS ULTIMATUM WITH SWORD; Greatest War In All Time." The paper subsequently focused on the navy's role in securing the sea lanes, explicitly emphasizing that the navy was "preparing to protect trade."[7] This was insightful, because, as of that date, Germany was the only sea power in the war; the British had not yet formally declared their intentions. However, with Germany's entry, Daniels anticipated that the conflict would spread to Britain and thus become a world war. The British would not allow the Germans to win the war on the continent and then leverage that victory into an expansion of their overseas empire at Britain's expense. Daniels understood that a war at sea, which meant a war on commerce, would follow from Britain's entry into the conflict, and he understood that US shipping would be caught in the crossfire between the Royal Navy and the Imperial German Navy.

And that is exactly what happened. The Germans threatened US trade directly by declaring the Atlantic a vast killing ground for their commerce-raiding navy and indirectly by eying bases in Haiti and the Dominican Republic, two more unstable regimes. Daniels openly worried about the Germans "obtaining bases in these near-by islands," thus threatening "the approaches to the Panama Canal."[8] The war in Europe threatened to spill across the Atlantic as the Germans soon employed their submarine fleet to blockade the British Isles. To prevent the establishment of foreign naval bases in the Caribbean, under Daniels' orders, US marines occupied Haiti and the Dominican Republic. Cuba was later added to the list. The Good Neighbor policy was dead, but the Germans were prohibited from establishing bases in the Western Hemisphere.

As Europe went to war, Wilson proclaimed US neutrality, calling upon Americans to be "impartial in thought as well as action," a position Daniels supported.[9] However, once the naval war between Britain and Germany commenced, neutrality became an impossible position to maintain. For many Americans, particularly those with close economic and cultural ties to the British and the French—a group that included Wall Street financiers and trade unionists for whom the war offered a profitable return on their capital and labor, as well as many high-ranking military officers, and eventually Wilson himself—neutrality was not even desirable. Wilson hoped to keep the country out of the war, but a more important objective was keeping Britain from losing it, an objective that would ultimately kill his neutrality policy.

Unlike Wilson, Daniels possessed no special affection for the French and British causes, especially as he saw those causes threatening freedom of the seas. Before the United States entered the war, Daniels argued the British were as culpable as the Germans when it came to violating the international laws covering war at sea. In his view, European problems were best left to the Europeans, and favoring one side of the fight would only threaten US trade with the other side. That threat would in turn directly harm the markets for North Carolina cotton and tobacco, commodities that would only end up at the bottom of the Atlantic or interned in a belligerent port.

Unfortunately, what happened in Europe did not stay in Europe. The United States ultimately entered the Great War because of Germany's indiscriminate use of submarines against commercial shipping. Although the Imperial German navy's surface fleet had grown rapidly in the decades leading up to the war, it was no match for Britain's Royal Navy. Thus, the Germans turned to commerce raiding with their U-boats. During Daniels' eight years as head of the navy, the U-boat war was his greatest challenge. From the outset, Daniels recognized the importance of protecting US shipping from the U-boats. Every US ship that went to the bottom of the ocean supplied the pro-war party with ammunition for its cause, and entry into the war would only further threaten US trade. Daniels filled his diary with passages related to the problems created by Germany's war on commerce, reminding himself and posterity that: "everything possible [must be] done . . . to protect American shipping . . . no cost & no effort spared to protect shipping."[10]

In protecting US commerce, Daniels confronted international law as it applied to naval warfare, as well as German and British violations of it. The law revolved around the so-called Cruiser Rules, two Hague Conventions (1899 and 1907), and the Declaration of London (1909).[11] The Cruiser Rules, which dated from the sixteenth century, covered (at least in theory) all Western countries at war with one another. They classified ships as belligerent or neutral, and goods as either absolute contraband (e.g., weapons and ammunition); conditional contraband (e.g., coal and petroleum); and noncontraband (e.g., food, raw cotton, and wool). Neutrals could trade freely with belligerents, but contraband was subject to confiscation. Absolute contraband could be seized. Conditional contraband could be seized only if a belligerent destination could be determined. Noncontraband could not be seized.[12] Blockades were legal under strict rules, which the British ignored by simply closing the English Channel and the North Sea outlet between Scotland and Norway, preventing anything from going in or out of Germany by sea. Furthermore, the British effectively declared just about every item destined for Germany, including noncontraband items such as cotton and foodstuffs, as contraband. The Royal Navy also extended the blockade to neutrals trading with other neutrals that in turn *might* conceivably trade with Germany. Thus, British policy could be summarized as follows: Nothing could go in or come out of Germany by sea, and nothing could go into the continent if its ultimate destination was determined to be Germany.

If left unchallenged, Daniels feared, this unilateral violation of the Cruiser Rules would damage the North Carolina economy. An outraged Daniels complained that in response to US protests the British would only agree to "generally [follow] the rules of the Declaration [of London] subject to certain modifications," which included the "steadily increasing definitions of lists of contrabands and . . . other radical modifications."[13] In short, the British blockade was a bald violation of international law. North Carolina tobacco and cotton could no longer be shipped safely to European destinations other than the United Kingdom and France. During the first few months of the war, the Royal Navy seized forty-five neutral ships leaving US ports for neutral destinations.

Wilson claimed it was "immoral to stifle commerce on the seas," and he voiced his objections to the British treatment of US shipping, but his protests were overly measured and lacked conviction. As for the Germans, their admiralty responded in the only way it could, by sending the U-boat fleet after merchant shipping. On February 14, 1915, Germany classified as a war zone the waters surrounding the British Isles; all enemy merchant vessels found in the zone would be destroyed without warning. Unrestricted submarine warfare, another naked violation of the Cruiser Rules, had begun.[14]

As Daniels feared, the struggle for control of the Atlantic sea lanes negatively impacted North Carolina's economy during the first year of the war. Although US manufacturers absorbed some of the blow to tobacco production, which fell by five percent, the volume of the state's cotton output declined by 24 percent. More damaging was the impact on prices; tobacco prices were down by more than 30 percent and those for cotton off by nearly 40 percent.[15] The combination of declines in price and quantity halved the incomes of cotton farmers. Wilson blamed the U-boats, but Daniels chafed at the hypocrisy of the British, who as they nakedly broke international law by sealing off the continent (and turning the North Sea into a giant minefield), demanded that the Germans follow it to the letter. Daniels wrote that the British were "insisting upon" adherence to international conventions that they themselves violated with impunity.[16]

Daniels saw that Wilson's tepid protests concerning Britain's blockade would bring the United States into conflict with the Germans. The German High Command could not simply continue to wage a mortal yet stalemated land war and wait until the Royal Navy starved Germany into submission. US public opinion hung in the balance; it was ultimately swayed by the sinking of the British passenger liner *Lusitania* on May 7, 1915. Wilson protested the act through formal diplomatic channels, and after much deliberation, to Daniels's relief German resolve faltered. Kaiser Wilhelm II, who had been vacillating between his bellicose admirals and his more cautious civilian advisors, ultimately swung towards minimizing open conflict with the United States. He declared neutral merchantmen and all passenger liners off limits to the Uboats, unless their captains followed rigorous stop-and-search procedures called for by the Cruiser Rules, an untenable practice for the U-boats. As a result of the Kaiser's decision, the Democrats could successfully run Wilson for reelection the following year by claiming that, while "He kept us out of war," he also defended American honor and the freedom of the seas.

Although the British blockade continued, the end of unrestricted submarine warfare dramatically improved North Carolina's economic outlook. Indeed, the disruption of world markets and the increased demand for US goods by the Entente and by neutrals that could no longer trade with the Central Powers led to an immediate recovery. The prices of cotton and tobacco rebounded in 1915 and 1916, and the production of both commodities returned to or exceeded pre-war levels.

Unfortunately, this was not the end of unrestricted submarine warfare. The war in the trenches and the British blockade continued for another eighteen months. The German High Command, which failed to win the war in the field even as the casualties reached the millions, sought an alternative to starvation on the homefront. Pressed by his military leadership, the Kaiser abandoned his earlier caution, and on February 1, 1917, the Germans announced the return to all-out submarine warfare in the Atlantic. The High Command erroneously gambled that the German navy could starve Britain before the United States could materially affect the war, either at sea or on land.

The German Foreign Ministry soon compounded the error by encouraging Mexico to join the Central Powers in return for territory in Texas, New Mexico, and Arizona, which Mexico had forfeited following the Mexican-American War. The message—the so-called Zimmerman Telegram—which vindicated Daniels' decision to interdict Germany's military shipment to Mexico in 1914, was intercepted by the Royal Navy and transmitted to Washington through official channels. On Inauguration Day, March 4, Wilson authorized Daniels to arm US merchant vessels under executive order. The deck guns offered little help against U-boats that did not surface, and they did nothing for US ships already at sea. Daniels noted that, "Within a few days of the inauguration, eight American vessels were sunk by U-boats."[17] Wilson then requested, and Congress passed, a declaration of war.

As a neutral, Daniels supported the Cruiser Rules, and he questioned both the legality of the British blockade and the preferential treatment the US government had extended to the British relative to the Germans. But as a combatant he now found the Cruiser Rules inconvenient and turned a blind eye to the Royal Navy's transgressions. After being briefed on the dire economic conditions in Great Britain, Daniels realized expediency would force the US Navy to also violate the rules. Daniels recognized that "after nearly three years of the most horrific slaughter in history, the war had become a kind of double-edge sword at the public throat. . . . [T]heir losses in lives and treasure had hardened the British against Germany, and this hardening rendered a compromise peace out of reach."[18] To many observers, Germany's war strategy appeared to be working. British losses at sea from the U-boat campaign could not be born indefinitely. Germany's victories on the Eastern Front opened up new channels for the supply of grain and raw materials. Daniels understood that the crisis faced by America's key ally resulted from two arithmetic relationships: Ships sank faster than they could be built, and the finite human capacity for endurance was a function of nutritional consumption.

Combating the U-boat menace consumed most of Daniels' efforts once the United States entered the war. This battle revolved around three key issues. One was Daniels' navy construction program, which included dramatic increases in the number of destroyers and sub-chasers, as well as an overall increase in the navy's size. A second issue involved the use of mines to reduce the number of U-boats that escaped into the Atlantic through the North Sea. The third was the organization of convoys to protect US shipping and troop transports. [19]

The building program was the most pressing problem because, without it, the other components would be less effective. Daniels' view of the size and role of the US Navy had taken a nearly 180–degree turn since Wilson had first offered him a cabinet position. Once happy to let the British rule the world's oceans, Daniels was now convinced that the United States must have a navy at least as large as the Royal Navy. Accordingly, he presented to the Congress a massive naval building program, one that would ultimately create a 2000–ship navy. Daniels maintained the same, pre-war pace of adding battleships to the fleet (roughly two per annum) but to that he added for immediate construction 275 destroyers, 447 sub-chasers, 99 submarines, and more than 200 additional support vessels. In contrast, when war was declared the navy had just over 300 vessels afloat. Daniels' plan represented an ambitious industrial and organizational objective by any historical standard. To offer one example, before the plan's implementation, US industry constructed a destroyer in 20–24 months. By the end of the war, they were being turned out in less than 50 days.

With the Democrats in control of Congress, the plan passed more or less intact, and Daniels turned to mining the North Sea to keep the U-boats out of the Atlantic. The Hague Convention (1907) recognized mining as a legitimate act of war. The convention declared mines could be deployed as "offensive" weapons in "hostile territorial waters."[20] Thus, they were viewed as components of the so-called close blockade, which was legal international law. Both the British and the Germans ignored the convention's constraints on mining. When first approached about assisting the British in expanding the mining campaign between Scotland and Norway, Daniels agreed with his Chief of Naval Operations, Admiral William Benson, that it was not a good idea for technological reasons.[21] Basically, mine laying was dangerous, costly, and time consuming, and the mines were not reliable enough to justify the effort. In his diary, Daniels shared his reservations, asking rhetorically: "North Sea too rough & will necessitate withdrawing all our ships from other work and then can we destroy the hornet's nest or keep the hornets in?"[22] Although the British had used mines excessively throughout the North Sea, they hesitated to adopt the mines as the primary means of closing the gap between Scotland and Norway. Their reservations had more to do with the state of mining technology than any qualms about further violations of the laws of war. Once the US Navy developed a new, more reliable mine, reservations on both sides of the Atlantic vanished, and the North Sea between Scotland and Norway was closed as the Allies turned it into a minefield.

As for convoys of merchant ships, Daniels was convinced that they were the best way of getting troops and supplies across the Atlantic. Since the war began, the British strategy had been to send single merchant ships out on the high seas. They argued that convoys offered the U-boats a more visible target. Furthermore, since a convoy could only travel as fast as its slowest member, the convoy system increased the collective exposure time of the ships in it. The British argued that the chances of a U-boat finding a single ship traveling as fast as it could were smaller than finding a group of ships traveling as slow as the slowest member. The addition of America's industrial might to the Entente's war effort, however, substantially lessened British reservations about convoying. With the capacity to produce a large number of destroyers and sub-chasers to accompany and screen the convoys, the Americans could use convoying as an offensive weapon against the U-boats. The destroyers, small escort vessels that were fast enough to attack a U-boat, could sink a submarine if it were caught on the surface, and if the U-boat submerged, the destroyer could sink it or force it to the surface with underwater explosives called "depth charges." The sub-chasers were even smaller, faster craft that also carried depth charges. The speed and shallow draft of these vessels made them difficult targets for the U-boats; they were, in words of one history of the period, "terriers to the U-boat's rats."[23]

When the United States entered the war, the majority view in Wilson's cabinet—and possibly among the U.S. population—was that defeating the U-boats and supplying the Entente with war materiel was all the United States would need to do to ensure victory. Daniels disagreed. He consistently argued that the war would be won only when the navy broke the Uboats at sea *and* when US ground forces broke the German Army in France. Daniels did not think the navy could choke off the German economy quickly enough to avoid political crises in the London, Paris, and Rome. At the time the United States entered the war, the British Admiralty was predicting that the U-boats would bring the British economy to its knees before the blockade strangled the German economy.[24] After reaching London that spring, Daniels' liaison to the Royal Navy, Admiral William Snowden Sims, confirmed the point in a report to Daniels. "The submarine issue is very much more serious than the people realize in America," Sims wrote, adding that the U-boats "constitute the real crisis of the war."[25]

After reviewing the data, Daniels concluded that the United States would have to feed the British immediately while simultaneously keeping the French armies supplied in the trenches. But he recognized that such expedients would only forestall a political crisis among the Entente. It followed that, for the war to end sooner rather than later, the US Army would have to be shipped to France. Persuaded by the War Department, Congress soon agreed, passing a conscription act on May 18, 1917. It would be Daniels' responsibility to deliver the troops across the Atlantic. After the war, when asked to assess the country's greatest achievement during the conflict, Daniels offered a two-part answer: One was raising an army of 4 million men and a navy of 600,000 men, and the second was transporting 2 million soldiers and marines to France, all within eighteen months. When the United States entered the war, Daniels summarized the problems faced by the Entente, writing presciently in his diary that the "stomach is the test." It was a test the German economy would fail in 1918 as the fifth winter of the war approached. It failed because the US Navy and merchant fleet supplied the Entente with more food, men, and war material than the German navy could sink. The war at sea and the war in the trenches were two sides of the same coin. Daniels had seen this since US entry became a possibility.

Meanwhile, America's entry into the war ushered in a golden age of North Carolina agriculture. Cotton prices had bottomed out at five cents a pound during the farm woes of the 1890s; they recovered to hover around ten cents a pound during the pre-war years, and tobacco prices were in the neighborhood of twelve cents a pound. By the end of the war, the prices of both had reached thirty cents a pound, a figure that would have been unimaginable only twenty years earlier.[26] Furthermore, North Carolina's production of tobacco nearly doubled following the war's initial disruptions, and cotton output increased by roughly 25 percent.[27] Average farm income among the state's tobacco and cotton farmers more than doubled between 1915 and 1919.

On January 8, 1918, Wilson offered his vision of peace in his Fourteen Points. "Freedom of the seas" was one of those points. It was an important one, as it had ultimately brought the United States into the war. Of course, when Wilson said "freedom of the seas" he meant an end to Germany's un-restricted submarine warfare, rather than an end to British (and now US) violations of international law. The finer points of international law associated with the Cruiser Rules could be worked out at some future date, but there was no room for unrestricted submarine warfare in whatever agreements might emerge from post-war diplomacy. Daniels recognized the hypocrisy of Wilson's position, as did the Kaiser and his High Command. To them, Wilson's call for freedom of the seas rang hollow. German General Erich Ludendorff summarized the connection between the war at sea and the one in France: "To allow ourselves to be deprived of our submarine weapon would amount to capitulation."[28]

In the spring and summer of 1918, Ludendorff orchestrated a series of campaigns on the Western Front, the intention of which was to break the Entente before the American army arrived. They failed; by the autumn, it was apparent the German army would not last another winter in the trenches. After consulting with Daniels, US Secretary of State Robert Lansing, and Army Chief of Staff Peyton March, on October 23, Wilson demanded the Kaiser's abdication before armistice negotiations could begin.[29] In doing so, Wilson had ignored Daniels' advice to seek an end to the fighting with whatever party controlled German forces, whether it was the Kaiser, parliamentarians, or the High Command. Wilson gambled—successfully as it turned out—that he could force Germany to become a republic as part of the price of peace. On Saturday, November 9, the Kaiser went into exile.

In his diary, Daniels summarized his thoughts: "I felt the first thrill of joy in years—in fact, I had not been without distress and anxiety and strain since the beginning of the fighting in 1914."[30] The Great War had sent nearly 20 million people to their graves.[31] The subsequent influenza pandemic, the spread and severity of which can be attributed to the war, killed at least another 50 million.[32] In a letter subsequently sent to a boyhood friend, Henry Groves Connor, Daniels ended his war correspondence with, "I feel something good must come out of all this suffering and travail."[33] Sadly for Daniels, who died in 1948, he would live long enough to be bitterly disappointed in what came out of the Great War.

Notes

1. As late as 1900 in North Carolina, agriculture's share of the labor force still hovered around 90 percent at a time when the national average was just 60 percent. Only five states—Idaho, Oklahoma, North Dakota, Mississippi, and Arkansas—had a larger share of their labor force in agriculture. See Lee A. Craig and Thomas Weiss, *Agricultural Labor Force by State, 1800 to 1900* (Lawrence: University of Kansas, 1998), computer files.

2. Josephus Daniels, *Tar Heel Editor* (Chapel Hill: University of North Carolina Press, 1939), 179.

3. W.J. Cash, *The Mind of the South* (New York: Vintage Books, 1941), 160.

4. Josephus Daniels, *Editor in Politics* (Chapel Hill: University of North Carolina Press, 1941), 49.

5. See Max Boot, *The Savage Wars of Peace: Small Wars and the Rise of American Power* (New York: Basic Books, 2002), 129–204; and George C. Herring, *From Colony to Superpower: US Foreign Relations Since 1776* (Oxford: Oxford University Press, 2008), 378–398.

6. Josephus Daniels, *The Wilson Era: Years of Peace—1910–1917* (Chapel Hill: University of North Carolina Press, 1944), 180–207; Boot, *Savage Wars of Peace*, 149–155; Herring, *From Colony to Super Power*, 378–398.

7. *News & Observer*, August 2, 1914, 1.

8. Daniels, *Wilson Era: Years of Peace*, 178.

9. Michael Kazin, *A Godly Hero: The Life of William Jennings Bryan* (New York: Random House, 2006), 233.

10. Josephus Daniels, *The Cabinet Diaries of Josephus Daniels: 1913–1921*, ed. E. David Cronon (Lincoln: University of Nebraska Press, 1963), 116–117.

11. Daniels, *Cabinet Diaries*, 97; Robert K. Massie, *Castles of Steel: Britain, Germany, and the Winning of the Great War at Sea* (New York: Random House, 2003), 504–506; Diana Preston, *Lusitania: An Epic Tragedy* (New York: Walker & Company, 2002), 70.

12. For an elaboration, see Massie, *Castles of Steel*, 504–506.

13. Josephus Daniels, *The Life of Woodrow Wilson—1856–1924* (New York: Will H. Johnson, 1924), 250.

14. On German naval strategy, see Paul G. Halpern, *A Naval History of World War I.* (Annapolis, MD: United States Naval Institute, 1994), 287–334.

15. Nannie May Tillie, *The Bright Tobacco Industry—1860–1929* (Chapel Hill: University of North Carolina Press, 1948), 354–356; and http://www2.census.gov/prod2/decennial/documents/17862820–1969ch01.pdf, accessed July 9, 2015.

16. Daniels, *Cabinet Diaries*, 97.

17. Josephus Daniels, *The Wilson Era: Years of War—1917–1923* (Chapel Hill: University of North Carolina Press, 1946), 19.

18. Lee A. Craig *Josephus Daniels: His Life and Times* (Chapel Hill: University of North Carolina Press, 2013), 330.

19. For an expanded version of the summary of the US Navy's strategy during the war, see Craig, *Josephus Daniels*, 325–339. For a more general summary of the war at sea, see Hew Strachan, *The First World War* (New York: Viking, Penguin Group, 2003), 201–230. For more comprehensive treatments, see Halpern, *Naval History*, and Massie, *Castles of Steel*.

20. Massie, *Castles of Steel*, 140.

21. Craig, *Josephus Daniels*, 334–335. The idea behind the close blockade was that the blockading navy had to actually station forces off the coast of the blockaded state. In other words, the British could not declare a blockade of Germany and then intercept ships leaving, say, Boston or Buenos Aires that might be destined for Germany. The mining program was championed by Daniels' assistant secretary, Franklin Roosevelt, who was supported by Wilson, the fleet commander, Admiral Henry Mayo, and the navy's representative in London, Admiral William Snowden Sims.

22. Daniels, *Cabinet Diaries*, 228.

23. Craig, *Josephus Daniels*, 335.

24. R. Ernest Dupuy and Trevor N. Dupuy, *The Encyclopedia of Military History from 3500 B.C. to the Present.* 2nd rev. ed. (New York: Harper and Row, 1986), 975.

25. Daniels, *Wilson Era: Years of War*, 69–70.

26. These are nominal figures; even adjusted for inflation, they were high by any historical standard.

27. Tilley, *Bright Tobacco Industry*, 354–356; http://www2.census.gov/prod2/decennial/documents/17862820–1969ch01.pdf, accessed, July 9, 2015.

28. Massie, *Castles of Steel*, 772.

29. Massie, *Castles of Steel*, 772.

30. Daniels, *Wilson Era: Years of War*, 335.

31. Dupuy and Dupuy, *Encyclopedia of Military History*, 990.

32. John Barry, *The Great Influenza: The Epic Story of the Deadliest Plague in History* (New York: Penguin Group, 2004), 4.

33. Joseph L. Morrison, *Josephus Daniels: The Small-d Democrat* (Chapel Hill: University of North Carolina Press, 1966), 103.

PART THREE

Memory

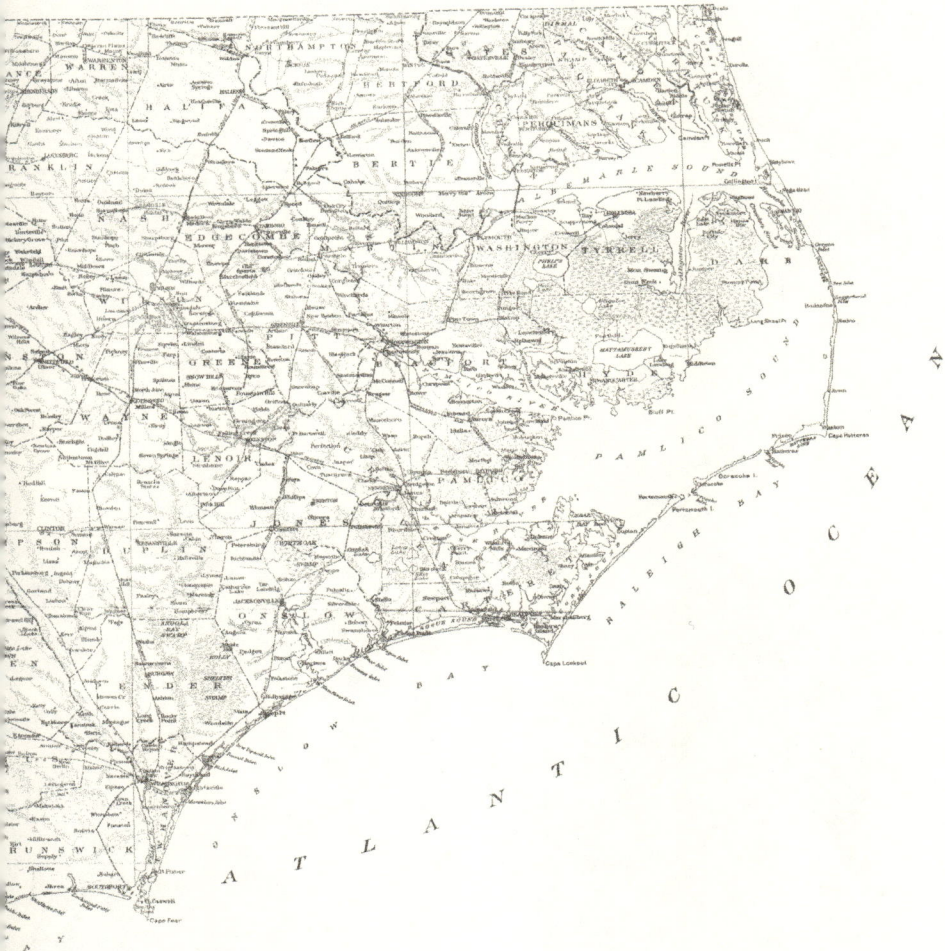

9

"Lest We Forget"

The Literary Works of North Carolina's First World War Soldiers

Melissa Edmundson

In the years following the First World War, there were numerous commemorations of North Carolinians who served in the conflict. The state erected war memorials, Armistice Day celebrations honored NC veterans, and regimental histories were written. However, there is also a unique group of literary works written by the soldiers themselves that provide an intimate portrait of their experiences. This chapter focuses on first-hand accounts of war in contemporary literature from North Carolinians who fought in Europe. These works were published both in wartime and in the years immediately following. Some were published regionally within North Carolina, while others were distributed by national publishing houses. Taken together, these personal narratives give us a unique glimpse into what soldiers were thinking and feeling while on the frontlines, as well as insight into combatants' ideas of honor, duty, and patriotism.

This chapter begins with the perspective of Benjamin Muse, who enlisted in the British Army before America entered the war and who became a German prisoner in 1917. Muse's *The Memoirs of a Swine in the Land of Kultur, or, How it Felt to be a Prisoner of War* (1919) and *Tarheel Tommy Atkins* (1963) took readers into the daily life of a prisoner of war (POW) and provide an eyewitness account of conditions "behind the lines" on the German homefront. Two of North Carolina's most celebrated soldiers, Kiffin Rockwell and James McConnell, also volunteered for foreign service before the United States entered the war, and both men wrote first-hand accounts of their pioneering service with the Lafayette Escadrille in France. Rockwell's numerous letters to family and friends were posthumously published as the *War Letters of Kiffin Yates Rockwell* (1925). McConnell's memoir, *Flying for France*, originally appeared in an abbreviated version in *The World's Work* in November 1916 and as a book the following year. The daring exploits of these two men guaranteed their status as war heroes, especially after their deaths, and captivated an American reading public eager for stories of the war "over there." Finally, this chapter examines the First World War writings of Paul Green. Before Green became one of North Carolina's most famous writers and a Pulitzer Prize-winning playwright, he encountered the desolation of No Man's Land and captured the horrific experiences of war on the frontlines of France in his war poems and letters, as well as in his anti-war play, *Johnny Johnson: The Biography of a Common Man* (1936).

Durham native Benjamin Muse was born on April 17, 1898. After leaving the army at the end of the First World War, Muse served for fourteen years as a US State Department diplomat. In *The Twentieth Century as I Saw It* (1982), Muse credited then-Secretary of the Navy Josephus Daniels with giving him his first opportunity in the diplomatic service. He stated, "Talking to his secretary, I recalled that I had once written Durham High School notes for Daniel's [sic] newspaper the *News and Observer* (Raleigh, NC). Then we got on the subject of my war experiences and he was fascinated. I got a five-minute interview with the Secretary of the Navy, who phoned somebody at State and asked him to find a place for me."[1] After retiring from the State Department in 1934, Muse began his career as an elected official. In 1935 he entered the Virginia Senate as a Democrat but resigned his seat the following year because of his opposition to Roosevelt's New Deal. At the same time, Muse switched to the Republican Party and in 1941 was the Republican nominee for governor of Virginia. Throughout the 1950s and 1960s, Muse gained national attention for his moderate views on southern racial policies. His commentaries were featured in the *Washington Post*'s "Virginia Affairs" column as well as in the *Nation* and the *New Republic*.[2]

Muse served in the Eleventh King's Royal Rifles before the United States entered the war and participated in the battles of Ypres and Cambrai. He was captured by German forces on November 30, 1917, and remained a POW until December 9, 1918. After his release, Muse published his earliest war account in *The Memoirs of a Swine in the Land of Kultur*.[3] In the book, Muse skillfully captured the day-to-day struggles of a POW, including quite a few humorous encounters along the way. After his capture, he described his trip to the German camp as "a hungry nightmare."[4] It was during this journey that Muse witnessed the extent of civilian suffering under German rule in occupied areas of France. Despite this, he remembered the generosity of the French people as they tried to smuggle the POWs as much food as they could spare from what little supplies they had. Upon his arrival at the German camp, Muse observed, "A prisoner of war camp had many characteristics in common with other communities of human beings. It had its social classes, its great and its humble citizens, its rich and poor."[5] He was lucky enough to be "adopted" by a French POW who had both valuable experience and an ample supply of hidden food and other provisions. The other eight hundred prisoners were not as fortunate and became "shabby, hungry, begging wanderers about the camp."[6] This suffering continued for the first few months of their captivity as Muse witnessed the physical and mental degradation of his fellow soldiers.

Despite continued hardships, the humanity that existed during the war is a recurring theme in Muse's narrative. After Muse failed at an escape attempt, a kindly German guard escorted him back to another farm. While the two were waiting for a train, the guard took Muse for a walk around Gadebusch, and the latter recalled meeting another English prisoner in a German home. The fellow POW was treated well by the family and was a particular favorite of the family's children. These depictions of POWs are in stark contrast to the prisoners described earlier in the memoir, and they highlight the shared experience of the war across nationalities. The ultimate balance between good and bad is also symbolized in Muse's description of "Mad Alek," a sergeant-major who was universally feared and despised by the POWs, and "Good Paul," a French–Alsatian guard who tried to help the prisoners. Muse wrote that he was "as well known to the habitués of the detention barracks as 'Mad Alek' and as cordially loved as the latter was hated."[7]

In his later memoir, *Tarheel Tommy Atkins* (1963), Muse went into further detail about his war experiences as he also demonstrated how his memories and impressions of the war changed over time. While still a student at Trinity College, he briefly supported pro-German causes, to the point of trying to sell subscriptions to *The Fatherland*, until the sinking of the *Lusitania* in May 1915 changed his mind about Germany. In this later re-envisioning of his war experiences, Muse gave greater emphasis to the problem of propaganda during the time. After seeing posters of Germans as the wicked "Huns," he recalled, "I wondered why we had not discovered the fact before. I found no such picture of Germans in books written before this war."[8] In the memoir, Muse also presented himself as a much more reflective person than in his earlier narrative, no doubt speaking from his many years of experience. He found bayonet practice troubling and "wondered sometimes if a civilization that could only be preserved by teaching youths to disembowel the living bodies of other human beings had not already ceased to be civilization."[9] In this retelling, readers also get a more detailed account of Muse's British Army service before he became a POW. He called the Third Battle of Ypres in July 1917 a place of tremendous loss of human life, and while being bombarded in the trenches, imagined that his death would make the front page of the *Durham* (North Carolina) *Morning Herald* and the *Durham Sun*. In November 1917, Muse also took part in the First Battle of Cambrai, and by the end of the month, was taken prisoner. He remembered, "The war in a sense was over for us. It was all a matter of a few seconds, but no war memory is more vivid for me than that of this moment of transition to the status of a noncombatant. I had a sudden feeling of relief at danger vanishing, and a flash of satisfaction at the new adventure that opened before me."[10] Another vivid memory was the announcement of the Armistice, about which he said: "Out of all the confusion this was a solid, comprehensible and wonderful event. I did not discuss it with any German, and I celebrated only a little while with my excited English comrades. My thoughts went back to North Carolina, and to the crowds that must be cheering in the streets of London and New York and Paris."[11]

After the war ended, Muse gained an even greater appreciation for the importance of moderation, something that defined his later career as a diplomat and politician. While spending time in London after leaving Germany, he witnessed the lingering lack of sympathy for Germany: "I found no spark of sympathy in England for the now prostrate and bleeding enemy. . . . Tommy Atkins was receiving the praise which he richly deserved, but all the slurs in the book were being heaped upon poor Fritz. No one suggested charity, or binding up Europe's wounds."[12] During this time, he also wrote to his father about how his time in Germany taught him to be more sympathetic: "I am disappointed in the attitude here—the gloating, and the abuse of the defeated enemy. It seems to cheapen the whole triumph, and lower the war from the level of a righteous crusade to that of a hideous, aimless brawl. Perhaps I have absorbed something of the German point of view."[13] Muse kept this letter his entire life as a symbol of the lessons he learned in the war. Through his writing—including his published memoirs, journalism, and books on the civil rights movement—he spent his life trying to convince others of the dangers of extremist views and the importance of cultural understanding.

Of all the North Carolinians who served in the First World War, Kiffin Rockwell inspired the most published tributes following his death in 1916. This includes Paul Rockwell's 1925 edition of his brother's letters, which give an even more complete picture of Kiffin's experiences in the war. He was born in Newport, Tennessee, on September 20, 1892. His father, James Chester Rockwell, was a native of Whiteville, North Carolina, and according to Paul, Kiffin "should have been born in Eastern Carolina, the country of his parents."[14] However, the family moved to eastern Tennessee before his birth for what was thought to be a healthier climate. When Kiffin was fourteen, his mother, Dr. Loula Ayres Rockwell, moved the family to Asheville, where he attended Asheville High School from 1906 to 1908. After his father's death when Kiffin was just six years old, Rockwell grew up listening to the war stories of his maternal grandfather, Enoch Shaw Ayres, and decided to one day pursue his own military career. In 1908, he entered Virginia Military Institute, but left in 1909 when he was awarded an appointment to the United States Naval Academy. Not seeing much opportunity for military action in the navy, Rockwell moved back to Virginia and joined Paul at Washington and Lee University where his favorite subject was history.[15]

Rockwell's letters to his mother reveal his motivations for volunteering to serve in the French Army and stand as an important example of wartime communications between battlefront and homefront. Writing from New York before sailing for Europe in early August 1914, Rockwell wrote, "You have always told me that you wanted me to live my life without interference and this opportunity is one that only comes once in a lifetime."[16] After receiving a letter from his mother, who pleaded with her two enlisted sons to come home, Rockwell wrote a prophetic letter in which he again tried to reassure his mother while also trying to convince her that fighting in the war was something that he must do: "If I should be killed in this war I will at least die as a man should and would not consider myself a complete failure."[17]

In a January 1915 letter to Paul, Kiffin described his anxiety and unhappiness with his current post in the French Foreign Legion, saying that the combination of physical and mental stress, combined with the seemingly endless hours of guard duty, was wearing him down. He asked his brother to obtain a transfer for him, anticipating his later requests to join the flying corps, and after that, to leave the Lafayette Escadrille for a French flying unit. After his time in the trenches, his purpose became clearer, and this desire to make a difference would become the single-minded tenacity he showed as a member of the Lafayette Escadrille. In November 1915, he wrote to Alice Weeks, the mother of a fellow soldier who died in the war and to whom Rockwell referred as his "second mother" and "Aunt Alice": "I feel that I have many scores to settle, and there is going to be more than one 'Boche' aviator to settle them, or I will not live to tell the tale."[18]

Rockwell's need to be understood and remembered as a person unselfishly sacrificing for the benefit of others extended to his letters to Weeks. Returning to active duty after being badly wounded in the leg, he wrote to her in an August 1915 letter saying that his injury gave him a renewed purpose to be as effective a soldier as he could. Rockwell reiterated that he was not afraid of dying because a death in war was the most honorable death he could imagine. This sentiment was echoed in a February 1916 letter to his mother, in which he assured her: "If I die, I want you to know that I have died as every man ought to die fighting for what is right. I do not feel that I am fighting for France alone, but for the cause of all humanity, the greatest of all causes."[19]

For all the frustration and doubt that Rockwell felt about wanting to make a difference in the war, his legacy as one of the greatest aviators of the First World War is assured. After his death, numerous memorial tributes appeared throughout the United States. In 1920, the North Carolina Society Daughters of the American Revolution published a booklet centered on "Great Events in North Carolina History." The concluding essay, written by Robert Burton House, discusses Rockwell. A native of Halifax County, House also experienced war first hand. He served as a lieutenant in the American Expeditionary Forces from 1917 to 1918. After the war, from 1919 to 1924, he served as archivist and Collector of World War Records for the North Carolina Historical Commission.[20] House prefaced his essay with the disclaimer that although Rockwell's story was more recent history, it deserved a place alongside the Colonial, Revolutionary, and Confederate eras. From the beginning of the essay, House foregrounded Rockwell's central importance in the Lafayette Escadrille. He listed the many "firsts" attached to Rockwell's name, such as being "the first North Carolinian to give his life in the world war, the first American volunteer for service in France, the first American to bring down a German plane," as well as being "the premier fighter of his time in the Escadrille Lafayette."[21] House described the many victories Rockwell had as the "Aristocrat of the Air" and concluded his essay by stressing Rockwell's symbolic importance to other American soldiers. [22]

Just as Kiffin Rockwell was born outside of North Carolina but later moved to the state, so too did James McConnell. He was born in Chicago on March 14, 1887, the son of Samuel and Sarah Rogers McConnell. Samuel McConnell worked as a lawyer and later as a circuit court judge, from 1872 to 1894. He then moved the family to New York City. In 1907 James McConnell enrolled at the University of Virginia. While he was at the university, McConnell was active in many clubs and organizations, including his role as president of the Aero Club of Virginia, which he co-founded in 1909. After leaving the university in 1910, McConnell moved to Carthage, North Carolina, joining his father at the Randolph and Cumberland Railway, where James served as the industrial and land agent. He also assumed a post as the secretary of the Carthage Board of Trade.[23] In this position, McConnell used his abilities as a professional writer to create promotional materials for Carthage and surrounding Sandhills areas.[24] In January 1915, McConnell volunteered as a driver for the American Ambulance Corps in France. He won the Croix de Guerre for his efforts with the corps and also pursued work as a war correspondent, writing for *Outlook* and *World's Work*.[25]

While he was recovering from a back injury sustained during a plane crash in August 1916, McConnell started the manuscript that would become *Flying for France* (1917). He continued to work on the manuscript while convalescing in Paris at the home of Alice Weeks. In early February 1917, McConnell wrote to Weeks confirming that Frank C. Page, editor of Doubleday Page and Company, had received the manuscript and that the book would be published on February 20.[26] *Flying for France* was well received by the public and is considered by many to be the best account of the Lafayette Escadrille. James Norman Hall and Charles Nordhoff, in their two-volume *The Lafayette Flying Corps* (1920), stated, "His sunny humanity, close and humorous powers of observation, and knack of vivid description lent an unusual charm to his writings, and his book 'Flying for France,' which appeared before our declaration of war, did genuine patriotic service in forming public opinion during the period preliminary to hostilities."[27] Likewise, Paul Rockwell called *Flying for France*, "The first, and by far the best book, written by a pilot of the Escadrille Lafayette." He claimed that it was a "simply and splendidly told story of the early days of the Escadrille . . . and when brought out in book form ran through many editions. Its winning and likeable style, characteristic of its author, made it extremely popular."[28] In writing his book, McConnell was contributing to a burgeoning area of fiction that was enjoying widespread popularity among readers. Robert Wohl notes that in the decade before the First World War, the aviation narrative emerged as a distinct literary genre and that "[f]lying and literature . . . were more compatible than anyone could have imagined."[29] These narratives combined the excitement of flying with the unique perspective of the pilot seeing objects on earth at a great distance and frequently interspersed autobiographical details about the pilots with descriptions of the reception they received once the plane landed.[30] Aviation narratives written during the war incorporate these general conventions with an added emphasis on the danger of flying missions over the battlefield.

In *Flying for France*, McConnell gave his readers a first-hand glimpse into the daily life of the Lafayette Escadrille members, from mundane daily routines to daring air battles. Early in the narrative, McConnell set the scene, describing how the American airmen looked to French infantry soldiers and highlighting the cultural anomaly these airmen represented when the escadrille was first founded: "Why is an aviator in a French uniform speaking a foreign tongue, they mutually ask themselves. . . . They learn that they are witnessing the return of the American Escadrille—composed of Americans who have volunteered to fly for France for the duration of the war—to their station near Bar-le-Duc, twenty-five miles south of Verdun." To McConnell, this "fascination" with the escadrille came from the combination of flying and fighting and the novelty of each. This same fascination appealed to McConnell, but he also stressed his need to make a difference in the war. He became increasingly dissatisfied with his position in the American Ambulance Service because he felt he was not doing enough to actively fight against the Germans.[31]

Like Kiffin Rockwell, McConnell took pride in fighting for the French, and he described his "elation" on his arrival to the airfield as "second only to my satisfaction at being a French soldier."[32] For the American newcomers, there was also a chance to restore individual personality. He recalled, "Warfare in the air was as novel to them as to me. For us all it contained unlimited possibilities for initiative and service to France, and for them it must have meant, too, the restoration of personality lost during those months in the trenches with the Foreign Legion."[33] However, with this excitement and special treatment came the reality of the dangerous nature of their work: "I thought of the luxury we were enjoying: our comfortable beds, baths, and motor cars, and then I recalled the ancient custom of giving a man selected for the sacrifice a royal time of it before the appointed day."[34] Death was mentioned only on rare occasions and was something on which the pilots tried not to dwell. This ability to deal with—and even to court—danger on a daily basis was fitting for the larger-than-life personalities represented in the escadrille.[35] For McConnell, there was a certain psyche that the *pilotes de chasse* possessed that made them unique. With his characteristic humor, he remarked, "In France, there's a saying that to be an aviator one must be a bit 'off.'"[36]

McConnell also provided detailed descriptions of what the landscape looked like from 13,000 feet in the air, and perhaps better than any other aviation narrative of the time, captured the experience of flying for his earthbound audience back home. Other planes became "the merest pinpoints against the great sweep of landscape below"; the clouds "appear as a solid bank of white," and it was "like being in an Arctic ice field" as the Alps became "majestic icebergs." From this height, the trenches resembled "a series of brown, woodworm-like tracings on the ground." Flying over the Verdun battlefield, McConnell described seeing the German planes as "a dull white in appearance, resembling sand flies against the mottled earth. High above them one glimpses the mosquito-like forms of two Fokkers."[37] Later in the narrative, McConnell provided an aerial description of Verdun. He said that though the pilots could not see details of the trenches, they could see the "broad, browned band" where the battle had taken place. He continued, "It is a great strip of murdered Nature. Trees, houses, and even roads have been blasted completely away. The shell holes were so numerous that they blended into one another and could not be separately seen."[38] When the escadrille arrived near the Somme battlefront, the action increased. The scene was complete with planes "darting like swallows in the shrapnel puffs of anti-air-craft fire," roaring motors, "the staccato barking of machine guns," and "the hollow whistling sound of a fast plane diving to earth." McConnell showed his skill as a writer as he described these sights and sounds as a "symphony of war notes."[39]

Several sections of *Flying for France* were devoted to McConnell's fellow North Carolinian, Kiffin Rockwell. He recalled Rockwell's first victory and the wound caused when an illegal explosive bullet hit his plane's windshield, resulting in several lacerations on his face.[40] McConnell also described Rockwell's death in detail, as well as his funeral and the effect his loss had on the morale of the escadrille. McConnell memorializes his close friend by focusing on Rockwell's legacy:

> No greater blow could have befallen the escadrille. Kiffin was its soul. He was loved and looked up to by not only every man in our flying corps but by every one who knew him. Kiffin was imbued with the spirit of the cause for which he fought and gave his heart and soul to the performance of his

duty. He said: "I pay my part for Lafayette and Rochambeau," and he gave the fullest measure. The old flame of chivalry burned brightly in this boy's fine and sensitive being. With his death France lost one of her most valuable pilots. When he was over the lines the Germans did not pass—and he was over them most of the time.[41]

Before and after their deaths in the skies above France, the aerial exploits of Kiffin Rockwell and James McConnell captured the public's attention on both sides of the Atlantic. Poetry was written about them, and newspaper articles and other memorials to their lives and military careers continued to be published into the 1920s and beyond. Statues were erected in Carthage and on the University of Virginia campus to honor McConnell, and a state historical marker in Asheville honors Rockwell's legacy. One hundred years after their deaths, the wartime writings of these men are still alive with the spirit and energy that defined the members of the Lafayette Escadrille.

In July 1917, Paul Green left the University of North Carolina, where he had enrolled as a freshman a year earlier, and enlisted in the North Carolina Engineers. After finishing basic training at Camp Sevier near Greenville, South Carolina, he quickly rose to the rank of sergeant by November. In May 1918, Green set sail for Europe, a journey that would take him far from Harnett County, where he was born on his family's farm on March 17, 1894, and where he graduated from Buies Creek Academy in 1914. The 105th Engineers of the 30th Division were tasked with setting up explosives, laying mines, and hanging communication lines. This work meant that they were constantly close to the frontlines, and the unit witnessed the intense fighting that led to the fall of the Hindenburg Line in September 1918. In October, Green was sent to Officers Candidate School in Langres, France. From December until June the next year, he served as a clerk in the US Army Purchasing Office with the rank of second lieutenant.[42]

Despite the rigors of camp life, Green remained devoted to his writing. While at Camp Sevier, he published several poems under the title, "Songs of a Soldier," in the Greenville *Daily News*. In November 1917, he wrote to his father, saying that the poems "ease me inside," and although they dominated his spare time, the poems "help me no little in mastering the English language." He then described how important writing was to him and to his future: "There are *only* two reasons that I especially wish to come safely through this war. One is for the sake of the homefolks; the other is that I may write something worthwhile."[43] In many ways, army life provided Green with the impetus to begin a professional writing career. During his time at Camp Sevier, Green paid for thirty copies of his collection of poems, *Trifles of Thought* (1917), to be published so that if he died, people would know that he intended to be a writer.[44]

Once Green saw the frontlines, he came to a greater understanding of the costs of war. He saw the shallow graves of soldiers while his unit was fighting near Ypres and recalled the deafening sound of continuous shell blasts. The unrelenting stress of No Man's Land eventually caused Green to suffer from shellshock. In late August, he wrote several entries in his diary that mentioned his mental state, saying that "the everlasting bombardments have put my head into a sort of shell-shock condition. Nervous! Nervous!"[45] During these times, writing poetry helped him relax, yet the haunting images of No Man's Land were always with him. In an August 1918 letter to his sister Erma, Green expressed his growing disturbance at witnessing the human cost of war: "Not long ago I was on an old battlefield. We were digging trenches. One could hardly push his spade into the ground without striking a bone of somebody's boy. Yes, horrible; but war. And a few days ago, I was at another place where 54,000 men 'went west' in one day. Awful! Yes, but war."[46] He finished this letter with a poem that would later become "A Thought in Ypres." In language reminiscent of John McCrae's "In Flanders Fields" (1915), Green's poem commemorates those lost in the war:

> If deep within the earth I lay
> And learned, old friends, that you had lost
> Or quit the game for which we paid
> Such bitter cost,
> I feel that death would fail to hold
> Me there in slumber with the dead,
> Tho' drowsy poppies held their cups
> Above my bed.[47]

Green's poetry written during this time showed his progression from naïve enlistee to hardened frontline soldier. His early poems were full of patriotic statements about what he and many other new soldiers thought was the grand fight ahead. In one of his earliest pieces, "Men of America," Green began with language befitting a propaganda poster, "Men of America! / The whole world breathless waits on thee / Arise and grasp thy vengeful steel / To save endangered liberty."[48] This same sentiment pervaded "And Slam the Bullets Home, Boys," in which Green depended on jingoistic abstractions that lack the personal elements of his later poems: "Uncle Sam and all his men / Have come across the sea / To beat the *Boches* back again, / And set the people free."[49] In "Who Knows the Worth?," Green again showed his distance from the battlefields, admitting, "But some have said that war is hell. / Perhaps it is; I do not know."[50] Once he was on the battlefront in France, this limited perspective was soon broadened, and with it, his poetry.

After only a month in the trenches, Green's writing became more personal and complex. In "They're Dying To-night," the realities of the battlefield take center stage from the opening lines: "They're dying to-night, they're dying to-night / Out where the S.O.S. flares bright. / Here in Flanders in the mud and rain,

/ Down on the Somme, the Marne, and the Aisne." The concluding lines stress the uncertain territorial gains amidst the more certain human losses: "And ye shall know when the battle's done / What the living gain when the dead have won."[51] During the summer and fall of 1918, Green's poetry took on an even more serious tone. In June 1918, he wrote "In the Dark Night," which ends with a vision of the mental abyss that the poem's speaker faces, "In the cold night I've seen vast things— / The black, black pit, an empty hungry space, / And lured unto its edge I've felt / The moths of death beat in my face."[52] This bears a striking similarity to Green's own experience with shellshock and his description of the dark pit that he imagined seeing on the battlefield.[53] The fear of an all-encompassing black hole followed Green from his childhood days and became even more foreboding during the war. Yet Green channeled his connection with North Carolina into other forms of poetic tribute. A fellow soldier from Harnett County, a close friend of both Paul and his brother Hugh, was killed in action in October 1918. "Rass Matthews" is Green's memorial to his friend:

> But who would weep for him, this glorious youth,
> So full of youth, so lithe, so brave, so great
> Altho' we'll never see his like again?
> His life was strong, his death a burning truth.
> And in my heart I'll keep inviolate
> The memory of a man who died for men.[54]

As the poet, Green will be the one to "weep" for Matthews and also capture his uniqueness, telling readers that "we'll never see his like again." In this passage, Green personalized the poem and foregrounded the importance of the individual among many. This one human loss represented a greater sacrifice, "a man who died for men."

In Green's later poems, written in November 1918, a deepening social consciousness is present. In "Sixteen Doughboys We Dumped in One Hole," Green concluded with the pessimism of one who had witnessed such an impersonal mass burial. He undeceived his audience, saying, "Writing your prayers on time's dark scroll, / Know ye, 'tis all a bootless pain. / As the cycles wheel and writhe and roll. / As the stars go out in the inky bowl."[55] "Voices from the Jug" concerns the harsh treatment of twenty-two American prisoners, who according to Green's note to the poem, "were kept in a hole large enough for six and fit for none." After cleaning latrines and loading trucks, they were consigned to their "dungeon" to "bed like the brutes." In this poem that prefigures the social consciousness that would become such a part of his later works, Green highlighted the inhumanity of war as well as the class divide that existed between officers and enlisted men: "Where once they have lived and were happy, / where once they were children and free, / And while we live here in our misery, the C.O. / will be taking his tea."[56]

Green later returned to the First World War in the three-act play *Johnny Johnson* (1936), a collaboration with Kurt Weill. Set during 1917 at the beginning of American involvement in the war, the play opens in a small southern town (no doubt inspired by Green's early years in Harnett County) with the unveiling of a monument to celebrate the colonial peace treaty between the white settlers and Native Americans. Johnny Johnson, a twenty-five-year-old monument artist, is applauded by the peace-loving townspeople until the mayor receives official word that President Woodrow Wilson has declared war on Germany.[57] Their isolationist principles quickly give way to war fever, but Johnny remains unsure about the war. He eventually enlists and is sent to the front where his attempts to end the war by peaceful means cause him to be labeled insane. Johnny Johnson's overall outlook is summed up early in the play when he states that "war is about the low-downest thing the human race can indulge in. Add up all the good in it and it's still a total loss."[58] Though Green had a low opinion of war strategy and the generals overseeing it, an opinion that he made clear in both his war poetry and *Johnny Johnson*, he did not waver in the ultimate goal of the war. He wrote in his diary, "Perhaps I'm worth more doing the job I am than I would be firing a rifle. Anyway, I will do anything that is asked of me for this the supreme cause. These days of horror and unthinkable happenings strike one mute."[59]

Yet North Carolinians who served in the First World War were not "mute." As early as 1917, John Wilber Jenkins claimed that North Carolina had "'done her bit' for the Allies on the firing lines."[60] A few years after the war's end, this sentiment was echoed in J. R. Graham's *Tar-Heel War Record* (1921): "North Carolina may well feel a strong thrill of pride when the noble enterprise of its men and women during the period of the great world conflict is rehearsed. . . . How many times a North Carolinian's name went down into imperishable fame for deeds of valor and self sacrifice in behalf of the greatest cause of all time."[61] In addition to "doing their bit" to help the war effort, Benjamin Muse, Kiffin Rockwell, James McConnell, and Paul Green also contributed a literary legacy to North Carolina in World War I. Their wide range of writings—from memoirs and letters to poetry and drama—stands as a testament to the bravery of the many North Carolinians who left small towns and family farms to travel thousands of miles to fight for their country. The first-hand narratives these soldiers left behind are important complements to the more general historical studies and biographies of the war. While these histories tell us about the vital role North Carolina men and women played in the First World War—both at the battlefront and homefront—the literature of war goes even deeper, giving modern readers an insight into the individual soldier's struggles, sacrifices, ambitions, and triumphs. These literary works also show the progression of memory itself. After millions of casualties on the battlefields of Europe, innocence was inevitably lost. The positive, uncomplicated war narratives such as Benjamin Muse's *Memoirs of a Swine in the Land of Kultur* and James

McConnell's *Flying for France*, which were published during the First World War and immediately following, could no longer be written. As Paul Green's play shows, by 1936, a society who had experienced the Depression and the rise of fascism and who saw another world war looming in Europe could no longer reminisce so easily about the "Great War," the war to end all wars.

Notes

1. Benjamin Muse, *The Twentieth Century as I Saw It* (New York: Carlton Press, 1982), 120.

2. Matthew D. Lassiter, "Benjamin Muse (1898–1986)," *Encyclopedia Virginia* (Virginia Foundation for the Humanities, April 7, 2011), http://encyclopediavirginia.org. During the 1960s, Muse continued to write about the civil rights movement in *Virginia's Massive Resistance* (1961), *Ten Years of Prelude* (1964), and *The American Negro Revolution* (1968).

3. *Memoirs* was published by Seeman Printery in Durham, North Carolina, which was founded in 1885. In 1917, Ernest Seeman took over the family business and ran the printery until 1923. In 1925, Seeman became head of Duke Press.

4. Benjamin Muse, *The Memoirs of a Swine in the Land of Kultur, or, How It Felt to be a Prisoner of War* (Durham, NC: Seeman Printery, 1919), 7.

5. Muse, *Memoirs*, 9.

6. Muse, *Memoirs*, 9.

7. Muse, *Memoirs*, 41.

8. Benjamin Muse, *Tarheel Tommy Atkins* (New York: Vantage Press, 1963), 12.

9. Muse, *Tarheel*, 30.

10. Muse, *Tarheel*, 71.

11. Muse, *Tarheel*, 130.

12. Muse, *Tarheel*, 136, 137.

13. Muse, *Tarheel*, 138.

14. Robert Burton House, "Kiffin Yates Rockwell," *The North Carolina Booklet* 19.4/20.1 (April–July 1920): 150–155; Paul Rockwell, "Introduction," *War Letters of Kiffin Yates Rockwell: Foreign Legionnaire and Aviator, France 1914–1916*, ed. Paul Ayres Rockwell (Garden City, NY: Country Life Press, 1925), ix.

15. Rockwell, "Introduction," *War Letters*, xiii, xv.

16. Rockwell, *War Letters*, 1.

17. Rockwell, *War Letters*, 7.

18. Rockwell, *War Letters*, 111. A native of Massachusetts, Alice Standish Weeks moved to Paris in 1915 to be closer to her son, Kenneth, who was fighting with the French Foreign Legion. After Kenneth's death in June 1916, Weeks became a surrogate mother for many of the American soldiers in Paris. She also helped to organize the Home Service for the American Soldiers. During the war, Weeks maintained correspondence with several American members of the Foreign Legion and the Lafayette Escadrille. She collected these letters in her book *Greater Love Hath No Man* (1939). For Weeks's biography, see Dennis Gordon, *Lafayette Escadrille Pilot Biographies* (Missoula, MT: Doughboy Historical Society, 1991), 259.

19. Rockwell, *War Letters*, 116.

20. William S. Powell, "Robert Burton House," *Dictionary of North Carolina Biography*, Vol. 3, ed. William S. Powell (Chapel Hill: University of North Carolina Press, 1988), 210.

21. House, "Kiffin Yates Rockwell," 151.

22. House, "Kiffin Yates Rockwell," 154.

23. Dennis Gordon, *Lafayette Escadrille Pilot Biographies* (Missoula, MT: Doughboy Historical Society, 1991), 39; Sarah McCulloh Lemmon, "James Rogers McConnell," *Dictionary of North Carolina Biography*, Vol. 4, ed. William S. Powell (Chapel Hill: University of North Carolina Press, 1991), 128.

24. Sarah McCulloh Lemmon, "James Rogers McConnell," *Dictionary of North Carolina Biography*, Vol. 4, ed. William S. Powell (Chapel Hill: University of North Carolina Press, 1991), 128; Thomas C. Parramore, *First to Fly: North Carolina and the Beginnings of Aviation* (Chapel Hill: University of North Carolina Press, 2002), 209–210.

25. McConnell's "With the American Ambulance in France" was published in the September 1915 issue of *Outlook* (111: 125–144). Another series of reports about life in the Lafayette Escadrille, which would later become part of *Flying for France*, was published in the November 1916 and March 1917 issues of *World's Work* (33: 41–53, 497–509).

26. Gordon, *Lafayette Escadrille*, 41.

27. James Norman Hall and Charles Bernard Nordhoff, eds., *The Lafayette Flying Corps*, 2 vols. (Boston: Houghton Mifflin Company, 1920), 343.

28. Paul Rockwell, "Writings of the American Pilots in the Escadrille Lafayette," *Ex Libris* 1.5 (November 1923): 131.

29. Robert Wohl, *A Passion for Wings: Aviation and the Western Imagination, 1908–1918* (New Haven: Yale University Press, 1996), 271.

30. Wohl, *A Passion for Wings*, 271.

31. James R. McConnell, *Flying for France: With the American Escadrille at Verdun* (Garden City, NY: Doubleday, Page, and Company, 1917), 7, 8.

32. McConnell, *Flying for France*, 16.

33. McConnell, *Flying for France*, 21.

34. McConnell, *Flying for France*, 26.

35. In a light-hearted passage, McConnell says that their daily routines often consisted of either excitement in the air or extreme boredom on the ground. When the group moved to Luxeuil in 1916, only five Nieuport planes arrived with them. He says that during this time, "It was about as much like war as a Bryan lecture. While I was in the hospital I received a letter written at this time from one of the boys. I opened it expecting to read of an air combat. It informed me that [Bill] Thaw had caught a trout three feet long, and that [Raoul] Lufbery [the Lafayette Escadrille's ace] had picked two baskets of mushrooms," 84.

36. McConnell, *Flying for France*, 70–71.

37. McConnell, *Flying for France*, 28, 29, 30, 58.

38. McConnell, *Flying for France*, 130.

39. McConnell, *Flying for France*, 118, 119.

40. An explosive bullet was also the cause of Kiffin Rockwell's death. According to McConnell, when Rockwell's body was found, "there was a hideous wound in his breast where an explosive bullet had torn through." Later, a surgeon who examined his body stated that Rockwell would most likely have been able to land if he had been shot with an ordinary bullet (*Flying*, 95).

41. McConnell, *Flying for France*, 96–97.

42. Laurence G. Avery, ed., *A Southern Life: Letters of Paul Green, 1916–1981* (Chapel Hill: University of North Carolina Press, 1994), xv-xvi.

43. Green quoted in Avery, *A Southern Life*, 6.

44. James R. Spence, *Watering the Sahara: Recollections of Paul Green from 1894–1937*, ed. Margaret D. Bauer (Raleigh: Office of Archives and History, North Carolina Department of Cultural Resources, 2008), 56.

45. Green quoted in Spence, *Watering the Sahara*, 71.

46. Green quoted in Avery, *A Southern Life*, 10.

47. Green quoted in Avery, *A Southern Life*, 13.

48. John Herbert Roper, ed., *Paul Green's War Songs: A Southern Poet's History of the Great War, 1917–1920* (Rocky Mount, NC: North Carolina Wesleyan College Press, 1993), 6.

49. Green, *War Songs*, 20.

50. Green, *War Songs*, 13.

51. Green, *War Songs*, 36.

52. Green, *War Songs*, 43.

53. For Green's description of this hole and how it symbolized his experience with shell-shock, see James R. Spence's interview in *Watering the Sahara,* 68–69.

54. Green, *War Songs*, 57.

55. Green, *War Songs*, 65.

56. Green, *War Songs*, 66.

57. In a February 1974 interview with Rhoda Wynn, Paul Green said that he wrote to the United States War Department inquiring about the most common name used in the army during the war. The response was that "more than 5,000 John Johnsons" had served in the American Expeditionary Forces (Green quoted in Spence, *Watering the Sahara*, 217).

58. Paul Green, *Johnny Johnson: The Biography of a Common Man* (New York: Samuel French, 1971), 24.

59. Green quoted in Spence, *Watering the Sahara*, 74.

60. John Wilber Jenkins, *North Carolina's Part in the War* (Greenville, NC: East Carolina Teachers Training School, 1917), 5.

61. J. R. Graham, *Tar-Heel War Record* (Charlotte: World War Publishing Company, 1921), 5.

10

"The Means of Instilling That Spirit of Americanism"

North Carolina, Cultural Memory, and the First World War

Shannon Bontrager

Northern memories had dominated American cultural memory since the Civil War.[1] North Carolina elites collaborated with citizens across the socio-economic spectrum to fashion a cultural memory from the First World War synchronizing their southern identity with a hegemonic national identity. North Carolinians selectively remembered a past that redefined the Great War as a national victory intimately tied to southern redemption. The World War I Collection at the North Carolina State Archives provides a snapshot of how this process was carried out. This collection not only contains the documents from which histories were made, but also includes the memories of people who experienced the war.[2] Thus this collection straddles the worlds of history and memory and provides details of the collaboration between state elites and citizens who sought to strategically maneuver the state into a position of historic national importance. But this came with the cost of alienating and even excluding the memories of families and individuals whose experiences failed to elevate southern identity in North Carolina and within the cultural memory of Americans.

Although archives served to support the history of the state, they often included the memories of people whose eyewitness accounts could potentially undermine, or at least critique, the cultural purpose of archival collections. The so-called "Archival Turn" articulated perhaps most famously by Jacques Derrida as "archive fever" but investigated recently and more rigorously by historians such as Ann Laura Stoler, suggests that scholars should view the archive not only as a repository of knowledge but also as a technological form that produced knowledge with a specific agenda in place.[3] Stoler encourages scholars to read "*along* the archival grain" first before "brush[ing] *against* the archive's received categories" to understand its "regularities, for its logic of recall, for its densities and distributions, for its consistencies of misinformation, omission, and mistake." Scholars must recognize the power dynamics of the colonial archive so that they can understand just "how much colonial history-writing has been shaped by nationalist historiographies and nation-bound projects."[4] By using the methods of the archival turn, scholars can view the World War I collection as a topography of colonialism within southern identity.

For those North Carolinians who operated the geopolitical levers and pulleys of the state to legitimate their own rule, the archives became a valuable institution of memory, knowledge, and power. They hoped to shape both their present and future by using the archives to show the origins and authority of a cultural memory of the state. Elites defined citizens' involvement in the First World War as a modified continuation of past collective memories stemming from the Lost Cause and the New South, both of which harkened back to the South's losing the Civil War. Now on the winning side of war, state leaders used the archives to document their success, which was embedded in memories of racial purity, "one hundred percent Americanism," and White Anglo-Saxon Protestantism. Remembering the role of North Carolina at the centenary of the First World War provides an important opportunity to assess the effectiveness of the archives and the collective memory built from them.

Progressive North Carolina officials attempted to modernize the state by building institutions that added structure, texture, and authority to North Carolina society.[5] Before the war, state elites were eager, suggests historian Catherine W. Bishir, to generate an "historical awakening" among citizens in the state. They used architectural styles and monumental depictions "as part of their reclamation of regional and national power." These elites, suggests Bishir, largely succeeded by publishing local histories and writing state history textbooks that eliminated alternative narratives. "With competing visions of the state's past, present, and future all but silent in official discourse, these leaders shared a powerful sense that both in politics and in the culture at large, matters had been returned to their correct alignment."[6] To the elites, the South's cultural tradition based on white, Anglo-Saxon, southern-male, Protestantism seemed under renewed assault after the war. The World War I collection was an extension of the pre-war attempts by North Carolina elites to control the history and memory of the state. Officials viewed the archive as an institution that would restore order and authenticity to the splintering memories that were proliferating in the post-war world. Just as the archives organized peoples' memories, they also housed the documents that would make history.

These efforts had their peculiar origins in President Woodrow Wilson's Council of Defense, in which federal authorities collaborated with state and local volunteers to support the war by raising money and materials. This federal institution helped state officials throughout the country build local chapters, and millions of people participated. North Carolina officials, like their counterparts in other states, organized citizens' domestic war efforts on the county level through the North Carolina Council of Defense. Communities in North Carolina were historically dispersed and had few institutions such as roads, libraries, and schools that connected the agrarian tobacco and cotton archipelagos to the state's urban centers of control. As progressive politicians gained influence in the state, they slowly tried to transform the topography in their state. The war and the accompanying Council of Defense expanded this process by aiding state officials who sought to shape the agrarian hinterlands that had remained largely out of their reach. The Council of Defense apparatus, government officials hoped, would traverse the geography of the state in ways that roads and libraries could not. Thus state officials sought out local rural elites who could reach out to their friends, families, and constituents, face to face, and then link them back to state officials in Raleigh.

Southern Progressive Governor Thomas W. Bickett organized the state's Council and put at its head Dr. Daniel Harvey Hill Jr. of Raleigh. The second son of Confederate General D. H. Hill, the new chairman held doctorate degrees in literature from Davidson College and law from the University of North Carolina. In 1916, he had resigned his position as President of the College of Agriculture and Mechanics Arts (now North Carolina State University) and now was a member of the North Carolina Historical Commission and United Daughters of the Confederacy (UDC). He had written several textbooks on the state's history and the Confederate military. He was positioned solidly within the elite pre-war "historical awakening" movement.[7] It was Hill's wartime task to line up local elites in each county to serve on committees responsible for doing the domestic work of supporting the war. County committees organized Four Minute Men programs; implemented fuel rationing policies; created War Bond drives; developed sanitation, conservation, and historical preservation policies; and established countless other ways to support the war. State officials naturally chose to keep the Council of Defense functioning after the war to support the post-war memory project they hoped would commemorate and document North Carolinian contributions to the war's success. The Council of Defense provided state officials with a network to collect post-war memories.

Even before the armistice, state officials were using this network to shape the memory of the state's fallen warriors. As early as June 1918, J. Bryan Grimes—Secretary of State, Board Member of the Council of Defense, and Chairman of the North Carolina Historical Commission—asked Hill to begin making arrangements with county chapters of the Council of Defense to erect memorial plaques listing the names of the men from each county who served and died in the war. Grimes believed that mistaken reports overestimating the number of dead might stymie homefront morale throughout the state. Hill used Council of Defense committees to sift through official records and correct false reports.[8] He insisted that local elite women head these committees. The Secretary asked the North Carolina Historical Commission to aid the Council of Defense in this task.[9] High-level participants of the conservative "historical awakening" movement thus used martial institutions to manage the way people on the homefront understood events happening on the warfront.[10]

Most counties erected these monuments despite an apparent lack of financial assistance from the state legislature. Local fundraising efforts largely supported these projects, demonstrating a collaborative effort between local and government officials to manage the homefront. But collaboration could become messy. Racial controversies arose quickly in some areas of the state. Beaufort County Council of Defense Chairman Junius D. Grimes, a partner in the Ward and Grimes law firm, was concerned about distinguishing between white and black soldiers on the plaques and turned to Hill for guidance. The chairman's response suggests that he had thought little about recognizing black soldiers. He noted that "the matter with what to do with the names of negro soldiers is a perplexing one." At first Hill recommended putting the names of black soldiers on the same tablets as white soldiers but designating them with the label "colored." But Hill then thought that "some of the negroes may object to this designation" so he directed Grimes to leave it up to the "county itself [to] find out the sentiment of its own people." Hill asserted "When a negro goes out and fights for his country and is killed, it looks as though it would not be needful to make any distinction but if the people feel differently about it, their wishes, of course, are entitled to consideration."[11] Of course, the committee members making these determinations were all white.

Grimes and his counterparts began work on the memorials, and the local committees placed tablets in county courthouses before the summer ended. Hill viewed this committee structure as a valuable tool that could continue aiding memorial efforts around the state. By November 1918, the war ended, and Hill sought to reallocate the work of county committees from wartime duties to post-war tasks of document collection. In a letter to A. H. Boyden in Salisbury, Hill congratulated Boyden on the local chairman's work of collecting and "preserving records in your county." He indicated that the Council of Defense would be "glad to keep a complete record of everything done in the county that contributed to the success of the war." This included, Hill proposed, records from county factories supplying war materials, Red Cross chapters, YMCA and YWCA chapters, Jewish Relief, Salvation Army, and Library Association and Belgian Relief activities. The chairman promised that he and others would coordinate the compiling, editing, and publishing of all these war records and stressed to Boyden the importance of this work.[12]

Hill thus supervised county commissioners who began collecting documents that local committees had produced throughout the war, and he tried to commemorate local soldiers who served and died in the conflict. Three observations can be made here. First, this was a civilian project, but it had its origins in a martial institution, the Council of Defense. Second, white committee members segregated the collected materials by race. Although national policymakers recommended that African Americans be included in the wartime Council of Defense through separate but parallel committees, North Carolinian officials—like those in several other southern states—refused to follow these federal guidelines and neglected to build committees that addressed African American roles during the war. This infrastructure remained after the war. Historians must be aware of the inherent colonialism in the state apparatus, in the work of the local and state committees, and in the organization of archival collections. The very infrastructure for obtaining a black civilian record of the war barely existed. Third, elites were well connected politically through various government agencies such as the Council of Defense, as well as culturally through the Historical Commission. These elites largely defined, at least officially, southern identity within the national context, and they worked hard to suppress alternative narratives. Despite this synergy of politics and culture, however, these officials had a daunting historical and geographical task ahead of them. With the state divided into one hundred counties, few roads to connect them, and so many geographically dispersed committees simultaneously producing overlapping work, capturing historical artifacts for state records was difficult. The sheer numbers of souvenirs, artifacts, documents, and memories to capture from each returning soldier added to this daunting task. In addition, there were no universal practices of collection and organization, and local elites had no practical motivation to keep their Council of Defense committees functioning now that the war was over. Since the federal government had no reason to support the Council of Defense, the statewide network became ineffective. To carry on the archival project and recover these objects of memory, elites would have to reorganize their institutions.

They accomplished this by convincing the state legislature, with whom commissioners were obviously well connected, to authorize the Historical Commission to hire a full-time Collector of War Records who would take over the informal work that the committees of the Council of Defense had been doing. Legislators created and funded legislation that decreed "the North Carolina Historical Commission is the legal agent of the State of North Carolina in all matters pertaining to State History, and into its hands has been delegated the responsibility of collecting and preserving the records of North Carolina in the World War." The individual who would hold the office of "Collector of War Records" had to be a trained historian able to collect documents that spoke to "the history of the contribution of North Carolina and of her soldiers, sailors, airmen, and civilians to the Great War." From these documents, the collector was to build an "artificial collection" and compile a book to be published by the state and placed in the state's schools, libraries, and public places.[13] The state legislature thus transferred the work of collecting memories and documenting history from a martial institution to the state's archives.

With the power of the state legislature behind them, the Historical Commission including Secretary of State Grimes and Chairman Hill chose someone they could trust to build the archival project. They found the perfect man to take on this project in recently discharged veteran Robert Burton House. Born on March 19, 1892 in Thelma, North Carolina, House graduated from the University of North Carolina in 1912 with a bachelor's degree and from Harvard University in 1917 with a master's degree in history. He enlisted in the US army in May 1917 and served as a machine gunner in the 103rd Infantry of the 26th Division based in New England. He went to France in August 1917 but returned to the United States in April 1918—just before the 103rd was sent into heavy combat—to serve as a machine gun instructor at Camp Gordon, Georgia. There he stayed through the end of the war with his colleagues as "glorified drill sergeants under tacit instructions to forget all that we may have learned in France. Theory was the watch word, together with red tape." Despite these misgivings, he married his fiancé within one week of returning from France in May 1918, and he received a promotion to Lieutenant in September 1918.[14] He was honorably discharged in December 1918 and, returning to North Carolina, accepted a teaching job with Greensboro schools, where he taught from January to June 1919. After this short stint as an educator, House agreed to become the North Carolina Historical Commission's Collector of War Records, serving until 1924.[15] He noted, "It is quite delightful work and gives me an opportunity to spend my time in doing what I like to do most."[16] House thus accepted the central role in building North Carolina's colonial archive of the First World War.

House was part of a new breed of southerner that historian Daniel Joseph Singal describes as "Modernists," who swept to power in the 1930s and reinvigorated the disciplines of history and sociology and whose scholarly adherents began re-investigating the social and historical frameworks of the South. This sociological turn stressed information and accuracy over experience and storytelling. The center of this sociological movement, according to Singal, was the University of North Carolina, and House presided over much of this process as the executive secretary (1926–34) and later dean (1934–45) of the Chapel Hill campus under President Frank Porter Graham's administration.[17] Graham transformed the campus into a major research center during the Great Depression, and House completed this process when he became the first chancellor of the consolidated campuses in 1945. Singal argues that the modernists were influenced more by Sigmund Freud and Charles Darwin than by proponents of the Old and New South. House, of course, was also significantly influenced by his experiences in the war. Singal claims this group believed in science, relativism, and positivism and that knowledge was "a shifting affair" in which "man was the human animal, [and] that the universe was inherently irrational, [and] that morality was embedded in history and not in immutable natural laws, and that personality was primarily determined by one's culture." He added, "theirs was an empirical approach that gathered in significant details unencumbered by the requirements of traditional mythology or moralism."[18]

Elites at the Historical Commission trusted House as a good southerner as well as a capable Collector of War Records. House embraced his southern heritage, celebrated both of his grandfathers who had been Confederate veterans, and joyfully received the Cross of Service from the UDC designating him in "perpetual memorial" as a "descendent of a Confederate Soldier" who "proved worthy of his lineage."[19] Yet House demonstrated his modern ability not to be overburdened with the southern past. After enlisting in the army, he had been sent to a training camp in Plattsburg, New York, with other New Englanders. "Just think of it," he wrote his mother, "I am in camp now with the sons of men who fought against my own people, and in hearty co-operation with them too." He had high hopes for the war and for national reunification. "After this war," he continued to his mother, "there will be no North and South in the sense of bitterness and prejudice I am hoping." Continuing, he said, "I can never be a New Englander. . . . They are not like us. But I can get on in the world with New Englanders in a better way now that I know more about them."[20] When not training, he attended lectures at the YMCA in town. One lecture in particular, delivered by Dean Brown from Yale especially influenced him. Brown spoke of Abraham Lincoln as "the greatest man of the 19th century" because "he saved the union; he freed the slaves; he secured the welfare of the American people."[21] The lecture impacted House enough for him to draw a similar parallel to Woodrow Wilson days later. House wrote that Lincoln was "the greatest example of simple strength on record" primarily because the Republican President had seen "the truth from the very first" and persevered through many challenges. But House noted that although Wilson "did not see the truth at first because is [sic] surprised him," Wilson, unlike Lincoln, provided "the greatest example of sheer analytical morals on record." House concluded: "Lincoln-Wilson; simple-complex; converse sides of one thing—greatness."[22] House's analysis of Lincoln and Wilson suggested that he was someone steeped in southern traditions but not burdened by them.

House also believed that northerners had respected him during his time in the North. He realized that despite the "most romantic notions about Southern plantations, colored mammys, and the other features of befo' de war stories,"

many of his northern friends believed that the "North had been acting ig-
norantly in most of its efforts to manipulate conditions among our people."
House particularly was aware of these signs of sectional reconciliation when
it came to the topics of race and immigration. He wrote to his mother that
"already the people here are beginning to realize that with their tremendous
tide of immigration the hope of the Anglo-Saxon American lies in the South
with its pure citizenship."[23] House found common ground with northerners
on the issues of race and pure Americanism, and this shaped his political
understandings of race, the war, and his role in it.

He developed these modern rearrangements of linking and unburdening
himself with the southern past even more while in France. For example, his
views on religion evolved particularly along these lines. "How superficial is
the culture that we think will last always," he noted in his journal. Then he
pondered, "Perhaps the very Christian religion that abhors war is the ideal
basis of war itself since the very essence of Christian martyrdom enobles
[sic] in part every war." "It may be," he continued, "that Christ showed us
not a model for each man to follow in his three score years and ten but for
the massed humanity of a million years to toil blindly toward through un-
told suffering of individual men." House was clearly coming to a critique of
his Christian thought based on his experiences. He wrote, "War may be the
working out of God's power in the life of man. But oh! the sad confession of
weakness in method if this be so." House was sick of war. It had become "a
thing to be endured in my life without letting it touch my soul. I will no more
make a philosophy of the beastly thing because I have to fight it than I will of
ignorance because I am not wise."[24]

Despite closing his soul to the war, he remained connected to his religios-
ity. While in France preparing his men for the trenches, House stayed in the
home of Monsieur and Madame Justin Humbloe, who had been married for
forty-five years. They were Catholic and kind, sharing their home and food.
House's Protestant upbringing could not completely comfort him during the
war so he went to Mass with the Humbloes on Sundays. After attending the
All Saints Day Mass, House informed his mother "now I am not a Catholic,
but I have a great respect for one thing I notice everywhere about Romanism:
it always has a church full of people who seem glad to be there, and it has a
service more beautiful I think than ours." His Catholic experiences seemed to
give him respite from the experience of war. A few Sundays later, House again
reported to his mother that he had been attending Protestant and Catholic
services. "I am of both faiths usually," he said, "because the Protestant is English and more understandable and the Catholic is music and more beautiful
so that by combining the two in genuine devotion I get the ideal worship of
Truth, Goodness, and Beauty."[25] Here the Catholic Mass facilitated his ability

to interpret the truth, particularly because he could experience the mass; his attendance at Protestant service was less of an interpretive experience. He came to a similar realization about French society. "Languages and customs differ the world over, but they all have root in the common soil of human nature."[26]

Thus House was able to negotiate old and new cultural landscapes in fairly sophisticated ways, and he translated these ways of thinking into his work as Collector of War Records. His experiences in army training camp allowed him to retain his southern identity while undergoing a transformation to a "Modern" southerner. House was not exclusively bound by the Victorian morality that had built the Cavalier and New South mythologies of the Southern Gentleman. House neither completely abandoned these mythologies nor completely embraced them. He understood the cultural landscapes of New England, the South, the federal government, and France in a way that tied his view of cultural memory to North Carolinian identity. His experiences prepared him to simultaneously win over the trust of the Historical Commission's elites and the returning soldiers. He collected the memories of the war by collaborating with state elites and white North Carolinians. Meanwhile, he came to be the Collector of War Records at the dawning of a new age of southern empiricism, an age in which the collection of memories became more important than the expression of memories. By examining the North Carolina State Archives and the artificial file Robert B. House built, historians can get a sense of the colonial structures and mechanisms built into this archival project.

Atomized memories could easily become lost in the traumatic chasms that the First World War produced. The war broke bodies, limited imaginations, and demythologized narratives. Elites sought to fill these craters with a documented cultural memory that they produced and that they interpreted for the rest of society. This project was more difficult than previous attempts by state elites to control historical awareness. The pre-war infrastructure was neither capable of capturing the memories of millions of individuals involved in the war, nor able to produce a ritualized mythology through which those memories could be understood. The number of memories to be collected was overwhelming, and "the means of the Historical Commission [were] too limited to pay for the vast amount of help necessary to collect records." Time was also a factor. "The work of the Historical Commission must of necessity be slow, whereas war records of value are being lost or destroyed every day. The Historical Commission confronts a task beyond its individual powers." Because the commissioners were not capable of completing the archival record, they had to rely on "each citizen [to] give what records he has, and secure a like response from his neighbors." Commissioners were no longer able to rely on the top-down Defense Council approach they had used to organize the state during the war. Thus they pleaded with the public, "Don't let any man fail to send in his record because he doesn't know it is wanted. Talk about the work. Announce it at the schools and Sunday schools[,] the movies, community fairs, soldiers' reunions[,] public meetings of all sorts."[27]

Before House could collect archival records, he had to build a more modern collection infrastructure, one that encouraged people to share their memories. When House accepted the job as archivist in the summer of 1919, he set to work immediately to capture splintered memories of the war by collaborating with the public. To accomplish this goal, he hoped to convince potential collaborators that their wartime documents and memories redefined the relationship between North Carolina identity and national politics. He began by first collecting divisional military histories from the War Department in Washington, DC, and sought to confirm the exact number of Congressional Medal awards given to Carolinians in the 30th Division, so he could dispute claims put forward by the 89th Division made up of Missourians that they had received more. He also initiated a search to document North Carolina airmen who might have become aces during combat.[28] House then began initiating document collection strategies using the teachers in the state's education system. He hoped to reach students training to be teachers at the North Carolina College for Women in Greensboro, the University of North Carolina in Chapel Hill, and the Agriculture and Engineering School in Raleigh before the 1919 summer school session ended and before they began teaching in the fall.[29] During the first few months, House also established a communication link with Julian Leavitt, who directed the Office of Jewish War Records in New York and coordinated record collection activities with A. A. Joseph, the Goldsboro-based Secretary of the Jewish Relief Committee in the state during the war.[30]

To complement these federal records, House collaborated with national institutions such as the American Legion. This institution was a political ally as much as a cultural one. He noted how the American Legion had run "down the I. W. W. [International Workers of the World] traitors on the western coast" in Centralia, Washington. He trusted that "should such conditions occur in North Carolina, or any other conditions wherein the American Legion might be of service," not only would the Legion intervene but that they would also make sure that "full records of this service . . . be preserved and sent to the North Carolina Historical Commission."[31] Thus the American Legion became a vital partner for House.[32] The UDC also became a partner, and he spoke at their annual convention at High Point.[33] House had no problems with the UDC's focus on Confederate lineage or the use of their own commemorative methods. In fact, he sought the institution's aid specifically to help identify Confederate descendants who fought in the Great War. He also encouraged UDC members to collect materials from soldiers even if they were not descendants of Confederates, particularly if these artifacts could "throw light on North Carolina history during the period of the war."[34]

In September 1919, House travelled to Washington, DC, to participate in the Conference of Representatives of State War Historical Agencies. The two-day conference resulted in the formation of the annual National Association of State War Historical Organizations conference. This allowed House to make contacts with like-minded counterparts from other states. They strategized over how to approach the US Navy and the US Shipping Board, received instructions about how to collect historical information from the US Food Administration, and learned how to use data from the upcoming 1920 census. State archivists and collectors from around the country shared methodologies, theories, and practices for working with archival institutions, the American Historical Association, and state legislatures to improve the collecting of documents and information.[35]

North Carolina's Collector of War Records took the knowledge he gained from this national conference and refined his strategies at the state level. Three months after his return from Washington, House initiated a conference for county historians. In a letter to county contacts, he admitted that during the war the "Historical Commission was unsuccessful in the State as a whole" in collecting records. He now urged county liaisons to attend a one-day conference in Raleigh on February 4, 1920. He promised to pay the expenses of each participant, and twenty people attended, almost all of whom were from either Raleigh or the central part of the state. No one attending came from west of Greensboro, and only two people came from the coastal region. House and other state officials were able to communicate the standards and the methods of collecting documents to the local volunteers who attended. House's county contacts provided valuable feedback to state organizers, and much of what they said exposed the weaknesses of collecting efforts around the state.

House and board members of the Historical Commission knew they were not getting the results that they wanted, and they hoped to use the conference to reinforce the structure they had built connecting local counties to a centralized overseer. J. Bryan Grimes and D. H. Hill attended the conference and made presentations, as did R. D. W. Connor who claimed that many county historians were having trouble persuading people, particularly soldiers, to donate their documents and share their recollections. Connor, the secretary of the North Carolina Historical Commission, believed soldiers were reluctant to give away their material objects because they were "not impressed with the importance of preserving in permanent form our experiences in the war." He admonished the county historians to see their work as "the most significant work that can be done in the United States." For Connor, the work of collecting documents was not just an exercise in historical preservation. "Upon the success of what we are trying to do will depend the work of Americanization," he asserted. Here Connor revealed the way he and others at the state level enlisted the county historians to promote the elite's version of the state's cultural memory. "Unless we can preserve the achievements and the ideals of the people of these times, we will not be able to preserve the spirit of Americanism—supplying to future generations the means of instilling that spirit of Americanism." According to Connor, documenting North Carolinians' memories of the war was a crucial step in perpetuating the cultural memory of the state and the nation to future generations.[36]

Local collectors were having mixed success. County Historian K. B. Council found some success in working with local school principals and the county superintendent. Council was able to get schoolteachers to develop classroom assignments that stimulated children's imaginations and sparked conversations at home. They in turn brought memorabilia into the school to supplement their reports and show-and-tell assignments. This way, Council secured documents from the students' homework and produced documents out of their essays. Meanwhile, Council organized schoolchildren to "plant a tree for each soldier and sailor who lost his life in the service and name it after him" to generate interest in the community about the project. But most local collectors reported that their work did not make as big of an impact as they had hoped. Others seemed confused about the entire process and had no real guidelines on how to go about capturing materials. Most attendees claimed that they certainly would be able to collect a complete history of their respective county, given enough time, but Brodie Jones of Warrenton was not so sure. Perhaps the youngest attendee, Jones asked, "What about the colored race?" He continued, "We have two colored men to one white. One colored boy won the croix de guerre [sic]." This question exposed a glaring weakness in the structure that the Historical Commission and House were building.

Black memories had not disappeared, but they remained undetected in North Carolina's cultural memory. House tried to overcome this limitation by creating a group of volunteer "Negro County Historians," asking them to collect letters, diaries, and other archival materials from black soldiers and civilians in each respective county. Here House had to rely on his white contacts—superintendents of county school systems—to provide him with names of black individuals who could serve. Superintendent of Yancey County Schools W. O. Griffith replied, "It is very hard to find a competent man or woman among the negroes in the county." His language dripping with the racial stereotypes of the day, Griffith thought it was unnecessary anyway because "there were but two or three drafted" from his county. He finally recommended Sul Griffith of Burnsville, but it seemed to be a half-hearted recommendation.[37] Others were more enthusiastic. R. W. Islay, the superintendent of Sampson County Schools, recommended John Kernegay of Newton Grove, who was a supervisor of rural schools and who Islay described as "honest and reliable. You can count on him doing the work well."[38] House was able to collect the names and enlist the help of African American men in fifty-seven of the state's one hundred counties.

House recommended to these collectors that they create committees in each community in the county and that committee members spread out to collect materials more easily. To Kernegay, House wrote, "The colored race had a notable and honorable part in the world war and should be fully represented in history." Then he urged Kernegay to collect as many records as possible through the "committee plan," including the role of African Americans in the Red Cross, Liberty Bond drives, pictures, letters, names of soldiers, and "war work of any sort." He implored the local collector to begin immediately because "records are being destroyed every day that are of great value, and you will thus see the necessity of losing no time."[39] But few materials collected from African Americans in the state arrived at the Collector of War Records' office. House had imposed a segregated order to collecting materials; each county hosted a white historian and a black one who worked independently from each other.

Despite embracing the emerging post-war sociological turn, House by the summer of 1920 had established a structure of collection that virtually ignored materials from whole sections and communities of the state, and this skewed the holdings of the archive he was building. House reformed the bureaucracy of collecting that had hampered efforts of local elites around the state from the beginning of the war, but the new elements within that bureaucracy, including black county historians, were not capable of overcoming the vast racial divide that permeated the North Carolina landscape. He also relied on traditional institutions whose interests were embedded in the racial hierarchies of counties throughout the state. Each institution—from the American Legion to the UDC to local county historians—brought their own interests and own agendas to their methodologies of collection. And this showed up in the materials that they collected and in the ways that they publicized their efforts. Despite being "modern," House effectively built an archival structure to which state and local elites could attach their own memories to North Carolina cultural memory while restricting black citizens from doing the same.

From this perspective, House's artificial collection essentially authenticated elite cultural memories of the war and the homefront. As scholars consider the war and its aftermath in North Carolina a century later, they would do well to consider how these authenticated memories worked. Rather than establishing a memory of the past, the archival collection more often than not established a pattern of remembrance that showcased southern Progressivism within the national identity of the United States. Criticism of these kinds of patterns would come much later in the twentieth century after scholars developed tools fashioned from more mature sociological and cultural turns to challenge the colonialism embedded in archival collections such as that of the World War I collection at the State Archives of North Carolina. Despite the skewed nature of the archives, some African Americans and women hid their memories within its foundation. What remains is for historians to read against the grain of this archive, to identify the nooks and crannies of this collection where oral histories of minorities, interviews of individuals, and documents critical of elites have been hidden from the cultural memory and the documented history of the state.

Notes

1. For a discussion of cultural memory, see Jan Assmann, Cultural Memory and Early Civilization: Writing, Remembrance, and Political Imagination (New York: Cambridge University Press, 2011); Marek Tamm, "History as Cultural Memory: Mnemohistory and the Construction of the Estonian Nation," Journal of Baltic Studies 39.4 (December 2008): 499–516.

2. For a discussion of history, memory, and ways historians can bridge the divide, see Jay Winter, Remembering War: The Great War between Memory and History in the 20th Century (New Haven: Yale University Press, 2006).

3. Jacques Derrida, Archive Fever: A Freudian Impression, trans. Eric Prenowitz (Chicago: University of Chicago Press, 1998), 1–2. See also Peter Fritzche, "The Archive," History and Memory 17 (Winter 2005): 13–44.

4. Ann Laura Stoler, "Colonial Archives and the Arts of Governance," Archival Science 2 (2002): 87–109, quote on p. 100.

5. See Robert Wiebe, The Search for Order, 1877–1920 (New York: Hill and Wang, 1966).

6. Catherine W. Bishir, "Landmarks of Power: Building a Southern Past in Raleigh and Wilmington, North Carolina, 1885–1915," ed. W. Fitzhugh Brundage, Where These Memories Grow: History, Memory, and Southern Identity (Chapel Hill: University of North Carolina Press, 2000), 149.

7. See bibliographical note of the Guide to Daniel Harvey Hill Papers at North Carolina State University Special Collections, accessed August 14, 2013, http://www.lib.ncsu.edu/-findingaids /mc00022#-CollectionSummary.

8. Committee Report, Dr. D. H. Hill, State Archives of North Carolina, World War I Collection, North Carolina Council of Defense Box, Memorials Folder.

9. Letter, Secretary of State J. Bryan Grimes to Chairman of the Council of Defense Dr. D. H. Hill, June 26, 1918, State Archives of North Carolina, World War I Collection, North Carolina Council of Defense Box, Memorials Folder; Caroline E. Janney, Burying the Dead But Not the Past: Ladies' Memorial Associations and the Lost Cause (Chapel Hill: University of North Carolina Press, 2012). By insisting that the members of these new local committees be women, Hill acknowledged that women traditionally had taken on the responsibility of memorialization since the days of the Civil War.

10. Jackson Lears, Rebirth of a Nation: The Making of Modern America, 1877–1920 (New York: Harper Perennial, 2010). Lears describes reformers during the Progressive Era as subscribing to a "militarist fantasy" in which they adopted military strategies and martial institutions to reshape the nation.

11. Letter, Dr. D. H. Hill to Junius D. Grimes, July 31, 1918, State Archives of North Carolina, World War I Collection, North Carolina Council of Defense Box, Memorials Folder; Letter,

Junius D. Grimes to Dr. D. H. Hill, July 30, 1918, State Archives of North Carolina, World War I Collection, North Carolina Council of Defense Box, Memorials Folder.

12. Letter, Dr. D. H. Hill to Colonel A. H. Boyden, November 18, 1918, State Archives of North Carolina, World War I Collection, North Carolina Council of Defense Box, Memorials Folder.

13. The term colonialism used above suggests that white North Carolinians built their collection with an internal/domestic cultural colonialism that resembled the archival collections that Germans of the nineteenth and twentieth centuries, as well as nineteenth century British overseers of India, constructed. See Peter Fritzche, "The Archive," *History and Memory* 17 (Winter 2005), 13–44. Fritzche claims, the German archives authenticate the elite political agenda and are used to distort history because they can only provide a re-presentation of the past in ways that project the concerns of the present and the future. Wilhelmine and Weimar historians, for example used German archives to define "Germanness" while the Nazis used the archives to define and identify "Jewishness," and the Stasi used them to define "Socialists." Similarly white North Carolinians inverted this domestic repertoire of colonial power by defining Americanness and Progressive southerness by segregating and suppressing African American material and cultural artefacts within the archives. See also Anjali Arondekar, "Without a Trace: Sexuality and the Colonial Archive," *Journal of the History of Sexuality* 14 (Jan–Apr 2005): 10–27. Colonial overseers suppressed reports of homosexual activity—preventing them from archival storage—because homosexual practices threatened the colonial order in India. These sorts of archival uses, claims Arondekar, provide an opportunity for regimes to empower the subject over the subjected because these impressions are "highly motivated" to suppress knowledge, practices, and ideologies that threatened the institution and the authority of the archives and of the political regimes that created them. Again white North Carolinians likewise employed similar repertoires of colonial power domestically to secure a white Progressive political regime within the state and to shape the knowledge of race and identity within the World War I Collection.

North Carolina Historical Commission, "Do Your Part," State Archives of North Carolina, World War I Collection, County War Records Box, Warren County Folder, 5. A "natural" collection conforms to a structure of order imposed by the donators and is handed over in totality to the archivist, whereas an "artificial" collection is collected and compiled by the archivists, who impose their own order on the records. Thus, an artificial collection is highly selective, and highly motivated, and reflects the archivist's values and interpretations much more than a "natural" collection.

14. Letter, Robert B. House to C. R. Cabbott, February 12, 1921, State Archives of North Carolina, World War I Collection, Private Collections, Robert B. House Papers, Box #6.

15. Robert B. House, "Letters and Diary of First Lieutenant Robert Burton House," State Archives of North Carolina, World War I Collection, Private Collections, Robert B. House Papers, Box #8.

16. Letter, Robert B. House to C. R. Cabbott, 12 February 12, 1921, State Archives of North Carolina, World War I Collection, Private Collections, Robert B. House Papers, Box #6.

17. William D. Snider, Light on the Hill: A History of the University of North Carolina at Chapel Hill (Chapel Hill: University of North Carolina Press, 2004).

18. Daniel Joseph Singal, The War Within: From Victorian to Modernist Thought in the South, 1919–1945 (Chapel Hill, University of North Carolina Press, 1982), 261–262.

19. United Daughters of the Confederacy Certificate of Award, State Archives of North Carolina, World War I Collection, Private Collections, Robert B. House Papers, Box #6.

20. Letter, Robert House to Sue Eldridge House, May 12, 1917, State Archives of North Carolina, World War I Collection, Private Collections, Robert B. House Papers, Box #8.

21. Robert B. House, "Unbound Scrapbook, entry May 20, 1917, State Archives of North Carolina, World War I Collection, Private Collections, Robert B. House Papers, Box #8.

22. Robert B. House, "Unbound Scrapbook, entry xxxix, State Archives of North Carolina, World War I Collection, Private Collections, Robert B. House Papers, Box #8.

23. Letter, Robert House to Sue Eldridge House, May 27, 1917, State Archives of North Carolina, World War I Collection, Private Collections, Robert B. House Papers, Box #8.

24. Robert B. House, "Unbound Scrapbook, entry xxiv, State Archives of North Carolina, World War I Collection, Private Collections, Robert B. House Papers, Box #8.

25. Letter, Robert House to Sue Eldridge House, undated, State Archives of North Carolina, World War I Collection, Private Collections, Robert B. House Papers, Box #8.

26. Letter, Robert House to Sue Eldridge House, undated, State Archives of North Carolina, World War I Collection, Private Collections, Robert B. House Papers, Box #8.

27. North Carolina Historical Commission, "Do Your Part, Make North Carolina's War Record Complete," State Archives of North Carolina, World War I Collection, County War Records Box, Warren County Folder, 5–8.

28. Letter, Robert B. House to Director of Historical Branch, September 16, 1919, State Archives of North Carolina, World War I Collection, Private Collections, Robert B. House Papers, Box #10, Adjutant Generals Office Washington Folder; Letter, Robert B. House to Adjutant-General's Office, August 26, 1919, State Archives of North Carolina, World War I Collection, Private Collections, Robert B. House Papers, Box #10, Adjutant Generals Office Washington Folder; Letter, Robert B. House, Aeronautical Division of the War Department, August 25, 1919, State Archives of North Carolina, World War I Collection, Private Collections, Robert B. House Papers, Box #10, Adjutant Generals Office Washington Folder.

29. Letter, N. W. Walker to R. D. W. Connor, July 5, 1919, State Archives of North Carolina, World War I Collection, Private Collections, Robert B. House Papers, Box #15, Teacher's Cooperation Folder; Letter, Robert B. House to Dr. W. A. Withers, July 1, 1919, World War I Collection, Private Collections, Robert B. House Papers, Box #15, Teacher's Cooperation Folder; Letter, W. C. Jackson to Robert B. House, July 5, 1919, World War I Collection, Private Collections, Robert B. House Papers, Box #15, Teacher's Cooperation Folder.

30. Letter, Robert House to Julian Leavitt, August 28, 1919, State Archives of North Carolina, World War I Collection, Private Collections, Robert B. House Papers, Box #12, Jewish War Records Folder; Letter, Robert House to A. A. Joseph, August 28, 1919, State Archives of North Carolina, World War I Collection, Private Collections, Robert B. House Papers, Box #12, Jewish War Records Folder.

31. Memo, Robert House to the American Legion, November 24, 1919, State Archives of North Carolina, World War I Collection, Private Collections, Robert B. House Papers, Box #10, American Legion Folder.

32. Letter, Henry Koonts to Robert House, November 28, 1919, State Archives of North Carolina, World War I Collection, Private Collections, Robert B. House Papers, Box #10, American Legion Folder; Robert House, "Historical Records of the American Legion in North Carolina," State Archives of North Carolina, World War I Collection, Private Collections, Robert B. House Papers, Box #10, American Legion Folder.

33. Letter, C. Felix Harvey to Robert House, February 14, 1920, State Archives of North Carolina, World War I Collection, Private Collections, Robert B. House Papers, Box #15, United Daughters of the Confederacy Folder.

34. Letter, Robert House to E. S. Clayton, February 18, 1920, State Archives of North Carolina, World War I Collection, Private Collections, Robert B. House Papers, Box #15, United Daughters of the Confederacy Folder.

35. Robert House, "Summary of Conference of Representatives of State War Historical Agencies," State Archives of North Carolina, World War I Collection, Private Collections, Robert B. House Papers, Box #13, National Association State War History Organizations Folder.

36. Robert House, "Summary of Conference of Representatives of State War Historical Agencies," State Archives of North Carolina, World War I Collection, Private Collections, Robert B. House Papers, Box #13, National Association State War History Organizations Folder. Robert Digges Wimberly Connor was a history professor at the University of North Carolina at

Chapel Hill and would go on to become the first archivist of the United States, presiding over the newly formed National Archives in 1934.

37. Letter, W. O. Griffith to Robert House, June 28, 1919, State Archives of North Carolina, World War I Collection, Private Collections, Robert B. House Papers, Box #14, Recommendation for Negro Historian Collectors Folder.

38. Letter, R. W. Islay to Robert House, July 5, 1919, State Archives of North Carolina, World War I Collection, Private Collections, Robert B. House Papers, Box #10, County Historians, Negro Folder.

39. Letter, Robert House to John Kornegay [*sic*], October 8, 1919, State Archives of North Carolina, World War I Collection, Private Collections, Robert B. House Papers, Box #10, County Historians, Negro Folder.

11

The First and Second World War Generations of North Carolina Political Leadership

Karl E. Campbell

The First World War had a significant impact on two different generations of North Carolina's political leaders. The war obviously helped to define the historical legacy of those Tar Heels who helped govern the state and nation between 1914 and 1920. The Great War also affected the political sensibilities of the doughboys who became the state's leading politicians in the 1940s and 1950s.

War impacts society long after the battles are done. Historians have acknowledged the influence of the Civil War on the generation of southerners who came afterwards. World War II served as a catalyst for the many political changes wrought by members of the so-called "greatest generation."[1] World War I had a similar impact. It helped shape the political history of North Carolina by altering the trajectory of the generation of politicians who led it and by shaping the generation of soldiers who fought it.[2]

These two generations have a particular significance in the political history of the Tar Heel state. During the first half of the twentieth century, North Carolina was under the control of an elite coalition of industrialists, businessmen, agriculturalists, and their lawyers. Political scientist V. O. Key famously called this ruling faction the "progressive plutocracy."[3] Two consecutive political machines—the first under Furnifold Simmons from 1900 to 1928 and the second run by O. Max Gardner and his followers from 1928 to 1960—managed North Carolina's state government by controlling patronage and determining who was next in line to run for important offices such as governor, congressman, and senator. Both the Simmons Machine and later the Shelby Dynasty—named for the town of Shelby, which was Gardner's home and political base—controlled the Democratic Party, which controlled the state. The World War I generation included many of the founders of this progressive plutocracy, including Simmons himself. Thirty years later the doughboy generation took over the reins of state government and extended the rule of the progressive plutocracy until the Civil Rights movement brought it to an end in the 1960s. Thus the two generations most influenced by World War I represent the beginning and the end of North Carolina's progressive plutocracy.[4]

Historians have struggled to present a balanced portrait of these political leaders. Impressed by the reformist tendencies and comparative moderation of North Carolina's statesmen, a cohort of scholars writing in the 1950s and 1960s praised them as the most progressive in the South. Regretfully, this description downplayed the virulent racism and sexism upon which the power of the progressive plutocracy depended. By the 1980s, a revisionist school of historians flipped the narrative. They dismissed North Carolina's moderation as mythology and attacked Tar Heel politicians for retarding social justice through a clever strategy of paternalism, tokenism, and civility. The revisionists correctly exposed the progressive plutocracy's repressive tendencies but underestimated its reform agenda. It is possible, however, for an interpretation of North Carolina politics to incorporate both racism and reform. The progressive plutocracy suppressed African Americans, workers, and women while also supporting public health, good roads, and education. An examination of the influence of World War I on North Carolina politicians—the wartime leaders who founded the progressive plutocracy and the doughboys who later sustained it—illustrates the patriotic but limited idealism of both generations.[5]

Compared to the destructive tides of war in Europe, North Carolina politics seemed a sea of tranquility in 1916. Even as the political failure across the Atlantic resulted in the deaths of millions, Tar Heel elections had settled into a quiet phase of predictable outcomes. In North Carolina there was little doubt that the progressive plutocracy ran the Simmons Machine, the Simmons Machine ran the Democratic Party, and the Democratic Party ran the state. Such was the case in the election of 1916. Simmons supported Democratic President Woodrow Wilson's reelection and allowed Thomas W. Bickett, a reform-minded member of his political machine, to run for governor. With Simmons' help, both Wilson and Bickett carried the state by comfortable margins.[6]

Simmons and the Democratic Party had gained control of Tar Heel politics eighteen years earlier in the traumatic election of 1898. Simmons and his conservative allies in the Democratic Party had crushed a biracial reformist coalition of Populists and Republicans through a vicious campaign of racist propaganda and vigilante violence followed by a bloody coup d'état in Wilmington. Two years later, in 1900, the Democrats solidified their power by electing Simmons to the US Senate and his ally, Charles Aycock, as governor. The Democrats also amended the North Carolina constitution to disenfranchise most blacks and many poor whites with a literacy test and poll tax. These events marked the beginning of the progressive plutocracy. Senator Simmons remained in Washington, DC for the next thirty years serving as the state's senior senator and political boss. Governor Aycock implemented both Jim Crow segregation and an aggressive program of school construction, making him the first in a long line of governors who earned controversial reputations as both white supremacists and progressive reformers.[7]

In the early years of the twentieth century. the progressive plutocracy's commitment to genuine reform was tenuous. North Carolina's Democratic Party promoted the expansion of public schools in part as a means to pacify illiterate whites worried that they would not gain access to the polls before the grandfather clause expired in 1908. But many Tar Heel Democrats distrusted the more liberal aspects of the national progressive movement. According to historian George Tindall, the South's version of progressivism was limited to just two basic components of the national reform ideology—government efficiency and the extension of its power to provide public services to the state's citizens. More liberal ideas such as democratization, corporate regulation, and social justice were all rejected by the progressive plutocracy. Tindall labeled this uniquely southern strand of the national reform movement "business progressivism."[8]

In North Carolina some members of the Simmons Machine thought that New South industrialism blended nicely with progressive ideas of good government, which promoted infrastructure needed by businesses and expanded educational opportunities and health programs for a more dependable workforce. Other Tar Heel elites, especially those more committed to agriculture, had little reason to support such ideas and initially resisted their implementation. World War I, however, marked the watershed in the progressive plutocracy's acceptance of business progressivism.[9]

America's entrance into the Great War brought new challenges to North Carolina's political leadership. Early debates over neutrality, taxation, and conscription exposed rifts within the Democratic Party. The most public demonstration of these tensions came in response to President Wilson's war message in April 1917. While most Tar Heel leaders quickly rallied to the cause, Claude Kitchin, a North Carolina congressman and the majority leader in the US House of Representatives, opposed the war resolution. Although Kitchin knew that his colleagues would overwhelmingly vote for war, he felt compelled to speak for peace.

The House of Representatives opened debate on the war resolution on April 5, 1917. Kitchin's speech came a little after midnight. Reading from a prepared text he explained: "[M]y conscience and judgment, after mature thought and fervent prayer for rightful guidance, have marked out clearly the path of my duty, and I have made up my mind to walk it, if I go barefooted and alone." He warned that voting for war meant entering a "vast drama of horrors and blood" and spoke eloquently of the need for the United States to remain "the last hope for peace on earth."[10] Kitchin was interrupted frequently by applause, but the outcome of the debate was never in question. The House passed the war resolution by a vote of 373 to 50. Although his speech brought a burst of initial criticism, Kitchin's promise to "work with all of my soul and might" in defense of the country earned the admiration of his fellow Tar Heels not only for the courage of his convictions but also for his patriotism in following the will of the majority. After the United States entered World War I, the progressive plutocracy united in support of Wilson's crusade to make the world safe for democracy.[11]

North Carolina had more influence in Washington, DC, during the Wilson administration than at any previous time in the state's history. Several Tar Heels made significant contributions to the war effort. Josephus Daniels, the editor of the *News & Observer* (Raleigh, NC), served as Wilson's Secretary of the Navy. Daniels pushed for a larger military before the United States declared war and then managed to transport more than two million American soldiers across the Atlantic without losing even one casualty to the German U-boats. Daniels oversaw a tremendous increase in the size of the navy while also serving as a political advisor to both President Wilson and the Democratic Party. Walter Hines Page, who served as the United States Ambassador to Great Britain before and during the war, gained international acclaim for his strengthening of Anglo-American relations. Page, who had been a North Carolina newspaperman before editing national journals such as the *Atlantic Monthly* and *World's Work*, was one of the state's best known progressive intellectuals. Angus W. McLean, a businessman from Lumberton, earned President Wilson's trust as a director of the powerful War Finance Corporation. Wilson later named him as his Assistant Secretary of the Treasury. McLean garnered a great deal of respect for his prudent management and was later elected governor of North Carolina in 1924.[12]

North Carolina's congressional delegation, all members of the progressive plutocracy, played a leading role in drafting important wartime legislation on the national stage. The demands of winning the war pushed all of them in a more progressive direction. Senator Lee S. Overman promoted legislation that greatly expanded the powers of the president to coordinate government agencies during wartime. Some critics attacked the Overman Act of 1918 for giving the president dictatorial powers, but the majority believed that the need for efficiency trumped civil liberties. Majority Leader Kitchin also served as the chair of the House Ways and Means Committee. He teamed up with Senator Simmons, chair of the Senate Finance Committee, to pass the Revenue Bill, which based most of the government's wartime spending on a graduated income tax. This progressive measure ensured that the burden of funding the war would not fall disproportionately on the poor. These and other examples demonstrate that the state's national leaders were embracing business progressivism and its central tenant—that government power should be expanded to serve the public good through efficient, businesslike management practices.[13]

World War I also contributed to the emerging progressive consensus back home in North Carolina. Bickett, the state's wartime governor, won election as a progressive reformer in 1916, but the coming of the war threatened his legislative plans. Bickett responded by enthusiastically embracing the war effort. The governor, a gifted speaker, traveled the state defending America's intervention as inevitable and describing the conflict as an opportunity "to mold and color the civilization of the whole world." "We must put all our moral power, all our money power, and all our man power into the fight," he told the student body at Chapel Hill in 1917. "Every blow delivered must carry the entire weight of the Nation. . . . [I]n the name of this dear old State that looks to you for the fruition of its hopes, I appeal to you to rise to the greatness of the hour."[14]

One example demonstrates the power of Bickett's oratorical skills particularly well. When word reached the governor in 1918 that forty deserters had fled into the mountains around Ashe County, he personally travelled to the town of Jefferson and delivered a patriotic speech lasting two-and-a-half hours. Appealing to the young men's mountain heritage, honor, and "the essence of Americanism," he promised that if they returned to duty he would vouch for their loyalty. North Carolinians, he explained, would understand they were not cowards but confused. Soon thereafter, all of the deserters turned themselves in, and the press wrote glowingly of Bickett's wartime leadership.[15]

Bickett wisely blended the themes of patriotism and progressivism in his speeches. The governor shamelessly argued that the General Assembly must pass his reform agenda at home to honor the troops fighting and dying overseas: "When the American soldier sacrificed every individual right, abandoned every personal pleasure and buried every personal profit for the common good, he breathed new life into the principle that no individual in the United States has any right the assertion of which would prove fatal to the welfare and happiness of all the people. . . . From every soldier's sepulcher there comes to this Nation the solemn warning, 'If you break faith with us who died, we shall not sleep.'" [16]

Historians point to the 1920s as the decade in which North Carolina emerged as the most progressive state in the South, but the turning point came during World War I. It became the first state in the Union to endorse a League of Nations and the first to ratify the federal prohibition amendment. During the war years, the state's legislators passed thirty-five of the forty-three measures Governor Bickett proposed; the new laws included creating the state's first public welfare system, increasing expenditures for teachers' salaries and state agencies, and extending the school term to six months.[17]

Not one to rest on his laurels, Bickett pushed through even more significant legislation during his last two years in office. During the 1919 and 1920 legislative sessions, the General Assembly granted the governor his request for major changes to the organization of the state government. It also passed a drastic restructuring of the tax system that included a revaluation of property, nicknamed the "Bickett Revaluation," which increased the assessed value of all property in the state from $1.1 billion to $3.1 billion in 1921. Additional revenue from a new graduated income tax resulted in a twelvefold increase in state funding by 1926, which helped to fuel expansion of state services up to the Great Depression.[18]

It is important to note, however, that the governor and other North Carolina progressives did not champion the rights of women, labor, or African Americans. Bickett opposed the Women's Suffrage Amendment, and the legislature declined to approve it, missing the opportunity to be the final state needed for ratification.[19] While he spoke often of the plight of workers, he did not support labor unions or strikes. Bickett also defended the white supremacy upon which southern progressivism was built, explaining: "In North Carolina we have definitely decided that the happiness of both races requires that white government shall be supreme and unchallenged in our borders."[20] Key's nickname for North Carolina's political leaders—the progressive plutocracy—was certainly an accurate summary: They would remain progressive only as long as their plutocracy remained unchallenged.

Governor Bickett was the quintessential business progressive. His administration's record of progressive reform stressed public service expansion and government efficiency while rejecting any significant democratization, social justice, or corporate regulation. The same can be said of North Carolina's representatives on the national level, including Daniels, Page, McLean, Overman, Kitchin, and Simmons, who all embraced a larger role for government during World War I. The war became a catalyst for the progressive plutocracy's acceptance of business progressivism, and it helped to define the generation of Tar Heels who led the state in the early twentieth century.

As the progressive plutocracy mobilized the state and nation for war, their sons and daughters responded to the call to arms. Tar Heel women joined various associations to support the war effort. Tar Heel men responded in unprecedented numbers, including a cohort of upper-class young men who would become the future political leaders of the state in the 1940s and 1950s. World War I marked their transition from youth to manhood and helped to form their views on morality, politics, and power.

There was a long delay between the war and these doughboys' ascension to power. Even after the progressive plutocracy shifted from the Simmons

Machine to the Shelby Dynasty in 1930, there was little opportunity for ambitious young men to break into the line of older machine politicians waiting their turn to hold office. R. Gregg Cherry, the first World War I veteran to serve as governor, was not elected until 1944. Thereafter every governor elected until 1960 had fought in the war. Likewise, Sam Ervin, the first World War I veteran to represent North Carolina in the US Senate, did not go to Washington, DC, until 1954. Every subsequent Tar Heel senator was a World War I veteran through 1972. In the three decades since these doughboys fought in the Great War, many other historical events had influenced their lives as well, including the roaring twenties, the Great Depression, World War II, and the beginning of the Cold War. Given such a long lapse of time, it is not surprising that the influence of World War I on this generation of political leaders has been overlooked.

There is reason, however, to consider the special role that the Great War played in shaping these young men's lives and careers. While the study of generations is certainly not an exact science, there is general agreement on the importance of early adulthood in determining lifelong worldviews. Studies in developmental psychology have shown that the most significant changes in political philosophy occur between the ages of 18 and 25 during the "emerging adult" stage of life.[21] North Carolinians who were born between 1880 and 1900 belonged to a generation of Americans that experienced the traumas of World War I during their formative years.

The most common description for the young men and women who came of age during World War I is "the Lost Generation."[22] Ernest Hemingway popularized this phrase for the disillusioned young writers of the 1920s who rebelled against the dominant social and artistic mores of the previous generation. While the Lost Generation is an accurate label for a specific group of influential intellectuals and artists, it does not accurately describe the majority of young adults living in the decades after the Great War, and it certainly does not apply to the Tar Heel soldiers from elite North Carolina families, such as Cherry and Ervin, who later rose to political prominence. These World War I veterans were not part of a Lost Generation but embraced the worldview and accepted the values of their elders who constituted the original progressive plutocracy, including their commitment to the paradoxical ideology of business progressivism.

Cherry was the first member of the doughboy generation to rise to statewide prominence. In 1944, during the final years of World War II, the Shelby Dynasty chose Cherry as its candidate for governor. The election turned out to be a bitter contest between Gardner's political machine and one of its most charismatic challengers, Ralph McDonald, a former professor at the University of North Carolina at Chapel Hill, and an outspoken member of the populist wing of the Democratic Party.[23] Cherry was a colorful figure as well. He had been orphaned at age seven and was raised by his uncle in Gastonia. After graduating from Trinity College (now Duke University), he earned a law degree and returned home to set up his own practice. In 1917 Cherry helped to organize local boys into a unit that became Company A of the 115th Machine Gun Battalion of the 30th Division, which served in France and Belgium. Cherry rose to the rank of major, and he followed the tradition begun a few generations earlier by former Confederate officers of maintaining the title "Major Cherry" for the rest of his life. During the attack on the Hindenburg Line on September 29, 1918, he barely escaped being crushed to death by an Allied tank that rolled over the top of his trench. After the war, Cherry returned to Gastonia where he practiced law; entered politics; and earned a reputation for talking tough, chewing tobacco, and drinking heavily. Cherry's friends joked that he was the best lawyer in town when sober and the second-best lawyer in town when drunk. A successful politician, Cherry became Speaker of the North Carolina House where he earned the nickname "Iron Major" for his strong leadership.[24]

During the gubernatorial election of 1944, Cherry's supporters considered his service in World War I to be an asset. He was the first politician to campaign as a veteran of the Great War, and he suggested that his experience would help him understand the needs of World War II soldiers when they returned home. But in the final weeks of the contest, McDonald's supporters accused Cherry of insulting World War I veterans at the American Legion state convention, saying he dismissed one delegate as "nothing but a private" and called the veteran's home chapter "one of the little and inconsequential posts of the State."[25] McDonald attacked Cherry as an elitist member of the Shelby Dynasty who was out of touch with regular Tar Heels, but Cherry denied the charges and held on to win the Democratic primary and later the general election.

In office, Governor Cherry exemplified the continuity between the earlier and later members of the progressive plutocracy. During his tenure, the state increased funding for government services in education, mental health, road construction, and veterans' programs. Having experienced the difficult economic transition after the First World War, Cherry had the foresight to purchase decommissioned military installations after the Second World War in order to transform them into hospitals, libraries, and even the first testing site in the country for experimental rockets. The governor's greatest contribution was reserving surplus funds the state had acquired during the war boom for the difficult post-war period when war industries closed, federal military money dried up, and returning GIs needed additional services. Unsurprisingly, he did not take any significant steps to protect black voting rights or regulate big business. Instead, Cherry's expansion of public services coupled with his efficient management of state government was textbook business progressivism.[26]

During the campaign to choose Cherry's successor in 1948, the divisions within the progressive plutocracy grew even sharper. Kerr Scott, a farmer and politician from Alamance County, mounted another liberal challenge to the Shelby Dynasty. But this time Scott and his political allies defeated the Old Guard by promising a Go Forward program to lift regular North Carolinians out of rural poverty. Unlike the other governors in this period, Scott was not greatly influenced by World War I. He served briefly as a private in the field artillery and did not leave the country. He was discharged at the end of the war before having a chance to attend officer training school. It was not the war but the state's agrarian populist tradition that influenced him the most.[27]

Scott's insurgency was significant but short lived. Like other governors in the progressive plutocracy, he expanded education and built roads, but unlike his predecessors he also tipped the balance of power a few notches away from the Piedmont industrialists and towards "the Branchhead boys," the nickname given to his supporters who lived in the countryside near the heads of the creeks and river branches.[28] Scott's success was more programmatic than political. He could not get his appointee to the US Senate, Frank Porter Graham, elected in 1950, and he was unable to put his chosen successor, Judge Hubert Olive, into the governor's mansion in 1952. Instead, the Shelby Dynasty reasserted its control over the progressive plutocracy by helping elect William Umstead as governor, Luther Hodges as lieutenant governor, and a few years later, Sam Ervin as a US senator. These three men were the core members of the doughboy generation who governed North Carolina during the 1950s. The businessman behind the Shelby Dynasty's return to power was Winston-Salem banker and Great War veteran Robert March Hanes.

Hanes inherited the leadership of the Democratic Old Guard soon after the death of O. Max Gardner in 1947, although he was more of a senior advisor than a political boss. Born into a wealthy tobacco and textile manufacturing family in 1890, Hanes studied in both the public schools and at the prestigious Woodberry Forest School in Virginia. He graduated from the University of North Carolina at Chapel Hill with honors in 1912 and studied at the Harvard School of Business during 1912–1913. He began his successful business career as the secretary-treasurer of the Crystal Ice Company the following year. When the United States entered the war, he married his sweetheart just a few weeks before enlisting in the army at age 27.[29]

World War I had a significant impact on Hanes. He served in France as a captain in the 113th Field Artillery and saw action at St. Mihiel, the Argonne, and with the First and Second Armies. Hanes wrote frequently to his new bride back home. Soon after arriving in France, he described the beauty of the countryside, "the loveliest country in the World," the boredom of camp, and his enthusiasm to get into "one more good drive before the whole show is over."[30] But the tone of his correspondence changed quickly once he faced the horrors of battle. Careful to leave out the goriest details, Hanes described endless marching at night, the rain and mud, an airplane battle and the subsequent crash nearby, the terror of incoming artillery shells, and the deaths of comrades "blown to nothing" right in front of him. German shells hit close enough to cover Hanes in debris and leave him temporarily deafened by the blast. Having had enough of war, he welcomed the armistice with relief and hope, calling it "the greatest day in history."[31]

Hanes returned to his wife and business career in 1919, joining Wachovia Bank and Trust Company where he was named president in 1931. He served several terms in both the North Carolina House and Senate where he worked closely with Governor Gardner on tax reform and other moderately progressive government initiatives. Hanes's civic engagement took him beyond the borders of the state to become the president of the American Bankers Association in 1939 and a top administrator of the Marshall Plan to rebuild Europe after World War II. In North Carolina he supported politicians such as Cherry, Umstead, Hodges, and Ervin who advanced business progressivism. He did not support the civil rights movement or organized labor. Still, at a banquet in his honor not long before his death in 1959, Hanes was praised for upholding "concepts such as duty, honor, citizenship, loyalty, and patriotism," all values more associated with the progressive plutocracy than with the Lost Generation.[32]

William B. Umstead became North Carolina's governor in 1953. He had been a long-time member of the Shelby Dynasty, having served three terms as a US congressman before Governor Cherry appointed him to fill a vacant seat in the US Senate in 1946. Two years later he failed to win a seat in the Senate and returned home to oppose Scott's liberal insurgency. Umstead's father was a prominent farmer and civic leader in Durham County, and William spent most of his early years on the farm. He was close to his parents, who raised their children in a rather strict Christian household. While attending the University of North Carolina at Chapel Hill, he earned a reputation as a skilled debater and campus politician, which was ironic given his quiet and sullen demeanor. A Raleigh newspaper once described him as "painfully lacking in personality."[33]

In the spring of 1917, after talking his decision over with his parents, Umstead resigned from a job teaching high school to enter military service.[34] He joined the 317th Machine Gun Battalion, a part of the "Wild Cat" Division, as a second lieutenant. Umstead trained at Camp Oglethorpe, Georgia, and then spent a year stationed in various stateside military camps where his skill at administration earned him promotion to battalion supply officer.

In his diary Umstead demonstrated the elitism and paternalism typical of the progressive plutocracy. Commenting on the first drafted men arriving in camp, he wrote:

Regular Duke's mixture as I expected. Men from all social castes, professions, and walks of life, brought together for a common purpose which many of them do not understand. It is both pitiful and inspiring to look at them. God knows they have my sympathy especially during the first few days. Thoughts of loved ones; of business left behind; the task of adjusting themselves to a new life, new duties, and new habits all together at once will be hard for them to handle. The officer who is not considerate at first must have a heart of stone, and should not have authority unless tempered by justice and patience.[35]

Umstead held Sunday school class in the camp and tutored illiterate soldiers. "My progress with the men who can't read and write in the company has been rather slow," he confided to his diary. "Yet all of them can now write their names, and can read simple sentences very well. I hope that I may be able to teach them enough to break the veil of ignorance so that they can add to their intelligence."[36]

Umstead deployed to France in August 1918, and spent the final eight months of his military duty serving as a supply officer in Europe. He petitioned the army for an early release in February 1919, to fulfill his "duty to care for father and mother in their declining years."[37] The following month he returned home and picked up his life more or less as he had left it. The war had not changed Umstead's worldview so much as reinforced it.

When he became governor in 1953, Umstead followed the business progressivism of his predecessors by proposing new programs for the undereducated and mentally ill. He was personally connected with the rise to power of two other members of the doughboy generation. In June 1954, Umstead named Sam Ervin to the US Senate, replacing Senator Clyde Hoey after he suffered a stroke. Senator Ervin remained in office for the next twenty years. In November 1954, Umstead died from a heart attack after a long illness, making his Lieutenant Governor, Luther Hodges, the new governor of North Carolina. Hodges served out Umstead's remaining two years and then won election to his own four-year term, allowing him to serve longer than any preceding governor in the state's history. Hodges and Ervin were two of the last remnants of the Shelby Dynasty. Thirty-seven years earlier, they both had left their studies at the University of North Carolina at Chapel Hill to fight in the First World War.

The day after President Wilson asked Congress for a declaration of war against the German Empire, University of North Carolina at Chapel Hill President Edward Kidder Graham told the students that the war was a crusade larger than the American or French revolutions. According to Graham, it would lead to "permanent peace" and world unity: "Our larger task is peace; our immediate task is war!"[38] Carolina students enlisted by the hundreds. Sam Ervin's father suggested that he finish his studies and wait until he was called up, but Ervin quit school and enrolled in officer training school at Fort Oglethorpe. Luther Hodges also decided to leave Chapel Hill for military service and traveled to Plattsburg, New York, for officer training where he was commissioned as a second lieutenant.

Hodges was a few years younger than Ervin and came from a very different background. While the Ervins were considered one of the leading families in Morganton, the Hodges lived a hard life in the textile mill village of Spray. In 1898 the Hodges family had moved from a failing tenant farm in Virginia when Luther was only a year old. Life was difficult. When his father started a small mercantile store, Luther was expected to work every hour that he was not in school, from sunrise to sunset. In many ways, his childhood resembled the plot of a Horatio Alger story. Like the heroes of those rags-to-riches novelettes, Hodges overcame hardship by applying Alger's formula for success—luck, pluck, and virtue—to every situation. He earned a conditional acceptance to the University of North Carolina at Chapel Hill and arrived with only sixty-two dollars and fifty cents to his name. Hodges worked three jobs to pay his own way through school. He left after his junior year to join the war.

Second Lieutenant Hodges was assigned to serve at Camp Grant, Illinois. Ironically, while at Camp Grant he learned hand-to-hand bayonet fighting from his commanding officer, Captain Robert E. Lee.[39] Hodges complained that he was going into debt because "it seems that an officer has got to get a certain amount of things before he is all equipped. I went out today and spent $30 for a bedding roll to sleep on and two blankets and I had already spent $200 or more getting a few clothes, Gee, it's some job to keep up with."[40]

Much to Hodges' dismay, he never got an opportunity to use his battle skills. The influenza epidemic descended on Illinois in 1918 and took a tremendous toll; over 1200 men died in Camp Grant that fall. Hodges was reassigned as a medic and remained in camp for the rest of the war, tending the sick and dying. He wrote to his sister that it was doubtful anyone from his unit would "stand a chance to get out until after the war and you need not worry about your big bother getting hurt or killed for darn it I don't believe that I shall get a chance to get out of the state of Illinois." He further wrote, "I want to get over there for that big drive next spring," but he realized that "it seems that we are going to finish it up by then."[41] Slowly Hodges lost his enthusiasm for the war. Denied his chance for glory, he wrote of his frustration with military life and its inefficient bureaucracy: "I shall be glad to get out of it and get back to civil life once again."[42]

World War I did not interfere with the upward trajectory of Hodges' life. He graduated from University of North Carolina at Chapel Hill, took a job as an assistant to a textile mill manager back home in Spray, and began a meteoric rise to fame and fortune. Twenty years after the war, he became vice president of Marshall Field and Company in charge of all the company's manufacturing interests in the United States. During World War II, Hodges volunteered in various capacities as a business consultant to the US government. After taking early retirement in 1950, he joined his friend Robert Hanes in post-war Europe as chief of the Industry Division in Germany during the Marshall Plan. Two years later he was elected Lieutenant Governor, and he became governor in 1954.

Hodges earned the nickname "the businessman governor," and his administration epitomized business progressivism. He started the industrial education centers that became the community college system, helped launch the Research Triangle Park, and passed the first minimum wage law in the South. Hodges surpassed all his fellow governors in recruiting new industry and was the first state executive to lead a delegation to Europe for that purpose. True to the racial conservatism of North Carolina's leadership, Hodges resisted the Supreme Court's desegregation ruling and fought against civil rights. His supporters praised the moderation he showed in leading the state's reaction to *Brown v. Board of Education* while his critics condemned the shrewdness he demonstrated in slowing racial integration. By the end of Hodges' administration, the African American struggle for freedom had successfully undercut the foundation of white supremacy upon which the Simmons Machine and Shelby Dynasty were built. Hodges was the last governor of the progressive plutocracy before it fell into competing factions in the 1960s.[43]

Hodges' classmate, Sam Ervin, had a very different experience in World War I. Of all the doughboys who later held high office in North Carolina, no one was more affected by the war than Ervin. In many ways, he was also the best example of how the conflict initially challenged but then reinforced the progressive plutocracy's traditional values and beliefs.[44]

After training at Fort Oglethorpe for several months, Ervin was commissioned as a second lieutenant and joined Company I, the 28th Infantry, First Division in France. In February 1918, the First Division, under the command of General John J. Pershing, took control of forward trenches across from the German lines near the village of Seicheprey. These were the first American troops assigned to the frontlines in the war. Ervin commanded a platoon assigned to some of the worst conditions along the line. Day after day they hunkered down in deep trenches filled with water, vermin, mud, and snow. Ervin's feet froze to the bottom of his shoes, thawed out, cracked, bled, and froze again. Gas bombs exploded overhead causing a mad scramble of men trying to put on gas masks before a mere whiff of chlorine or mustard gas led to terrible suffering. The reality of trench warfare was a long way from the idealistic speeches back home. To make matters worse, Ervin came down with the flu, the same strain of influenza that kept Hodges stuck in Illinois and took the life of Edward Kidder Graham in Chapel Hill.[45]

Ervin "went over the top" on May 28, 1918, in the battle of Cantigny, the first battle fought by Americans in World War I. He was assigned to a "carrying party" moving ammunition and barbed wire from the rear into the heart of the battle. During several trips back and forth, Ervin came under intense enemy fire. At one point, German artillery shells rained down so heavily that he had to take cover in a hole with several engineers who were trying to set up barbed wire fences. An American was hit just a few feet away, and Ervin crawled forward to help him. A shell flew over his head and landed in the hole he had just left, killing all the engineers.[46] As Ervin turned back toward his own lines, machine gun fire sprayed through the field of tall grass he was crossing. Down below him he saw an injured German soldier with a broken arm. Ervin tried to make a splint for the wounded man, but as he knelt down an enemy bullet pierced through his foot. The German shouted, "Wir sind verdammte Schweine," (we are damn swine) in apology. Ervin hobbled back to an aid station, where he later learned that the Americans had successfully defended the town of Cantigny from the German counterattack. After the war, the Army awarded Ervin the Silver Star for his "courage and perseverance" under fire.[47]

Ervin spent several weeks in the hospital before returning to his company. His timing could not have been worse. Just days later, the First Division of the 28th Infantry Division led the charge in the battle of the Soissons. It was a turning point in the war, stopping the last German offensive, but victory came at a terrible price. On July 18, 1918, Ervin's company entered the battle with about 180 men. Five days later, only 38 of them remained alive and unwounded.[48] After fighting through a swamp, the platoon fell under heavy fire from a German machine gun nest that was threatening to mow down the American troops up and down the line. Ervin hit the ground and waited, but no one else was in a position to take out the German gun. He called for volunteers and led the attack himself.[49]

Ervin and four other men jumped up and ran straight toward the machine gun in a 100–yard suicide sprint. First one of his men was hit, then a second. Both men died instantly. Ervin fired his automatic rifle, killing one of the Germans. Seconds later he felt a weight hit his upper leg as he was smashed into the ground just short of the machine gun. Shell fragments had cut through his ammunition case and tore deep into his bone. The two remaining men reached the embankment and killed the gunners. They rushed back to Ervin, bandaged his wounds as best they could, and tried to carry him back their platoon. Realizing the three of them would be a clear target, however, Ervin ordered the men to go on. He crawled into an abandoned trench just before a French tank rolled over the top of the ditch. Just seconds later a shell hit and destroyed the tank. For Ervin, the war was over. After several terribly painful days, he rode in an ambulance to a hospital where doctors removed the shell fragment from his bone marrow. He spent months moving from one hospital to another fighting a series of infections in his leg.[50]

Ervin returned to Morganton a few months later. When his family explained how worried they had been when some of their letters were returned, Ervin joked that he was never lost: "I knew where I was all the time."[51] But his behavior over the next few months suggested that he had been, and still was, more lost than he would admit. Ervin was no longer as sure of himself and his place in the world as he had been back in Chapel Hill before the war. He was nervous, fidgety, and would not talk about his wartime experiences. He responded to frequent questions with vague responses. Everyone in Morganton was surprised when years later, in 1932, the War Department awarded Ervin the Distinguished Service Cross for his heroic conduct at Soissons.[52]

Ervin recovered from the trauma he experienced in World War I to become one of North Carolina's best known political leaders. After graduating from Harvard Law School, he had successful careers as a lawyer, judge, North Carolina Supreme Court Justice, and US Senator from 1954 until 1974. A staunch opponent of civil rights—he voted against every civil rights bill introduced during his twenty years in the Senate—Ervin also earned a reputation as a champion of civil liberties. He is most often remembered as the "old country lawyer" from the Senate Watergate Hearings in the summer of 1973. During those televised hearings, Ervin became a national hero not only for standing up against the imperial presidency of Richard Nixon but also for helping restore the nation's faith in constitutional government. Many who watched Ervin on television delighted at his twitching eyebrows that seemed to fly up and down his forehead whenever he became agitated. Little did they know that this nervous condition was one of several that sprung from an anxiousness that began during the First World War.[53]

Ten years after the Armistice, in 1929, the graduating classes of 1917 and 1918 held a joint reunion in Chapel Hill. As the alumni went around the room sharing what they had been doing with their lives, a ten-year-old boy was introduced to the gathering as the son of Oliver Ranson. A classmate of Ervin's, Ranson died in action during the war, leaving behind a bride who had become a wife, widow, and mother within a year. This boy was the son that Oliver Ranson had never seen. Without hesitation Ervin sprung to his feet and delivered a poetic tribute to the boy's father and the patriotic spirit which had moved him to:

> Pour out the red,
> Sweet wine of youth; give up the years to be
> Of work and joy, and that unhoped serene
> That men call age.

Witnesses to the speech marveled at Ervin's power to stir a cynical post-war audience by citing Rupert Brooke's romantic war poetry. Clearly Sam Ervin did not belong to the Lost Generation.[54]

As Ervin prepared to retire from the Senate in 1974, he sat down with Paul Clancy, his first biographer, to talk about the Great War. He explained that he had never questioned Wilson's reasons for leading America into war, nor did he ever doubt his own responsibility to serve. "That was what you were expected to do," he said simply, "and so that's what you naturally did." If America had not gone to war, he said, Europe would have been crushed. "I think the lights of liberty in Europe would have been extinguished."[55]

The War in Vietnam presented the Senator with a different problem. In private he confessed his doubts about the wisdom of continuing the war, but in public he remained a steadfast "hawk" supporting nearly every request for military appropriations. "I have seen war, and I hate war," he said in a speech on the Senate floor. "But sometimes war is the only road to peace and safety." And, as Senator Ervin did so often, he summarized his opinion with a quote, this time from John J. Crittenden who declared during the Mexican War, "I hope to find my country in the right; however, I will stand by her, right or wrong."[56]

The Dutch historian Pieter Geyl concluded that "[w]ars usually have the effect of speeding up the process of history."[57] In North Carolina, the First World War served as a catalyst for the rise of business progressivism among the elite politicians who led the war effort. Governor Bickett and the reformers among the first generation of the progressive plutocracy took advantage of wartime idealism to push their ambitious agenda while the more conservative members of the Simmons Machine, including Senator Simmons himself, accepted increased government power as necessary to win the war. The Great War also shaped the moral and political worldview of the generation of doughboys who fought in it. The elite young men who joined President Wilson's crusade to make the world safe for democracy drank deeply from the cup of progressive idealism during their early adulthood. The wartime values of patriotism, duty, honor, and service resurfaced decades later when they led the progressive plutocracy in the 1940s and 1950s. Governors Cherry, Scott, Umstead, and Hodges all followed the paternalistic tenants of business progressivism during their administrations, as did businessman Robert Hanes and Senator Sam Ervin. Regretfully, the doughboy generation also inherited the racism and plutocracy of their political forbearers; these fissures and faults ran throughout the whole structure of the political system and eventually brought it crashing down in the 1960s. The story of North Carolina politics in the twentieth century is dominated by the rise and fall of the progressive plutocracy. World War I helped to define the destiny of two critical generations of these Tar Heel leaders.

Notes

1. Tom Brokaw, *The Greatest Generation* (New York: Random House, 1998), xxx, 11–12.

2. On the complicated question of what constitutes a generation, see William Strauss and Neil Howe, *Generations: The History of America's Future, 1584 to 2069* (New York: Harper Collins, 1992).

3. V. O. Key Jr., *Southern Politics in State and Nation* (New York: Alfred A. Knopf, 1949), 205–228.

4. On North Carolina politics, see Rob Christensen, *The Paradox of Tar Heel Politics* (Chapel Hill: University of North Carolina Press, 2008).

5. For a sampling of the debate over the reputation of the progressive plutocracy, see Thad L. Beyle, "The Paradox of North Carolina," *in* ed. Thad L. Beyle and Merle Black, *Politics and Policy in North Carolina* (New York: MSS Information Corp., 1975), 12; H. G. Jones, "North Carolina, 1946–1976: Where Historians Fear to Tread," in ed. Jeffrey J. Crow and Larry E. Tise, *Writing North Carolina History* (Chapel Hill: University of North Carolina Press, 1979), 211–18; William H. Chafe, *Civilities and Civil Rights: Greensboro, North Carolina, and the Black Struggle for Freedom* (New York: Oxford University Press, 1980); Paul Luebke, *Tar Heel Politics 2000* (Chapel Hill: The University of North Carolina Press, 1998), 1–18.

6. Hugh Talmadge Lefler and Albert Ray Newsome, *The History of a Southern State: North Carolina* (Chapel Hill: University of North Carolina Press, 1973), 572.

7. Christensen, *Paradox of Tar Heel Politics*, 14–45.

8. George B. Tindall, "Business Progressivism: Southern Politics in the Twenties," *South Atlantic Quarterly* 62 (Winter 1963): 92–106.

9. Tindall, "Business Progressivism"; Christensen, *Paradox of Tar Heel Politics*, 48–61.

10. Kitchin quoted in Alex Mathews Arnett, *Claude Kitchin and the Wilson War Policies* (Boston: Little, Brown and Company, 1937), 229.

11. Kitchin's opposition to the war and his speech are discussed in William Link, *North Carolina: Change and Tradition in a Southern State* (Wheeling, IL: Harlan Davidson, 2009), 315; Arnett, *Claude Kitchin and the Wilson War Policies*, 227–240.

12. Sarah McCulloh Lemmon and Nancy Smith Midgette, *North Carolina and the Two World Wars* (Raleigh: Office of Archives and History, North Carolina Department of Cultural Resources, 2013), 30–36; Lee A. Craig, *Josephus Daniels: His Life & Times* (Chapel Hill: University of North Carolina Press, 2013), 289–344; Steven Niven, "Walter Hines, Frank Jr., and Robert N. Page," in eds., Howard E Covington Jr. and Marion A. Ellis, *The North Carolina Century: Tar Heels Who Made a Difference, 1900–2000* (Charlotte: Levine Museum of the New South, 2002), 503–506.

13. Lemmon and Midgette, *North Carolina and the Two World Wars*, 26–28; David M. Kennedy, *Over Here: The First World War and American Society* (New York: Oxford University Press, 1980), 106–113, 125–126; Arnett, *Claude Kitchin and the Wilson War Policies*, 259–270; Michael Sistrom, *North Carolinians and the Great War*, "Introduction," accessed July 7, 2016, http://docsouth.unc.edu/wwi/introduction.html.

14. Thomas Bickett, "Address at the University of North Carolina on Founders' Day, 1917," in *Public Letters and Papers of Thomas Walter Bickett, Governor of North Carolina, 1917–1921* (Raleigh: Edward & Broughton, 1923), 161–164.

15. Bickett, "The Ashe County Case," in *Public Letters and Papers*, 172–181. See also Michael Sistrom, *North Carolinians and the Great War*, "The Ashe County Case," accessed July 7, 2016, http://docsouth.unc.edu/wwi/bickettashe/summary.html.

16. Bickett, "A Debt of Honor," November 11, 1919, *Public Letters and Papers*, 208.

17. Bickett, "An Inspiring Record," *Public Letters and Papers*, 287–292; "Governor Bickett's Administration Represents New High Record of Legislative Achievement," *News & Observer*, April 20, 1919, in Bickett, *Public Letters and Papers*, 283.

18. Tindall, "Business Progressivism," 98; Lefler and Newsome, *North Carolina*, 574–575.

19. Bickett, "Women's Suffrage," *Public Letters and Papers*, 62.

20. "Legislation for Negroes," Seventh Message of Governor T. W. Bickett to the Special Session of the General Assembly of 1920, August 23, 1920, *Public Letters and Papers*, 72–73.

21. Jeffrey Jensen Arnett, "Emerging Adulthood: A Theory of Development from the Late Teens Through the Twenties," *American Psychologist* 55 (May 2000): 469–480.

22. Craig Monk, *Writing the Lost Generation: Expatriate Autobiography and American Modernism* (Iowa City: University of Iowa Press, 2008), 1–3.

23. For more on McDonald's challenge to the Shelby Dynasty, see Christensen, *Paradox of Tar Heel Politics*, 91–101.

24. Thomas S. Morgan, "Cherry, Robert Gregg," in ed. William S. Powell, *Dictionary of North Carolina Biography*, (hereafter cited as NCPedia), accessed July 7, 2016, http://ncpedia.org/biography/cherry-robert-gregg; "R. Gregg Cherry, Essay," North Carolina Highway Historical Marker Program, accessed July 7, 2016, http://www.ncmarkers.com/Markers.aspx?sp=Markers&sv=O-56.

25. Lemmon and Midgette, *North Carolina and the Two World Wars*, 179–184.

26. Ibid., 212–214.

27. William D. Snider, "The Scotts of Haw River," in Covington and Ellis, *The North Carolina Century*, 518–522.

28. Christensen, *Paradox of Tar Heel Politics*, 114.

29. T. Harry Gatton, "Robert March Hanes," NCPedia, accessed November 25, 2013, http://ncpedia.org/biography/hanes-robert-march. See also Stan Brennan, "The Hanes Family," in Covington and Ellis, *The North Carolina Century*, 149–152.

30. Correspondence, Robert Hanes to wife, June 19, 1918, November 2, 1919, in Robert March Hanes Papers (#4534), Southern Historical Collection, Wilson Library, University of North Carolina at Chapel Hill (hereafter cited as Hanes Papers, SHC). Hanes' experiences in war are also recounted at http://docsouth.unc.edu/wwi/soldiersintro.html, accessed January 3, 2014.

31. Correspondence, Robert Hanes to wife, November 11, 1918, Hanes Papers, SHC.

32. John C. Whitaker, "Robert M. Hanes, Citizen Banker, Statesman," address to the Newcomen Society of North America, Charlotte, April 13, 1956, North Carolina Collection, Wilson Library, University of North Carolina at Chapel Hill (hereafter cited as NCC).

33. Quoted in Michael Hill, "William Bradley Umstead," NCPedia, accessed November 25, 2013, http://ncpedia.org/biography/governors/-umstead.

34. William Umstead, "My Diary, A Soldier's Record," August 29, 1917, Folder 1091, William Bradley and Merle Davis Umstead papers (#4529), Southern Historical Collection, Wilson Library, University of North Carolina at Chapel Hill (hereafter cited as Umstead Papers, SHC).

35. Umstead, "My Diary," September 5, 1917, Folder 1091, Umstead Papers, SHC.

36. Ibid., January 11, 1918.

37. Memorandum, William Umstead to Adjutant General of the Army, February 9, 1919, Folder 1096, Umstead Papers, SHC.

38. Paul Clancy, *Just A Country Lawyer: A Biography of Senator Sam Ervin* (Bloomington: University of Indiana Press, 1974), 57.

39. A. G. Ivey, *Luther H. Hodges, Practical Idealist* (Minneapolis: T.S. Denison & Co., 1968), 67.

40. Correspondence, Luther Hodges to "Dearest Sister," n.d. 1918, Luther H. Hodges Papers, Folder 1, (#3698), Southern Historical Collection, Wilson Library, University of North Carolina at Chapel Hill, (hereafter cited as Hodges Papers).

41. Correspondence, Luther Hodges to "Dearest Sister," September 30, 1918, Hodges Papers, Folder 1, SHC.

42. Correspondence, Luther Hodges to J. J. Hodges, April 1918, Hodges Papers, Folder 1, SHC.

43. On Governor Hodges' political career, see Luther Hodges, *Businessman in the Statehouse: Six Years as Governor of North Carolina* (Chapel Hill: University of North Carolina Press, 1962). On Hodges and civil rights, see Anders Walker, *The Ghost of Jim Crow: How Southern Moderates Used Brown v. Board of Education to Stall Civil Rights* (Oxford: Oxford University Press, 2009), 49–84.

44. Karl Campbell, *Senator Sam Ervin, Last of the Founding Fathers* (Chapel Hill: University of North Carolina, 2007), 35–42.

45. Dick Dabney, *A Good Man: The Life of Sam J. Ervin* (Boston: Houghton Mifflin, 1976), 67; Ervin Corrections to Dabney, Samuel J. Ervin Papers, B., Folder 1159–1160, Southern Historical Collection, Wilson Library, University of North Carolina at Chapel Hill (hereafter cited as Ervin Papers).

46. Dabney, *A Good Man*, 71–72.

47. Clancy, *Just a Country Lawyer*, 67–68; Ervin, *Preserving the Constitution*, 23–24.

48. Ervin, *Preserving the Constitution*, 24.

49. Fred Hardesty, "Little Known Stories About Well-Known People," *The State*, (April 1967): 20; Ervin Corrections to Dabney, Ervin Papers, B., Folder 1160.

50. Clancy, *Just A Country Lawyer*, 72–73.

51. Jean Conyors Ervin interview, with the author, March 17, 2001, 2–3; Ervin quoted in Albert Coates, "Three North Carolinians Who Stood Up to Be Counted for the Bill of Rights," Speech to the North Carolina Democratic Club in Washington, DC, October 18, 1973, 23, NCC.

52. Ervin, *Preserving the Constitution*, 24–26.

53. Campbell, *Senator Sam Ervin*, 1–10, 71.

54. Albert Coates, "Three North Carolinians Who Stood Up to Be Counted for the Bill of Rights."

55. Clancy, *Just a Country Lawyer*, 76.

56. Ibid., 76–77.

57. Pieter Geyl, *Debates with Historians* (Cleveland: Meridian, 1958), accessed July 7, 2016, https://www.google.com/search?q=https%3A%2F%2Fwww.cite.ly%2Fquotes%2Fwars-usually-have-the-effect-of-speeding-up-the%20%20&ie=utf-8&oe=utf-8&aq=t&rls=org.mozilla:en-US:official&client=firefox-a&channel=np&source=hp.

Camden County Council of Defense patriotic celebration poster for an event held on July 14, 1917, in Camden, North Carolina. From Box 31, Folder 8, WWI 1, WWI Papers.

Handmade poster display for a war savings stamp drive during WWI by schoolchildren of the Uncle Sam War Savings Stamps Society at Murphey School.

SEPTEMBER, 1917   **PLEASE POST**   POSTER BULLETIN No. 8

North Carolina State College of Agriculture and Engineering, North Carolina Department of Agriculture, North Carolina Experiment Station, and United States Department of Agriculture, Cooperating

AGRICULTURAL EXTENSION SERVICE
B. W. KILGORE, Director, Raleigh and West Raleigh

Grow More Oats for Hay

| The Time and Place for Oats | A Good Start for Oats | Thorough Preparation Always Pays |

Oats planted this Fall will save money in the Spring. Timothy hay cost $30.00 per ton this Spring. It may go higher. Oat hay is better. Save by growing it at home. When handled properly, oats may provide much good grazing during the early Spring. If mixed with vetch or crimson clover, the grazing and hay are much improved.

Oat Hay Comes In When Other Hays are Scarce and Expensive

| Breaking the Open Fields | | Preparing a Good Seed-bed |

The Oat Crop Comes Off in Time to Plant Soybeans or Cowpeas

| Open Furrow Planting in Cotton | A Good Place for Farm Manures | A Two-ton Hay Crop After Cowpeas |

HINTS ON GROWING OATS. Use the Best Home-grown Seed of the Best-yielding Varieties. Generous Applications of Farm Manures and Properly Balanced Fertilizers will Produce Good Returns. It will Pay to Treat the Seed for Smut Before Sowing. Broadcast Oats are Usually Injured by Cold. Open-furrow Seeding Stands Severe Freezing Best. Use Ample Supply of Seed in Planting. Be Sure the Land is Well Prepared and Thoroughly Drained Before Seeding.

BEST YIELDING VARIETIES

For Mountain Section for Spring Seeding:	For Piedmont Section for Fall Seeding:	For Coastal Plain for Fall Seeding:
Burt	Appler	Fulghum
Fulghum	Fulghum	Red Appler
	Red Rust Proof	Red Rust Proof
	Virginia Turf	

For Further Information Regarding the Growing of Oats, write to the

DIVISION OF AGRONOMY, AGRICULTURAL EXTENSION SERVICE, WEST RALEIGH, NORTH CAROLINA

Agricultural Extension Service poster touting the benefits of Oat Hay, September 1917.

Back of a 1918 post card sent from the brother
of Margaret Leach to Pittsboro, North Carolina.

Camp Greene panorama, 1915.

Surry County war events poster.

Community Cannery, Asheville.

Second Lieutenant Paul Green in
France. Used by permission, Paul
Green Foundation, Chapel Hill,
North Carolina.

Lt. Thomas J. Bullock of Wilmington,
ca. 1917.

North Carolina's cotton farming and textile industries.

North Carolina's cotton farming and textile industries.

North Carolina's cotton farming and textile industries.

North Carolinians worked in various capacities,
including nursing, farming, and education.

North Carolinians worked in various capacities,
including nursing, farming, and education.

North Carolinians worked in various capacities,
including nursing, farming, and education.

North Carolinians worked in various capacities,
including nursing, farming, and education.

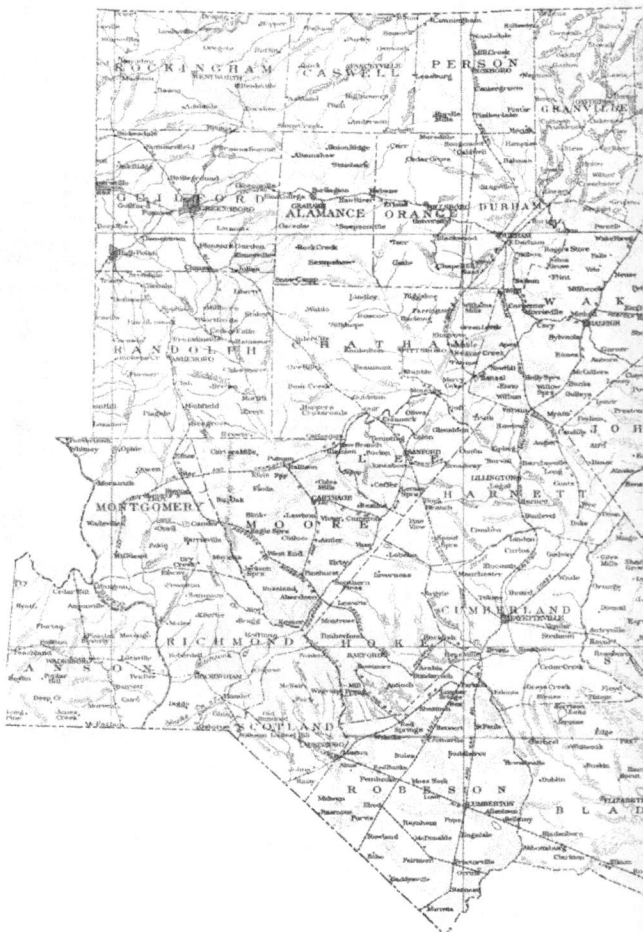

PART FOUR

Homefront

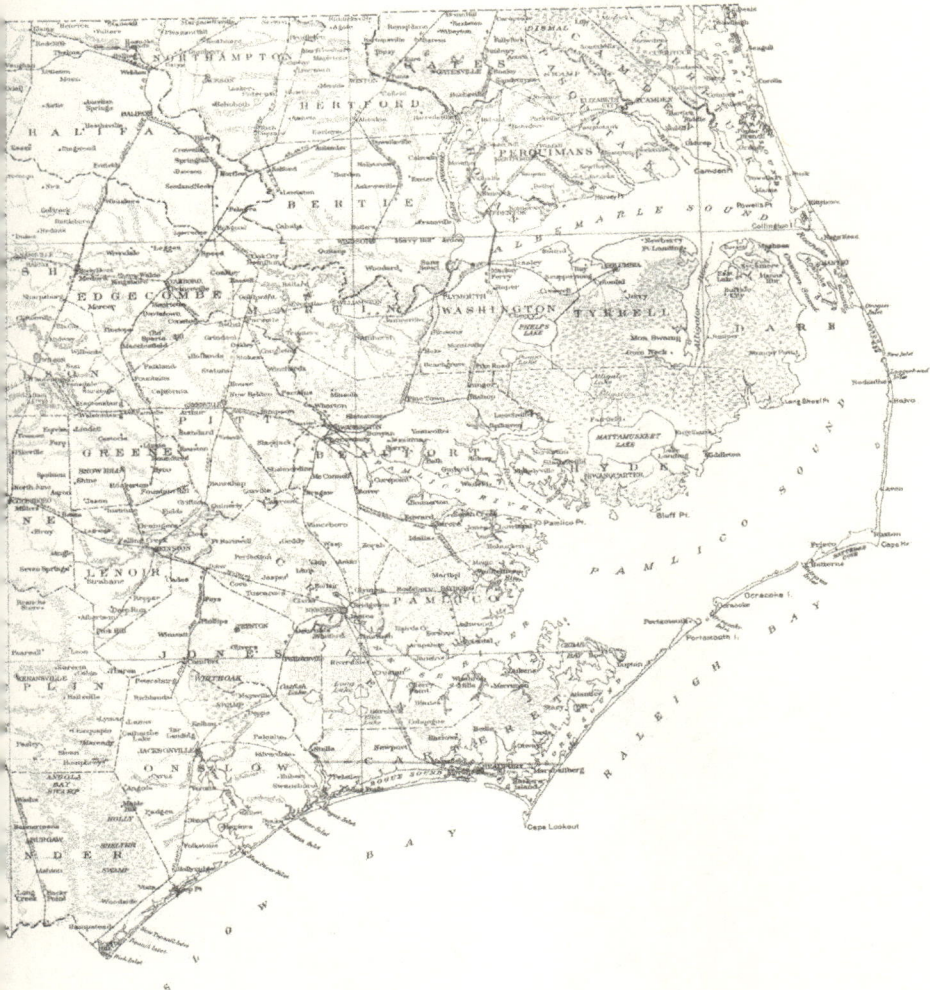

12

"The American Legion Will Come to My Rescue"

Disability in North Carolina's Great War

Pamela C. Edwards

North Carolina sent 86,457 soldiers to fight in the First World War. Of these, 833 died in combat or from wounds sustained in combat, 1,542 died of disease, and 3,655 wounded soldiers survived to return home to the Tar Heel state.[1] Some North Carolina doughboys arrived home with their disability status determined, but others began the process years later, when war-related trauma surfaced to disrupt their lives, livelihood, and health. Between the Civil War and 1919, reform fostered change in multiple social and political arenas, gaining momentum during World War I as professionals from all walks of life focused on the anticipated needs of disabled veterans.[2] The veterans' health care and benefits delivery systems they shaped linked North Carolina with the federal government to a degree not experienced since Reconstruction, but in their initial form, these new institutions proved inadequate to the challenge of meeting the rehabilitation and medical needs of all veterans, particularly those of racial minorities and the mentally ill. In response, North Carolina's disabled veterans and their friends, families, and advocacy groups participated in grassroots efforts to improve and broaden the institutions and programs formed to serve them.[3]

Federal and state benefits programs established for Civil War veterans influenced those who planned for the care of disabled veterans during the First World War. After the Civil War, Congress established a pension system for disabled and, ultimately, all veterans of the Union forces as well as their widows and children. Patriotic nostalgia and the growing political power of veterans led to the expansion of services for the aging boys in blue well into the twentieth century.[4] The South's veterans did not receive these benefits. Veteran care established by the Confederate government collapsed during the war, as did initial efforts by most southern states during Reconstruction.[5] This was not the case for North Carolina, which established a program sustained by state tax revenues to supply prosthetic limbs and pensions for veterans.[6] Both federal and state programs expanded to the point that benefits offered to Civil War veterans and their dependents dominated the federal budget as well as those of the former Confederate states, including North Carolina. While some called for expanding old-age pensions to nonveterans, others claimed that Civil War veterans' benefits were bloated by political corruption, fostered dependence, and undermined American masculinity.[7] Historian Beth Linker identifies two prominent North Carolinians who criticized the federal pension system prior to the First World War: journalist-turned-ambassador Walter Hines Page and Trinity College and Duke University economist William H. Glasson.[8] To correct what they considered mistakes of the Civil War era, free-trade and anti-union progressives like Page and Glasson supported alternative pension systems focused on insurance and education. They believed each disabled veteran should be medically repaired and rehabilitated for employment to live as independently as possible. As the views of Page and Glasson reveal, turn-of-the-century progressives spanned the political spectrum, though few escaped society's prevailing racism and prejudice against the disabled.[9]

Rejecting Civil War era pension systems, Progressive Era professionals shaping what became the U.S. Department of Veterans Affairs (VA) drew on other nineteenth century social experiments, including industrial training schools, workmen's compensation, protective labor laws for women and children, and public health care systems for disabled children and tuberculosis patients. At the federal level, the War Risk Insurance Act of 1917 deducted financial support for wives and dependent children from the paycheck of married soldiers, gave each recruit the opportunity to purchase life and disability insurance, and in case of a war-related disabling injury or disease, guaranteed set rates of compensation, medical care, and vocational rehabilitation in addition to insurance claims.[10] Additionally, the Smith-Hughes National Vocational Education Act (1917) and the Smith-Sears Veterans Rehabilitation Act (1918) established educational rehabilitation programs and mandated medical care, ultimately leading to formation of the Federal Bureau of Vocational Education (FBVE), the American Legion, and the VA.[11] The goal of employment for disabled veterans reflected unquestioning commitment to medical science and technological innovation and a gendered understanding of labor and the patriarchal family. For middle-class reformers, reconstructing and reemploying disabled veterans secured each soldier's masculine place in society, avoiding the perceived pitfalls of existing pension systems.[12] This white middle-class construct of masculinity sought to secure white male patriarchal dominance in their homes, jobs, and society.[13]

Although the War Risk Insurance Act passed with unanimous support, related congressional hearings and publications indicated that not everyone believed that the legislation prevented the continuation or expansion of the existing federal pension system. To the contrary, some congressmen predicted that First World War veterans would seek additional support after the war, and even the author of the act, Judge Julian Mack, acknowledged that the legislation would likely evolve with time. Survivors of both the Civil War and the Spanish– American War demonstrated that medical complications often surfaced years after a conflict, and the political power of and popular support for veterans encouraged them and their dependents to seek more generous benefits.[14] Additionally, American doctors and surgeons who visited Europe's battlefields knew the tremendous medical challenges posed by modern warfare. The physical damage to soldiers' bodies and the psychological trauma associated with prolonged exposure to bombardment on the Western Front had been seen in previous conflicts, but recent advances in medical treatment allowed soldiers to survive wounds that proved fatal in the Civil War.[15] Because they survived with more severe injuries and illnesses, First World War veterans often faced complicated and long-term health care needs. New chemical weapons caused blindness and severe respiratory problems, often fostering lifelong struggles with tuberculosis. Private Terry Brady of Halifax County recalled, "The gas was dreadful. . . . Some of the boys' lips began to bleed; some lost eye sight; many were knocked out completely. . . . Not any of us were equipped with gas masks."[16] Despite advances, some fields of medicine were more advanced than others; psychiatry, for instance, was still in its infancy in 1917. American soldiers suffering from "shell shock" were brought behind the frontlines just long enough to restore a degree of rationality, and then they were returned to their units as quickly as possible. Instead of helping, this "frontline" psychological treatment method based on the "principles of proximity, immediacy, and expectancy" or "P.I.E." often deepened and extended the trauma veterans experienced.[17] In this and other situations, the idealism of reformers fell short of reality, and disabled veterans had to challenge medical experts and government officials before they received adequate care and financial support.[18]

Drawing on the experiences of Europeans, the US Army Medical Corps responded to the rehabilitation mandates of the War Risk Insurance Act by recruiting physicians, surgeons, and nurses and by engineering a system of field hospitals, recovery centers, and medical ships to bring wounded soldiers home.[19] Corpsmen and ambulance drivers located and treated the wounded on the battlefield, providing stop-gap first aid before transporting them to aid posts and then to field hospitals. Mobile field hospitals consisted of a few tents where one or two doctors worked with about twenty-five medical corpsmen and nurses. The military organized two hospital units with North Carolina personnel, including the 4400–bed Base Hospital 65, which was established behind the frontlines in France.[20] Ambulances moved stabilized but severely wounded soldiers from field hospitals to evacuation centers in port cities where hospital ships waited to transport them home.[21] Stateside, amputees went to specialized wards in major research hospitals where teams of orthopedic surgeons, nurses, and therapists directed healing, therapy, prosthetic fitting, and initially, vocational training. In 1917 the army established the Division of Special Hospitals and Physical Reconstruction, and in 1918, Walter Reed Army Hospital opened its Artificial Limb Lab. To foster innovation, lab administrators encouraged formation of the Artificial Limb Manufacturers and Brace Association. As the list of war-related disabilities expanded, the Army Medical Department added medical specialists and specialized care centers in psychiatry, neurology, psychology, ophthalmology, and tuberculosis.[22] In addition, federal employees interacted with state governments, setting up regional administrative and medical facilities to serve veterans throughout the nation.

The FBVE's District 5 served the Southeast and was headquartered in Atlanta. While directives and oversight radiated out from the Atlanta offices, disabled veterans returning to North Carolina received rehabilitation and vocational training in facilities scattered throughout their home state, including the Oteen Veteran's Hospital in Asheville, the Veteran's Bureau Vocational School in Waynesville, and sanatoriums in Black Mountain and Asheville.[23] Raymond W. Ferris, first Acting District Vocational Officer in Atlanta, set up a Case Board to advise the FBVE, with the assistance of T. E. Whitaker, a southern labor union activist associated with the US Department of Labor.[24] FBVE representatives cooperated with trade schools throughout North Carolina to identify training space for disabled veterans' vocational education; these trade schools included the Normal and Industrial Institute in Albemarle, the Asheville Farm School, the Brevard Institute, the Southern Industrial Institute in Charlotte, the US Indian Industrial School in Cherokee, and the Eastern North Carolina Industrial School Company in New Bern.[25] Vocational advisers stationed at military medical facilities, including those in Azalea, Waynesville, and at Camp Green in Charlotte, made contact with disabled veterans, informed them of vocational education opportunities, and assisted them in applying for admission to FBVE programs.[26] Ideally, a superintendent of employment followed up with each veteran to make sure he secured a permanent job.[27] Administrators and Case Board members also scoured the countryside making contact with prospective employers, high schools, colleges, and universities to identify types of labor and training facilities suitable for the diverse population of disabled veterans. One effort attempted to secure land for those who wanted to begin or continue farming.[28] The list of occupations in which veterans indicated interest continued to grow and included accountant, motion picture machine operator, radio operator, auto mechanic, electrician, carpenter, plumber, optometrist, lawyer, physician, journalist, businessman, minister, textile manufacturer, salesman, teacher, and banker.[29] Once a veteran signed up for training, the FBVE paid transportation and housing expenses incurred while attending a vocational education program.[30]

While administrators seemed dedicated to enrolling all disabled veterans and ensuring each man gainful employment, they encountered multiple difficulties in implementing vocational education programs. Even FBVE officials seemed confused as to when and through which programs veterans should receive compensation, training, or both.[31] The goal was to contact all disabled veterans before they left medical facilities, to enroll them in training programs, and to follow their progress through visits and employment surveys. Working out of FBVE offices in larger cities, such as Charlotte and Asheville, neither regional nor state facilities employed enough staff members to handle the geographically dispersed workload.[32] In December 1922, the Charlotte office employed 7 men to deal with recruiting, advising, and supervising some 277 disabled veterans. In that same year, supervisors in the Asheville subdivision received a severe critique when an audit of files revealed poor record keeping and infrequent followup visits.[33] Additionally, setting up new training facilities proved expensive, and many existing facilities did not have enough space to accommodate disabled trainees using wheelchairs or other enabling technologies. Many facilities did not have the recommended or functioning equipment to provide hands-on training. One auto mechanic training facility did not have a cylinder regrinding machine, although learning to use it was a required part of the standardized curriculum.[34] Some training programs were little more than correspondence schools, such that North Carolina veterans trained to be superintendents, poultry farmers, postal clerks, and salesmen by corresponding with schools based in Pennsylvania and Illinois.[35] During a conference held at FBVE district offices in Atlanta, W. I. Hamilton reported that many attendees complained about inadequate facilities, and some rejected the entire concept of vocational training, declaring "that the South knows best what is good for the South, and the ingrown idea that training is 'book-learning'" contributed to "a very difficult and possibly a hopeless situation."[36] He and others at the conference found available facilities for industrial training so poor that on-the-job apprenticeships seemed the only viable option.[37] In fact, supervision reports for farmer trainees in North Carolina indicate that many disabled soldiers "trained" on their own or their father's farms while receiving FBVE payments.[38]

Beyond administrative and logistical issues, the diverse population of disabled veterans in District 5 did not have equal access to benefits programs. Different disabilities required different types of vocational training. North Carolina's existing facilities for the blind served only children, so most blind (and many deaf) veterans went out of state to acquire training if they pursued it at all.[39] Tuberculosis and mental health patients faced difficulties in taking advantage of educational programs and sustaining employment afterwards. Training officers reported that "tuberculous men . . . are to a serious extent, breaking down and many will . . . have to stop training and return to a sanatorium . . . because of failing . . . health." J. Foster Searles recommended developing a treatment and recovery center in North Carolina's Appalachian Mountains for veterans with tuberculosis who could not complete training.[40] Mental health patients also raised unique challenges for the VA system. A veteran might qualify for rehabilitation training based on physical disability, but if his "mental condition unfits him for training," he would be "turned at large to 'shift' for" himself unless his home state made provisions for his care. According to one vocational officer, "provisions . . . for men suffering from any mental disarrangement" were "meager and inadequate."[41] African American veterans fared worst of all in this system; they received less care and training, and they had applications for disability status rejected at a significantly higher rate than white veterans.

It is important to note that the medical and administrative professionals who developed the policies and programs intended to serve disabled veterans did so during the era of Jim Crow, when some scientists embraced the racial hierarchies of eugenics. Discrimination began with recruitment and continued through training and deployment, ultimately impacting the care received by disabled African American veterans.[42] Officials often attributed the health problems of black soldiers to hygiene, diet, or other personal shortcomings, making it more difficult for blacks than for whites to document and prove war-related disabilities.[43] Vocational education in the Southeast was segregated, which initially required disabled black veterans from North Carolina to enroll in out-of-state training programs at Tuskegee Normal and Industrial Institute in Alabama and Hampton Normal and Agricultural Institute in Virginia.[44] Eventually segregated in-state facilities, including the Normal and Industrial Schools in Clinton and Edenton, the Agricultural and Technical College in Greensboro, and the Shaw University Department of Industries in Raleigh, became available.[45] Health care facilities were also segregated and often out of state; as one memo circulated to district-five administrators noted, "negroes are being sent to the Marine Hospitals at Ft. Stanton [in New Mexico] and St. Louis. Some are also to be sent to a Sanatorium at Battle Hill, Atlanta."[46] Segregated facilities in distant locations made administrative followup more difficult and less likely to occur, making it more probable that disabled African American veterans would fail to receive adequate health care or full access to available benefits.

Despite the system's inherent racism, some FBVE supervisors ably and energetically assisted North Carolina's African American veterans. Rolland Tyson Winstead of Rocky Mount, who completed his medical degree at historically black Meharry Medical College in Nashville, thanked FBVE staff for the support he received.[47] In an early memo, FBVE district director Ferris called attention to low literacy rates among African American disabled veterans. What they needed most, he suggested, was elementary education. Ferris wanted the FBVE to pay local teachers to tutor black veterans after hours, teaching them to read and write, "the fundamental operations of arithmetic and the rudiments of geography, American history and civics" before drawing them into vocational training.[48] Administrators ultimately rejected his suggestion as too complex because it involved the issue of funding and segregation of education throughout the South. Literacy proved to be a widespread problem for southern disabled veterans, white and black; FBVE appointees expressed shock at some veterans' low levels of educational achievement.[49]

As medical doctors and administrators worked with disabled veterans during the war, they also expanded definitions of disability to encompass the physical assessment and training of recruits. Army officers measured male candidates on an "able-ness" spectrum ranging from fit enough for military duty to not meeting minimal requirements for soldiering. Records of the Headquarters Sanitary Detachment in Sevier, South Carolina, where many North Carolinians were stationed, reveal that soldiers with serious health problems often enlisted, while others were injured during training. Depending on how it interfered with a soldier's ability to perform assigned duties, any injury, illness, or handicap might lead to a disability discharge application and review.[50] One recruit, Tebe Woodell of Monroe, came into the military with epilepsy, and as his condition deteriorated, he grew weaker and suffered "recurring attacks of unconsciousness."[51] Woodell's clinical history documented in his discharge review indicated that he experienced seizures for almost three years before joining the military.[52] Health assessments conducted at his recruitment failed to gather a comprehensive medical history, and this was not an isolated incident. Months after enlistment and the beginning of training, numerous soldiers were identified as "mentally defective."[53] At other times, health issues such as flawed vision, extensive varicose veins, chronic ear infections, heart disease, rheumatism, and lung trouble led to disability discharge reviews.[54] The variety of health problems identified as potentially disabling suggest that the US military developed a flexible and broad definition of able-ness centered on the ability of a recruit to carry out assigned duties. This definition, however, was itself corrupted by racial and class-based conceptions of manhood and wellness. Despite expressed concerns for racial balance in all branches of the military, examiners accepted a greater percentage of African American recruits despite higher rates of poverty, malnutrition, and more serious health issues. Black recruits received minimal training before becoming the earliest soldiers transported to Europe, and while in the military, they experienced substandard housing, services, and medical care.[55]

Experience with enlisting and discharging recruits with disabilities raised concerns about the physical preparedness of the general population, which compelled officials to discuss public health and national security concerns in tandem. The recognition that health was an issue central to the war effort surfaced in multiple ways. Since the War Risk Act required federal authorities to offer each soldier the opportunity to obtain insurance, they needed a way to send information and forms directly to recruits and draftees. Each state formed a Council of Defense made up of prominent citizens, and state councils in turn organized and worked with local Councils of Defense at the county and municipal levels. Volunteers staffed all levels of the councils of defense in North Carolina. Local branches formed Soldiers' Business Aid Committees to take care of anticipated needs of deployed soldiers, assisting them in writing wills, protecting property, and checking on their families. They helped recruits take out war risk insurance policies and arranged for paycheck deductions for their wives and dependents. The committees also offered additional aid to military families in the form of health care, food, and child care. These preparatory services stopped when county councils encountered communitywide health care crises, such as outbreaks of typhoid fever and influenza, requiring a statewide response coordinated with the state Board of Health and multiple medical facilities.[56] The ramifications of total war brought home the message that health care began on the local level and was closely associated with preparedness.[57] The First World War expanded already existing conceptions of public health, and heightened awareness of disabled veterans drew attention to degrees of able-ness in the general population.

The most prevalent cause for extending disability discharges to enlisted soldiers during the war was tuberculosis (TB), which spread easily in the unsanitary conditions encountered in crowded military camps and on the frontlines.[58] Gas attacks, which damaged soldiers' lungs, made them more vulnerable to TB, and veterans contracting TB during the war often faced a lifetime of poor physical and intellectual health. Neighbors and friends of John C. Haithcox of Monroe noted dramatic changes in the young man after he returned from Europe having survived a gas attack. According to C. J. Jones, Haithcox suffered from "a constant cough, hawking and expectorating. . . . [W]hen he was working he was constantly sitting down from feeling weak and nervous, hurting in [his] chest, and [a] light headache. . . . [B]eing sick consumed at least half of his time."[59] Constant and severe fatigue and pain, coughing, difficulty breathing, and problems with memory and depression were typical symptoms of TB and disrupted work and daily activities.[60] Administrators in Atlanta worked with the Red Cross and the Anti-Tuberculosis Society to identify between 800 and 900 veterans suffering from TB in District 5 alone.[61]

While tuberculosis was the most documented cause for a disability discharge, the most prevalent wartime injury was what is now labeled Post Traumatic Stress Disorder (PTSD). During and following the First World War, medical professionals had little knowledge about PTSD or traumatic brain injuries (TBIs), but there was a recognition that some soldiers experienced "shell shock" or "neurasthenia" after spending long hours in underground bunkers during big-gun shelling campaigns or after extended exposure to combat. These soldiers exhibited a variety of symptoms including hysteria and anxiety, paralysis, limping and muscle contractions, blindness and deafness, nightmares and insomnia, heart palpitations, depression, dizziness and disorientation, and loss of appetite.[62] Many veterans continued to experience side effects long after the war, which is also the case for those diagnosed with PTSD and TBIs today. Symptoms of PTSD, in particular, often grew more intense with the passage of time and confused those closest to the veteran, who had seemed fine for years after his combat experience.[63] Identifying mental health issues associated with PTSD and/or TBI among veterans, particularly after they returned to civilian life, proved challenging. Those suffering from PTSD often isolated themselves from their families and communities, making diagnosis, treatment, and compensation more difficult to secure.[64]

Despite the fact that veterans' emotional and psychological illnesses often went undiagnosed and untreated, some surviving letters and medical records document the difficulties faced in identifying and responding to their mental health issues. For instance, on December 11, 1928, Charles L. Dunkel composed a letter to the North Carolina Department of the American Legion from Broughton Hospital in Morganton. Admitted against his will into the state mental institution, he explained: "I am a married man having a wife and 2 small children. I had purchased a home in Greensboro, bought a house full of nice furniture and was getting along happily—I was succeeding in business, having managed a sales force for a Chicago Corporation for the entire state."[65] According to his own report, Dunkel's life was going well, but then "suddenly I became sick as a result of my war wounds had to go to a hospital —where I used up all my savings. Suddenly my wife became cold & deserted me took my baby to her mother's &. . . had me railroaded to the 'Big House.'" Several points in his narrative raise questions. He began by noting that he was incarcerated and then "railroaded here for ulterior motives after false allegations had been made concerning my sanity." He lost his job, his money, and his wife "suddenly" and seemed to have no clear understanding as to why these misfortunes came his way. Later, when he described the trial, Dunkel again claimed "false allegations were made from sinister sources . . . to get rid of me. A fake alienist [sic] who had never before in his life saw me for a moment made in 3 minutes examination of me. In spite of an affidavit from the Veterans Bureau to the effect that I was sane the Judge denied my motion for a release."[66] All of this may have been true, but his grievances may also indicate a break with reality characterized by paranoia and delusions of persecution, all typical symptoms of PTSD. In another case, Edith G. Barton wrote from an American Legion Auxiliary in Tennessee to Mrs. John A. Porter, President of the American Legion Auxiliary in Concord, North Carolina. Barton hoped to find a home for the young son of veteran Paul Caudle who had admitted himself to the Soldier's Home in Johnson City. He arrived with his seven-year-old son, "in a very pitiful condition," and she hoped to reconnect the child with his grandfather in Kannapolis.[67] Caudle sought treatment at a hospital for nervous men, and Barton did "not think the child should be left with him for he wanders all over the country." Caudle could not work or care for the boy and was "most impatient . . . and may change his mind any time. He has tramped from Kannapolis to Baltimore and back here in the last two months. . . . The child was very dirty and rather neglected when he arrived."[68] Caudle and Dunkel's post-war experiences document the overlapping challenges faced by veterans suffering from shell shock, including emotional instability; homelessness; unemployment; and difficulties sustaining relationships with spouses, family, and friends.

While the military discharged some soldiers with a 100% or total disability rating, most received a degree of disability assessment; this appeared on discharge papers as a ratio intended to represent the severity of the veteran's disability. Methods of calculating the ratio changed in 1917, 1924, and again in 1933, but through most of the inter-war years, the degree of disability was based on "the average impairment in earning capacity" or the "average loss of earnings for all occupations performing manual labor."[69] If the soldier received, for example, a 10/100 ratio, he was considered 10% disabled, and compensation payments reflected this assessment. Although this assessment and compensation system had its origins in Civil War veterans' pensions and workmen's compensation settlements, tools for measuring degrees of disability became more precise after 1918, as VA medical administrators created detailed mathematical tables in an effort to standardize the assessment process. For decades the manual of disability tables was closely guarded, hidden from veterans and congressmen alike. Calculated by committees of experts, the tables attempted to quantify the work-related impact of every conceivable type of wartime wound or disease.[70] As experts applied standards of description and the language of mathematical percentages to the wounded bodies and minds of veterans, they defined and redefined disability to encompass a spectrum based on an idealized average, an almost mechanized, human form and capacity. Institutional willingness to parse and measure the bodies of disabled veterans sometimes broached absurdity, as the case of one North Carolina veteran, J. J. Thomas, indicates: "gun shot wound, elbow, 15%; gun shot wound, right ankle, 28%; gun shot wound, left thigh 22%; gun shot wound, left scrotum 0%; gun shot wound, chest, 0%; combined ratings 51% permanent partial. . . . It is noted that the veteran complained of pains in his chest. The last examination failed to show any respiratory disability and it failed to show that there was any nerve involvement, loss of muscle, limitation of motion, or adhesions of the scar on chest."[71]

The military took pains to determine if a soldier came into the service with a disabling condition as opposed to becoming disabled in the line of duty, qualifying him for a disability status and payments after the war.[72] While young soldiers undoubtedly valued a fully-abled status upon discharge, their situations often changed dramatically in decades following the war. What initially appeared to be a controllable condition could grow worse, eroding the veteran's ability to work and function with the same degree of skill and energy. When this happened, veterans, such as Leland Brown of Rich Square, applied to the VA to establish a disability status. Brown sustained a lung injury diagnosed during the war as bronchitis and pharyngitis subacute exacerbated by his battlefield injuries. He secured a disability allowance of $12.00 per month, but this came just before passage of the Disability Allowance Act cancelled further payments.[73] Under the 1933 law and executive order, both signed by Franklin D. Roosevelt, nonservice-connected disability warranted a pension payment only if it was permanently and totally disabling.[74] To receive disability benefits, Brown had to reapply and either prove that his disability was service related or demonstrate 100% disability. Brown's most recent diagnosis was bronchiectasis, different than his wartime diagnosis, and therefore, according to reviewers, not a service-related disability. Brown appealed the decision, arguing, "my condition has become more acute since I was discharged from service. . . . I am unable to engage in regular employment of a gainful kind and [am] gradually becoming worse. I was in good health when I entered service as my service record shows; I was not in good health when I was discharged."[75] Brown's civilian physician submitted a supporting affidavit, reporting, "I did treat Mr. Leland Brown in the year of 1919 following his discharge from the army for a chronic bronchitis and have off and on each year since, and for the past two years it has developed into a bronchial asthma. I am sure it is not improving any under my treatment." [76] His case dragged on for years, evidence that disability benefits were not easy to obtain.

It is likely that other North Carolina veterans struggled to gain access to benefits they thought were legally and ethically theirs.[77] Like Brown, many of them found support from comrades in local American Legions throughout the state. Marion Crawford, Executive Secretary of the American Legion Auxiliary in Greensboro, commented on the plight of veteran Clyde Thacker who contacted the local Legion for help. Discharged "with 25% disability . . . in line of duty," Thacker was "in a very nervous condition and we assisted him in filling out forms" to file a compensation claim, but Thacker did not wait to get the results. Crawford records that Thacker "left Greensboro and we were unable to locate him."[78] Thacker showed up again some five years later, "stating that his condition was exceedingly bad, that he was very nervous and wished to be entered in a government hospital."[79] At times local officials or health care providers, some of whom may have been veterans, contacted the local American Legion on behalf of a veteran they knew was in trouble. A. T. Walston, Clerk of Superior Court in Tarboro and a Legion member, wrote to the Superintendent of the State Hospital in Raleigh seeking help for a North

Carolinian jailed after release from the Veterans Hospital in Perryville, Maryland, noting that his "mental condition is such that we cannot permit him to be at large, for he is what I consider a dangerous man in his present mental condition."[80]

Delayed diagnosis and compensation and the social stigma associated with the poverty accompanying those delays had detrimental consequences for veterans and their families. Even when a veteran received some percentage of disability, compensation might not be enough to support a family and create a stable home. Diagnosed with "mental deficiency," Tucker Perry of Pittsboro drew $16.00 per month compensation, which surprised the reviewing officer because "under the World War Veterans Act there is no compensation allowed for mental deficiency."[81] To receive disability benefits for tuberculosis, John C. Haithcox had to apply to the VA within five years of the armistice. The five-year limit was somewhat arbitrary as officials estimated that any tubercular symptoms associated with wartime experiences would manifest themselves in that time, but this also assumed that the veteran was aware of the deadline.[82] By 1928 the year of Haithcox's application, officials associated with the US Veterans Hospital in Oteen issued a statement outlining inconsistencies in the disabilities compensation application process for those suffering from TB and the inequities in treatment those inconsistencies created. Tubercular symptoms differed from one veteran to the next; those with mild infections might have few manifestations of the disease before a rapid onset of severe symptoms years later. Thus, a veteran contracting the disease during the war but not displaying symptoms until 1926 was not eligible for disability compensation, a severe blow to his personal and family finances.[83]

While disability benefits often were difficult to attain, being diagnosed with emotional or mental competency issues carried social and legal stigmas that also posed lifelong problems for veterans. Frank B. Leake wrote to the State Commander of the American Legion in Raleigh: "I am a disabled exService man. . . . I was wounded . . . and have been treated in Various Bureau Hospitals. I was adjudged incompitant [sic] by Medical Board."[84] This new status prevented his legal marriage in North Carolina because state laws allowed an appointed guardian to oversee decisions impacting the estate or income of "any non-sane person."[85]

Between 1919 and 1921, the American Legion formed a Committee on Rehabilitation to address the long-term negative impacts of poverty and social stigma on veterans, their wives, children, and extended family members fostered by delayed diagnoses of combat-related disabilities and receipt of benefit payments. The national convention concluded that "problems connected with the care of our disabled comrades have not yet been solved. Thirty thousand of them are today in hospitals, a greater number than at any time since the Armistice. Acute diseases and minor injuries have been successfully dealt with, but of those in hospitals today, a large majority are suffering from serious disorders which may result in their death or in lifetime invalidism."[86] Throughout the 1920s, the Committee on Rehabilitation lobbied for centralization of veterans' care under the VA and became the gadfly overseeing VA interactions with veterans, appointing subcommittees of experts on mental and nervous disorders, tuberculosis, medical and surgical cases, vocational training, compensation, and insurance. While the Legion itself was hierarchical and characterized by large regional offices that mirrored the VA's administrative structure, local American Legion clubs served as centers of support for individual veterans and their families.[87] Many veterans trusted the American Legion, and when their backs were against the wall, they turned to local Legion members for help. When federal officials invalidated Leland Brown's initial disability allowance, it was J. G. Madry, a District Commander in the American Legion and a fellow Rich Square resident, who advocated on Brown's behalf.[88] In his letter to the American Legion, Charles Dunkel expressed desperation but also his trust in the organization: "Being a disabled world war veteran & a former member . . . I am writing you in the belief that the American Legion will come to my rescue."[89] But the American Legion did not serve all veterans equally and "set no nationwide standards for admission of blacks but permitted each state organization to make its own rules." Some southern states, including North Carolina, permitted segregated posts for African American and Native American veterans, but "these were not permitted to send representatives to state or national conventions and their members were not eligible for office above the local level."[90] In other words, minority posts could not influence priorities and did not receive a fair share of the jobs or health care benefits wrought by the white power structure of the largest and most recognized veterans' advocacy organization.

As Walter Hines Page predicted, a nationalized health care system for disabled veterans drew former Confederate states like North Carolina back into the national mainstream, fostering regional medical and educational reform. While Page and other progressive reformers sought to replace Civil War era pensions with compensation, rehabilitation, and vocational education for disabled veterans, they were only partially successful. Their ambitious undertaking placed too much confidence in technology and training, creating a system that could not adequately respond to the complex medical needs of the Great War's veterans. Reformers committed to a vocational rehabilitation response to wartime disability drew on conceptions of manhood and masculinity that privileged households headed by white males, as well as middle-class cultural norms that sustained racialized and gendered stereotypes and stigmatized those suffering from mental as opposed to physical wounds. Much like the incremental expansion of veterans' benefits in the nineteenth century, additional legislation and public support expanded health care access and compensation for growing numbers of veterans. This required long-term and coordinated pressure from veterans and their advocates before the United States achieved a comprehensive and permanent veteran's health care system that incorporated pensions, health care, and rehabilitation. It would take still longer for civil rights and mental health advocacy to challenge discriminatory practices impacting the care of African American, Native American, and mentally ill veterans. The voices of North Carolina's disabled veterans emerge in the letters they wrote and in the activism of veterans' and civil rights groups organized to challenge and demand a response from government officials, health care professionals, and the broader community.[91] Over the long course of the twentieth century, this combination of advocacy by politicians, medical professionals, and citizens on behalf of disabled veterans resulted in improved health care for all North Carolinians and fed a slow but expanding consensus that a national health care system could contain costs, reach more citizens, and foster a stronger, healthier democracy.

Notes

1. R. Jackson Marshall III, *Memories of World War I: North Carolina Doughboys on the Western Front* (Raleigh: North Carolina Division of Archives and History, 1998), 170.

2. Beth Linker, *War's Waste: Rehabilitation in World War I America* (Chicago: University of Chicago Press, 2011), 3–8; Theda Skocpol, *Protecting Soldiers and Mothers: The Political Origins of Social Policy in the United States* (London: Belknap Press of Harvard University Press, 1992), 160–171.

3. K. Walter Hickel, "Medicine, Bureaucracy, and Social Welfare: The Politics of Disability Compensation for American Veterans of World War I," in ed. Paul M. Longmore and Lauri Umansky, *The New Disability History: American Perspectives* (New York: New York University Press, 2001), 252–258.

4. Linker, *War's Waste*, 11–17; Skocpol, *Protecting*, 102–115.

5. David A. Gerber, "Introduction: Finding Disabled Veterans in History," in ed. David A. Gerber, *Disabled Veterans in History* (Ann Arbor: University of Michigan Press, 2012), Kindle location [kl] 655–776; R. B. Rosenburg, "Empty Sleeves and Wooden Pegs: Disabled Confederate Veterans in Image and Reality," in ed. David A. Gerber, *Disabled Veterans in History*, kl 4986–5541; Megan Kate Nelson, *Ruin Nation: Destruction and the American Civil War* (Athens: University of Georgia Press, 2012), kl 2827–3914; Eric T. Dean Jr., *Shook Over Hell: Post-Traumatic Stress, Vietnam, and the Civil War* (Cambridge: Harvard University Press, 1997), 142–153.

6. Ansley Herring Wegner, *Phantom Pain: North Carolina's Artificial-Limbs Program for Confederate Veterans* (Raleigh: Office of Archives and History, North Carolina Department of Cultural Resources, 2004), 3, 19–35; Guy R. Hasegawa, *Mending Broken Soldiers: The Union and Confederate Programs to Supply Artificial Limbs* (Carbondale: Southern Illinois University Press, 2012), 75.

7. Wegner, *Phantom Pain*, 32–35; Skocpol, *Protecting*, 120–130; Linker, *War's Waste*, 17–27.

8. Linker, *War's Waste*, 14–27; Troy L. Kicker, "Walter Hines Page (1855–1918)," North Carolina History Project, accessed August 14, 2014, http://www.northcarolinahistory.org; "William Henry Glasson, 1874–1946," William S. Powell, ed. *Dictionary of North Carolina Biography* Vol. 2, D-G (University of North Carolina Press, 1986) Documenting the American South, (University Library. The University of North Carolina at Chapel Hill, 2004) (hereafter cited as DocSouth), accessed August 12, 2014, http://docsouth.unc.edu; William H. Glasson, *Federal Military Pensions in the United States* (Oxford: Oxford University Press, 1918), https://archive.org.

9. Linker, *War's Waste*, 27–35, 59–69; Hickel, "Medicine, Bureaucracy," 236–245; Robert J. Rusnak, *Walter Hines Page and the World's Work, 1900–1913* (Washington, DC: University Press of America, 1982), 75–131.

10. Samuel McCune Lindsay, "Purpose and Scope of War Risk Insurance," *Annals of the American Academy of Political and Social Science* 79 (September 1918): 52–68; Economic Systems, Inc., VA Disability Compensation Program: Legislative History, (VA Office of Policy, Planning, and Preparedness, December 2004): 1–48; Richard G. Cholmeley-Jones, "War Risk Insurance," *Scientific Monthly* 12:3 (March 1921): 228–235; John L. Todd, "The Duty of War Pension," *North American Review* 210:767 (October 1919): 449–511.

11. Economic Systems, Inc., VA Disability Compensation Program, 30, 33–49; Linker, *War's Waste*, 147–165.

12. Hickel, "Medicine, Bureaucracy," 242–244; Skocpol, *Protecting*, 205–215, 350–361; Linker, *War's Waste*, 27–51; Michael J. Lansing, "Salvaging the Man Power of America: Conservation, Manhood, and Disabled Veterans During World War I," *Environmental History* 14 (January 2009): 32–50; Mark Aldrich, *Safety First: Technology, Labor and Business in the Building of American Work Safety, 1870–1939* (Baltimore: Johns Hopkins University Press, 1997), 76–121; Paul K. Longmore, "The League of the Physically Handicapped and the Great Depression: A Case Study in the New Disability History" and "Why I Burned My Book" in ed. Paul K. Longmore, *Why I Burned My Book and Other Essays on Disability* (Philadelphia: Temple University Press, 2003), 53–101, 230–259.

13. Arthur E. Barbeau and Florette Henri, *The Unknown Soldiers: Black American Troops in World War I* (Philadelphia: Temple University Press, 1974), 111–163; Chad L. Williams, *Torchbearers of Democracy: African American Soldiers in the World War I Era* (Chapel Hill: University of North Carolina Press, 2010), 7–68; Gerald Horne, *Black and Brown: African Americans and the Mexican Revolution, 1910–1920* (New York: New York University Press, 2005), 92–109.

14. United States Congress, Senate Committee on War Risk Insurance H.R. 5723, Hearing Before the Subcommittee of the Committee on Finance 65th Congress, First Session (September 18, 1917); K. Walter Hickel, "War, Region, and Social Welfare: Federal Aid to Servicemen's Dependents in the South, 1917–1921," *Journal of American History* 87:4 (March 2001): 1369; Julia C. Lathrop, "The Military and Naval Insurance Act," *The Nation* 106:2745 (February 7, 1918): 157–158; George E. Ide, "Governmental War Insurance and War Taxation," *The Nation* 106:2745 (February 7, 1918): 158–160; Mark Sullivan, "One Year of President Harding," *World's Work* 43:1 (November 1921): 31.

15. Thomas Fleming, "Nurse on the Edge of No Man's Land," *MHQ: Quarterly Journal of Military History* 17:4 (June 1, 2005): 34–41; Dean, Jr., *Shook Over Hell*, 51–52, 78–80.

16. K. May, Private Terry Brady, Box 7, Halifax – Biographical Sketches, North Carolina County War Records, WWI 2, WWI Papers [WWI], Military Collection (MC), State Archives of North Carolina (SANC), Raleigh, NC.

17. Dean Jr., *Shook Over Hell*, 30–34.

18. Hickel, "Medicine, Bureaucracy," 245–255; Longmore, "Disability Watch" and "The Life of Randolph Bourne and the Need for a History of Disabled People" in *Why I Burned My Book*, 53–101, 230–259.

19. Linker, *War's Waste*, 51–59.

20. Biography of Capt. Paul C. Carter, Box 7, Halifax – Biographical Sketches, North Carolina County War Records, WWI 2, WWI, MC, SANC; Hoffman, History of Base Hospital #65 and Bane, Mission Accomplished! Experiences in World War One, Ione B. Bain Papers, WWI 61, WWI, MC, SANC; Sarah McCulloh Lemmon and Nancy Smith Midgette, *North Carolina and the Two World Wars* (Raleigh: Office of Archives and History, North Carolina Department of Cultural Resources, 2013), 77–78.

21. Brown to "Dearest Cousin" (August 15, 1918), Donald D. Brown Letter, Cumberland County Soldier's Letters, North Carolina County War Records, WWI 2, WWI, MC, SANC.

22. Linker, *War's Waste*, 6, 79–119; Dean, Jr., *Shook Over Hell*, 30–34.

23. List of Cases Receiving Compensation (1918), Correspondence April 18–September 18, 1918, Veteran's Administration Rehabilitation Division District 5 [VARD5], Record Group 15 (RG15), US National Archives and Records Administration, Atlanta, GA; Office of Medical

History, US Army Medical Department, *The First World War Volume V Military Hospitals in the United States* Chapter XXVI General Hospitals, Nos. 9–18, http://history.amedd.army.mil.

24. R. W. Ferris to Kidner (August 31, 1918); R. W. Ferris to Walter G. Cooper, Secretary, Atlanta Chamber of Commerce (September 3, 1918), Correspondence, April 18–September 18, 1918, VARD5, RG15, US National Archives and Records Administration, Atlanta, GA.

25. List of Trade Schools attached to Acting Chief to Dear Sir (August 30, 1918), Correspondence April 18–September 18, 1918, VARD5, RG15, US National Archives and Records Administration, Atlanta, GA; Chandler to Ferris (December 9, 1918); R. W. Ferris to Chandler (December 7, 1918), Correspondence, December 1918, VARD5, RG15, US National Archives and Records Administration, Atlanta, GA.

26. R. W. Ferris to J. A. C. Chandler, Chief of Division of Rehabilitation (October 22, 1918), Correspondence October 1918, VARD5, RG15, US National Archives and Records Administration, Atlanta, GA; Chief, Division of Research, to J. Foster Searles, Placement Officer, Atlanta (November 19, 1918), Correspondence November 1918, VARD5, RG15, US National Archives and Records Administration, Atlanta, GA; R. W. Ferris to E. C. Graham, Special Agent (November 14, 1918); Foster Searles to Chief, Division of Rehabilitation (December 23, 1918), Correspondence December 1918, VARD5, RG15, US National Archives and Records Administration, Atlanta, GA; J. A. C. Chandler to J. F. Searles, Atlanta (January 2, 1919), Correspondence January–March, 1919, VARD5, RG15, US National Archives and Records Administration, Atlanta, GA.

27. H. L. Brunson, Superintendent of Employment, to Chief of Rehabilitation Division (October 22, 1918), Correspondence October 1918, VARD5, RG15, US National Archives and Records Administration, Atlanta, GA.

28. R. W. Ferris to J. A. C. Chandler, Chief of the Division of Rehabilitation (October 19, 1918), Correspondence October 1918, VARD5, RG15, US National Archives and Records Administration, Atlanta, GA; J. A. C. Chandler to D. V. O. District 5 (March 12, 1918), Land Settlements, 1919–1921, VARD5, RG15, US National Archives and Records Administration, Atlanta, GA.

29. R. W. Ferris to Chief of Division (October 25 1918); Superintendent of Employment to District Vocational Officer (Oct. 28, 1918); Acting Chief, Division of Rehabilitation, to Acting D. V. O. District 5 (October 3, 1918), Correspondence October 1918, VARD5, RG15, US National Archives and Records Administration, Atlanta, GA; J. A. C. Chandler to Acting District Vocational Officer (November 8, 1918); R. W. Ferris to J. A. C. Chandler (November 8, 1918), Correspondence November 1918, VARD5, RG15, US National Archives and Records Administration, Atlanta, GA; H. L. McCoy, Chief, Rehabilitation Division, to Manager, Regional Office, Charlotte, NC (June 24, 1925), Correspondence 1925, VARD5, RG15, US National Archives and Records Administration, Atlanta, GA.

30. R. W. Ferris to Dolan, Disbursing Officer (December 11, 1918); R. W. Ferris to Acting D. V. O. District 5 (December 11, 1918), Correspondence December 1918, VARD5, RG15, US National Archives and Records Administration, Atlanta, GA.

31. R. W. Ferris to Chief of Division of Rehabilitation (circa December 2, 1918), Correspondence November 1918, Correspondence, VARD5, RG15, US National Archives and Records Administration, Atlanta, GA.

32. R. W. Ferris to J. A. C. Chandler (December 1, 1918), Correspondence December 1918, VARD5, RG15, US National Archives and Records Administration, Atlanta, GA.

33. John L. Davis to J. C. Wardlaw, Chief, Rehabilitation Division (February 1, 1922); E. J. Bilk and [illegible] B. Knight to N. Bryson, Manager District 5 (December 11, 1922), Evaluation of Rehabilitation Charlotte (March 1920–August 1924), Placement Training, 1922, VARD5, RG15, US National Archives and Records Administration, Atlanta, GA.

34. M. Bryson, District Manager, to H. V. Stirling, Assistant Director, Rehabilitation Division (February 19, 1923), Equipment January–June 1923, VARD5, RG15, US National Archives and Records Administration, Atlanta, GA.

35. Section 400 with Pay and Section 402 (n.d.), Charlotte, NC, VARD5, RG15, US National Archives and Records Administration, Atlanta, GA.

36. W. I. Hamilton, Superintendent, Advisement and Training, to Chief, Division of Rehabilitation (November 6, 1919), Correspondence, 1918–1919, Blind Deaf Speech, VARD5, RG15, US National Archives and Records Administration, Atlanta, GA.

37. Men in Placement Training in North Carolina, Evaluation of Rehabilitation Charlotte (March 1920–August 1924), Placement Training, VARD5, RG15, US National Archives and Records Administration, Atlanta, GA.

38. Supervision Reports (August 1923–July 1924), VARD5, RG15, US National Archives and Records Administration, Atlanta, GA.

39. J. A. C. Chandler to All District Vocational Officers (December 10, 1918), Correspondence December 1918, VARD5, RG15, US National Archives and Records Administration, Atlanta, GA; G. W. Weaver to Acting D. V. O District 5 (November 16, 1918), Correspondence November 1918, VARD5, RG15, US National Archives and Records Administration, Atlanta, GA; C. G. Schulz to Chief, Division of Rehabilitation (August 13, 1919), Correspondence July–September 1919, VARD5, RG15, US National Archives and Records Administration, Atlanta, GA; Uel W. Lamkin to District Vocational Officers (May 5, 1920), Correspondence April–June 1920, VARD5, RG15, US National Archives and Records Administration, Atlanta, GA.

40. Hickel, "Medicine, Bureaucracy," 247–255; Katherine Ott, *Fevered Lives: Tuberculosis in American Culture since 1870* (Cambridge: Harvard University Press, 1996), 146–149; J. Foster Searles, D. V. O., to Dr. H. A. Pattison, FBVE (May 9, 1919), Correspondence April–June 1919, VARD5, RG15, US National Archives and Records Administration, Atlanta, GA.

41. C. G. Schulz, D. V. O., Suggestions of changes in the Rehabilitation Act, Correspondence January–March 1920, VARD5, RG15, US National Archives and Records Administration, Atlanta, GA.

42. Barbeau and Henri, *The Unknown Soldiers,*48–88; Williams, *Torchbearers of Democracy,* 7–103.

43. Linker, *War's Waste*, 87–88, 115, 135–138; Hickel, "Medicine, Bureaucracy," 255–258; Douglas C. Baynton, "Disability and the Justification of Inequality in American History," in eds. Longmore and Umansky, *The New Disability History*, 45–48; Kim Nielson, "Helen Keller and the Politics of Civic Fitness," in eds. Longmore and Umansky, *The New Disability History*, 277–282.

44. Acting Chief to Dear Sir (August 30, 1918), Correspondence April 18–September 18, 1918, VARD5, RG15, US National Archives and Records Administration, Atlanta, GA.

45. List of Trade Schools attached to Acting Chief to Dear Sir (August 30, 1918), Correspondence April 18–September 18, 1918, VARD5, RG15, US National Archives and Records Administration, Atlanta, GA; J. A. C. Chandler to R. W. Ferris (December 9, 1918), R. W. Ferris to J. A. C. Chandler (December 7, 1918), Correspondence December 1918, VARD5, RG15 US National Archives and Records Administration, Atlanta, GA.

46. J. A. C. Chandler to D. V. O. District 5 (December 16, 1918), Correspondence December 1918, VARD5, RG15, US National Archives and Records Administration, Atlanta, GA.

47. R. W. Ferris to J. A. C. Chandler, Chief of Division (October 26, 1918), Correspondence October 1918, VARD5, RG15, US National Archives and Records Administration, Atlanta, GA; J. A. C. Chandler to Acting D. V. O. (November 2, 1918), Correspondence November 1918, VARD5, RG15, US National Archives and Records Administration, Atlanta, GA; Rolland T. Winstead to Mr. C. G. Schulz, D. V. O. (December 6, 1919), Correspondence October–December 1919, VARD5, RG15, US National Archives and Records Administration, Atlanta, GA; Meharry Medical College, Catalogue of 1922, 1923, Announcement for 1923, 1924, Meharry Medical College Archives.

48. R. W. Ferris to Kidner (October 1, 1918), Correspondence October 1918, VARD5, RG15, US National Archives and Records Administration, Atlanta, GA.

49. Chief of the Division of Rehabilitation to Acting D. V. O. District 5 (October 7, 1918); R. W. Ferris to Chief of Division (October 21, 1918), Correspondence October 1918, VARD5, RG15, US National Archives and Records Administration, Atlanta, GA; J. A. C. Chandler to Acting D. V. O. (November 2, 1918); R. W. Ferris, Acting D. V. O. District 5 to J. A. C. Chandler (November 8, 1918), Correspondence November 1918, VARD5, RG15, US National Archives and Records Administration, Atlanta, GA; J. A. C. Chandler to D. V. O. District 5 (December 20, 1918),

Correspondence December 1918, VARD5, RG15, US National Archives and Records Administration, Atlanta, GA.

50. Correspondence and forms with Certificate of Disability for Discharge of James R. Galloway (1917), 30th Division, Military Organizations, WWI, MC, SANC; Brown to "Dearest Cousin" (August 15, 1918), WWI 2, WWI, MC, SANC.

51. Memo from Wooddell [*sic*] to C. G., 30th Division, Camp Sevier, SC (December 15, 1917); Proceedings of Board of Medical Officers. . .Wooddell (December 29, 1917); Correspondence and forms accompanying Certificate of Disability for Discharge of Tebe Woodell, 1917–1918, 30th Division, Military Organizations, WWI, MC, SANC.

52. Clinical History of Tebe Woodell (December 27, 1917), 30th Division, Military Organizations, WWI, MC, SANC.

53. Certificate of Disability for Discharge of Clarence Propst, (July 21, 1917); Certificate of Disability for Discharge of Robert Bowling, (January 16, 1918), 30th Division, Military Organization, WWI, MC, SANC.

54. Christian E. Mears, 1st Lieutenant 113th F. A., Commanding Battery E, to Commanding General, 30th Division (February 5, 1918); Correspondence with subject line indicating Discharge Account of Disability (1918); Memo from the Adjutant of the 113th F. A. to the Adjutant General of North Carolina, Camp Sevier, Greenville, SC (February 5, 1918); Memo from Jacob A. Mack, 113th F. A. to the Surgeon General of the Army (February 27, 1918), 30th Division, Military Organizations, WWI, MC, SANC.

55. Barbeau and Henri, *The Unknown Soldiers*, 34–55; Williams, *Torchbearers of Democracy*, 95–98, 195–196.

56. William J. Breen, "The North Carolina Council of Defense during World War I, 1917–1918," *North Carolina Historical Review* 50 (1973): 11, 23–24.

57. The term "total war" is often used in conjunction with World War I and World War II to stress the full mobilization of military, industrial, natural, and human resources in the conduct of a war effort by a nation's government and people. For an extended definition of the term, see "Total War" entry in *Encyclopedia Britannica*, https://www.britannica.com.

58. Correspondence and forms with Certificate of Disability for Discharge of Gilbert Falls (1917); Correspondence and forms with Certificate of Disability for Discharge of Andrew M. Johnston, (1918), 30th Division, Military Organizations, WWI, MC, SANC.

59. Affidavit of C. J. Jones to "Whom It May Concern," Monroe (August 16, 1928); Affidavit of C. D. Olinger to "Whom It May Concern," Haywood (August 16, 1928), Rehab 1928, American Legion–North Carolina Department (AL-NC), Organization Records 12 (ORG 12), SANC.

60. "Tuberculosis (TB) – Symptoms," *NHS Choices: Your Health, Your Choices* (November 30, 2012), http://www.nhs.uk; Mayo Clinic Staff, "Tuberculosis: Treatment and Drugs," *Mayo Clinic: Health Information*, http://www.mayoclinic.com; A. M. Doherty et al., "A Review of the Interplay between Tuberculosis and Mental Health," *General Hospital Psychiatry* 35, no. 4 (July–August 2013), 398–406.

61. R. W. Ferris to T. B. Kidner (August 31, 1918), Correspondence April 18–Sept. 18, 1918, VARD5, RG15, US National Archives and Records Administration, Atlanta, GA; Colonel Munson to Captain Keller (excerpt from Frank K. Boal) (December 27, 1918), Correspondence December 1918, VARD5, RG15, US National Archives and Records Administration, Atlanta, GA.

62. Steve Bentley, "A Short History of PTSD: From Thermopylae to Hue Soldiers Have Always Had A Disturbing Reaction To War," *The VVA Veteran: The Official Voice of Vietnam Veterans of America* (March/April 2005), http://www.vva.org; "Shell Shock," *Inside Out Extra: BBC Home* (March 3, 2004), http://www.bbc.co.uk; Dr. Edgar Jones, "Shell Shocked: Time Capsule," *American Psychological Association* 43, no. 6 (June 2012): 18, http://www.apa.org.

63. Nebraska Department of Veterans' Affairs, "What is PTSD?" Post Traumatic Stress Disorder (Lincoln: Nebraska Department of Veterans' Affairs, 2007), http://www.ptsd.ne.gov.

64. W. F. Lancaster, Ward-O-2, Oteen to Gen. Albert L. Cox, American Legion, Raleigh (November 5, 1927), Rehab March–December 1927, AL-NC, ORG 12, SANC.

65. Charles L. Dunkel, State Hospital, Morganton to NC Department of American Legion, Office of the Commander, Raleigh (December 11, 1928), Rehab 1928, AL-NC, ORG 12, SANC.

66. Dunkel to NC Department of American Legion, Office of the Commander, Raleigh (December 11, 1928), SANC.

67. Edith G. Barton to Mrs. John A. Porter (December 13, 1928), Rehab 1928, AL-NC, ORG 12, SANC.

68. Correspondence, Barton to Porter (December 13, 1928), SANC.

69. Economic Systems, Inc., VA Disability Compensation Program, 33–45.

70. Hickel, "Medicine, Bureaucracy," 243–252.

71. F. A. Hutchinson, State Service Officer, Charlotte to J. A. Nicholas Jr., Department Adjutant, American Legion, Richmond, VA (February 9, 1928), Rehab 1928, AL-NC, ORG 12, SANC.

72. Correspondence and forms for individual veterans (1917–1918), 30th Division, Military Organizations, WWI, MC, SANC; Correspondence and Degree of Disability determinations for individual NC veterans (1919–1933), AL-NC, ORG 12, SANC.

73. Jack P. Lang, Assistant State Service Officer, Department of Labor, State of North Carolina, to Leland Brown, Rich Square (circa December 1933), Leland Brown Papers, WWI 52, WWI, MC, SANC.

74. F. A. Hutchinson, NC State Service Officer, Charlotte, Department of Labor to J. G. Madry, District Commander, American Legion, Rich Square (February 13, 1934), Leland Brown Papers, WWI 52, WWI, MC, SANC; Economic Systems, Inc., VA Disability Compensation Program, 43–45.

75. Claimant Appeal to Administrator of Veterans' Affairs, (circa December 11, 1936); R. G. Coldwell, Adjudication Officer, Veteran's Administration, Charlotte, to Leland Brown, Rich Square (January 21, 1935), Leland Brown Papers, WWI 52, WWI, MC, SANC.

76. Claimant Appeal to Administrator of Veterans' Affairs, (circa December 11, 1936), SANC.

77. J. S. Pittman, Manager, Veterans Administration, to S. Russell Lane, Rich Square, NC (December 11, 1936), Leland Brown Papers, WWI 52, WWI, MC, SANC.

78. Marion Crawford, Executive Secretary, Greensboro to Daniel F. Krass, Jr., Acting Post Service Officer, Niagara Falls, NY (May 8, 1928), Rehab 1928, AL-NC, ORG 12, SANC.

79. Crawford to Krass (May 8, 1928), SANC.

80. Walston, Clerk Superior Court, to Anderson, Superintendent of State Hospital, Raleigh (May 11, 1928), Rehab 1928, AL-NC, ORG 12, SANC.

81. R. C. Powell, Department Adjutant, to F. A. Hutchinson, State Service Officer, Charlotte (May 11, 1928), Rehab 1928, AL-NC, ORG 12, SANC.

82. Robin Kirby to Commander Albert L. Cox, Charlotte (August 11, 1928), Rehab 1928, AL-NC, ORG 12, SANC.

83. Charles F. Cole, United States Veterans Hospital, Oteen, to General Albert L. Cox, Commander of State Department, American Legion, Raleigh (August 4, 1928), Rehab 1928, AL-NC, ORG 12, SANC.

84. Frank B. Leake, Perry Point, MD, to State Commander, American Legion, Raleigh (March 9, 1928), Rehab 1928, AL-NC, ORG 12, SANC.

85. Leake to State Commander, American Legion, Raleigh (March 9, 1928), SANC. Correspondence between Albert L. Cox, Department Commander, to Franck C. Leake, US Veterans Hospital, Perry Point, MD (March 12, 1928), indicates that the North Carolina General Assembly passed the law restricting Leake's civil liberties in 1924. A search of the "Public Laws and Resolutions Enacted by the Extra Session of the General Assembly in 1924" suggest this letter refers to "An act to amend section 2296 of the Consolidated Statutes of North Carolina, relating to estates of insane persons," which linked a "non-sane persons" marriage status to inherited property and other financial resources. While the 1924 anti-miscegenation law passed in North Carolina does not refer to the disabled, such laws often combined prohibition of mixed-race marriage and restrictions on the marriage rights of people with cognitive or psychiatric disabilities (Session Laws of North Carolina http://ncgovdocs.org/guides/sessionlawslist). For information on the relation between white supremacy, anti-immigration politics and

legislation, anti-miscegenation, disability, mental illness, retardation, and eugenics in the early 20th century, see: "Racial Integrity Act of 1924" Wikipedia accessed July 16, 2017; Victoria Brignell, "When America Believed in Eugenics" *New Statesmen* (December 10, 2010) http://www .newstatesman.com; Brendan Wolfe, "Racial Integrity Laws (1924–1930) *Encyclopedia Virginia* https://www.encyclopediavirginia.org. Chapter 6, "Three Generations of Imbeciles Are Enough: The Progressive Era, 1890–1927," of Kim E. Nielsen, *A Disability History of the United States* (Boston: Beacon Press, 2012), 100–130, specifically addresses the impact of such discriminatory legislation, policies, and ideology on veterans on page 129.

86. National Rehabilitation Committee, *History of the Organization and the Duties of the National Rehabilitation Committee of the American Legion* (Washington, DC: National Rehabilitation Committee, The American Legion, 1933), 7; National Executive Committee of the American Legion, *Education and Vocational Training of the War Orphans* (Indianapolis: American Legion, 1927), Rehab 1928, AL-NC, ORG 12, SANC.

87. National Rehabilitation Committee, *History of the Organization and the Duties,* 3–31.

88. Hutchinson to Madry (February 13, 1934), SANC; Newton G. Wilson, Madison, to R. C. Powell, Department Adjutant, American Legion, Raleigh (May 28, 1928), Rehab 1928, AL-NC, ORG 12, SANC.

89. Dunkel to NC Department of American Legion, Office of the Commander, Raleigh (December 11, 1928), SANC.

90. Barbeau and Henri, *The Unknown Soldiers,* 173–174; Tom Belton, "American Legion" in ed. William S. Powell, *Encyclopedia of North Carolina,* http://www.ncpedia.org.

91. Linker, *War's Waste,* 20–27, 120–166; Skocpol, *Protecting,* 3–11, 531–539; Hickel, "Medicine, Bureaucracy," 248–258.

13

W. S. Rankin and the Creation of Public Health in North Carolina, 1909–1925

William P. Brandon and Lauren A. Austin

This chapter studies the growth of North Carolina's public health system from the late nineteenth century through the early 1920s. It provides a context for the development of this critical aspect of the homefront during World War I and for understanding the impact of the "Spanish" influenza epidemic that devastated North Carolina along with the rest of the nation in 1918–1919. The chapter focuses on the transformative role that Watson Smith Rankin, MD (1879-1970), the State's first full-time public health officer, played in building the state's public health infrastructure. It shows an evolution from his focus on population and environmental measures to control disease and disability in the early years to the addition of clinical public health services and concern for health care resources in the state by the end of the era. The public health structures that exist today originated during the decade of World War I and the early 1920s. The achievements in public health in this period were an important if often overlooked aspect of the transformation of North Carolina into "the Wisconsin of the South."[1] Often left unexamined in the background of this history and continuing to our own day is tension and fundamental disagreement about the appropriate role of government and of organized healthcare professionals with their tradition of using professional power to control the organization, delivery and financing of healthcare.

Before exploring the public health institutions that Rankin built between 1909 and 1925, it is necessary to grasp the difficult problems that residents of North Carolina and therefore its chief medical officer faced in the late nineteenth and early twentieth centuries. This congeries of difficult problems and appalling conditions can be summarized as four sorts of "bad": bad health conditions, bad health care, bad provisions for public health, and bad medical education. Rankin effectively addressed many of the bad health conditions by laying the foundation for strong public health infrastructure. The sorry state of medical education exacerbated the shortages of qualified health providers. Together these factors meant that most North Carolinians would get second-rate care if they received any at all. As a young man, Rankin participated in a revolution in medical education that occurred in the decades around the turn of the century. This revolution created the kind of medical care we experience today. It also created challenges that Rankin would face both as North Carolina's chief medical officer and also later in his professional career as the Duke Endowment's major executive responsible for using its considerable resources to improve health care in North and South Carolina.

During the last half of the nineteenth century numerous outbreaks and epidemics plagued North Carolina's white and black citizens alike, due in part to poor socioeconomic conditions. One of the most prevalent chronic health problems was hookworm. The parasite thrived in the South's humid climate and poor hygienic conditions; southerners suffered as the result of minimal or absent sanitary conditions, the use of night-soil (the process of fertilizing with human feces), a widespread lack of footwear and clothing options, poor nourishment, and inadequate housing. By the end of the century, investigations showed that hookworm had infected as many as 7.5 million southerners and demonstrated a strong negative correlation between agricultural income per capita and rate of hookworm infection.[2] Malaria was also endemic in the South. Most prevalent in humid areas with many bodies of standing and stagnant water, malaria threatened the South more than any other region of the United States. According to the 1850 US Census, 45.7 out of every 1000 deaths in the nation resulted from malarial fevers, one of the leading causes of death in that period. Furthermore, research on Civil War soldiers has suggested that individuals who lived in counties with high levels of malarial outbreaks developed weaker immune systems and were more prone to infection or chronic diseases later in life.[3] North Carolina consistently suffered unduly high malaria mortality rates through 1920; during some years, the state experienced rates more than fifteen times greater than the overall national mortality rate (Table 13.1).

By the turn of the twentieth century, tuberculosis became the leading cause of death in the United States, especially in the tenements of large cities. Due to its unknown origin and initial mislabeling as a hereditary, constitutional disease instead of a contagious one, a wide variety of largely ineffective treatments emerged.[4] The most popular treatment called for relocation of the patient to an environment that boasted clean air, sunshine, low humidity, and cool night temperatures. Western North Carolina's temperate climate attracted tuberculosis sufferers, especially after new railroad construction

Table 13.1. Disease in North Carolina: NC and US Crude Selected and All-Cause Mortality, 1910-1920.

	1910	1911	1912	1913	1914	1915	1916	1917	1918	1919	1920
					(per 100,000 population)						
Overall Death Rate											
US	400.7	386.3	360.0	375.6	361.8	359.0	375.7	380.9	657.0	401.9	380.5
NC	633.6	631.3	556.2	559.9	595.5	547.1	381.8	405.8	673.8	420.2	383.7
Typhoid											
US	23.5	21.0	16.5	17.9	15.5	12.4	13.3	13.5	12.6	9.2	7.8
NC	57.6	69.6	39.7	56.4	56.5	40.8	28.9	29.5	22.8	17.5	12.5
Malaria											
US	2.2	3.0	3.1	2.5	2.2	2.3	3.0	3.2	3.1	3.8	3.6
NC	33.1	23.1	34.1	18.6	21.8	13.9	13.9	10.9	7.6	7.9	8.1
Tuberculosis											
US	139.7	138.0	130.0	127.9	128.2	128.2	124.3	129.4	133.4	111.3	100.8
NC	247.3	228.1	209.3	200.2	221.4	207.6	133.3	124.5	127.6	111.5	106.4
Influenza											
US	14.4	15.7	10.3	12.2	9.1	16.0	26.5	17.3	300.8	98.8	71.0
NC	28.1	24.2	20.5	18.1	18.6	19.1	26.1	16.3	320.4	149.6	116.2
Diahhrea/Enteritis (<2yr)											
US	100.8	77.5	70.4	75.2	66.0	59.8	65.8	64.3	58.8	44.2	44.0
NC	137.6	149.3	135.5	112.3	133.9	118.0	76.9	95.8	79.7	55.5	54.2

Source: Department of Commerce, Bureau of the Census, *Mortality Rates: 1910-1920* (Washington, DC: Government Printing Office, 1923), Table 111.

in the 1880s. Many sanatoriums opened in the Asheville area, bringing thousands of tuberculosis patients to the state. Yet despite the healthy climate, roughly 75% of patients in sanatoriums died within five years.[5] This influx of tuberculosis patients from other states may have contributed to North Carolina's high tuberculosis mortality rate, which consistently exceeded the national average until 1917 (Table 13.1). However, crowded living conditions experienced by large, impoverished families both in rural North Carolina and in the expanding mill villages in its many small towns constituted environmental conditions where tuberculosis bacilli easily spread.[6]

While hookworm, malaria, and tuberculosis were the principal endemic diseases in the South, the rural and underdeveloped nature of North Carolina in the decades before the First World War often disproportionately exposed its residents to other diseases such as typhoid fever, dysentery, and yellow fever, all of which originated in human waste or stagnant water. Inadequate toilets known as "insanitary privies" acted as one of the largest factors contributing to the emergence and spread of these diseases. The privies were surface toilets, open in back from the seat to the ground, which resulted in excrement being deposited on the ground surface; rain, flies, birds, animals, and even farmers using night-soil as fertilizer then introduced the excrement into local food and water supplies. As we shall see, Rankin made improving sanitary conditions an early and continuing objective of his public health program. Yet despite its inherently unsanitary features, the open surface toilet remained the type of toilet most commonly used in the state until the General Assembly passed the 1919 Act to Prevent the Spread of Disease from Insanitary Privies.[7]

Inadequate nutrition also caused major problems. Pellagra, a disease of poverty due to insufficient niacin in the diet, was especially common in the white laboring class living in mill villages; its heaviest toll was felt by children and nonworking women, perhaps because pregnancy and nursing further depleted the body's reserves. Its cause was identified by Dr. Joseph Goldberger, a US Public Health Service Officer, in the years immediately before the United States entered World War I, and the first effort at nutritional education was begun by southern public health officials in 1916. Recognition of nutritional disease was slow because by the early twentieth century, American physicians and laymen alike had finally come to accept the germ theory of disease. Consequently, those arguing for an alternative etiology often encountered considerable skepticism, especially from mill owners, managers, and their physicians, who had no incentive to recognize the devastating effects of economic inequality. In an era when Southern elites fought national efforts to improve working conditions, such as restricting child labor in textile factories, they found it easy to dismiss the connection of nutritional disease to poverty and low wages when workers were unhealthy. The boom in wages during the war years—when even workers' families could afford milk, fresh meat, and vegetables—led to greater consumption of dairy products and eggs which greatly diminished pellagra. With the wrenching cutbacks in textile wages in the 1920s, however, pellagra again became a major problem that required attention from public health authorities.[8]

Despite the disproportionate spread of infectious and parasitic disease prior to 1920, the Tar Heel state had few hospitals. Even in 1925, American Medical Association (AMA) data showed North Carolina to be fortieth among the 48 states and the District of Columbia in general hospital beds per population.[9] Beginning in 1856, the state did support a psychiatric hospital (later named Dorothea Dix Hospital); previously the severely mentally ill could rely only on locally supported alms houses and jails. North Carolina was among the last of the East Coast states to assume the responsibility of caring for mental patients. Even where hospitals existed, typically only those who could not afford in-home health care sought treatment at hospitals. Before the flu epidemic of 1918–1919, most North Carolinians viewed hospitals as last-resort treatment facilities for the destitute. The outbreak of influenza in 1918 did create a surge of hospital attendance: records show rural doctors could not keep up with demand, and many who were infected opted for hospital assistance over none at all. Aside from the flu epidemic, hospitals did not begin to steadily attract individuals from all economic strata until general medical knowledge and treatment technology began greatly expanding in the 1930s and 1940s.[10] Even during the First World War, North Carolina's hospitals remained subpar, lacking in standardization and shunned as viable treatment options whenever alternatives were available. Therefore, the state's burgeoning medical community faced an uphill battle at the dawn of the century as physicians determined how best to fight the spread of infectious diseases and foster a better public health environment. Most citizens and medical practitioners viewed government provision or even regulation of medical treatment as taboo and showed little sympathy for regulation in the interest of health promotion. Rankin's focus in the early years on broad *population*-based health interventions such as provision of clean drinking water had the advantage of minimizing opposition from medical professionals, who feared competition from government delivery of individual health services, and quelling the anger of a conservative public who rejected the very idea that government should provide health care. Moreover, in the third-world-like conditions existing in North Carolina before the war, environmental interventions in the interest of public health could produce quick and visible victories by reducing morbidity and mortality for relatively small expenditures.[11]

As suggested in the introduction, antipathy to overt government involvement in health and health care is a recurring theme in American history. Perhaps less appreciated is the long-standing distrust of medical professionals and the perception that they seek to control health care in their own interest as well as that of patients. Eighteenth-century English guild-like regulation, which distinguished apothecaries, surgeons, physicians, man-midwifes and women-midwives as much by social status and gender as by medical competence, did not flourish in the American colonies and expired completely in the anti-regulatory environment of Jacksonian democracy in the 1830s. Great antipathy to both the pretenses of allopathic or "scientific" physicians and government regulation slowly gave way in the late nineteenth century to not-very-demanding state licensing that was largely controlled by the allopaths organized as state and local medical societies and the American Medical Association (founded in 1846). As the chief professional beneficiaries of the revolution in medical education discussed later in this chapter, organized medicine, which enjoyed the benefits of the "learned professions" exclusion from anti-trust legislation until *Goldfarb v. Virginia State Bar* (1975), supported a regulatory regime that reinforced its power. Ever fearful of losing control through "third-party payment," organized medicine always fought government efforts to finance health care for patients who might be able to pay doctors for care in the professionally dominated market. For most of the twentieth century this concern also led organized medicine to make sure that typically underfunded public health systems did not provide care to any but the most indigent patients.[12]

A brief account of the state's public health history prior to the Great War shows how daunting were the tasks faced by the first generation of public health officials. The North Carolina General Assembly did not create a state board of health until 1877 when the legislature declared that the entire membership of the North Carolina Medical Society constituted the NC Board of Health and appropriated $100 to cover its expenses.[13] Massachusetts had created the first state board of health in 1869.[14] However, North Carolina's initial Board was barely functional and nearly useless due to severe underfunding and the resulting lack of resources necessary to collect data and disseminate important medical information.[15] In 1879 the legislature reformed the law, creating a nine-member Board of Health that would function as a part of the state government and mandating that each county organize its own local board of health to maintain and distribute vaccines for infectious diseases.[16] The legislation also required that the Board of Health start maintaining vital statistics for the state's population. Unfortunately, no enforcement of this or any other requirement existed at the local level. Therefore, with no incentive to spend the time or resources necessary to track vital statistics, the majority of county leaders refused to act. This underreporting resulted in the US Census Bureau's refusal to recognize as accurate or to utilize North Carolina's reported annual vital statistics until 1916, three years after Rankin had successfully overhauled the state's statistical record maintenance and enforcement.[17]

Frequent outbreaks of diseases related to substandard sanitary conditions and the general disregard for the state's existing public health regulations led medical professionals in North Carolina to begin calling for stronger public health laws by the early 1890s. Sanitary reports and reforms carried out in other parts of the country also fueled these calls for reform. In 1850, Lemuel Shattuck of Boston wrote the first comprehensive plan for an integrated state program of public health in the United States in his *Report of the Sanitary Commission for Massachusetts*. It called for improved water sanitation and waste disposal, control of communicable diseases, more efficient building construction, and a decrease in pollution as ways to reduce disease outbreaks.[18] The official 1864 sanitation survey conducted by the New York City Council of Hygiene and Public Health of the Citizens' Association, the first of its kind in America, was another influential report.[19] This survey provided maps and tables outlining the precise locations of outbreaks of infectious diseases and stagnant conditions brought about by insufficient sewage drainage and lack of access to clean water. These reports signaled to state boards of health that state and county governments not only needed to take larger steps to impede outbreaks of infectious diseases but also that these actions could actually decrease mortality rates.

In light of sanitation reforms elsewhere, a large group of medical experts and policymakers gathered in Raleigh in January 1893 to compare North Carolina public health policies with those of other states and to determine where major deficiencies existed and how best to overcome them. This conference produced the North Carolina Public Health Law of 1893. The law's two main goals were to better protect citizens against contagious diseases and to standardize public health regulations at the local and state levels. It required annual inspections of all public institutions, routine inspections of all inland water sources, and the creation of approved treatment facilities for sewage and water supplies. The legislation also expanded the State Board of Health's powers to promulgate additional regulations or restrictions necessary to protect citizens from disease during epidemics and included enforcement provisions with legal penalties.[20]

The 1893 law also pushed the Board to develop governing bodies to oversee desired changes in specific public health functions. Bureaus of Epidemics, Water Supply and Drainage, Hygienics of Public Schools, Climatology, Adulteration of Food and Medicines, Sanitary Conditions of State Institutions, and Vital Statistics all emerged within the final decade of the nineteenth century. Further legislation in 1899 and 1903 required that all public water suppliers adhere to standards set, regulated, and inspected monthly by the State Board of Health.[21] The creation of these bureaus, offices, and safety standards in North Carolina no doubt stemmed from the positive outcomes of numerous sanitation and public health measures carried out in cities like New York and Boston. These developments also likely reflected Rankin's visit to the canal construction in Panama in 1905 to learn the latest in malaria prevention through mosquito control.[22]

At the dawn of the twentieth century, North Carolina's public health officials and experts initiated a robust effort to fight infectious diseases caused by widespread water contamination by increasing the state's role in the creation and maintenance of public water systems. Unfortunately, while these efforts produced positive results in some urban areas, many rural areas without access to such systems fell short of the new sanitization standard. County boards of health, where they existed, remained too disconnected from each other and lacking in clear lines of communication with the state Board of Health and its bureaus in Raleigh to effectively achieve widespread success in implementing these fundamental public health measures prior to World War I. Indeed, despite the state's clear desire for county governments to create full-time public health departments and the provision of state funding at least from 1917, only 38 of North Carolina's 100 counties had established health departments in 1928.[23] Consequently, until at least 1916 continual outbreaks of diseases such as typhoid, malaria, tuberculosis, influenza, dysentery, and diarrhea in children under 2 years old contributed to significantly higher death rates in North Carolina than in many other states (Table 13.1).

The uneven quality of medical education and practices constituted another hurdle faced by North Carolina's emerging public health sector. Entry into the profession of medicine in post-Civil War America required little education and few resources; consequently, most allopathic physicians had low social status and earned lower middle class incomes. Many proprietary medical schools[24] accepted almost any tuition-paying student (including some who had not completed high school) into two-year programs with short terms of didactic instruction that earned the participant an MD degree. Future physicians then spent a few years essentially apprenticed to an established physician, who might be considered a good and effective physician in the local community but was unlikely to be familiar with advances in bacteriology coming out of European labs. Thus, except for the few elites whose family wealth allowed them to study in Europe, most new doctors, especially in rural areas, were limited to the knowledge their teachers possessed and consequently remained largely ignorant of scientific or medical advances. Although 160 medical schools existed across the country by 1901, no nationwide standards or templates for medical school entrance requirements, curriculum, or grading rubrics existed. However, a revolution in medical education began in 1893 with the opening of a medical school by Johns Hopkins University that required entering students to hold a college degree. Its curriculum required two intensive years of preclinical study of medical and laboratory sciences and two clinical years, thereby binding together the bedside, laboratory, and classroom. A key element was the University's ownership of the Johns Hopkins Hospital, opened in 1889, which together with impressive faculty put American medicine on a path that generated modern medicine and its culture.[25] Yet the other 159 American medical schools granted medical degrees completely at their own discretion, resulting in an unacceptably wide range of educational quality and knowledge acquired by their graduates.[26]

The AMA, which had pushed to upgrade the social status and incomes of physicians, created the Council on Medical Education in 1904 to restructure medical education in the United States. The council adopted two important standards: a minimal prior educational requirement for admitting students to medical schools and the expectation that medical education should consist of two years of training in both anatomy and physiology followed by another two years working in a teaching hospital. To determine exactly how well the nation's 160 medical schools already met these requirements, the council tasked the Carnegie Foundation for the Advancement of Teaching to conduct a survey. The foundation chose research scholar Abraham Flexner to conduct it. Flexner toured all 160 medical schools in the United States and Canada, and reported in a 1910 summary to the AMA that the general state of affairs of America's medical education was dismal indeed. Flexner labeled most schools as "indescribably foul" for falling far short of the ideal medical education set forth by the Council of Medical Education.[27] North Carolina had four medical schools, all of which received visits from Flexner in February 1909. Two of these schools awarded medical degrees: North Carolina Medical College, a proprietary stock company in Charlotte (previously located in Davidson), which had 94 students, and Leonard Medical School of Shaw University in Raleigh, an African American university enrolling 125 medical students. The other two, Wake Forest (then located in the small town of Wake Forest north of Raleigh) and the University of North Carolina (in Chapel Hill), were "half-schools" that merely prepared students to pursue clinical training at other institutions and enrolled 53 and 74 students, respectively.[28] Only the latter two schools survived. The faculty at the University of North Carolina at Chapel Hill had established a medical department in Raleigh where third- and fourth-year students could receive clinical training under many of the white physicians who taught at Leonard Medical School in Raleigh, but only the half-school at Chapel Hill survived the contraction in medical education that occurred in the decade following the publication of Flexner's report.[29] In *Medical Education in the United States and Canada*, Flexner remarked that North Carolina's population of 2.14 million had a reasonable supply of doctors with physician-to-population ratios of 1:1216 or 1:1110 (depending on source). "But," Flexner continued, "this may . . . be due to the fact that practitioners, unlicensed and unregistered, exist undisturbed in the remote districts. It is futile to maintain a low standard in order to prepare doctors for those parts."[30] Between the end of World War I and the opening in 1930 of the four-year Duke University School of Medicine (one of the medical schools newly founded after Flexner's report), North Carolina had no institution that conferred medical degrees. Arguably, greater numbers of physicians were most needed during US involvement in World War I and the flu epidemic.[31]

Thus, North Carolina had to depend on the two half-schools of Wake Forest and University of North Carolina at Chapel Hill to bring to the state the educational revolution that created not only the science but also the organization, practice, and culture of modern medicine that now constitutes the international standard for health care. The Wake Forest College School of Medicine, founded only in 1902, was praised by Flexner, who was hosted in February 1909 by its young dean, W. S. Rankin. Flexner would have felt right at home with Rankin. Flexner was a southerner who earned his own undergraduate degree from the Johns Hopkins University, and his brother and lifelong confidant Simon did postgraduate work in pathology under founding Johns Hopkins Medical School Dean William Henry Welch and became the first director of the Rockefeller Institute for Medical Research in 1901. The young dean belonged to the cadre of young physicians like Simon who trained at Johns Hopkins before World War I and then propagated the new medical school model on faculties of university medical schools that wished to reform and upgrade.[32]

Born in Mooresville in 1879, Rankin attended both the North Carolina Medical College for two years and the University of Maryland, from which he received a medical degree in 1901. He then did postgraduate work at the Johns Hopkins Medical School, which Flexner regarded as the model for medical education, followed by residencies in obstetrics and pathology in Maryland.[33] In 1903 Rankin accepted a position as a professor at Wake Forest and two years later became dean of the medical school, a position he held until his appointment in 1909 as the first full-time public health officer in North Carolina.[34]

In his new job as the head of North Carolina's nascent state public health agency, Rankin spent a great deal of his time between 1909 and 1917 visiting towns and cities in North Carolina to assess health services and offer guidance for improving local public health facilities; he also wrote extensively about his findings and their implications. In 1913 he wrote that "vital statistics are the right arm of the health officer, and, in my opinion, the greatest defect in our Southern States in promoting sanitary progress is the absence of vital statistics."[35] Given Rankin's passion for accurate statistics as a way to show both communities and public health officials where health care procedures were deficient, it is no surprise that the overhaul of North Carolina's vital statistics program occurred in 1913 during the time Rankin was State Health Officer. Under Rankin's vigorous leadership, North Carolina was among the thirteen states qualifying as contributors of mortality statistics maintained by the Federal Bureau of the Census in the decade 1911–1920; by 1920, thirty-four states and the District of Columbia participated.[36]

In the journal articles "The Standardization of Public Health Work" (1915) and "Rural Sanitation: Definition, Field Principles, Methods, and Costs" (1916), Rankin advocated the standardization and implementation of rural sanitation laws and practices.[37] These topics were critically important in the early years of the twentieth century because over 80% of North Carolina residents lived in rural areas untouched by larger state sanitation reforms.[38] Rankin acknowledged that rural sanitation should be initiated by the state but implemented at the county level, that each county should be able to implement changes in ways that best suited its residents, that sanitation must be cost efficient for poorer counties, and that policies and implementation must take into consideration the individualism of rural inhabitants. However, he also noted that "in any attempt at standardization of health work the county is the field of election" and that successful implementation of state-issued public health standards was dependent on the cooperation of both the county health officials and local governments for which they worked.[39] To encourage and coordinate local public health efforts and especially the creation of county departments of health, in 1917 the Board of Health established the North Carolina Bureau of County Health Work staffed with professionals to liaison with counties.[40]

When Rankin toured North Carolina, he personally visited and evaluated county health facilities and met with county politicians and administrators, offering advice to correct shortcomings and encouraging them to take a more active role in sanitation standardization. He urged county leaders to watch and anticipate the health care needs of their citizens and not to wait on national or state directives if needs arose.[41] He also imported Dr. Henry Carter's successful method of mosquito control from Panama, producing a rapid decline in the incidence of malaria within the state.[42] However, despite the robust changes regarding the standardization of medical education and state licensure advocated by the AMA and the leaps forward made by Rankin in North Carolina, by 1918 the ravaging impacts of both the First World War and the flu epidemic exposed continuing failures in the state's public health system. More sweeping changes were needed in both access to and distribution of public health care.[43]

Because the influenza epidemic of 1918—1919 has received so much attention in the last forty years, an entire chapter ("Pandemic and War, 1918—1919") in this volume is devoted to exploring its scope and magnitude; here the focus is on how the epidemic affected public health. Anecdotal accounts report that the 1918–1919 flu epidemic generated overwhelming numbers of requests for clinical assistance, which the Board of Health was unable to provide. Yet publications of the Board and the record of new state initiatives during 1918–1919 suggest that the flu epidemic was a public health emergency that demanded and received attention but did not greatly divert the leadership from the task of building public health institutions that would make the state a leader in public health for the next half-century. Thus, the epidemic was reported in only one issue of the newsletter that the Board regularly distributed to the public.[44] From the perspective of the twenty-first century, the epidemic seems to stand out as the most memorable health issue of the First World War era; to contemporaries it must have been important at the time, but officials were balancing numerous demands. Moreover, the public had repeatedly experienced deadly infectious disease epidemics during their lifetime. Perhaps it is not surprising that once the epidemic waned, it seemed to lack continuing impact on popular consciousness.[45] Nonetheless, the end of the war years can be seen as the harbinger of a change in the mix of services provided by state health authorities.

By the last year of the war, state authorities had begun to offer more programs that affected the individual health status of North Carolinians. Governors Thomas W. Bickett (1917–1921) and Cameron Morrison (1921–1925) oversaw a drastic increase in state expenditures (847 percent during 1915–1925) along with an expansion of taxes and the state's bonded debt.[46] In 1918 the Assembly established the Bureau of Medical Inspection of Schools, which worked closely with school officials primarily through the introduction of in-school nursing staffs. The Bureau identified poor dental health as the most prevalent health issue among school-aged children, placed oral hygiene lectures in state public schools, and created volunteer portable dental clinics in schools and other facilities. The legislators also established the Bureau of Venereal Disease and the Bureau of Public Health Nursing and Infant Hygiene. In 1919 they created the Bureau of Sanitary Engineering and Inspection, which inspected and licensed privies and closed down all that failed to meet the Board's standards. The same legislation also granted the new bureau broader powers to enforce public health laws and more closely monitor public water systems.[47] This period saw North Carolina leading the South by establishing the first state welfare agency in 1917, an important potential collaborator with public health institutions facing diseases of poverty, such as hookworm and pellagra, and child hunger. An important milestone was the creation in 1920 of the School of Public Welfare at the University of North Carolina at Chapel Hill, led by acclaimed sociologist and social welfare advocate Howard W. Odum.[48] In contrast, public health was incorporated into higher education in North Carolina as a division in University of North Carolina at Chapel Hill's medical school in only 1936; it achieved independent school status in 1939, becoming the first school of public health in a state university.

Federal assistance after the First World War also contributed to the birth of modern health care in North Carolina. Newly available data gathered in examinations of potential soldiers provided insights into population health status that served as a forceful wake-up call for national leaders. With nearly one-quarter of the US population infected with chronic disease or disability, a national death toll of approximately 650,000, a plunge in the average US life expectancy during 1917–1918, and far more American casualties due to flu than war battles, Congress acted to help the states improve their health care systems.[49] In explaining the Duke Endowment's plans for health care in the Hospital Section's first *Annual Report*, Rankin himself referred to the high rate of "defects" found in males undergoing physical exams as part of the World War I draft.[50] Recognition of these national shortcomings and setbacks took the shape of increased access to federal funding for the establishment and maintenance of state public health programs. The General Assembly utilized these federal funds to create numerous public health bureaus and offices.[51]

Along with greater state and federal funding passing through the State Board of Health to local authorities came more control by state officials. Previously, counties and cities that assumed public health functions could largely take measures that they designed themselves. Limited improvement occurred in counties where local officials were uninterested or actively opposed to progressive public health measures. At best, state public health officials could only cajole and offer modest incentives, except in clear emergencies such as the 1918–1919 flu pandemic. This power imbalance explains why in his early years as State Health Officer Rankin and his lieutenants invested so much time in outreach to counties at a time when only train travel between main towns was easy. However, the new federal legislation—with its appropriation of significant amounts of money for states willing to implement federal policy and its acceptance by the North Carolina General Assembly—gave the state greater ability to compel action in matters of public health.[52]

An excellent example of this development was the creation of the Board of Venereal Disease within the State Board of Health. The federal Chamberlain-Kahn Act, enacted on July 9, 1918, responded to a perceived epidemic of venereal disease (VD). [53] The rationale for federal action to generate state implementation was the need to protect soldiers from women who might be infected with VD, especially syphilis and gonorrhea. Health authorities believed that the South had the highest incidence of VD, and North Carolina hosted several camps for training soldiers. While officials targeted red light districts and sex workers, they also focused more broadly on young women who were perceived to have a penchant for immoral behavior; soldiers and other male clients of sex workers were not targets of this legislation.[54] The Maternity and Infancy Act (formally the Sheppard-Towner Act) of 1921, which was allowed to lapse in 1929, is a somewhat better-known early example of federal legislation providing financial support to states if they implemented programs following federal guidelines. [55] Title V of the Social Security Act of 1935 reinstituted grants-in-aid to states to establish Maternal and Child Health Programs and Crippled Children's Services. [56]

Although the effect of laws such as Chamberlain-Khan and Sheppard-Towner would only be felt in the aftermath of the war and fewer than five grant programs for the "social welfare, health, and security" categories were established prior to the New Deal, the larger significance should not be underestimated. [57] These grant-in-aid programs constituted early trials of what became the peculiarly American workaround for the fundamental flaw in the nation's version of federalism. In its commerce clause and grant of authority over money, the US Constitution gave the federal government the power to regulate the national economy. In contrast, Congress seemed to lack authority to ameliorate the many social problems created by rapid industrialization and periodic economic catastrophe. Sheppard-Towner was a harbinger of large-scale, ongoing transfers of funds dispersed with federal oversight of state activities and periodic policy changes that became the signature of New Deal social welfare policies. Grants-in-aid were the mechanism that allowed the United States to escape the minimalist straightjacket of the Constitution and become a modern state.[58]

Northern philanthropies seemed to have a greater impact than the federal government on the development of public health in the South. Private donors, led by the Rockefeller philanthropies, began earlier and instituted carefully planned programs. The US Public Health Service in this era was largely focused on specific public health threats such as VD, mosquito control, and pellagra. In contrast, the International Health Board of the Rockefeller Foundation (and its predecessor) learned from its pioneering work on hookworm that building local public health institutions was critical to achieve success. The Rockefeller philanthropies spent over a million dollars to support local health departments in the South between 1913 and 1930, and at the end of the period the eleven southern states had 347 of the nation's 553 county departments of public health.[59] North Carolina was the favorite southern state of the US Public Health Service, Rockefeller philanthropies, and Rosenwald Fund. In the 1920s the Rockefeller philanthropies alone invested about $150,000 in North Carolina but only $78,000 in Georgia and $111,000 in South Carolina. [60]

North Carolina's relatively progressive actions on race, an issue so central to any consideration of the South in the twentieth century, help to explain why the state enjoyed a favored position among southern public health programs. Unlike South Carolina, it adequately funded the construction of its tuberculosis sanatorium for blacks in 1919 with $100,000 and benefited children of both races by fully tapping all available Sheppard-Towner funding, including those provisions for medical services to children that required state funding. Both black and white school children received physical exams and, even more significantly, the state mandated that children found to have a problem should be treated at government expense if the family could not afford to pay. In a society with limited opportunities for black professionals, North Carolina led the South in hiring a black dentist at the state level in 1920 and successfully pushed local health departments to hire black nurses.[61]

Rankin deserves much of the credit for setting North Carolina apart from other southern states, both for his public health professionalism that recognized black as well as white needs and the leadership abilities that enabled him to secure the necessary support from others, especially the North Carolina General Assembly.[62] Historian Edward H. Beardsley characterized Rankin's views on race:

> Privately he *might* [our emphasis] have shared the outlook of other white North Carolinians, accepting segregation as a given, but . . . his personal views did not affect his professional outlook. As a medical officer, strongly imbued with the research ethic, he was interested only in biological facts. The primary fact was there were a great number of people in North Carolina who were sick and in need of primary and preventive medical care. That

some were black and some white made not the slightest difference. . . .
[T]here were problems to be solved and people to be helped. . . .He did
recognize that blacks suffered to a greater degree than whites and while he
made no special appeals in their name, he strove consistently to improve
delivery of services to them.[63]

Whatever Rankin's undocumented private views on race *may* have been, it
is clear that his actions set him apart from other southern public health
chiefs, thereby placing the Old North State in the nation's eye as the most
forward looking of the former Confederate states in public health. Building
on Beardsley's comments, avoidance of overt advocacy for blacks might have
been a necessary condition for securing equal provision of services for the
black community while serving the white constituents who elected the white
political leaders.

Of course, factors other than the availability of philanthropic and government funds were important to increasing access to health care. Automobile
ownership was burgeoning by the 1920s when Cameron Morrison, the "Good
Roads Governor," persuaded the state legislature to enact the Highway Act
of 1921, which made highway construction a state responsibility and provided funds from the first gas tax (one cent per gallon) and new state bond
authority. During Morrison's governorship, 5500 miles of paved highways
were built using $65 million of borrowed money and the gas tax.[64] In addition
to emphasizing the importance of the automobile and improved roads, the
Duke Endowment's 1926 *Annual Report* discussed the importance of rural
telephones for medical practice.[65]

The progressive legislation and other reforms continued in the 1920s
as the General Assembly created the Bureau of Maternity and Infancy and
mandated standards for bedding materials. North Carolina became one of the
first states in which health departments and public hospitals provided family
planning assistance.[66] Influenced by the lessons of the war and flu epidemic
and the sweeping changes brought about by state lawmakers, the State Board
of Public Health, philanthropic efforts, and federal funding, North Carolina
became a leader in sanitization and public health matters, especially family
planning. By the time Rankin retired from the state board in 1925, North
Carolina reported more counties with full-time public health officers than
any other state.[67] The results were impressive. By 1935 the state had declined
to or below the average crude rate for all-cause mortality and for mortality
from most specific infectious diseases (Table 13.1).[68]

Founded by James B. Duke in 1924, the Duke Endowment was a major
source of hospital planning and expansion that confined its activities to North
and South Carolina. Duke's grand vision was to support health care and child
welfare as well as spiritual life and higher education in the Carolinas with
$40 million in funding. One of the Duke Endowment's original provisions

supported the growth of private nonprofit hospitals. Impressed by Rankin's ideas and writings, Duke agreed that North Carolina's post-war budgetary problems greatly hindered the state's ability to build more hospitals and expand physician care across the state. Therefore, he allocated 32% of the spendable earnings of the Trust to support nonprofit hospitals that served both blacks and whites.[69] Upon Rankin's 1925 retirement from the State Board of Health, Duke made him the trustee heading the Hospital and Orphans Section of the Endowment and, therefore, responsible for the creation and funding of these hospitals.[70]

Just as Rankin focused on developing a system to produce accurate vital statistics in the early years of his tenure as North Carolina's chief public health officer, so too did he and his colleagues meticulously survey North and South Carolina hospitals at the end of 1924 to determine the baseline for measuring their future activities. They recorded fifty whites-only general hospitals with 3,160 total beds, twenty blacks-only hospitals with 557 total beds, and seventy hospitals with 3,467 total beds that served both whites and blacks. The 93 "private" (i.e., doctor-owned) nominally for-profit hospitals constituted two-thirds of all general hospitals in the two states but provided only 51 percent of the beds. Hospitals were small in this era; only six general hospitals had 100 beds or more. There were 1486 general hospital beds for blacks in North and South Carolina and 4,698 for whites,[71] despite the fact that blacks made up 30 percent of North Carolina's population and 51 percent of South Carolina's in the 1920 Census.[72]

Establishment of the Duke Endowment began to change access to modern hospitals. Its administrators helped communities purchase private doctor-owned hospitals throughout the state and convert them into community hospitals for both races. By 1950 North Carolina's Public Health Office reported that 130 nonprofit hospitals in the state received funding from the Endowment.[73] Doctors who previously balked at the idea of working in what they considered to be the backwoods of North Carolina now found themselves more willing to serve in areas of medical shortage if they and their patients could access new and modernized facilities.[74] In addition to helping communities establish general hospitals by conversion to private nonprofit status or new construction, Rankin used Endowment funds to subsidize those hospitals' operating budgets. The Duke Endowment provided one dollar per day only to community hospitals for the care of charity patients who could not pay for inpatient hospitalization. The Endowment also encouraged a surge of medical fieldwork and stronger ties between the state and agencies such as the Red Cross; those ties, in turn, helped make local public health officials more knowledgeable and better able to disseminate health care information to area citizens.[75]

Greater access to public health assistance and physician care made a huge difference in rural North Carolina. The presence of more hospitals and doctors insured much wider availability of vaccines, treatments, and professional advice. The distribution of existing vaccines for diseases such as smallpox increased significantly across the state, and health care workers found it easier to treat diseases such as diphtheria, malaria, measles, mumps, influenza, polio, scarlet fever, typhoid fever, and yellow fever as medical knowledge advanced and new vaccines became available.[76] North Carolina's doctors

Table 13.2. The Evolution of Public Health Focus in Papers by Dr. W. S. Rankin, 1912–1926.* Published in the American Journal of Public Health (AJPH).

On health statistics (1912), which he termed "vital statistics," but meant to include much more than birth and death records;

On the conduct or "standardization" of work in public health (1914) and again in 1924 when he placed more emphasis on evaluating public health efforts;

On sanitation (1915), which for Rankin included immunization and infectious disease control, health education of students and their parents, and health screening;

On the relation of state and provincial boards of health to federal U.S. and Canadian public health authorities (1919);

On the need for public health to shift from prevention to health promotion in light of its successes in controlling communicable diseases (1922);

On the roles of medicine and public health and the appropriate relations between the two and the need for increasingly specialized and reductionist medical knowledge to be leavened by a broad "social outlook" and commitment to act collectively to ameliorate problems in providing needed health care for everyone (two 1923 papers);

On "rural medical and hospital services" where Rankin, now a Director at the Duke Endowment, addressed the need for physicians and hospitals in appropriate numbers (1925 or 1926).

*Date of publication often lagged the initial oral presentation.

Sources (in order, all by W.S. Rankin): "The Practical Value of Vital Statistics in the South," *AJPH* 3 (1913): 453—456; "The Standardization of Public Health Work," *AJPH* 5 (1915): 1024—1028; "The Fly in the Ointment," *AJPH* 14 (1924): 819-826; "Rural Sanitation: Definition, Field, Principles, Methods, and Costs," *AJPH* 6 (1916): 554–558; "A Dangerous Tendency in Public Health Administration," *AJPH* 9 (1919): 567–571; "Emphasis Shifting from Disease Prevention to Health Promotion," *AJPH* 12 (1922): 999–1005; "Report of the Committee of the State and Provincial Health Authorities on Relations of Medical Men and Health Officials," *AJPH* 13 (1923): 753–756; "The Medical Profession and the Laity from the Standpoint of the Health Officer," *AJPH* 13 (1923): 360-363; "Rural Medical and Hospital Services," *AJPH* 17 (1927): 15–20.

quickly adopted the medical technology either developed or improved by military doctors in Europe during World War I. Such technology included nondirect blood transfusion; X-rays to locate foreign objects in the body; and more effective ways to treat tissue damage, infected wounds, burns, and contagious diseases.[77] The influx of new medical knowledge brought back by military medical personnel returning from the warfront undoubtedly helped North Carolina's new community hospital system to flourish.

The picture that emerges from this review of the 1909–1925 era is of a forceful and persuasive leader. Rankin was a systematic and orderly thinker who could both conceptualize long-term plans and attend to the small details necessary to realize them. Early in his tenure at the Board of Health, he focused on the state's ability to generate valid and reliable health statistics. As a representative of the new clinical medicine who had come to appreciate issues of population health, he clearly believed in "evidence-based" public health. He knew that success in public health in North Carolina required local, county-based institutions serving blacks as well as whites, and he therefore made sustained efforts as the chief state health officer to convince local communities to create public health structures that possessed current public health knowledge and worked closely with experts at the state level. By focusing on hookworm (with the help of resources external to the state) and the reduction or elimination of endemic diseases like malaria, Rankin pursued visible victories early in his term. With his transition to the Duke Endowment, where he remained for the rest of his professional career, Rankin completed an evolution from a focus on the pure population health issues of prevention (e.g., securing clean community water supplies) to the more clinically focused issues of health-promoting medical services (such as providing prenatal care through public health departments) and of planning for the availability of and access to clinical medical services for the general public. This evolution of Rankin's agenda can be traced in a series of papers delivered at national professional meetings and published in the *American Journal of Public Health* (Table 13.2). In "Rural Medical and Hospital Services," published in 1927 when he was responsible at the Duke Endowment for fostering hospitals in North and South Carolina, Rankin himself summarized this evolution: " . . . the predominant interest of public health has moved farther and farther away from the environment and nearer and nearer to man himself, [h]aving cleaned up his surroundings. . . . So today, especially in the more advanced health departments, we find an increasingly larger part of the budget going into prenatal clinics, infant welfare clinics, medical inspection of schools, and periodic health examinations."[78] In other words, public health departments in the future, he believed, would need to emphasize medical services for individuals.

Notes

1. George Brown Tindall, *The Emergence of the New South, 1913–1945*, vol. 10, *A History of the New South*, (Baton Rouge: Louisiana State University Press, 1967), 225, quoting Neil Battle Lewis in the *News & Observer* (Raleigh, NC), January 20, 1924. Wisconsinites Robert M. La Follete and John R. Commons pioneered progressive policies.

2. Rebecca Kreston, "Blood Money: Hookworm Economics in the Postbellum South," *Discover*, April 25, 2011, http://blogs.discovermagazine.com/bodyhorrors/2011/04/25/blood-money-hookworm-economics-in-the-postbellum-south/#.VqE4iVKHhlQ.

3. Sok Chul Hong, "The Burden of Early Exposure to Malaria in the United States, 1850–1860: Malnutrition and Immune Disorders," *Journal of Economic History* 67.4 (December 2007): 1012; Robert Lamb, "10 Worst Epidemics," *Discover*, September 18, 2013, http://www.seeker.com/10-worst-epidemics-1767852043.html#news.discovery.com.

4. "Tuberculosis in Europe and America, 1800–1922: Harvard University Library Open Collections Program," http://ocp.hul.harvard.edu/contagion/tuberculosis.html.

5. "Sanitariums: North Carolina Digital History," http://www.learnnc.org/lp/editions/nchist-newsouth/5504.

6. Tuberculosis' etiology was discovered in the 1880s; by 1900 laboratory tests could identify it. But dissemination of new medical knowledge in the United States was slow, and development of successful therapies for tuberculosis was even slower. Paul Starr, *Transformation of American Medicine* (New York: Basic Books, 1982), 137–138, 187–197; George Rosen, *A History of Public Health, expanded edition with introduction by Elizabeth Fee* (1958; reprint, Baltimore: Johns Hopkins University Press, 1993), 361–365.

7. "Sanitariums: North Carolina Digital History."

8. Edward H. Beardsley, *A History of Neglect: Health Care for Blacks and Mill Workers in the Twentieth Century South* (Knoxville: University of Tennessee Press, 1987), 54–60. Litigation blocked Congress' effort in 1916 to end factory labor by children younger than 14 using the Constitution's commerce clause, when the United States Supreme Court secured for Roland Dagenhart the right of his two young sons to enjoy unrestricted labor in a Charlotte cotton mill (*Hammer v. Dagenhart*, 247 US 251 (1918)). Congress then tried to restrict child labor using federal taxing power, but the Supreme Court again ruled the legislation unconstitutional in *Bailey v. Drexel Furniture Co.* (259 US 20 (1922)). Drexel has long been a famous brand in North Carolina furniture. In finding the Affordable Care Act ("Obamacare") constitutional, Chief Justice John Roberts based the majority's acceptance of the individual mandate to secure health coverage on the federal taxing power after using a restricted interpretation of the interstate commerce clause to deny its relevance. *National Federation of Independent Business v. Sibelius* 567 US 519 (2012).

9. North Carolina hospitals had one bed per 517 persons; the US ratio was 1:291. South Carolina had the worst ratio in the country with 1:797. The Duke Endowment, *Annual Report of the Hospital Section, 1925* (Charlotte: Duke Endowment, 1926), 50–55, 85, Tables 13 and 14, citing data from *Journal of the American Medical Association* 86.14 (April 1926): 1009–1064.

10. "Winston-Salem's Early Hospitals: North Carolina Digital History," http://www.learnnc.org/lp/editions/nchist-newcentury/5784.

11. New revolutionary governments, such as the Soviet Union, the Peoples' Republic of China, and Castro's Cuba have repeatedly demonstrated the truth of this claim, thereby helping to consolidate their hold on power and the allegiance of their citizens. Perhaps Vladimir Lenin said it best in his succinct slogan at the Seventh Congress of Soviets in 1919, in the midst of the devastating typhus epidemic: "Either the lice defeat socialism or socialism defeats the lice." Mark G. Field *Soviet Socialized Medicine: An Introduction* (New York: Free Press, 1967), chap.

4, 49–74 (Lenin quote, p. 52); Victor W. Sidel and Ruth Sidel, *Serve the People: Observations on Medicine in the People's Republic of China* (New York: Josiah Macy Jr. Foundation, 1973), 22–23; Edgar A. Porter, *The People's Doctor: George Hatem and China's Revolution* (Honolulu: University of Hawaii Press, 1997).

12. The authors wish to thank the thoughtful editor at the University of Tennessee Press and Thomas W. Hanchett, public historian of North Carolina extraordinaire, who both urged us to make explicit this continuing tension in the history of U. S. health policy. Goldfarb v. Virginia State Bar is found at 421 U.S. 773 (1975); Barbara Brandon Schnorrenberg, "Is Childbirth Any Place for a Woman? The Decline of Midwifery in Eighteenth-Century England," in Studies in Eighteenth-Century, vol. 10, ed. Harry C. Payne (Madison: University of Wisconsin Press, 1981), 393–408; Starr, Transformation, passim, especially 54–59, 180–197; Elton Rayack, Professional Power and American Medicine: The Economics of the American Medical Association (Cleveland: World Publishing Co., 1967).

13. Anne M. Dellinger, Jeffrey S. Koeze, and Vicki Winslow, "Public Health," in *State and Local Government Relations in North Carolina: Their Evolutions and Current Status*, ed. Charles D. Liner, 2nd ed. (Chapel Hill: University of North Carolina at Chapel Hill Institute of Government, 1995), 123–137.

14. Massachusetts Department of Public Health, *State Board of Health of Massachusetts: A Brief History of its Organization and its Work, 1869–1912* (Boston: Wright & Potter, 1912), 8–9. https://archive.org/details/stateboardofheal00mass; "Agency History 1755–1990s: Government Records Branch of North Carolina Department of Health and Human Services," http://www.stateschedules.ncdcr.gov/AgencyHistory.aspx?L1=Department%-20of%20Health%20and%20Human%20Services.

15. "Agency History 1755–1990s."

16. Dellinger, Koeze, and Winslow, "Public Health," 123–137.

17. "Agency History 1755–1990s."

18. Lemuel Shattuck, *Report on the Sanitary Condition of Massachusetts* (Boston: Dutton & Wentworth, 1850), 149–166, http://biotech.law.lsu.edu/cphl/history/books/sr/.

19. Suellen Hoy, *Chasing Dirt: The American Pursuit of Cleanliness* (New York: Oxford University Press, 1996), 78–80.

20. "Agency History 1755–1990s."

21. "Agency History 1755–1990s."

22. Mattie U. Russel, "Rankin, Watson Smith," in *Dictionary of North Carolina Biography*, vol. 5, ed. William S. Powell (Chapel Hill: University of North Carolina Press, 1994), 174–175.

23. Dellinger, Koeze, and Winslow, "Public Health," 123–137.

24. Proprietary or for-profit enterprises are distinguished from nonprofit ventures by the fact that the former have identifiable owners—individual or institutions—which can legally receive profits from them. Both for-profit and non-profit entities are private as distinct from government. Nowadays all medical schools in the U.S. are either private nonprofit institutions or government-sponsored, but North Americans established profitable proprietary medical schools in the Caribbean in the second half of the last century to attract American students who wished to become doctors but failed to gain admission to a U.S. medical school. The markets for both hospital and nursing home care are unusual in that for-profit and non-profit enterprises are often found competing head to head in the same market. Alternative theories explaining non-profit organizations and their differences from for-profits are: Henry B. Hansmann, "The Role of Nonprofit Enterprise," in *The Economics of Nonprofit Institutions*, ed. Susan Rose-Ackerman (New York: Oxford University Press, 1986), 57–84; Lester M. Salamon, "Of Market Failure, Voluntary Failure, and Third-Party Government: Toward a Theory of Government-Nonprofit Relations in the Modern Welfare State," in *Shifting the Debate: Public/Private Sector Relations in the Modern Welfare State*, ed. Susan A. Ostrander et al., (New Brunswick: Transaction Books, 1987), 29–49.

25. "American Medical Association Timeline: American Medical Association," http://www
.ama-assn.org/ama/pub/about-ama/our-history/ama-history-timeline.page; Starr, *Transformation*, 112–127; Rosen, *A History of Public Health*, 361–365; Rosemary Stevens, *American Medicine
and the Public Interest* (New Haven: Yale University Press, 1971), chap. 2, 34–54.

26. The standardization of medical education took years to accomplish as Flexner himself
complained. Daniel M. Fox, "Abraham Flexner's Unpublished Report: Foundations and Medical
Education, 1909–1928," *Bulletin of the History of Medicine* 54: 4 (Winter 1980): 489, citing A.
Flexner, transcript to talk, n.d. but likely 1922, General Education Board Papers, I, 5, Box 702.

27. "Back to the Flexner: Medical Education in America by American Medical Student Association," http://getmeducated.weebly.com/back-to-the-flexner.html.

28. Abraham Flexner. *Medical Education in the United States and Canada: A Report to the
Carnegie Foundation for the Advancement of Teaching* (New York: Carnegie Foundation, 1910),
279–281.

29. University of North Carolina at Chapel Hill, School of Medicine, "History." http://www
.med.unc.edu/www/about/about-the-school-of-medicine-1/history; Todd L. Savitt, "Medical
History: A Medical School for African-Americans in 19th Century North Carolina," *Department
of Medical Humanities Newsletter* (East Carolina University) 2.2 (Fall 1999).

30. Flexner, *Medical Education*, 281.

31. "Association News," *American Journal of Public Health* 9.10 (October 1919): 787.

32. Flexner. *Medical Education*, 280–281.

33. Flexner. *Medical Education*, 12, 234–235, 239.

34. Russell, "Rankin," 174–175; "Association News," *American Journal of Public Health* 9.11
(November 1919): 868.

35. W. S. Rankin, "The Practical Value of Vital Statistics in the South," *American Journal of
Public Health* 3 (1913): 456.

36. "Agency History 1755–1990s"; Gary W. Shannon and Gerald F. Pyle, *Disease and Medical
Care in the United States: A Medical Atlas of the Twentieth Century* (New York: Macmillan, 1993), 4.

37. W. S. Rankin, "The Standardization of Public Health Work" *American Journal of Public
Health* 5.10 (October 1915): 1024–1030; Watson Smith Rankin, "Rural Sanitation: Definition, Field
Principles, Methods, and Costs" *American Journal of Public Health* 6.6 (June 1916): 554–558;
David L. Cockrell, "'A Blessing in Disguise': The Influenza Epidemic of 1918 and North Carolina's
Medical and Public Health Communities," *North Carolina Historical Review* 73.3 (July 1996):
309–327.

38. Authors' calculation from 1920 US Census data. US Bureau of the Census, "Fourteenth
Census of the United States, vol. 3, *Population - North Carolina, Table I*, 730.

39. Rankin, "Standardization," 1025; Cockrell, "Blessing," 311–312.

40. Cockrell, "Blessing," 312.

41. Rankin, "The Evolution of County Health Work," *American Journal of Public Health* 7.12
(December 1919): 998–999; Russell, "Rankin," 174–175.

42. "Henry Rose Carter: 1852–1925: University of Virginia Historical Collections at the
Claude Moore Health Sciences Library," http://exhibits.hsl.virginia.edu/yellowfever/henry
-rose-carter-1852–1925–2/; Watson Smith Rankin, *W.S. Rankin Papers* (Durham: Manuscript
Department, Duke University Library, 1905).

43. Cockrell, "Blessing," 320; W. S. Rankin, "Next Step for State Health Departments," *American Journal of Public Health* 12.12 (December 1922): 1000; for details regarding death rates see
U.S. Department of Commerce, Bureau of the Census, *Mortality Rates: 1910–1920* (Washington,
DC: Government Printing Office, 1923), Table III, http://www.cdc.gov/nchs/data/vsushistorical
/mortrates_1910–1920.pdf.

44. The publication was *The Health Bulletin of the North Carolina State Board of Health* 33.5
(November 1918): 38–39; Cockrell, "Blessing," 311. See also Lauren A. Austin and William P.
Brandon, "Pandemic and War, 1918–1919: Preliminary Analysis of New North Carolina Influenza

Data," in *North Carolina during the First World War*, eds. Shepherd W. McKinley and Steven Sabol (Knoxville: University of Tennessee Press, 2018).

45. Alfred W. Crosby highlights his astonishment that the epidemic faded from public memory by retitling the second edition of his book *America's Forgotten Pandemic: The Influenza of 1918* (New York: Cambridge University Press, 1989), first published as *Epidemic and Peace, 1918* (Westport CT: Greenwood, 1976). Both editions, which are exact duplicates with identical pagination, contain an insightful chapter (chap. 14, 295–308) in which Cosby considers the cultural context in which the epidemic was quickly forgotten, whereas the world continued struggling to understand how it could have become engulfed in such a devastating war.

46. Tindall, *Emergence,* 225. According to Tindall, tax revenues rose 554 % between 1913 and 1930.

47. Cockrell, "Blessing," 321–327; Rankin, "Next Step," 1005.

48. Tindall, *Emergence,* 283.

49. "The Deadly Virus: The Influenza Epidemic of 1918: US National Archives and Records Administration," https://www.archives.gov/exhibits/influenza-epidemic/.

50. Duke Endowment, *Annual Report,* 1925, 20–22 and Tables 28, 28A, and 28B, 96–101. Rankin also used draft boards' findings that 28% of those examined were "disqualified for *active* military service," p. 22, emphasis in original. Rankin put great store by the "government supervised" examinations of 2,753,922 men for 269 "defects" that would exclude the man from military service. Defects not relevant to service and therefore not recorded included "defects of vision, teeth, focal infection [i.e., one localized to a specific part of the body], uncured venereal disease." Moreover, Rankin was careful to point out that finding one defect leading to exclusion ended the exam, so other defects would not be recorded. Duke Endowment, *Annual Report,* 1925, 21. For recognition of the need for federal participation and better coordination in response to the medical need, see W. S. Rankin, "A Supreme National Need: Coordination and Enlargement of Federal Health Activities," *American Journal of Public Health* 9.11 (1919): 819–822.

51. "Agency History 1755–1990s."

52. Karin L. Zipf, "In Defense of the Nation: Syphilis, North Carolina's 'Girl Problem' and World War I," *North Carolina Historical Review* 89.3 (July 2012): 283–285.

53. 40 Stat. I, 886.

54. Karen L. Zipf, "In Defense," 276–300. Although public health implemented the medical side of disease control, over time the effort became an interdepartmental initiative with the Interdepartmental Social Hygiene Board directing funds to a state reformatory for women. Zipf tells the story of this reformatory in *Bad Girls at Samarcand: Sexuality and Sterilization in a Southern Juvenile Reformatory* (Baton Rouge: Louisiana State University Press, 2016).

55. P.L. 67–97.

56. P.L. 74–271.

57. James A. Maxwell, "Brief History of Grants," in *Federal Grants and the Business Cycle*, ed. J. A. Maxwell (Cambridge, MA: National Bureau of Economic Research, 1952), 1–13.

58. In contrast to twentieth-century grants-in-aid, most nineteenth-century grants to states involved one-time gifts of land or the proceeds of land sales to support education or highway building; the most notable, of course, was the Morrill Act of 1862, which established land-grant universities, which fostered modernization of agriculture. Robert Jay Dilger, "Federal Grants to State and Local Governments: A Historical Perspective on Contemporary Issues," CRS Report R40638, March 5, 2015, (Washington, DC: Congressional Research Service); Maxwell, "Brief History of Grants," 1–13; David B. Walker, *Toward a Functioning Federalism* (Cambridge MA: Winthrop Publishers, 1981), 46–99.

59. Tindall, *Emergence*, 276–281. Fredrick Taylor Gates, philanthropic advisor to the Rockefellers (Senior and Junior) and mastermind of institutionalizing their philanthropy, believed that the hookworm campaign, originally organized as the US Sanitary Commission

to assuage southern sensitivity about the region's backwardness and the source of funding, was by the time it became international "the most extensive public benefaction ever undertaken by man." He explained that North Carolina's Sandhills region was chosen for the first demonstration efforts to eliminate the South's "lazy bug," because "North Carolina then as always since the Reconstruction days [was] the most progressive of the Southern States." Frederick Taylor Gates, *Chapters in My Life* (New York: The Free Press, 1977), 226–230 (quotations on pp. 230 and 229, respectively). C. Vann Woodward, who emphasized the role of philanthropy in developing education, social welfare, and public health in the South prior to the Great War, stressed the role of North Carolina journalist and politician Walter Hines Page (1855–1918) in securing support for the hookworm campaign in the South from the General Education Board. C. Vann Woodward, *Origins of the New South, 1877–1913: A History of the South,* vol. IX (Baton Rouge: Louisiana State University Press, 1951), 425–428.

60. Beardsley, *History of Neglect*, 141, 148–149.

61. Beardsley, *History of Neglect*, 140–147.

62. Beardsley, *History of Neglect*, chap. 6, 139–155.

63. Beardsley, *History of Neglect*, 146–147.

64. Michael Hill, "Cameron Morrison," in ed. William S. Powell, *Dictionary of North Carolina Biography*, NCPedia, http://ncpedia.org/biography/-governors/morrison; Douglas Carl Abrams, "Cameron Morrison (1869–1953)," North Carolina History Project, http://northcarolinahistory. org/encyclopedia/cameron-morrison-1869–1953/; Bryan Mims, "North Carolina is the Good Roads State," *Our State Magazine* (July 2014), https://www.ourstate.com/good-road-state/.

65. Duke Endowment, *Annual Report of the Hospital Section, 1926* (Charlotte: Duke Endowment, 1927), 33.

66. "Agency History 1755–1990s"; Centers for Disease Control, "Achievements in Public Health, 1900–1999: Family Planning," *Morbidity and Mortality Weekly Report* 48.47 (December 1999): 1073–1080.

67. Thomas C. Ricketts, Jim Vickers, and Sarah McEwan, *Family and Friends: Rural Health Policy in North Carolina* (Chapel Hill: North Carolina Rural Health Research Program, Cecil G. Sheps Center for Health Services Research at the University of North Carolina at Chapel Hill, 1998), 1–35.

68. US Department of Commerce, US Bureau of the Census, *Vital Statistics of the United States, 1940: Part 2* (Washington, DC: Government Printing Office, 1943), http://www.cdc.gov /nchs/data/vsus/VSUS_1943_2.pdf.

69. Robert F. Durden, *Lasting Legacy to the Carolinas: The Duke Endowment, 1924–1994* (Durham: Duke University Press, 1998), 11–12, 17; Barry D. Karl and Stanley N. Katz, "The American Private Philanthropic Foundation and the Public Sphere: 1890–1930," *Minerva* 19.2 (June 1981): 259–263.

70. Durden, *Legacy*, 13, 30.

71. Duke Endowment, *Annual Report,* 1925, Tables 28, 28A, and 28B, 96–101. Table 28 makes it clear that hospitals serving both whites and blacks had specifically designated beds for blacks. It would be naïve to think that the facilities, with features such as separate hospital wings, were equal.

72. US Bureau of the Census, "Population - North Carolina: Table I," 730; U.S. Bureau of the Census, "Fourteenth Census of the United States, Volume Three, "Population - South Carolina, Table I," 924.

73. Durden, *Legacy*, 110–111.

74. Rankin, "A Million Dollars a Year for Carolina Hospitals," *Review of Reviews* 73 (April 1926): 406–408; Rankin, "Rural Medical and Hospital Services," *American Journal of Public Health* 17.1 (January 1927): 19.

75. Durden, *Legacy,* 33–34 et seq.; Cockrell, "Blessing," 322.

76. Cockrell, "Blessing," 321, 324.

77. L. G. Walker Jr, "Alexis Carrel's Contribution to the Care of the Wounded: 1914–1918 and the Role of Rockefeller Institute in Medical Advances in World War I," in *Glimpsing Modernity: Military Medicine in World War I*, eds. Stephen C. Craig and Dale C. Smith (Newcastle upon Tyne, UK: Cambridge Scholars Publishing, 2015), 173–198; "North Carolinians and the Great War," Documenting the American South, North Carolina at Chapel Hill Libraries," http://docsouth .unc.edu/wwi/.

78. Rankin, "Rural Medical," 15.

14

"Doing Their Big Bit": North Carolina's Women on the Homefront

Angela Robbins

Many American women stood poised in 1914 to provide aid to war-ravaged Europeans because they were already organized in the interest of social reform or as volunteers providing resources to the needy and vulnerable in their own communities. Women's club members and college students across North Carolina immediately began collecting funds and supplies to send to Belgian mothers and their children, and they committed countless hours to working with the Red Cross. When the United States entered the war in 1917, women encouraged and supported one another to "do their bit" through service with their existing organizations and by providing leadership to newly formed state and national organizations. They added to their duties such undertakings as putting together care packages for soldiers, growing and preserving food in the wake of severe shortages, and raising funds through Liberty Bond drives. At war's end, North Carolina's women could also point to victories in various Progressive reform efforts, including prohibition, establishing an institution for "wayward" girls, and woman suffrage. Often unified in purpose yet divided by identity, many Tar Heel women emerged from the conflict with confidence in their ability to influence the state's direction while others, owing to their race or socioeconomic status, found their social footing unimproved.

Men's and women's clubs and organizations pulled their leadership from the best educated and most accomplished, who would bring their skills to bear in the war effort. The National Council of Defense, organized to meet the goals of mobilizing the nation for war, included members of President Woodrow Wilson's cabinet and prominent men in industry, commerce, finance, and education. At the state level, North Carolina's most recognizable and accomplished professionals and politicians accepted appointments and applied their expertise to committees on matters of finance, public information, law, conservation, labor, and transportation. Of the fifteen committees initially established was one on women's work. The head of the Woman's Committee and the North Carolina Council's sole woman member, Mrs. J. E. (Laura) Reilley of Charlotte, had been active in the North Carolina Federation of Women's Clubs (NCFWC) since its founding in 1901 and served as president of the organization in 1910 and 1911. Through the NCFWC, which had ten thousand members representing over two hundred clubs by 1922, women gained valuable leadership experience. Reilley herself had served on several committees, presided at meetings and state conventions, and presented special programs and talks to the group. To assist her in her wartime position, Reilley solicited the services of the state's most tireless women philanthropists and reformers, including such figures as Mrs. William Neal (Kate Bitting) Reynolds of Winston-Salem, wife of the future president of R. J. Reynolds Tobacco Company. Described as a woman of "executive ability" and "vision," Reynolds also served as chairman of the National Woman's Liberty Loan Committee for the state of North Carolina during the second Liberty Loan drive.[1]

When the war began, women's club members and college women fit war work into their existing structure for reform, volunteer work, and community service. Like so many other women's clubs of the early twentieth century, the Orange Church Community Club had organized prior to the war as part of the national Progressive movement to improve their local school building in the interest of the health and safety of the children. When the United States entered the war in 1917, they turned their attention and resources to war work. Likewise, the Chapel Hill Community Club "offered its services as an organized body of women to the Government of the United States, through the County Council of Defense," and reported that "all the activities of the club as a whole have been concerned with the war."[2] When the NCFWC opened its Sixteenth Convention in Raleigh on May 28, 1918, its members declared that this "was not to be a social function, but a meeting of serious minded women," with a keynote address on war service. Governor Thomas W. Bickett administered the oath of allegiance to the club members in attendance so that they might "reiterate and impress" their loyalty at a time when patriotic calls to service engaged every American. A point of particular gratification for the club women that year was that the members of the Raleigh Woman's Club, having just completed the construction of their new clubhouse, immediately turned the facility into a Red Cross center.[3]

Traditionally, women's reform and charitable organizations operated separately from men's, even when working toward the same goals.[4] Observing this custom, the North Carolina Council of Defense set up the Woman's Committee to work independently as an auxiliary. The state council remarked upon the "patriotic service" of women and the committee's "endeavor to unify the manifold activities of the women," but it appears to have provided little in the way of direction or close supervision.[5] The state council provided funds on a monthly basis to help the Woman's Committee carry out its duties; however, such funding was generally inadequate nationwide, and women's clubs and organizations found it necessary to capitalize on their skills and experience to pursue creative ways to raise money. Nonetheless, the National Council insisted that activities be coordinated, noting, "The dividing line between men's and women's war work is so slight" that "success . . . depends largely upon their working together harmoniously."[6]

Such harmony would be achieved precisely because women engaged in "social housekeeping," not politics, and society's expectation was that women would observe tradition rather than adopt new roles and responsibilities, even in war.[7] Women's organizations generally focused on issues of social welfare and reform that seemed most fitting to their status and associated with their domestic roles.[8] During the war, the General Federation of Women's Clubs, in conjunction with the Treasury Department, listed among the "housewife's relation to municipal affairs" the cleanliness of sidewalks, air, and water; food inspection and waste disposal; safety, such as police, fire, and health services; general welfare, including hospitals and jails; infant care; and education.[9] The NCFWC divided its responsibilities into ten departments that represented its members' common interests and goals: art, civics, conservation, education, health, home economics, library extension, literature, music, and social service.[10] Attesting to the scope and nature of women's Progressive reform efforts in North Carolina, Sallie Southall Cotten, founder and long-time leader of the NCFWC, thought it "interesting to record that the work of the (women's) clubs extended from the care of County Homes to the Study of Shakespeare; from the civic conditions of their communities to the real problems of Public Welfare . . . the betterment of the world was their concern as well as the betterment of their homes."[11]

As women's organizations were separate from men's in order to not violate social norms and customs, so African American and white organizations were segregated in the Jim Crow South. North Carolina's women were accustomed to working in segregated groups, yet they had also coordinated to achieve similar goals, one of the most significant being the prohibition of alcohol. By the late nineteenth century, a growing army of reformers labored to break down the public's love affair with alcohol through various local referendums. As early as 1877 the cities of Asheville and Greensboro prohibited alcohol, while voters in Wilson, Franklinton, and Raleigh opted for regulation of alcohol through licensing. Women could not yet vote, but they nonetheless influenced this wave of legislation by actively campaigning, and they were often quite visible on election day, as when "fifty ladies attended the polls and worked all day for prohibition" in Monroe.[12] Historian Janette Thomas Greenwood argues that through the prohibition movement of the 1880s, a coalition of black and white members of the better classes in Charlotte "briefly shaped a new kind of politics outside of traditional party channels." Through their joint efforts, Charlotte became dry in 1881. White women had encouraged the participation of black women in segregated temperance societies, and the number of temperance activists in the state swelled to over fifteen hundred in the 1890s.[13] Armed with arguments about the destruction alcohol brought to individuals, families, and society at large, prohibitionists in North Carolina succeeded in making the state the first in the union to enact statewide prohibition of alcohol in 1908. Within a year after the war ended, the eighteenth amendment established prohibition as the law of the land.[14]

Political shifts put an end to interracial cooperation among prohibitionists and influenced the ways in which white and black women worked together during the war. North Carolinians had only recently been rocked by the Wilmington Race Riot, in which white Democrats violently attacked the city's black citizens to remove black officeholders and their political allies. In the wake of the riot, Democratic legislators revised the state constitution to include literacy tests and poll taxes to disenfranchise African American voters and stultify black leadership. Most of the members of black women's clubs were married to the state's most prominent black men—middle class, educated professionals who would have risen to political power had these mechanisms not been in place.[15]

Since the North Carolina Council opted not to establish a separate Negro council, it was left to white women's clubs to determine how they would include African American women in their war efforts. Leaders of both black and white women's clubs facilitated interracial cooperation. Yet, in keeping with the racial order, contemporary accounts always delineated the work and achievements of black women. Separate "colored" auxiliaries and committees existed for every single type of work in which women were engaged, whether through their association with the Red Cross, the YMCA, or Liberty Loan drives. African American women put together "comfort kits" specifically for segregated African American soldiers because black men would not receive such care and attention from white women. Regardless of the independent nature of the work of Orange County's African American committees, a white woman, Mrs. I. H. Manning, served as chair of the "Colored Circles" and provided the report on behalf of the group. Such circumstances only reinforced assumptions that black women merely followed the lead of white women and, given their relationship as members of subcommittees, that they had simply been incorporated into white women's organizations. Hoping to correct this misperception, African American women's organizations pushed for separate Negro state councils, to no avail. In North Carolina, Miss Mamie McCullough and other black women who had been taking on war work in Charlotte were "aching" to establish command of their work but were refused.[16] Nationwide, African American leaders had encouraged patriotic war service at home and abroad out of a belief that it would improve race relations and the status of blacks generally, but whites went to almost any length to maintain the status quo. This fact was made shockingly clear when at least two hundred African Americans lost their lives to white violence in the both the North and the South between 1917 and 1919.[17]

As was true of Progressive reform generally, the goals of the state's middle class women's club members often smacked of social control, as they doled out lessons on morality along with their charity. During the war, the NCFWC secured the facilities and funding for an ongoing project, an institution for white "delinquent girls" in rural Moore County. The stated purpose of Samarcand Manor was to provide "firm yet kind discipline" so that "fallen" girls could "begin to live morally," and concern for the honor of these underprivileged citizens went hand in hand with efforts to improve their general living conditions. Bible study and lessons in cleanliness accompanied vocational training in traditional female skills such as sewing, laundry work, and agricultural work in an effort to ensure that when the girls and women were released they could earn a living. However, most Samarcand residents could only hope to improve their quality of life in the most limited way, since their training prepared them for pitifully low-paying jobs. By the 1930s, Samarcand was sterilizing young women its staff deemed beyond reform, part of a broader state-sponsored eugenics campaign to weed out those white citizens who, it was argued, "weakened" the white race. Significantly, while they provided their subjects an education that promoted continued economic dependence and took from them their reproductive rights, the college-educated women who ran the institution enjoyed greater opportunities and experiences that increased their own independence. Educated women with specialized training made up the majority of Samarcand's board, a rarity in government institutions, and from this position white, middle class women wielded significant authority over social conditions and government reform, as well as maintaining white supremacy, in the state.[18]

Women rose to leadership at Samarcand precisely because assisting in the uplift of the poor, the disadvantaged, and the vulnerable were among those Progressive reform activities deemed most appropriate for women given their presumed innate abilities for nurturing. Women often took the lead in efforts to improve the welfare of children and other women. In 1914, "America's Christmas Gift to Europe" included twelve hundred tons of clothing and toys. The NCFWC allocated funds for aid to French and Belgian orphans. The student body at State Normal and Industrial College—later the North Carolina College for Women and currently the University of North Carolina at Greensboro—provided funds to the Red Cross for the purchase of a bale of cotton to go to Belgium, and they made a layette for a French baby.[19] The class of 1915 at Meredith College in Raleigh earmarked its class gift for Belgian relief, and the faculty performed concerts at the college for the benefit of Belgian citizens burned out of their homes during the war. These efforts were spurred not only by reports of German atrocities in newspapers but also by the first-hand experience of the director of Meredith's School of Music, Miss Charlotte Ruegger, who had served with the Red Cross in Belgium. Students in sewing classes made clothing for Belgian relief, and Miss Ruegger sent along with the donation a letter addressed to the Belgian ambassador. She later received a royal response. "The student body was thrilled," related one account, "by a letter of thanks from Maria, Queen of Belgium."[20]

Beginning with the first Liberty Loan drive in April 1917, women's organizations also threw themselves into raising money through the selling of war bonds. A National Woman's Liberty Loan Committee sold government-issued bonds to citizens, who would receive modest interest on the bonds in the future, to fund a war estimated to cost $14 billion in its first year alone. The committee characterized the "enthusiastic and patriotic" efforts of women as essential to the success of the bond drives.[21] The NCFWC reported selling nearly $3 million of bonds in the second Liberty Loan drive and over $7 million in the third.[22]

Talk of collecting money for war bonds preoccupied North Carolina's college students. Twenty-eight members of the Meredith College graduating class of 1918 purchased a $200 liberty bond, and the entire student body bought $800 in bonds.[23] The small group of undergraduate women only recently admitted to the University of North Carolina at Chapel Hill made contributions to the war that included $154 for the purchase of war bonds.[24] An audience of more than 5000 Greensboro residents, including State Normal students, rallied behind movie star Charlie Chaplin as he promoted the Third Liberty Loan drive in 1918. Chaplin wended his way across the state visiting Rocky Mount, Wilson, and Raleigh before stopping in Greensboro on April 13th to lead a parade on campus that included a large contingent of the students from both State Normal and Greensboro College. Impressing the crowd with his patriotism, the funny man "tried hard to be serious" as he stressed the need for a "big response to this call."[25] By the following spring, State Normal students had grown a bit weary of the sacrifices required of them, complaining that abandoning the Junior–Senior banquet was "one of the biggest disappointments of our entire college course." Their sense of personal loss was allayed upon their discovery "that by not having the banquet we could increase the war fund by three hundred and fifty dollars."[26]

Building on prevailing notions of women as caretakers with a special duty to their homes and communities, federal publications made clear the expectation that all homemakers modify their shopping lists and their families' diets to assist in the war effort. Growing their own food, learning home canning techniques, and making substitutions for in-demand items were expressed as high priorities in government pamphlets that also provided step-by-step instructions and advice written by home economics experts. In addition to the general information in the War Garden Commission's manual, such as how to rid gardens of "enemy plotters" like cabbage worms and potato bugs, southern gardeners found a planting table suited to the region's climate.[27] The many women for whom these demands were new and challenging could send their questions to the Department of Household Science where "technically trained workers, of practical experience" awaited their inquiries. Some southern home-makers did just that when the recommended cold pack method for canning failed. However, government experts concluded that they made no mistakes, faulting instead the home canner's "lack of care in following the instructions."[28]

County home demonstration agents were also ready to assist North Carolina's women if they struggled with government recommendations. These female state government employees traveled the county to offer their expertise in the management of the home, particularly to rural, less prosperous wives and mothers who had not had the advantages of an education to learn the modern practices routinely offered in home economics classes at women's colleges. Demonstrations by agents enhanced the knowledge of farmwomen in areas such as preparing nutritious and sanitary food, growing tomatoes and other produce, and the relatively new practice of preserving food through home canning. During the war, more than 8000 demonstrations reached over 800,000 citizens, and these efforts resulted in over 8 million cans of food produced in 1917 alone.[29] Orange County women's club members secured their county's first Home Demonstration Agent during the war, and this shored up their confidence in their ability to organize "country" women. The isolation of rural women might prevent them from working side by side on a regular basis with the club women who routinely gathered at Red Cross chapters in the state's towns and cities, but it did not keep them from "doing their bit" by knitting bandages and other materials needed by hospital patients or contributing to food production and preservation.[30]

American households sacrificed those food items that US soldiers and allies in Europe needed most, namely wheat, meat, dairy, and sugar. "Food Will Win the War" became the rallying cry on posters and in publications. The specter of starving women and children in Belgium was an effective tool in the push for alterations to the American diet and purchasing habits throughout the war. Across the nation, citizens were to observe Tuesdays as "meatless" and Wednesdays as "wheatless" days. Housewives could find guidelines for buying in bulk, selecting cheaper cuts of meat, and preparing substitutes from one of the many recipes offered, such as the mixture of gelatin, milk, and oleomargarine to replace butter.[31]

Most importantly, not only would every woman cut costs and consumption through her thrift, she would "be rendering a distinct patriotic service to her country at this critical time."[32] The United States had entered the war to make the world safe for democracy, and the head of the United States Food Administration, Herbert Hoover, viewed relief efforts and food conservation as critical to defeating anarchy, "the handmaiden of Hunger." Lady Liberty implored citizens to "Be Patriotic" and "sign your country's pledge to save the food."[33] Over twenty million did just that. The Chapel Hill Community Club's activities typified those of many other women's groups across the nation, as it had "assisted the County Food Administrator in the distribution of Federal Food Membership and Kitchen Cards . . . the signing of the Food Pledge Cards . . . and placed hundreds of Food Administration bulletins in the homes of town and township."[34] Meredith College students were inspired by the imperative to "Clean your plate and lick the Kaiser."[35] Students at State Normal took pride in calling themselves "Hooverites," who were careful not to waste food in the dining room; made a point to cut back on spices; and applauded each other on the fact that "a goodly number of patriotic souls among us are learning to drink tea and coffee without cream and sugar—some of them have even come to like it!"[36]

While the national sentiment was that such contributions were vital, some women argued that women could, and should, take a more active and unconventional role in the war effort. Women, the student editors of the *State Normal Magazine* advocated, should not only be more efficient consumers, but they should *produce* the nation's food as well. Students at the college had consistently done what was asked of them—reducing their consumption of sugar by a barrel each week, sewing and knitting clothing and other supplies for the Red Cross, providing trench candles to troops, and raising thousands of dollars for the war fund—but the editors challenged their classmates to stop congratulating themselves and do more, namely, to sacrifice their summer vacations. They promoted the formation of campus Farmerettes on the model of Vassar, Mount Holyoke, Wellesley, and other women's colleges across the nation, where students had worked on farms for eight hours a day beginning at 4:30 a.m. in the summer of 1917.[37] This particular expectation proved quite challenging to those unaccustomed to farming and gardening. In an effort to buoy the spirits of those frustrated by their new tasks, the editors used gardening as a metaphor to underscore the need for college women to cultivate leadership skills.[38]

Initially organized independently of government agencies, which had only promoted war work for women that reflected prevailing notions of appropriate domestic roles, the Farmerettes program proved so successful that the Department of Labor formed the national Woman's Land Army in the winter of 1918. Twenty-one states and ten thousand women, the majority of them college students, were engaged in this work by the summer of 1918, alleviating severe food shortages abroad and rising food prices at home. They replaced male farmers and workhands at large commercial operations, on dairy farms, in poultry production, in the teaming of livestock, and—in perhaps was what seen as the most manly of tasks—driving tractors and harvesters, technology that had only recently been introduced on most farms. Following a brief training period, these women laborers dug in and worked full days on the farm. Self-supporting and highly efficient, they often arranged their own transportation to and from campus or lived in tents when necessary, and they made their own meals from the fruits of their labor rather than relying on farm wives to cook for them, as had been customary among male laborers. Marrying traditional women's work with their new duties, they also carved out time to can food. Through their efforts, they encouraged a "change in attitude on the part of the farmers from scepticism (*sic*) or incredulity regarding the ability of women to do the work to enthusiastic appreciation of the help given." Farm owners declared this "experiment" in employing women on the farm as "entirely successful"; described their new laborers as conscientious, reliable, and capable; and enthusiastically coordinated with the Farmerettes for their return the following season.[39]

State Normal's Farmerettes joined the tens of thousands of other women engaged in this work and headed out to the fields in the summer of 1918. The class of 1920 produced a special "War Time Features" segment of the yearbook, *Pine Needles*, choosing the image of a Farmerette to symbolize the war efforts that had consumed their college years. When the country needed them, the yearbook staff inquired,

> . . . what did they do? Why, just jump right in to middies and khaki suits and begin mowing lawns and farming with a vengeance. Planting and spraying potatoes, cultivating tomatoes, weeding and thinning corn—mowing, raking, hauling, stacking! What an inexhaustible bunch! And what a picture in their khaki middy suits, brogans, and old country farm hats! Then, when the fruits of this fine harvest were reaped, new enthusiasm came in with the new supplies, and right away another bunch began canning. Why, the corn and beans and potatoes that were saved by these young patriots would alone have won the war—doubtless.[40]

Not only were Farmerettes working the land in summer and preserving the produce in fall, other students committed to mow the lawn and otherwise maintain the grounds, and campus organizations such as the YWCA and literary societies nourished debate and discussion about international events. The world had changed, and the students had changed with it. Acknowledging that "American, and particularly Southern men are slow to break time honored precedents," the magazine's student editors expressed hope that both reluctant farmers and the larger community would come to recognize that this work, while unconventional, was a meaningful and measurable way in which women could fulfill their patriotic duty to the country. "The girls," they concluded, "are doing their *big* bit."[41]

Women "doing their bit" during the war was what suffragists across the nation hoped would finally secure their goal. Dr. Anna Howard Shaw and Carrie Chapman Catt, prominent leaders of the National American Woman Suffrage Association (NAWSA), also provided leadership to the Woman's Committee of the National Council of Defense. Breaking with the more mainstream NAWSA, members of the National Woman's Party (NWP), including North Carolinian Virginia Arnold, picketed the White House throughout the war and declared President Wilson a hypocrite for portraying himself the defender of democracy while he opposed the constitutional amendment on woman suffrage. Both the war service and protests of suffragists swayed Wilson to support the Susan B. Anthony amendment to the US Constitution by war's end.[42]

Mainstream national suffrage leaders like Catt spoke of the "double duty" of women to both serve their country and continue efforts to win the vote, and not even the "gentlemen's agreement" struck among members of Congress to table general legislation in favor of war measures halted the work of suffragists in the halls of the House of Representatives and the Senate. While they kept lobbying to a minimum so as not to appear unpatriotic, suffragists successfully moved forward with their plan to convince the House Rules Committee to form a committee on woman suffrage. Maud Wood Park, chair of NAWSA's Congressional Committee, reflected on her engagement with two of North Carolina's congressmen in this uncertain atmosphere. She credited Democrat Edward William Pou, chairman of the House Rules Committee, as the only true states' rights supporter she ever met in Congress. Pou approved the formation of a committee on women's suffrage despite his own opposition to the federal amendment; he supported suffrage, but, in keeping with his ideology, Pou preferred that it be achieved through state legislation. Park found House Majority Leader Claude Kitchin, Pou's fellow Democratic congressman, to be less genial and forthright. She complained about his "tricks" to shuffle the committee due to his opposition to women's suffrage in any form.[43]

Reluctance on the part of the NCFWC to endorse the suffrage amendment is indicative of the reality that not all women reformers—certainly not the majority of southern women—viewed their volunteer and community work as necessarily political. Anti-suffrage men and women fought instead to reinforce traditional gender roles, which they argued were essential to national security.[44] Although members of the federation had discussed the importance of publicly announcing support for the suffrage amendment, they had declined "in respect to many, who believed in it but thought the time for action had not come" to formally bring the issue before the convention. They finally did so in May 1918. The timing was not only right that spring, but the issue was pressing, given that the suffrage amendment was being debated on the Senate floor. The resolution on suffrage was the thirteenth, and last, to be heard at the convention that year and "after some discussion the Resolution endorsing Suffrage for women was passed amidst great applause." The corresponding secretary immediately drafted a telegram to Lee Overman and Furnifold Simmons, North Carolina's anti-suffrage senators, who along with the majority of the Senate, defeated the amendment. Their commitment now unwavering, the convention met the following year on "the eve of enfranchisement," as once again the nation waited for the Senate vote. The hall was abuzz in Hendersonville, the location of the 1919 convention, when Gertrude Weil, President of the North Carolina Suffrage League, came forward to relate the news from Capitol Hill, adding, "Victory will not be ours until North Carolina has ratified."[45]

Although women's club members questioned the wisdom of supporting women's suffrage in the conservative South, North Carolina's college women enthusiastically embraced the "double duty" of war work and suffrage work. State Normal students staged a suffrage parade in February 1915 featuring the "suffrage band," which included members from the orchestra as well as "amateurs, who . . . performed lustily on comb and tissue paper," and traversed campus with "Votes for Women" banners, ending in front of Spencer dormitory, where the 250 students in attendance listened to "convincing" speeches.[46] Of the 84 members of the class of 1917, 77 made known their commitment as "suffragettes" whose "very souls . . . revel in . . . stumping the state for suffrage." Four of their classmates who did not support the cause were rebuffed by "not allow(ing) their names to be read."[47] As part of Meredith College's Class Day celebration, seniors performed an original play exemplifying their commitment to both war service and community service while challenging classmates to work for suffrage to demonstrate their belief "that without the women (America) can do nothing." Among the photographs of student organizations appearing in the yearbook was the Equal Suffrage League, with 74 proud members displaying a banner declaring their patriotism.[48]

Upon receiving the news that the House had passed the suffrage amendment and it would move forward to the Senate, State Normal students held a mock election in which they elected the nation's first female president. "It was only fitting and proper," *The Greensboro Daily News* quoted one of the celebrants, "that the first woman president should come from the State Normal of North Carolina. Accordingly at a very spirited mass meeting, Miss Eliza Collins was unanimously elected to that position." Two graduates of the class of 1918 who compiled a report on "Women and the War in North Carolina" included among the student body's accomplishments the petition on woman suffrage bearing the signatures of 576 of their classmates sent with the hope of influencing Senators Overman and Simmons to vote for the amendment.[49]

Faculty and administrators also encouraged a continual push for suffrage and invited prominent suffragists to speak at the college. In May 1917, State Normal invited Helen Guthrie Miller, the first vice president of NAWSA, to be the college's first woman commencement speaker. As the United States had only entered the war a month earlier, Miller's speech focused on ways in which students could reduce waste.[50] Jeanette Rankin, representative from Montana and the first woman to serve in Congress, visited campus in April 1918.[51]

Dr. Shaw traveled to State Normal numerous times to speak about both suffrage and the duties of women in wartime. Following her address on democracy in 1917, motivated students asked, "Who . . . is better qualified to speak of and for democracy than she who has given forty years of a magnificently full life to securing and establishing democracy?"[52] In 1918 her message was about women's duties during war, and she also "reaffirmed [the students'] faith in the Cause of Woman Suffrage."[53] Shaw made her final visit to campus as commencement speaker in May 1919, one month before the suffrage bill was approved in the Senate. She urged the students to set great goals for themselves and keep in mind that "the rights of women will be gained . . . if only they will aspire to noble things." Having recently earned the Distinguished Service Medal, she expressed that despite being the only woman honoree, and her frustration in her role as chair of the national Woman's Committee over the "enormous demand for women's work without a corresponding appreciation of the value of that work, or recognition of its relative worth to the Government," she believed that women's service in the war had "led [men] to respect us." The graduating class left in their "Last Will and Testament" two Liberty bonds worth $150 and a large portrait of Shaw, "the greatest woman in America," to hang in the library. Shaw died just one month after Senate approval of the suffrage amendment. State Normal, having only recently been christened the North Carolina College for Women, paid tribute to Shaw in 1921 by naming a dormitory after her.[54]

Armistice celebrations in November 1918 were brief, even nonexistent in some cases due to the influenza outbreak and the quarantines that followed in the fall of 1918 and winter of 1919. Governing authorities prohibited public assemblies for weeks on end, schools and churches closed, and citizens suspended their work to gather funds for the fourth Liberty Loan drive.[55] Some students had not been able to go home for the holidays and watched as the lunch room on the campus of State Normal transformed into a supply station for sick residents of Guilford County.[56] The YWCA brought Christmas shops to campus so quarantined people could prepare for the holidays and also left stockings for those students who remained on campus. Students walked to the nearby Children's Home to fill stockings there but did not have direct contact with the children under the circumstances. Limited Christmas parties that year included a visit to the Greensboro YWCA and the Guilford Court

House Battleground Park. In addition to personal sacrifices, students pledged another $5000 to the War Fund Campaign, which continued until all of the soldiers returned home.[57] At Meredith College, the quarantine was in effect in October and continued until the scheduled winter break. "The necessity of keeping up the morale and physical vigor of several hundred girls cooped up on the diminutive campus" resulted in the organization of an army-style training program for students, complete with officer rankings. It worked to keep their spirits up and helped them push through yet another fundraiser in November, this time through the United War Work Campaign. Students sacrificed new outfits and coats, repairing and making do with existing clothing instead, and they decided to forego trips in order to pledge $2000 to the fund. When students and faculty returned from their Christmas break, 50 of them fell ill with the flu, and efforts to prevent its spread began again.[58]

Service and sacrifice are the words that best capture the experiences of North Carolina's women during World War I. As professionals and homemakers, as students and women's club members, and as reformers both traditional and forward looking, women assessed the importance of their wartime contributions primarily in terms of what they were able to do for others. While many of their Tar Heel sisters continued to struggle in a post-war landscape marked by institutionalized racism and generational poverty, white and educated women, armed with the right to vote and secure in their ability to shape their world through activism, emerged from the war as new women, finding that what they had done for others was just as remarkable in terms of what it helped them accomplish for themselves.

Notes

1. "The North Carolina Council of Defense Plan of Organization" (Raleigh: Commercial Printing Co., 1917), 2–5, 12, *"Documenting the American South,"* 2002, University Library, University of North Carolina at Chapel Hill (hereafter cited as *DocSouth*), http://docsouth.unc.edu/wwi /nccod/nccod.html; Sallie Southall Cotten, *History of the North Carolina Federation of Women's Clubs, 1901–1925* (Raleigh: Edwards & Broughton Printing Co., 1925), 34–46, passim, *DocSouth*, 2001, http://docsouth.unc.edu/nc/cottenss/cottenss.html; Nellie Roberson, "The Organized Work of Women in One State," *Journal of Social Forces* 1, no. 1 (November 1922): 50–55; "Mrs. William Reynolds," *Sky-Land Magazine*, 2 no. 3 (June 1915), 221-222; Treasury Department, "Report of National Woman's Liberty Loan Committee for the First and Second Liberty Loan Campaigns 1917" (Washington, DC: Government Printing Office, 1918), 9, accessed July 25, 2012, https://archive.org/details/-reportofnational00natirich; Michele Gillespie, "Edith Vanderbilt and Katherine Smith Reynolds: The Public Lives of Progressive North Carolina's Wealthiest Women," in ed. Michele Gillespie and Sally G. McMillen, *North Carolina Women: Their Lives and Times – Volume 1* (Athens: University of Georgia Press, 2014), 346.

2. Annie Sutton Cameron, *A Record of the War Activities in Orange County, North Carolina. 1917–1919*, 12–14, Orange County (NC) World War I Activities Record, *DocSouth*, 2002, http:// docsouth.unc.edu/wwi/cameron/cameron.html.

3. Cotten, *History*, 117–119.

4. Anne Firor Scott, *Natural Allies: Women's Associations in American History* (Urbana: University of Illinois Press, 1991); Glenda Elizabeth Gilmore, *Gender and Jim Crow: Women and the Politics of White Supremacy in North Carolina, 1896–1920* (Chapel Hill: University of North Carolina Press, 1996); Janette Thomas Greenwood, *Bittersweet Legacy: The Black and White "Better Classes" in Charlotte, 1850–1910* (Chapel Hill: University of North Carolina Press, 1994).

5. "Plan of Organization," 9.

6. "First Annual Report of the North Carolina Council of Defense," North Carolina Council of Defense (Raleigh: Commercial Printing Co., 1918), 18, *DocSouth*, 2002, http://docsouth.unc.edu /wwi/nccod1918/nccod.html; "Second Annual Report of the Council of National Defense," 28–31, accessed August 25, 2012, https://archive.org/details/-firstfourthannu00defegoog.

7. Elaine F. Weiss, *Fruits of Victory: The Woman's Land Army of America in the Great War* (Washington, DC: Potomac Books, 2008), 223–224; David M. Kennedy, *Over Here: The First World War and American Society* (New York: Oxford University Press, 1980), 284–286.

8. Scott, *Natural Allies*, 169–171.

9. "Ten Lessons in Thrift," US Treasury Department, prepared in cooperation with the Social and Industrial Conditions Department of the General Federation of Women's Clubs (Washington, DC: Government Printing Office, May 1919), 14, World War I Pamphlets Collection, University of North Carolina at Greensboro (hereafter UNCG), accessed July 1, 2012, http:// libcdm1.uncg.edu/cdm/landingpage/collection/WWIPamp.

10. Roberson, "The Organized Work," 52–53.

11. Cotten, *History*, 29. On the women's club movement, see Anne Firor Scott, *Natural Allies* and *The Southern Lady: From Pedestal to Politics, 1830–1930* (Chicago: University of Chicago Press, 1970); Anastasia Sims, *The Power of Femininity in the New South: Women's Organizations and Politics in North Carolina, 1880–1930* (Columbia: University of South Carolina Press, 1997).

12. "Prohibition—License" and "Prohibition Election," *Raleigh Register*, June 12, 1877.

13. Greenwood, "Bittersweet Legacy," 77–113; Scott, *Natural Allies*, 102–103. On African American women's club members in North Carolina, see Gilmore, *Gender and Jim Crow*, and on the coordinated efforts of black and white women's club members in the state specifically, see 147–202. On the national African American clubwomen's movement, see Dorothy Salem, *To Better our World: Black Women in Organized Reform, 1890–1920* (Brooklyn, NY: Carlson Publishing, 1990); Anne Firor Scott, "Most Invisible of All: Black Women's Voluntary Associations," *Journal of Southern History* 56, no. 1 (February 1990): 3–22; Stephanie Shaw, "Black Club Women and the Creation of the National Association of Colored Women," *Journal of Women's History* 3 (Summer 1991): 10–25.

14. Sarah Wilkerson-Freeman, "Stealth in the Political Arsenal of Southern Women: A Retrospective for the Millennium," in ed. Melissa Walker, Jeanette R. Dunn, and Joe P. Dunn, *Southern Women at the Millennium: A Historical Perspective* (Columbia: University of Missouri Press, 2003), 47–48; Kennedy, *Over Here*, 185.

15. David S. Cicelski and Timothy B. Tyson, *Democracy Betrayed: The Wilmington Race Riot and Its Legacy* (Chapel Hill: University of North Carolina Press, 1998); Gilmore, *Gender and Jim Crow*, 58–59; Jeffrey J. Crow, Paul D. Escott, and Flora J. Hatley Wadelington, *A History of African Americans in North Carolina* (Raleigh: NC Department of Cultural Resources, Division of Archives and History, 1992), 127–129.

16. Cameron, "A Record," 13 and passim; Gilmore, 195–96; William J. Breen, "Black Women and the Great War: Mobilization and Reform in the South," *Journal of Southern History* 44, no. 3 (August 1978), 428–29.

17. Kennedy, *Over Here*, 279–284.

18. Cotten, *History*, 107–112; Julian M. Pleasants, "Samarcand Manor," in ed. William S. Powell, *Dictionary of North Carolina Biography*, NCPedia, accessed June 20, 2013, http://ncpedia .org/samarcand-manor. A 1938 report showed that the institution had just over two hundred students enrolled and had sterilized 127 over the previous four years. See the *Tenth Biennial Report of the Board of Directors and Superintendent of the State Home and Industrial School for*

Girls, Samarcand Manor, Eagle Springs, N.C. (1938), 280–283, accessed June 20, 2013, https://
archive.org/details/biennialreportof1938stat; Karen L. Zipf, *Bad Girls at Samarcand: Sexuality
and Sterilization at a Southern Juvenile Reformatory* (Baton Rouge: Louisiana State University
Press, 2016), 3, passim. See also Melton Alonza McLaurin and Anne Russell, *The Wayward Girls
of Samarcand: A True Story of the American South* (Wilmington, NC: Bradley Creek Press, 2012).
Samarcand has been variously listed as Samarkand in some sources, including Google Maps.

19. Cotten, *History*, 125; *State Normal Magazine*, December 1914, 100, and January 1915, 135,
Magazines and Periodicals Collection, Martha Blakeney Hodges Special Collections and University Archives, University Libraries, UNCG, accessed July 1, 2012, http://libcdm1.uncg.edu/cdm
/landingpage/collection/Coraddi; *Pine Needles* (1920), 83, 232, University Yearbook Collection,
University Archives, UNCG, accessed July 1, 2012, http://libcdm1.uncg.edu/cdm/landingpage
/collection/PineNeedles.

20. Mary Lynch Johnson, *A History of Meredith College* (Raleigh: Meredith College, 1972),
135, 154, 159.

21. "Report of National Woman's Liberty Loan Committee," 7.

22. Cotten, *History*, 120–121.

23. "Meredith College Quarterly Bulletin," November 1917, 15–16, and May 1918, 7–9, accessed July 12, 2013, https://archive.org/details/meredithcollegeq1915mere.

24. Cameron, "A Record," 16.

25. *State Normal Magazine*, May 1918, 291–292, University Archives, UNCG; "Buy WWI
Liberty Bonds, Chaplin told 5,000 on Campus," *Campus Weekly*, accessed July 1, 2012, http://
ure.uncg.edu/prod/cweekly/2012/06/12/chaplinoncampus/.

26. *Pine Needles* (1920), 83–84, University Archives, UNCG.

27. "War Gardening and Home Storage of Vegetables for the Southern States" (Victory
Edition, 1919), National War Garden Commission, WWI Pamphlets, UNCG; "War Vegetable
Gardening and the Home Storage of Vegetables," National War Garden Commission (1918),
WWI Pamphlets, UNCG.

28. "Home Canning and Drying of Vegetable and Fruits," National War Garden Commission,
1918, 1–27, WWI Pamphlets, UNCG.

29. LuAnn Jones, *Mama Learned Us to Work: Farm Women in the New South* (Chapel Hill: University of North Carolina Press, 2002), 107–169; Archibald Henderson, *North Carolina Women in
the World War* (Raleigh: North Carolina Literary and Historical Association, 1920), 8, *DocSouth*,
2002, http://docsouth.unc.edu/wwi/henderson/henderson.html.

30. Cameron, "A Record," 9.

31. "War Economy in Food with Suggestions and Recipes for Substitutions in the Planning
of Meals," United States Food Administration (Washington, DC: Government Printing Office,
January 1918), 5–9, WWI Pamphlets, UNCG; "Hints to Housewives," Mayor Mitchel's Food Supply
Committee (New York: June 1917), 1–11, WWI Pamphlets, UNCG; *Pine Needles* (1920), 232, University Archives, UNCG.

32. "Hints to Housewives," 1.

33. "'Food Will Win the War,' 1917," The Gilda Lehrman Institute of American History, accessed
July 1, 2013, http://www.gilderlehrman.org/history-by-era/world-war-i/resources/%E2%80%9C
food-will-win-war%E2%80%9D-1917; "Be Patriotic – Sign Your Country's Pledge to Save the Food,"
Prints and Photographs Online Catalog, Library of Congress, accessed July 1, 2013, http://www
.loc.gov/pictures/item/96515511.

34. Cameron, "A Record," 14.

35. Johnson, *Meredith College*, 159.

36. "Are You a Hooverite?," *State Normal Magazine*, November 1917, 27, University Archives,
UNCG.

37. "We're With You, Mr. Hoover," *State Normal Magazine*, December 1917, 63, University Archives, UNCG; "Thanksgiving Service," and "Our Pledge Paid," *State Normal Magazine*, January,

1918, 137, 139, University Archives, UNCG; Mabel Tate and Naomi Neal, *Women and the War in North Carolina* (Greensboro: State Normal and Industrial College, 1918), 5–6, *DocSouth*, 2002, http://docsouth.unc.edu/wwi/tate/tate.html; "Stop Congratulations," *State Normal Magazine*, February 1918, 145–146, University Archives, UNCG.

38. "War Gardens," *State Normal Magazine*, March 1918, 178–179, University Archives, UNCG.

39. "Woman's Land Army of 1918," Woman's Land Army of America (New York: 1918), WWI Pamphlets, UNCG; "What the Farmers Say about the Work of the Woman's Land Army of America in 1918," Woman's Land Army of America (New York: 1918), WWI Pamphlets, UNCG; Alice Campbell, "Eight Hours a Day on the Vassar Farm," Eastern States Exposition and Dairy Show (Springfield, MA: 1917), WWI Pamphlets, UNCG. On the organization and accomplishments of the Woman's Land Army, see Weiss, *Fruits of Victory*.

40. *Pine Needles* (1920), 231–232, University Archives, UNCG. Photographs show students in their uniforms at work in the fields and canning food, 233–235.

41. *State Normal Magazine*, June 1918, 298–300, University Archives, UNCG.

42. "The Woman's Committee. United States Council of National Defense" (Washington, DC: Government Printing Office, 1920), 9–12, accessed July 25, 2012, https://archive.org/details /womanscommittee00blaigoog; Kimberly Jensen, *Mobilizing Minerva: American Women in the First World War* (Urbana, Chicago, and Springfield: University of Illinois Press, 2008), 15–18, 165–166; Scott, *Natural Allies*, 171; Doris Stevens, *Jailed for Freedom* (New York: Boni and Liveright, 1920), 94-96, passim.

43. Maud Wood Park, *Front Door Lobby*, ed. Edna Lamprey Stantial (Boston: Beacon Press, 1960), 11, 62, 74–79, 87–95, 99–127.

44. Elna C. Green, *Southern Strategies: Southern Women and the Woman Suffrage Question* (Chapel Hill: University of North Carolina Press, 1997); Marjorie Spruill, *New Women of the New South: The Leaders of the Woman Suffrage Movement in the Southern States* (New York: Oxford University Press, 1993); Jensen, *Mobilizing Minerva*, 20.

45. Cotten, *History*, 127, 135–138.

46. *State Normal Magazine*, March 1915, 219, University Archives, UNCG.

47. *State Normal Magazine*, May 1917, 241–42, University Archives, UNCG.

48. *Oak Leaves* (1918), 68–72, 133, accessed July 12, 2013, https://archive.org/details/-oak leaves1918bapt.

49. *State Normal Magazine*, February 1918, 174 (reprint of *Greensboro Daily News* story), University Archives, UNCG; Tate and Neal, 5–6; *State Normal Magazine*, March 1918, 211, University Archives, UNCG. Senator Simmons was a leader of the white supremacy campaign of 1898 and had also pulled funding from state colleges, including State Normal; see Ronnie W. Faulkner, "Furnifold McLendel Simmons," *NorthCarolinahistory.org: An Online Encyclopedia, North Carolina History Project*, http://northcarolinahistory.org/encyclopedia/furnifold-mclendel -simmons-1854-1940/ (accessed July 12, 2013).

50. *State Normal Magazine*, May 1917, 247–248, University Archives, UNCG.

51. *State Normal Magazine*, April 1918, 253, University Archives, UNCG.

52. *State Normal Magazine*, May 1917, 258, University Archives, UNCG.

53. *State Normal Magazine*, June 1918, 331–332, University Archives, UNCG.

54. *State Normal Magazine,* May-June 1919, 232, 241, 242–244, University Archives, UNCG; Wilkerson-Freeman, "Stealth in the Political Arsenal," 60–63; Weiss, *Fruits of Victory*, 223–24; Kennedy, *Over Here*, 284–86.

55. Cameron, "A Record," 59, 64–65.

56. *Pine Needles* (1920), 84, University Archives, UNCG.

57. *State Normal Magazine*, December 1918, 104 and January 1919, 136, 139–140, University Archives, UNCG.

58. Johnson, *Meredith College*, 160–162.

15

Pandemic and War, 1918–1919

Preliminary Analysis of New North Carolina Influenza Data

Lauren A. Austin and William P. Brandon

War and pestilence together constitute a deadly duo that has produced shudders ever since Thucydides so vividly described the plague in Athens in the second year of the Peloponnesian War (430 BCE).[1] Thus, no account of North Carolina during the First World War can be complete without a chapter devoted to the "Spanish influenza." Looking back upon the last century, it is no small irony that the plague year of 1918–1919 experienced by combatant and neutral states alike stands out as almost the only pre-modern aspect of a conflict that introduced industrial warfare for the first time. A conflict waged with complex machinery—U-boats, machine guns, tanks, aeroplanes, and chemical weapons—generated new battlefield tactics and strategic innovations to exploit the potential of industrialized warfare. On the homefront, mobilization to sustain industrial warfare and assembly-line slaughter was required to a much greater extent even in the United States than previously known. In contrast to the mechanized lethality introduced by the Great War, its consort with even more lethal disease is almost the only traditional element of the first of the century's world wars. Indeed, this preindustrial aspect of the war puts the noncombatant survivor in North Carolina much nearer the Athenian survivor of the plague than to survivors of subsequent twentieth-century conflicts.

During the First World War, North Carolina hosted several military training camps, served as a transportation hub for thousands of American servicemen travelling to and from European fronts, and produced and shipped wartime textiles and armored materials from factories throughout the state.[2] North Carolina also had substandard public health care practices, largely due to its predominantly rural nature. The combination of poor health care resources and the increased transportation of war goods meant that North Carolina's citizens faced elevated risks during the 1918–1919 epidemic as the disease swept largely unchecked through most of the state in a short time period.[3] The epidemic brought the medical and health care systems of both North Carolina and the nation to their knees, causing many people to doubt that doctors, hospitals, or other medical resources were able to protect them from this or perhaps any other new disease. Unfortunately, as the epidemic spread, professionals themselves began to doubt that they had the ability to provide relief or assistance at the level required. The epidemic helped reveal the need for a complete overhaul of the public health system, especially in North Carolina where W. S. Rankin proved to be a highly effective and adaptable chief public health officer.[4]

These generalizations about the flu epidemic, based on contemporary accounts, anecdotes, and secondary sources, have become commonplace since the popular and scholarly rediscovery of the twentieth century's most devastating epidemic at the time of the 1976 swine flu scare.[5] The remarkable scientific forensics involved in the genetic studies of the virus recounted by Gina Kolata have not yet been matched with similar progress in social scientists' understanding of the epidemic's morbidity and mortality in large US populations.[6] This chapter provides the first look at a newly collected database constituting all the death certificates for the state of North Carolina at the beginning and end of the epidemic. The chapter identifies three testable hypotheses in a lengthy general introductory account of North Carolina's experience with the second wave of the influenza epidemic. It then describes the first statewide database of flu deaths, the study methodology, empirical findings, and limitations of the quantitative investigation. The analysis that concludes the chapter is only a first look at a rich database; subsequent publications will contain more sophisticated statistical analysis. Yet the relatively simple epidemiological analysis provided is sufficient to constitute valid quantitative tests of the current historical consensus about who died from flu in the unusual pandemic of 1918–1919.

In the fall of 1918, residents of North Carolina waged war on two separate fronts: on the Western Front where soldiers fought against the Central Powers and on the homefront where citizens fought against a rapidly spreading strain of influenza.[7] Scholars still debate the origin of the epidemic. Many researchers trace the initial reports of the 1918 flu strain to Camp Funston in Kansas during spring of that year, while others point to China, Japan, or France as the origin.[8] The 1918 strain is often and erroneously called the Spanish Flu. During the spring of 1918 many countries in Europe as well as the United States and Asia experienced a flu outbreak, but only Spain, still neutral in the midst of war, did not censor its news reports. Thus, Spain's flu outbreak became public knowledge whereas other countries regarded news of the devastating disease as critical intelligence to be suppressed; consequently, the flu became branded as the "Spanish influenza."[9] Whatever its origin, the influenza quickly spread throughout Asia, Europe, and North America in three distinct waves between 1918 and 1919.[10] The first wave struck during the spring and early summer of 1918 followed by the second wave in August 1918 and the third wave during the winter of 1918–1919.[11]

Because typhoid fever and tuberculosis combined caused more than 2,200 deaths in North Carolina in the first nine months of 1918, the first wave of the influenza epidemic went largely unnoticed. It did not claim an abnormally high number of lives, and people assumed it to be an older, rarely deadly form of the flu that doctors often called "la grippe."[12] However, North Carolina's second wave, which started in Wilmington in September 1918, garnered almost immediate attention.[13] Within a week of the first cases, so many residents of Wilmington found themselves afflicted that the James Walker Memorial Hospital overflowed with patients, and officials had to open many temporary facilities.[14] This new strain of influenza, unlike other flu epidemics, targeted the robust immune systems of the young (ages 20–40) and healthy as well as the elderly and unhealthy, whose elevated mortality was expected; the resulting W-shaped epidemic curve contrasted with the usual U-shaped age curve where the highest flu death rates were in children and the elderly.[15]

Approximately twenty percent of the epidemic's victims contracted a mild case and recovered without much incident. However, the other eighty percent of victims experienced one of two terrifying patterns. Some victims became deathly ill almost immediately, their lungs quickly filling with fluid as they struggled to breathe. These victims died in a matter of days, sometimes even hours, their bodies ravaged by a high fever, gasping for breath, until they lapsed into unconsciousness until death. For the remainder of the victims, the illness initially presented itself as the ordinary flu complete with chills, fever, and muscle aches. However, by the fourth or fifth day of the illness, pneumonia developed, filling the victims' lungs with bacteria that either killed them or led to an exceptionally long period of convalescence.[16] The prevalence of blue-tinted skin among the victims caused observers to label this particular strain of influenza the "Blue Death."[17] There were also widespread reports of continued and persistent lethargy experienced by those who survived the flu. Many survivors, including President Woodrow Wilson, experienced sluggish mental abilities, paranoia, and depression following their recovery from the flu.[18]

Unfortunately, the epidemic struck the world at the worst possible time. During the massive upheaval caused by World War I, people traveled more extensively and frequently than ever before, and many soldiers found themselves assigned either overseas or to military training camps, often returning home for visits. The camps produced environments ripe for the influenza strain, as many young and robust bodies sheltered together in overcrowded barracks.[19] By mid-October 1918, the flu was present in every state in America.[20]

Normally, the largely rural demographics of North Carolina would slow the transmission of a virus. However, due to the surge of military movement along the railroad lines brought about by US war mobilization and the fact that the state housed numerous military camps, the Blue Death quickly spread westward from Wilmington into other counties and eventually other states, according to the current historical consensus.[21] After the United States entered World War I, North Carolina became home to three military training camps that trained 86,457 soldiers: Camp Greene near Charlotte, Camp Bragg near Fayetteville, and Camp Polk near Raleigh.[22] In addition, the state's workers gathered in large groups to produce Navy warships in Wilmington, airplane propellers in High Point, artillery shells in Raleigh, and Army-issued blankets, tents, and socks in textile mills in many towns and cities. This hotbed of war activity for the eighteen months that the United States participated in the war facilitated the growth and rapid spread of this uncommonly deadly flu virus in North Carolina.[23]

Densely populated areas, including larger cities, university communities, and military training camps, suffered higher numbers of fatalities during the flu epidemic than did sparsely populated rural areas. However, the dire sanitary conditions still prevalent in many areas of North Carolina in 1918 only made the situation worse. After visiting Camp Greene in Charlotte prior to the first flu wave, US Congressman Sherman E. Burroughs (R-NH) told the New Hampshire House of Representatives in February 1918 about the poor conditions of North Carolina's military camps.[24] He explained that due to the dense clay formation of the soil, the melting snow and rainy weather combined to make the entire camp a "veritable bog" with "mud knee-deep in roads throughout." He saw standing water "in large pools and ponds all over the surface of the camp" and kitchen and latrine waste accumulating in ditches because soldiers had no wood to burn it and garbage contractors could not cross the mud to collect it. Burroughs then blasted the camp's military officials for having no sewage system, an oversight that likely led to typhoid fever and diphtheria outbreaks in the summer.[25] Not surprisingly, the influenza strain hit soldiers stationed at the camp particularly hard. During the outbreak of 1918, observers noted that coffins of soldiers who contracted and succumbed to the flu filled Camp Greene's railroad station from floor to ceiling.[26]

At the peak of the influenza epidemic, the virus infected at least twenty percent of North Carolina's population.[27] The state did not have the resources to care for so many sick individuals. On October 3, 1918, Governor Thomas Bickett issued a statement urging citizens not to "share eating or drinking utensils," "sneeze or cough without covering," or engage in any other form of "swapping spit" in an effort to slow down the spread of the virus. Officials also instituted mandatory quarantining for people suffering from influenza. On October 4, the State Board of Health imposed a ban on almost all social interaction that made it illegal for anyone to hold an event that would draw a crowd.[28] On the same day, Burlington placed a ban on public gatherings for two weeks in an effort to keep the number of flu cases low. The mayor of High Point died of influenza on October 14, and officials closed Winston-Salem's tobacco houses three days later. The state quarantined the entire city of Charlotte on October 24 due to an outbreak at Camp Greene. The vigorous president of the University of North Carolina at Chapel Hill, Edward Kidder Graham, died of the flu on October 26, just after turning 42. On October 30, all stores within three miles of the city limits of Winston-Salem were ordered closed immediately.[29]

Quarantine measures and closures did not stop or even slow the spread of the virus. The situation worsened, and the office of W. S. Rankin, North Carolina's chief public health official, was inundated with pleas for help. One such request from the village of Stonewall stated that, "Our people are dying, the doctors are overworked and cannot do justice to the situation and we need help." Rankin's office could only respond: "No nurse available. You should insist on community organizations as advised three weeks ago." The federal government met pleas for help from North Carolina with similar responses.[30] The state, which over the past few decades had played catch up in controlling outbreaks of infectious diseases now found itself isolated by the federal government and forced to confront the influenza outbreak alone.

Without federal assistance for flu victims, the North Carolina Board of Public Health organized several grassroots volunteer campaigns to shuffle aid to places where it was most needed. State officials reassigned home economic volunteers, created a wartime physician pool, and moved volunteers from county to county based on demand. The Red Cross helped establish temporary hospitals and soup kitchens to augment the overflowing regular hospitals. Even though many of them were sick, students at the University of North Carolina at Chapel Hill came together to make 286 face masks for the doctors and nurses in various emergency hospitals as well as 170 armbands for hospital attendants.[31] Physicians threw themselves wholeheartedly into the battle against influenza by tending patients in spite of the risks. According to the North Carolina Medical Society, seventeen physicians died while trying to help others during the influenza epidemic, but this number reflects only physicians who were active members of the society during the epidemic. Consequently, the number is probably much higher.[32] However, most of these efforts proved too localized and limited to reach the state's rural majority.

The State Board of Health published a monthly newsletter, *The Health Bulletin*, and sent it to any citizen of North Carolina upon request. The only substantive information about influenza during the actual epidemic appeared in *The Health Bulletin* in November 1918. In an article titled, "Influenza and What You Should Know About It," the Board encouraged people to keep away from crowds; avoid people who sneeze, cough, or spit; not to use common drinking cups or utensils; keep their bowels open; snuff Vaseline up their noses three times a day; gargle with warm salt water; sleep with their windows open; and get as much sunshine as possible.[33] Officials urged people to use judgment and common sense and to not get "unduly alarmed" during the epidemic. Residents were also encouraged to immediately contact a doctor should they develop flu symptoms, but the article acknowledged that some people did not have access to a doctor for any number of reasons. These individuals were encouraged to stay in bed with plenty of covers to keep warm and to keep open every window in the home, freely take medication to open the bowels, and eat milk, eggs, and broth every four hours.[34]

Due to the state's rural nature and its lack of local state-of-the art medical care, many North Carolinians faced the influenza outbreak without the aid of qualified physicians and without access to hospitals or treatment centers. Dead bodies filled morgues, deceased families remained undiscovered for weeks and sometimes months, and bodies remained unburied. The state public health system floundered under the strain of such great medical need. The influenza epidemic in the state ultimately claimed a reported 13,644 lives, many of whom never received physician or hospital care during their illness.[35] Dan Tonkel, a child living in Goldsboro during the epidemic, recalled the fear that pervaded the population during the autumn of 1918 and winter of 1918–1919:

> I felt like I was walking on eggshells. I was afraid to go out, to play with my playmates, my classmates, my neighbors. I was almost afraid to breathe. I remember I was actually afraid to breathe. People were afraid to talk to each other. It was like—don't breathe in my face, don't even look at me, because you might give me germs that will kill me. Farmers stopped farming, merchants stopped selling. The country more or less just shut down. Everyone was holding their breath, waiting for something to happen. So many people were dying, we could hardly count them. We never knew from one day to another who was going to be next on the death list.[36]

By spring 1919 the epidemic abated on its own, and life in North Carolina returned to near-normal with schools and businesses reopening and people less afraid to socialize. However, fears regarding new outbreaks lingered. The third wave of the flu crested in early January 1919, leaving many school districts hesitant to reopen even though the state quarantine on public gatherings had been lifted. While most North Carolina school districts decided to restart classes in early spring, authorities in Lenoir were undecided about bringing the students back; the local school board called a public meeting to allow townspeople to vote on the issue. The next day's *Charlotte* (North Carolina) *Observer* headline read: "Lenoir Public Schools Closed till Next Fall: People So Decide by Vote of 150 to 70 After Bitter Fight. 'Flu' the Reason."[37] Many Lenoir residents objected, arguing that without any spring classes their children could not advance to the next grade when the next school year began. Litigation ensued. The case finally made its way to the North Carolina Supreme Court, which ruled in favor of the school district's right to close the school until fall 1919 due to the school board's desire to promote "public welfare."[38]

These accounts of the 1918–1919 flu and the path it took through North Carolina suggest three hypotheses that can be tested with data generated by collecting and coding death data for all one hundred counties and securing the 1920 US Census data necessary to calculate mortality rates. The three hypotheses are:

1. Vulnerable Young Adults: That in North Carolina young adults died in numbers greater than or equal to the death rates of young children and the elderly.
2. Spatial Diffusion: (2A) That the flu initially spread along the train lines emanating from Wilmington, NC and (2B) that it spread differentially over the state with hard-hit areas early in the epidemic having lower mortality relative to other counties in the last months of the epidemic.
3. Vulnerable Concentrations: That institutions or activities involving large concentrations of vulnerable individuals suffered disproportionally greater mortality. Counties with (3A) large military training camps and (3B) manufacturing centers, especially cotton mills, experienced greater flu mortality in proportion to their population than did other North Carolina counties.

These hypotheses can be subjected to empirical verification by examining newly collected data for all recorded deaths in October 1918, the month with the highest mortality, and March 1919, the last month when mortality had declined in the familiar pattern of epidemics. Numerator data for calculating flu mortality rates were coded from all North Carolina death certificates for October 1918 and March 1919.[39] Denominators for mortality rates came from the 1920 US Census, which was taken on January 1, 1920.[40] Intentional sampling based on 100 percent of recorded deaths in the two important months allowed the investigators to observe temporal and spatial patterns. A study with the county as the unit of analysis required hundred-percent samples to obtain sufficient numbers of cases in counties with small populations and to enable analyses that drilled down to narrow intervals for such important population parameters as age.

Analysis involved presenting data for each month in a form that allowed valid comparisons of flu mortality among one hundred counties with very different population structures. Because crude death rates (i.e., flu-caused deaths for a given period divided by total population at risk) are notoriously misleading when populations differ in demographic characteristics such as age, sex, and race, it was necessary to standardize mortality data for all one hundred counties. Standardization, or age, sex, race adjustment was accomplished using the direct method applied to county populations reported in the 1920 census.[41] The 1920 state population was the standard population used to compute age, sex, and race adjustments for each county. No adjustment was made in the analysis of state data. (Comparisons of crude mortality rates can be made between different populations using narrow age intervals, which minimize distortion due to age, but our analyses involve no comparisons between states.)

The first hypothesis, that young adults died of flu in equal or greater numbers during the epidemic than did the usual victims of flu, young children and the elderly, is sometimes described as a "W" rather than the U-shaped configuration typical of graphs representing deaths by age in normal flu seasons. This hypothesis was tested using unadjusted state-level data showing mortality rates by six age intervals in North Carolina in October 1918 and March 1919 (Table 15.1). Although non-flu mortality and all-cause mortality are included in this table, the comparison between the flu mortality rates for age intervals 0–1 and 2–9, 20–39 and 60+ is especially important for testing the received opinion. In October 1918, young adults 20–39 suffered higher mortality rates (379.41 per 100,000) than the 2–9 and 60+ age groups (149.06 and 96.94 per 100,000, respectively), but lower mortality rates than the 0–1 age group (606.41 per 100,000). In contrast, young adults had far lower non-flu mortality (82.24 per 100,000) than infants aged 0–1 (530.79 per 100,000) and the elderly (383.31 per 100,000) in October 1918. Flu mortality constituted 69.22 percent of all deaths in the state in October 1918, but a far different picture is revealed in March 1919, when flu mortality fell to 17.92 percent of all mortality. In March 1919, flu deaths among young adults were 22.28 per 100,000, while mortality for the 0–1 age group was 73.44 per 100,000; for the 2–9 age group was 9.86 per 100,000; and for the elderly was 39.54 per 100,000. The non-flu mortality remained roughly the same for March 1919 with infants aged 0–1 experiencing a 611.50 per 100,000 mortality rate; children aged 2–9

Table 15.1. North Carolina Unadjusted Mortality Rates by Age, October 1918 and March 1919

Age	OCTOBER 1918			MARCH 1919		
	Flu mortality	Nonflu mortality	All-cause mortality	Flu mortality	Nonflu mortality	All-cause mortality
0–1	606.41	530.79	1137.20	73.44	611.50	684.94
2–9	149.06	42.54	191.60	9.86	18.33	28.19
10–19	153.44	30.79	184.23	11.40	17.86	29.26
20–39	379.41	82.24	461.65	22.28	54.59	76.87
40–59	158.42	95.37	253.79	20.57	82.28	102.85
60+	96.94	383.31	480.26	39.54	415.84	455.38
Population Mortality	238.18	105.90	344.07	20.53	94.03	114.56

(Per 100,000 Persons)

Sources: Authors' Calculations. Death certificates accessed from www.ancestry.com; Population in 1920 Census (www.usa.ipums.org).

Table 15.2. North Carolina Counties Comprising Each Geographical Region

Mountains (24 counties)

Alleghany, Ashe, Avery, Buncombe, Burke, Caldwell, Cherokee, Clay, Graham, Haywood, Henderson, Jackson, Macon, Madison, McDowell, Mitchell, Polk, Rutherford, Surry, Swain, Transylvania, Watauga, Wilkes, Yancey

Piedmont (35 counties)

Alamance, Alexander, Anson, Cabarrus, Caswell, Catawba, Chatham, Cleveland, Davidson, Davie, Durham, Forsyth, Franklin, Gaston, Guilford, Granville, Iredell, Lee, Lincoln, Mecklenburg, Montgomery, Moore, Orange, Person, Randolph, Richmond, Rockingham, Rowan, Stanly, Stokes, Union, Vance, Wake, Warren, Yadkin

Coastal Plain (23 counties)

Bertie, Bladen, Columbus, Cumberland, Duplin, Edgecombe, Gates, Greene, Halifax, Harnett, Hertford, Hoke, Johnston, Lenoir, Martin, Nash, Northampton, Pitt, Roberson, Sampson, Scotland, Wayne, Wilson

Tidewater (18 counties)

Beaufort, Brunswick, Camden, Carteret, Chowan, Craven, Currituck, Dare, Hyde, Jones, New Hanover, Onslow, Pamlico, Pasquotank, Pender, Perquimans, Tyrrell, Washington

Source: Alfred Stuart and Douglas M. Orr, eds. *The North Carolina Atlas: Portrait for a New Century* (Chapel Hill: University of North Carolina Press, 2000).

**Table 15.3. North Carolina County Standardized Mortality
Quintile Rankings by Geographical Region, October 1918 & March 1919**

	(Number, Percent of Region's Counties in Each Quintile)				
	REGIONS				
MONTH	**Mountains**	**Piedmont**	**Coastal Plain**	**Tidewater**	**TOTAL COUNTIES**
	(N = 24)	(N = 35)	(N = 23)	(N = 18)	(N = 100)
Highest					
October 1918	3, 12.5%	3, 8.6%*	8, 34.8%	6, 33.3%	20, 20.0%
March 1919	5, 20.8%	7, 20.0%	6, 26.1%*	2, 11.1%*	20, 20.0%
Mid-high					
October 1918	3, 12.5%	4, 11.4%	5, 21.8%	8, 44.4%*	20, 20.0%
March 1919	1, 4.2%*	8, 22.9%	6, 26.1%	5, 27.8%	20, 20.0%
Middle					
October 1918	3, 12.5%	9, 25.7%	7, 30.4%*	1, 5.6%*	20, 20.0%
March 1919	4, 16.7%	5, 14.3%	7, 30.4%*	4, 22.2%	20, 20.0%
Mid-low					
October 1918	6, 25.0%	10, 28.6%	3, 13.0%	1, 5.6%*	20, 20.0%
March 1919	4, 16.7%	11, 31.4%*	2, 8.7%*	3, 16.7%	20, 20.0%
Lowest					
October 1918	9, 37.5%*	9, 25.7%	0, 0%*	2, 11.1%	20, 20.0%
March 1919	10, 41.6%*	4, 11.4%	2, 8.7%	4, 22.2%	20, 20.0%
TOTAL	24, 100%	35, 100%	23, 100%	18, 100%	100, 100%

*Denotes regions that scored above or below the standard deviation of the mean for each monthly quintile and are therefore considered highly or lightly impacted regions for that month.

Sources: Authors' calculation of age-, sex-, and race-adjusted county mortality rates. Death certificates accessed from (www.ancestry.com); Population in 1920 Census (www.usa.ipums.org)

experiencing an 18.33 per 100,000 mortality rate; young adults aged 20–39 experiencing a 54.59 per 100,000 mortality rate; and the elderly experiencing a mortality rate of 414.56 per 100,000. Based on the above mortality rates, it can be seen that the "W" shape epidemiology curve is evident in October 1918 with one abnormality: elderly North Carolinians seemed to experience some form of protection during the height of the epidemic since the expected spike for the 60+ age group is not evident in the epidemiological curve for October (Figure 15.1). Thus, there is evidence to support the theory that elderly residents were somewhat protected from the deadly 1918 influenza strain due to immunity gained by having survived an earlier epidemic of a similar strain in 1889.[42] However, by March 1919 the curve had settled back into the more normal, albeit somewhat lopsided, U-shaped influenza epidemiology curve that is most often seen during normal flu cycles, with the 20–39 age group being only slightly elevated and the 60+ age group being slightly lower than expected (Figure 15.2).

The second hypothesis, spatial diffusion and dispersion, had two parts. The hypothesis (2A) that the initial spread of the 1918 flu was along rail lines from Wilmington must be modified. If the generally acknowledged claim that the deadly second wave of the flu first appeared in North Carolina in Wilmington (New Hanover County) is accepted, the counties containing three rail lines leading out of Wilmington ought to show disproportionately high incidence of flu deaths if rail lines themselves were the disease vectors. This outcome was tested by examining the map in Figure 15.3 to see whether the counties between New Hanover (Wilmington) and Mecklenburg (Charlotte), Wake (Raleigh), and Craven (New Bern) showed more elevated mortality at the beginning of the epidemic in October 1918 than did other counties not near these major transportation routes. Unlike the state data in Table 15.1, this county-level data was standardized to allow valid comparisons undistorted by difference in age, sex, or race that might be associated with differential vulnerability. The map for October 1918 does not show higher levels of flu mortality along the railroad lines between the railroad hubs; no pattern of dispersion is evident as the counties between the hubs fall in all quintiles of the mortality rates. However, the map does show that the counties containing the nearest major terminal or transshipment hub—Mecklenburg, Wake, and Craven—were all in the highest quintile of flu deaths in October 1918. Mecklenburg and Wake also placed in that highest quintile in March 1918 (Figure 15.4), when flu mortality was much lower across the state than it had been in October 1918.

Spatial dispersion of the epidemic across the state's 100 counties (hypothesis 2B) can be measured in terms of the relative mortality of counties in each of the four regions that modern geographers delineate (Table 15.2): Mountain (24 counties), Piedmont (35 counties), Coastal Plain (23 counties), and Tidewater (18 counties).[43] The regions stretch from southwest to northeast in serial stripes between the South Carolina and Virginia borders. Although similarity in physical features defined the four regions, the difficulty in East–West transportation in North Carolina prior to the construction of serviceable, paved east-west highways in the 1930s also makes these county groupings relevant for epidemiological purposes. To determine regions of very high and very low mortality, the threshold of a deviance above or below the standard deviation from the mean for each quintile was chosen, thereby generating a unique above/below threshold specific to each quintile. For example, the twenty counties suffering the greatest flu mortality in October 1918 are displayed in the first row of Table 15.1, which shows that among those twenty counties only those contained in the Piedmont (asterisk) fall below the standard deviation threshold, and no region exceeds the threshold on the positive side of the quintile mean. The standard deviation of the mean for each quintile was obtained by running a one-sample t-test for each quintile. Thus, regions equal to or falling below or above the calculated standard deviation of counties in the highest or lowest quintiles were considered to be highly or lightly impacted regions. By this stringent measure, while both the Coastal Plain (34.8% of 23 counties) and Tidewater (33.3% of 18 counties) felt the greatest impact of the epidemic in October 1918 (Table 15.3 and Figure 15.3), they did not exceed the standard deviation from the mean (35.98%) for the highest quintile. However, only two counties (Currituck and Jones) in the Tidewater region and no counties in the Coastal Plain region fell into the lowest emphasizing the burden that these two regions felt during October. The Piedmont region, in contrast, was disproportionately spared, with less than 9% of its 35 counties in the most severely impacted quintile, and it was in fact the only region in the highest quintile for October that fell either above or below the standard deviation from the mean. Although the Piedmont did have an elevated number of counties in the lowest quintile (25.7%), only the Mountain region exceeded the standard deviation threshold for relatively untouched counties (37.5% of its 24 counties).

In the familiar pattern of epidemics, when incidence falls as the vulnerable population that has not yet become ill shrinks, far fewer North Carolinians died from flu in March 1919 than had succumbed in October 1918. Table 15.3 and Figure 15.4 show that relative flu mortality was somewhat more evenly dispersed across the four regions. The Coastal Plain region (26.1%) is the only one that exceeded the standard deviation threshold in March 1919, and the Tidewater region (11.1%) is the only region to fall below that threshold. In terms of the quintile lowest in relative mortality, the Mountain region with 41.6% of 24 counties in the lowest quintile even exceeded its favorable situation in October 1918. The Coastal Plain, which had suffered increased mortality in October 1918, still placed less than 10% of its 23 counties in the lowest quintile. In summary, the spatial analysis leads to the general conclusion that (1) the counties in the Coastal Plain suffered the greatest overall mortality in the two sample months and (2) the counties in the Mountain region felt the lightest impact. However, noting the *relative* leniency of the flu mortality in the mountain counties should not be interpreted as minimizing the suffering experienced by many families in that region. The 1918–1919 flu epidemic was devastating throughout the state; no region escaped unscathed.

The third hypothesis, that training camps and manufacturing centers were particularly hard hit, can only be assessed for the months of October 1918 and

March 1919. If the epidemic took its toll in the intervening months, it would escape detection in Figures 15.3 and 15.4. By far the largest training camp was Camp Greene in Mecklenburg County, which contemporary accounts report was hard hit by the epidemic; by March 1919 it was no longer in use.[44] (Although authorized in August 1918 as an artillery training center, Fort Bragg did not become fully operational during the war as initial construction was not completed until February 1, 1919).[45] Figures 15.3 and 15.4 show that indeed mortality in Mecklenburg was among the highest in the state in October 1918, but surprisingly, the county also ranked among the highest in flu mortality in March 1919. A third training camp, Camp Polk, was located in Raleigh and served as a tank training facility from 1918 to 1919. The location of Camp Polk in Wake County undoubtedly contributed to that county being placed in the highest quintile for both October 1918 and March 1919.

The account of North Carolina's experience of the flu epidemic that opened this chapter mentions Wilmington (New Hanover County), High Point (Guilford), and Raleigh (Wake) as centers of war material production. These three counties show mixed results during the months of October and March. New Hanover and Wake placed in the highest quintile in October while Guilford placed in the middle quintile (Figures 15.3 and 15.4). In March, Wake remained in the highest quintile while both New Hanover and Guilford fell to the second lowest quintile. This finding is unsurprising because by March 1919 the war was over and these particular counties were most likely not producing and shipping goods as frequently as they had been in October 1918. The exception to this is Wake, which remained a major transportation hub for both people and goods even after the war ended and consequently appeared in the highest quintile for both months examined.

Finally, Annette Cox's chapter on textile manufacturing in North Carolina during the war emphasizes Alamance, Cabarrus, Durham, Gaston, and Guilford Counties as especially important centers of cotton textile manufacturing.[46] She suggests that the epidemic may have taken an especially heavy toll among mill workers and their families. However, no clear pattern emerges from our analysis; Alamance, Durham, and Guilford place in the middle quintile for October 1918 mortality rates while Cabarrus and Gaston place in the second highest quintile. None of the textile manufacturing centers place in the highest quintile for October 1918 (Table 15.3 and Figure 15.3). The picture for March 1919 in Figure 15.4 is no clearer; Durham and Guilford placed in the second lowest mortality quintile, Alamance and Gaston placed in the second highest, and Cabarrus placed in the highest quintile. Because epidemics tend to peter out as the supply of those who have escaped the illness dwindles, one would not expect to see concentrated mortality at the end of the epidemic. This analysis used the flu mortality for the entire county population, which might have masked flu impacts on vulnerable subpopulations. Future analyses will permit the investigators to limit comparison mortality rates for working-age whites who supplied the workforce in those mills.

Several potential limitations in this study should be noted. First, the database includes only deaths for which death certificates were written and archived. Especially in sparsely populated counties, flu victims may have been buried without authorities being notified or death certificates being issued. A second potential limitation might result from missing or incorrect data, including misdiagnosed cause of death. Death certificates in the World War I era asked health providers to write two causes of death; if either gave flu as a cause, the death was counted as a flu death. Sometimes pneumonia, the actual cause of death in many cases of flu morbidity, appeared on the death certificate and no mention was made of flu. The small number of such death certificates—310 in October 1918 and 143 in March 1919—were not counted as flu deaths. A third source of potential data problems might stem from the use of the 1920 Census as the denominator in calculating mortality rates. It was taken on New Year's Day, 1920, so significant population change occurring in the fifteen months after October 1, 1918, and the ten months after March 1, 1919, would distort the mortality rate. Technically, the denominator in calculating mortality and morbidity should be the population at risk during the period when numerators were collected. Thus, the deaths occurring between October 1, 1918, and January 1, 1920, and between March 1, 1919, and January 1, 1920, should ideally be included and births occurring after the index months excluded. However, the stability of relatively large populations in the county units of analysis should mitigate the danger that reliance on 1920 Census data distorts the findings, except where the war's end caused large population shifts in counties. Thus, the end of military training at Camp Greene might mean that mortality rates for Mecklenburg County in October 1918 are overestimated; the authors are unaware of other significant population changes in the relatively brief period before the 1920 Census.[47] Finally, as indicated above, more granular comparisons of specific county subpopulations (e.g., restricted to specific races or ages) may reveal elevated or reduced mortality that was masked in examining mortality of the entire county population.

The effort to bring together the qualitative research and quantitative analysis in this chapter has significantly advanced our knowledge of the 1918–1919 epidemic. A moderate amount of traditional historical research has generated broad generalizations such as the W-shaped mortality curve and the idea that the epidemic spread along the railroads. Most of the generalizations about the flu epidemic appear in contexts that seem to suggest that they apply to the entire nation. Little archival research on the epidemic has focused specifically on North Carolina. In any case, as far as the investigators know, no one has previously tested these broad generalizations using a large quantitative statewide database. Our initial work with the data has already confirmed the insight that the W-shaped mortality curve is partially true in North Carolina, although those 60 years old and above did seem to be somewhat protected, which may have come from exposure to an earlier flu strain that provided a modicum of resistance. The evidence also found that counties with major transportation hubs in North Carolina experienced high mortality rates relative to other counties. In contrast, we could not find support for the perception produced by qualitative historical research that the counties where cotton mills were concentrated experienced especially high mortality. Our most important discovery, however, is one that no one previously appears to have apprehended: regional differences in flu mortality. The eastern part of the state, especially the Coastal Plain, suffered disproportionate mortality, whereas the Mountain region experienced relatively less mortality in both October 1918 and March 1919. This chapter reporting our initial quantitative analysis has yielded significant new findings, but it is important to emphasize that they have emerged from careful but unsophisticated direct observation of the data. Further analysis of this rich dataset will use sophisticated statistical techniques that should reveal unexpected findings that could never be gleaned from traditional archival methods.

The perceived failure of the state's health system during the epidemic greatly undermined the people's trust. Medical professionals at the time recognized the system's deficiencies, especially the need for more hospital beds for both urban and rural populations. North Carolina's influenza mortality rate exceeded the national average (320.37 deaths per 100,000 persons versus 300.84 in 1918 and 149.6 deaths per 100,000 persons versus 98.8 in 1919), a fact that highlighted the state's shortcomings and exposed lower levels of preparedness than states with more established public health and hospital infrastructure. [48] The influenza epidemic severely impacted every region of the state, with normally healthy young adults aged 20–39 experiencing the significantly increased mortality rates in both October 1918 and March 1919. The Coastal Plain region of the state was the most significantly impacted during the epidemic while the more remote Mountain region fared the best, although it still experienced significant losses. These dismal facts created a positive legacy by spurring a boom in hospital construction and a renewed attention to health care reform throughout the state in the years after the First World War.

In light of the current awareness of the devastating impact of the 1918–1919 flu pandemic generated by the 1976 swine flu crisis, it is puzzling how rapidly the pandemic faded from the public mind after World War I, especially when memories and consequences of the war continued to weigh so heavily throughout the 1920s.[49] Indeed, David L. Cockrell, who chronicles the pandemic in North Carolina, remarks, "Amazingly, the pandemic was scarcely mentioned in the *Health Bulletin*," the house publication of the Board of Health.[50] His account shows how W. S. Rankin, the state's chief public health official, attended to the broad range of ongoing health issues such as sanitation while struggling to foster the institutionalization of public health at the county level through the local creation and funding of public health departments. The flu pandemic, to which Rankin and his colleagues responded as best they could, was certainly a public health emergency that severely taxed the capacity of North Carolina's nascent public health infrastructure and overwhelmed available medical resources. But like other emergencies it abated, leaving health officials to deal with the perennial problems of public health in a poor state with limited government capacity.

Prior to the First World War and the influenza epidemic of 1918–1919, North Carolina's health system was almost entirely the result of individual choices and local market forces; only occasionally before the war did the social capital of civil society undertake the planning and financing of a community hospital. However, the more than 13,000 North Carolinians lost during the epidemic—along with the shocking health status of young American males, revealed by the physical exams conducted as part of World War I

Figure 15.1. Influenza Mortality Rate by Age, North Carolina, October 1918 (Unadjusted State Mortality Rate per 100,000 Persons)

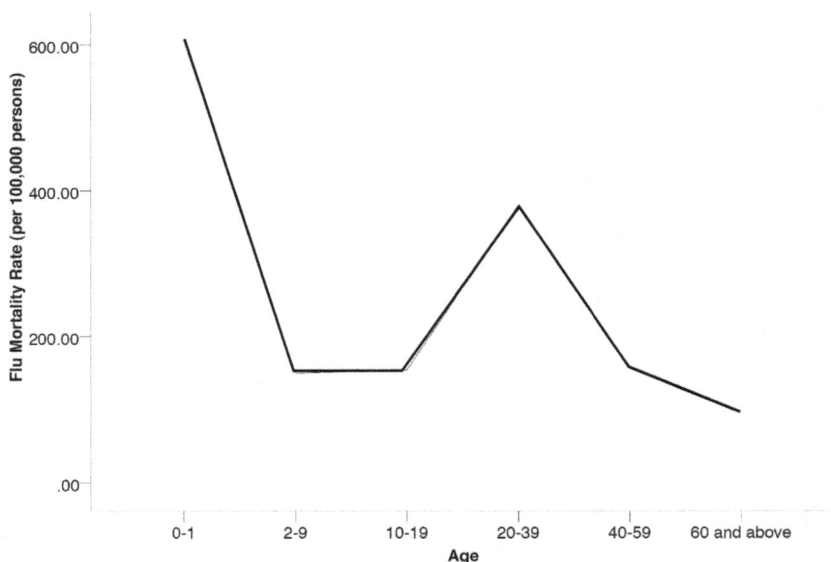

Source: Death Certificates from www.ancestry.com. Population in 1920 Census, ipums.org.

Figure 15.2. Influenza Mortality Rate by Age, North Carolina, March 1919 (Unadjusted State Mortality Rate per 100,000 Persons)

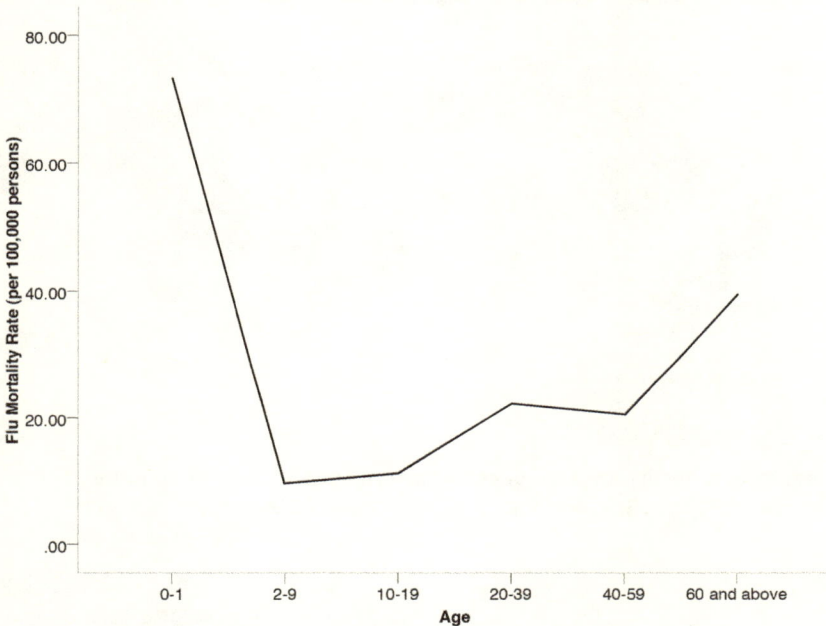

Source: Death Certificates from www.ancestry.com. Population in 1920 Census, ipums.org.

conscription—highlighted the need for the planning, expansion, and funding of medical, dental, and public health services.[51] In particular, greater access to hospital and physician services was required. Not until the federal government increased funding for welfare programs after the epidemic and the Duke Endowment began operation in 1925 did North Carolina's health care system change significantly.[52] A steady growth in the number of hospital beds began, especially in hospitals organized on a community basis, and local officials and ordinary citizens increasingly embraced the knowledge and practices suggested by public health campaigns. As Rankin noted in 1919, this new "progressive attitude" towards public health emerged "due to the great cost in human suffering, health, and life [during] epidemic conditions and the need for providing against such conditions as impressed on our people by the recent influenza epidemic."[53] In this way, the war and the epidemic served as "blessings in disguise" to North Carolina's public health system and the future health and well-being of the state's citizens.[54]

Figure 15.3. North Carolina County Influenza Mortality Rate by Quintile, October 1918 (Age-, Sex-, and Race-Adjusted County Mortality)

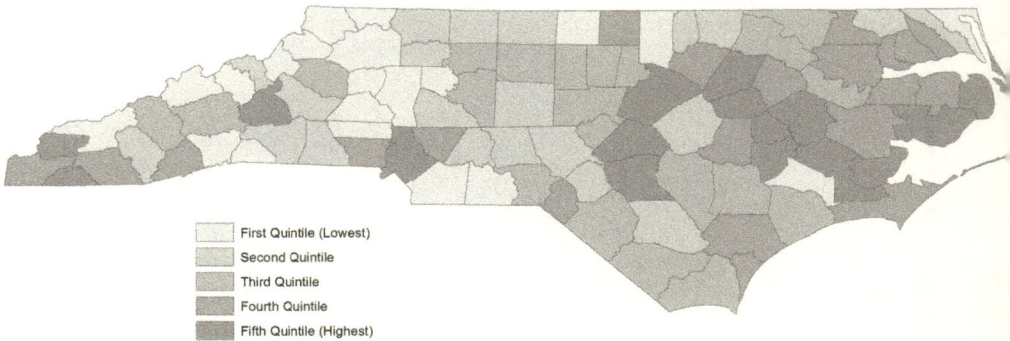

First Quintile (Lowest)
Second Quintile
Third Quintile
Fourth Quintile
Fifth Quintile (Highest)

Figure 15.4. North Carolina County Influenza Mortality Rate by Quintile, March 1919 (Age-, Sex-, and Race-Adjusted County Mortality)

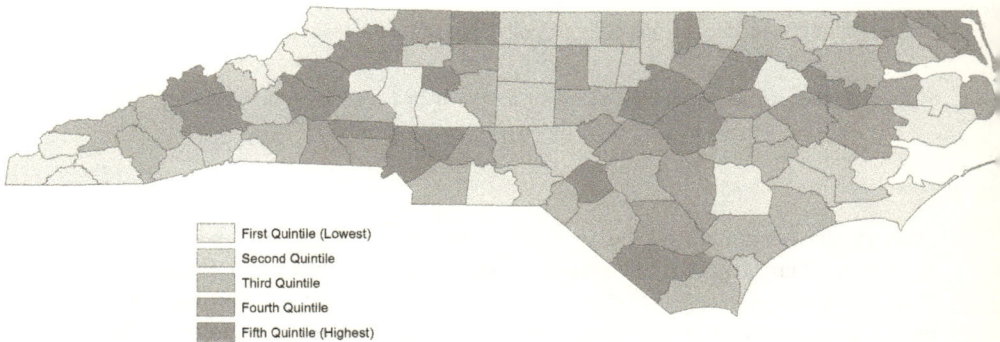

First Quintile (Lowest)
Second Quintile
Third Quintile
Fourth Quintile
Fifth Quintile (Highest)

Notes

1. Thucydides, *History of the Peloponnesian War*, rev. ed., trans. Rex Warner, introduction by M. I. Finley, (Harmondsworth, Middlesex England: Penguin, 1972), 151–156.

2. "World War I: North Carolina Digital History," http://www.learnnc.org/lp/editions/-nchist -newcentury/3.0.

3. David L. Cockrell, "'A Blessing in Disguise': The Influenza Epidemic of 1918 and North Carolina's Medical and Public Health Communities," *North Carolina Historical Review* 73.3 (July 1996): 309–327.

4. William P. Brandon and Lauren A. Austin, "W.S. Rankin and the Creation of Public Health in North Carolina, 1909–1925," in *North Carolina during the First World War*, eds. Shepherd W. McKinley and Steven Sabol (Knoxville: University of Tennessee Press, 2018).

5. The forgetting and subsequent remembering of "swine" flu and the remarkable scientific forensics contributed by virologists and pathologists since the Ford administration would make a fascinating historiographical essay. It would presumably start with Alfred W. Crosby's well-timed *Epidemic and Peace, 1918* (Westport CT: Greenwood, 1976) republished and tellingly retitled by Cambridge University Press (New York) as *America's Forgotten Pandemic: The Influenza of 1918* in 2003; see also William P. Brandon, "In the Age of Bioterrorism, an Affair to Remember: The Silver Anniversary of the Swine Flu Epidemic that Never Was," *Politics and the Life Sciences* 20.1 (March 2001): 85–90.

6. Gina Kolata, *Flu: The Story of the Great Influenza Pandemic of 1918 and the Search for the Virus that Caused It* (New York: Farrar, Straus and Giroux, 1999).

7. Cockrell, "'A Blessing,'" 309–327; Robert Mason, "Surviving the Blue Killer, 1918," *Virginia Quarterly Review* 74.2 (April 1998): 343; "North Carolina and the 'Blue Death': The Flu Epidemic of 1918: North Carolina Digital History," http://www.learnnc.org/lp/editions/nchist-newcentury /4974; Selena W. Sanders, "The Big Flu," *The State: Down Home in North Carolina* 44.7 (December 1976).

8. Alfred W. Crosby, *American's Forgotten Pandemic: The Influenza of 1918*, Second Edition (New York: Cambridge University Press, 2003), 19; Kolata, *Flu*, 9–11; Gerald F. Pyle, *The Diffusion of Influenza: Patterns and Paradigms* (Lanham, MD: Rowman & Littlefield), 40.

9. Kolata, *Flu*, 10.

10. Jeffrey K. Taubenberger and David M. Morens, "1918 Influenza: The Mother of All Pandemics," *Rev Biomed* 17 (2006): 71.

11. Pyle, *The Diffusion*, 41; Taubenberger and Morens, "1918 Influenza," 71.

12. Cockrell, "'A Blessing,'" 309–327; Mason, "Blue Killer," 343; "North Carolina and the 'Blue Death'"; Sanders, "The Big Flu."

13. Kolata, *Flu*, 12–13.

14. Cockrell, "'A Blessing,'" 311.

15. Pyle, *The Diffusion*, 40.

16. Subsequent research has revealed that a significant proportion of the deaths in the epidemic resulted from pneumococcal or other bacterial infections that took advantage of flu-weakened immune systems. See Kolata, *Flu*, 12, 303–305; Taubenberger and Morens, "1918 Influenza," 74.

17. Cockrell, "'A Blessing,'" 309–327; Mason, "Blue Killer," 343; "North Carolina and the 'Blue Death'"; Sanders, "The Big Flu."

18. Susan Kingsley Kent, *The Influenza Pandemic of 1918–1919: A Brief History with Documents* (Boston: Bedford/St. Martin's, 2013), 20–22; Elizabeth Outka, "'Wood for the Coffins Ran Out': Modernism and the Shadowed Afterlife of the Influenza Pandemic," *Modernism/modernity* 21.4 (November 2014): 942.

19. Crosby, *America's Forgotten Pandemic*, 62–64.

20. Crosby, *America's Forgotten Pandemic*, 65.

21. Cockrell, "'A Blessing,'" 31; Crosby, *American's Forgotten Pandemic*, 63.

22. "World War I: North Carolina Digital History."

23. "World War I: North Carolina Digital History."

24. Hon. Sherman E. Burroughs, *"Conditions at Camp Greene," speech given in New Hampshire House of Representatives, "Documenting the American South," February 22, 1918* (Washington, DC: Government Printing Office, 1918), 3–4, http://docsouth.unc.edu/~wwi/burroughs /burroughs.html.

25. Burroughs, *"Camp Greene,"* 3–4.

26. "North Carolina and the 'Blue Death.'"

27. Cockrell, "'A Blessing,'" 310.

28. H. Garrett Adams, "A Local Chronicle of the Influenza Epidemic of 1918: As Gleaned from Newspaper Accounts of the Day (Part 1)," *North Carolina Medical Journal* 25 (August 1964): 352.

29. Adams, "A Local Chronicle," 353–354; Adams, "A Local Chronicle," *North Carolina Medical Journal* 26 (September 1964): 397–398; "The United States in 1918–1919, The Great Pandemic: North Carolina," http://www.flu.gov/pandemic/history/1918/your_state/-southeast/northcarolina.

30. Rupert Blue to Watson Smith Rankin, *Correspondence, 1918* (Raleigh: Records of North Carolina State Board of Health, October 11, 1918).

31. Annie Sutton Cameron, "A Record of the War Activities in Orange County, North Carolina: 1917–1919," Manuscript Department, Southern Historical Collection, University of North Carolina at Chapel Hill, 26.

32. "Transactions of the Medical Society of the State of North Carolina, Sixty-Sixth Annual Meeting," (Raleigh: Edwards and Broughton, 1919), 284–285.

33. The North Carolina State Board of Health, "Influenza and What You Should Know About It," *The Health Bulletin* 33.5 (November 1918): 38–39.

34. State Board of Health, "Influenza," 39.

35. Cockrell, "'A Blessing,'" 311; Mason, "Blue Killer," 343; "North Carolina and the 'Blue Death'"; Sanders, "The Big Flu."

36. "The United States in 1918–1919, The Great Pandemic: North Carolina."

37. "Lenoir Public Schools Closed till Next Fall: People So Decide by Vote of 150 to 70 After Bitter Fight. 'Flu' the Reason," *Charlotte Observer*, January 9, 1919, 11.

38. James Marisa, "Local Governance and Pandemics: Lessons from the 1918 Flu," *University of Detroit Mercy Law Review* 85 (Spring 2008): 361.

39. www.ancestry.com provided copies of the originals for all North Carolina death certificates during the study period in PDF format.

40. https://usa.ipums.org/usa/complete_count.shtml provided the 1920 US Census Data in SPSS format.

41. Thomas D. Koepsell and Noel S. Weiss, *Epidemiologic Methods: Studying the Occurrence of Illness,* (Oxford: Oxford University Press, 2003), 247–252.

42. Kolata, *Flu,"* 14.

43. Alfred Stuart and Douglas M. Orr, eds., *The North Carolina Atlas: Portrait for a New Century* (Chapel Hill: University of North Carolina Press, 2000).

44. See Kurt Geske, "Where Johnnie Got His Gun: Charlotte and Camp Greene," in *North Carolina during the First World War*, eds. Shepherd W. McKinley and Steven Sabol (Knoxville: University of Tennessee Press, 2018).

45. Mathew Shaeffer, "Fort Bragg: North Carolina History Project," http://northcarolina history.org/encyclopedia/fort-bragg/.

46. Annette Cox, "Towels, Socks, and Denim: World War I and North Carolina's Cotton Mills," in *North Carolina during the First World War*, eds. Shepherd W. McKinley and Steven Sabol (Knoxville: University of Tennessee Press, 2018).

47. Future investigation will include sensitivity analysis to address this possible limitation.

48. US Department of Commerce, Bureau of the Census, *Mortality Rates: 1910–1920,* Table III (Washington, DC: Government Printing Office, 1923), http://www.cdc.gov/nchs/-data/vsus historical/mortrates_1910–1920.pdf.

49. The combination of the swine flu scare and immunization program of 1976 and several important books about the 1918–19 flu educated professionals and the public about the pandemic. Moreover, since the "Swine Flu Affair," biological archeology has given us much greater understanding of the 1918 virus. See Crosby, *Epidemic and Peace*, chap. 15; Kolata, *Flu;* Richard E. Neustadt and Harvey V. Fineberg, *The Epidemic That Never Was: Policy-Making and the Swine Flu Affair* (New York: Vintage, 1983); Brandon, "In the Age of Bioterrorism," 85–90.

50. Cockrell, "'A Blessing,'" 321. This account was given in the November 1918 article previously mentioned.

51. Board of Trustees, *Duke Endowment Annual Report of the Hospital Section, 1925* (Charlotte: The Duke Endowment, 1925), Tables 28, 28A and 28B, pp. 96–101.

52. See Brandon and Austin, "W.S. Rankin and the Creation of Public Health."

53. Watson Smith Rankin, "Health Legislation by the General Assembly," *Correspondence, 1919* (Raleigh: Records of North Carolina State Board of Health, 1919).

54. Cockrell, "'A Blessing,'" 327.

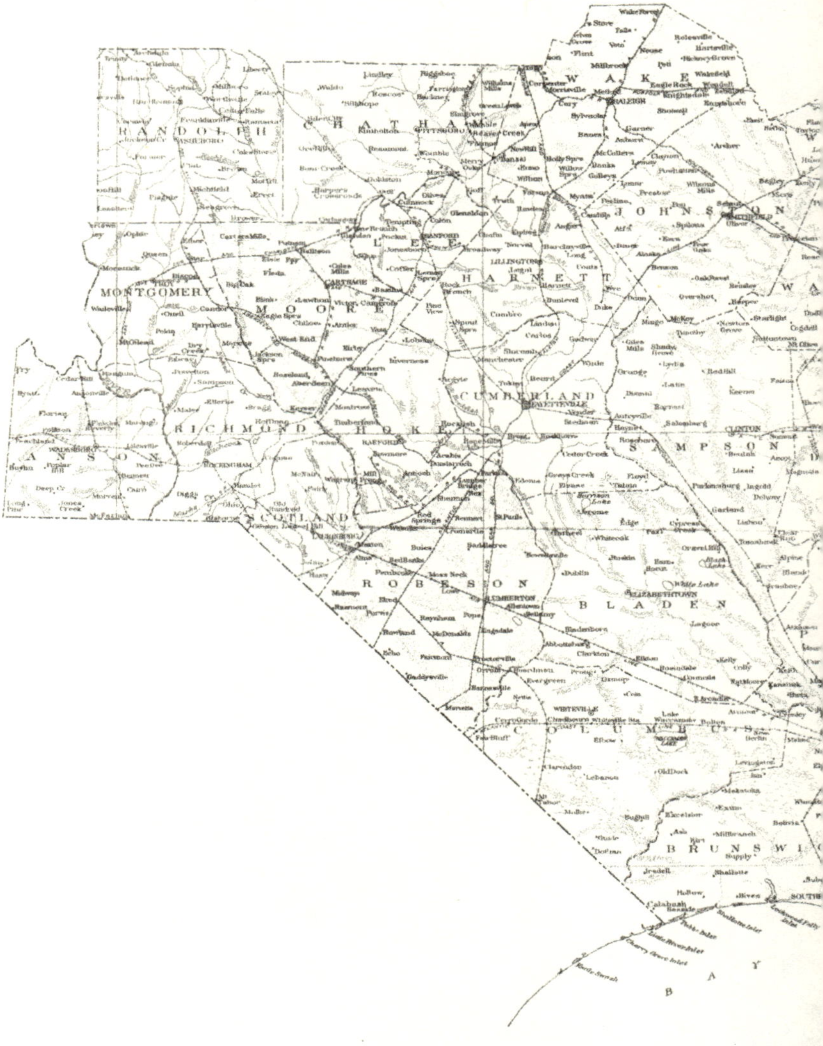
RANDOLPH
CHATHAM
WAKE
JOHNSON
MONTGOMERY
MOORE
LEE
HARNETT
CUMBERLAND
SAMPSON
RICHMOND
HOKE
ANSON
SCOTLAND
ROBESON
BLADEN
COLUMBUS
BAY

PART FIVE

Business and Labor

16

Years of Promise

Tobacco Agriculture and the Great War

Evan P. Bennett

The tobacco was green in North Carolina when Gavrilo Princip shot Archduke Franz Ferdinand and his wife Sophie in June 1914. It was yellowing and ready to be harvested when the German army swept into Belgium and France that August; curing season was nearly done when the Allies halted its advance at the Marne in September. As farm families prepared their crops for auction, most in the tobacco business assumed the war would bring hard times. Even before the auctions opened, North Carolina's Secretary of State pleaded with the federal government for funds to support tobacco farmers ruined by low prices. Local boards of trade, which controlled the auction schedule, postponed opening the warehouses to prevent gluts on the market. When the auctions finally started, the pessimists were proved right: prices were 20 percent lower than the previous year in Wilson, the leading market in the eastern part of the state; in Winston-Salem, in the western Piedmont, they were down 29 percent. In Danville, Virginia, where farm families all along the state line sold their crops, prices were nearly half what they had been in 1913.[1] Frustration lingered into 1915. Low prices had left a "great scarcity of money," and there was "no prospect of improved conditions," a *New York Times* correspondent noted. "The year . . . has indeed been a trying one," wrote the president of the Danville Tobacco Association, expressing the feeling all along Tobacco Road.[2]

Still, he saw silver linings in the war clouds. The war had already created "active demand for stocks" of bright tobacco from abroad, he said, and this "will redound to the benefit of Virginia and North Carolina tobacco for years to come long after the sanguinary strife between Christian brethren shall happily be over."[3] His prayer proved prophetic. Demand in 1916 was higher, and it grew every year after through the war's end. By 1919 North Carolina tobacco farmers received more than four times as much per pound as they had in 1914.[4] The Great War proved to be a turning point for North Carolina's

tobacco farms. Before the war, the Piedmont led the way in tobacco production; by its end, the Coastal Plain had taken pride of place. Before the war,
tobacco agriculture in North Carolina was archaic, more craft than science;
by its end, business and government attention to developing new techniques
and technologies opened the door for modernization. Before the war, farming
tobacco was, for most, a path to poverty; by its end, North Carolina farm
families were no longer willing to accept that tobacco had to make them
poor. Wartime prosperity imbued North Carolina's tobacco farmers with the
confidence that tobacco could pay. This confidence inspired a generation to
search for new ways of organizing the tobacco economy and ultimately to
support the New Deal's sweeping reforms.

In the 1910s, American Tobacco Company and R.J. Reynolds Company
spent a lot of money trying to convince consumers that small inputs made
big differences in their products. Camel cigarettes, Reynolds proclaimed,
were made from the highest-quality leaves to please the most discerning
smokers, while American Tobacco touted that toasting the leaves made Lucky
Strike cigarettes smoother. There were, no doubt, real differences between the
brands, but the advertising hid, and was largely the result of, one fact: both
used the same kind of tobacco as their primary ingredient. Bright tobacco
had been popular for making cigarettes and smoking tobacco since the late
nineteenth century, and it remains the primary ingredient in American cigarettes today. The curing process is largely what differentiates bright tobacco
from other varieties. To make bright tobacco, farmers cured raw leaves with
intense indirect heat in barns built with flues; hence, it is also called flue-cured
tobacco. Curing them this way turns the leaves a brilliant yellow color and
gives them a light texture and a mild flavor. The color first made the variety
desirable as a wrapper for plug tobacco, but as smoking became more popular
than chewing, manufacturers were attracted more to these latter qualities,
extending the market for the leaves.[5]

Before World War I, almost all bright tobacco was grown in Virginia
and North Carolina. Planters and slaves in the Piedmont counties along the
Virginia–North Carolina border near Danville first grew the crop in the years
before the Civil War. In the 1870s, small farmers throughout North Carolina's
border Piedmont counties began cultivating it. As cotton prices fell in the
late nineteenth century, creditors pressured more farmers to take up bright
tobacco as a supplemental, or even replacement, crop. By 1910, bright tobacco
was grown in two distinctive "belts": the Old Bright Belt of the Piedmont and
the New Bright Belt of the Coastal Plain.[6]

The Old Bright Belt was the cultural heart of bright tobacco agriculture.
The techniques and technologies for making bright tobacco had developed
there, as had the ideologies of bright tobacco agriculture. The design of curing
barns, the seasonal work rhythms, the use of farm tools—or, as much, the reluctance to use some—the assumptions about proper farming, and the unique

language of bright tobacco farming was nurtured there. It was, for the most part, a conservative culture, one that prized folk wisdom and local experts. The adoption of new techniques progressed slowly and unevenly, almost always against a current of traditionalism. When Coastal Plain farmers proved more willing to adopt new methods, some Old Bright Belt growers dismissed them as neophytes who did not truly understand bright tobacco agriculture or chalked up their own unwillingness to change to the peculiarities of their region.[7]

One of the most famous institutions that followed bright tobacco out from the Piedmont was the auction method of selling tobacco. The auctions were a spectacle in which an auctioneer led buyers from pile to pile of tobacco across a large warehouse floor, taking bids on each lot with the speed of a machine. In less than a minute, the fruits of a family's labor changed hands, and the fate of a year's work was sealed. Most had mixed feelings about the auction warehouses and felt they were exciting but uncertain. Auction time was a good time to go to town and visit with people, to go shopping and maybe take in some entertainment. But it was also a time for reckoning.[8]

In theory, a good crop could always make a farm family money, but by the early twentieth century, the reality was far bleaker. After 1890, the American Tobacco Company, having established a near-monopoly on the American tobacco market, reduced the number of buyers competing for farm families' crops and drove down prices. While the breakup of American Tobacco in 1911 offered some relief, farm families still found themselves at a structural disadvantage: They had to sell their crops while manufacturers, who could store their supplies indefinitely, did not have to buy them. Only by gaining control of the supply could they do anything substantive to raise prices.[9]

For several decades, many tried to do exactly that. While they channeled their frustration with the market through numerous organizations—from the Grange in the 1870s to the Farmers' Alliance and Colored Farmers' Alliance in the 1880s, to local cooperatives around the turn of the century to the Farmers' Union after 1905—their primary goal remained the same: figure out some way to limit the amount of tobacco at auction so that companies had to pay more for the crops. They tried voluntary cutbacks, buying their own auction warehouses, pooling and holding their crops, and even building their own tobacco factories, but nothing worked. Manufacturers remained too powerful and farm families too diffuse to do anything about it.[10]

The war changed the dynamics of the market, or better said, the cigarette changed them. People smoked cigarettes long before the Great War, but the war turned Americans into cigarette smokers. "World War I," historian Allan M. Brandt has explained, " . . . mark[ed] a critical watershed in establishing the cigarette as a dominant product of modern consumer culture." Once maligned as the "dirty habit" of "disreputable men," cigarette smoking became a sign of masculine vigor during the war years.[11] The military gave smokes as rations, the YMCA doled them out to keep bored soldiers from pursuing worse vices, and propagandists made donating them a measure of patriotic fervor. During the war years, the value of American cigarettes produced more than tripled to nearly $400 million.[12] By 1920 Americans smoked 48 billion cigarettes a year—up from 16.5 billion in 1914—and consumption only grew over the next half-century.[13]

During these years, North Carolina, home to the makers of the two most popular brands, rode this demand curve to become the Cigarette Capital of the World. In Durham, the American Tobacco Company churned out Lucky Strike cigarettes, while in Winston-Salem, the R. J. Reynolds Tobacco Company produced Camel cigarettes. During the war years, American Tobacco and Reynolds expanded production by nearly 900 percent, to more than 28 billion cigarettes in 1919. The value of goods made in these two cities alone accounted for 29 percent of the value of the state's total manufactures. Between 1910 and 1920, Durham's population grew by a fifth while in Winston-Salem, where the R.J. Reynolds Company found it necessary to construct housing for its workers, the population more than doubled, rising to nearly fifty thousand.[14]

Wartime demand did for farm families what generations of organizing never could—raise prices. Overnight, it seemed, tobacco companies needed all the tobacco they could get, and prices followed demand. Farm and political leaders who had only recently counseled farmers to limit production in favor of home production now told them it was their patriotic duty to grow more tobacco. North Carolina farm families listened and doubled down on tobacco. Between 1914 and 1920, the acreage devoted to tobacco more than doubled to almost six hundred thousand acres; the number of tobacco farms increased by 90 percent.[15] Much of this growth was in the Coastal Plain where farm families abandoned cotton for tobacco. By 1920 the New Bright Belt extended from Halifax County south to the South Carolina line. By the end of the war, the sleepy town of Wilson (population 13,569) auctioned more tobacco within its city limits than any other municipality in the United States—perhaps even the world—reflecting the growing importance of North Carolina in the nation's tobacco economy.[16]

At the level of the individual tobacco farm, the war years brought immense change, too. Farm families saw a general improvement in their conditions. They paid long-standing bills, purchased land, bought cars and houses, and bragged a little more about how they made their livings. In Surry County, one observer noted that "most of the farmers are getting out of debt" and "buying new homes" thanks to "high priced tobacco."[17] In Davidson County, the Extension Service agent reported that he had received many calls from the "tobacco section" of the county for "help in the selection of water and light systems for the farm home."[18]

While white landowning farmers with larger acreages accrued most of the benefits of the boom, landless farmers and African American farmers (both landowners and tenants) enjoyed better times, too. Black landownership increased, and those with some land added even more.[19] "The young boys are not satisfied working on some other man's land . . . ," reported Wake County's black Extension Service agent, "so many of their fathers are buying land in order to keep their sons with them on the farm."[20] Two decades after the war, black farmer Walter Corbett recounted how he and his family planted a "big crop" in 1915 to buy their twenty-acre farm. "I was in debt for the land and the only chance I had to pay the debt lay in that tobacco," he explained. Fortunately, their gamble paid off. "I had nearly six hundred dollars and a load of tobacco ready to sell. After selling that load I paid off the note. I was one happy man that day. I had become a landowner!" Continued high prices in 1917 and 1918 allowed him to buy fifty more acres.[21]

The cigarette revolution that took place during the war years also drove changes in farming practices. The most important of these was the adoption of priming as the method of harvesting leaves for curing. For centuries, tobacco farmers had allowed plants to mature completely in the fields before cutting and curing the entire plant. By the late nineteenth century, however, priming, or pulling the leaves off as they ripened and curing the loose leaves in small bunches, became more popular. So long as market pressures did not force change, however, convincing long-time farmers to adopt the technique was difficult. Priming required them to work more and to work faster. Instead of waiting for the tobacco to ripen and making one trip through the field, farmers would have to return several times as the leaves ripened. Farmers also had to pick enough leaves to fill a curing barn, since it required as much fuel to cure a half-empty barn as a full one, and to pick on a tight schedule, since primed leaves deteriorated quickly.[22]

Cigarette manufacturers preferred primed leaves because they more consistently matched the qualities they sought. When demand for these leaves rose, farm families responded, and priming became more common. In Granville County, where bright tobacco had a long history and traditional methods were common, the county Extension Service Agent reported that priming was "growing rapidly into practice," and he took credit for a change the market had more likely produced by claiming he had "induc[ed] 80% of the tobacco farmers of the county" to prime their crops.[23]

While a seemingly mundane change, the practice of priming altered the calendar of work on the tobacco farm, speeding up the harvest season and increasing the need for laborers in the late summer and early fall. Before the war, landowning tobacco farmers of most classes (except large landowners) exploited the labor of their own families to see a crop through. Most might swap labor with neighbors, and those with some resources might bring on a sharecropping family or hire a few wage laborers, but most hired no labor at all. During the war years, however, their ability to rely solely on their own hands declined as the migration from the countryside to the cities reduced the rural labor pools. By 1917 farmers in every North Carolina county reported that labor was scarce, and the need grew only more acute as the war went on.[24]

The widespread adoption of priming, combined with labor shortages, opened more opportunities for women to participate in tobacco agriculture. Black women and poor white women had always worked in tobacco, but many middling farmers felt it was inappropriate for white women to work tobacco. To many, the presence of white women and girls around the fields or the barns was a sign that a family had fallen on hard times. (No doubt the era's racism and its rituals surrounding the interactions of white women and black men shaped this assumption as well.) Priming, however, opened a new task: tying leaves. When entire plants were cured, they were nailed to the sticks, but it did too much damage to the leaves to do this to them. Instead, the leaves would be bunched into groups of three or four and then tied together at the stem with a string attached to a long stick. It was a time-consuming task that needed to be done skillfully—lest any leaves fall off and catch fire—and with alacrity. It was also a task that needed to be timed with priming to make sure the leaves were cured as soon as they were harvested. Farm women increasingly handled this task because they could combine the work with other, more traditional chores like cooking and child care. In time, tying became women's work on most farms, and biological justifications—women's hands were smaller and more dexterous—were offered for this gendering of labor. Nevertheless, the culture of bright tobacco agriculture shifted ever so subtly.[25]

Despite labor shortages, North Carolina tobacco farmers strode confidently through the war years, sure that their crops would not fail them. Confidence bred hubris, and hubris led to disaster. In 1920 North Carolina farm families doubled production just as demand slackened. Prices fell by half. While still higher than they had been before the war, they were not high enough to cover the debts many had accrued during an era of rising confidence. Thousands stood ruined, their credit overextended and their farms on the foreclosure dockets. The year 1921 proved a little better, but not by much.[26]

Immediately a new wave of protests started, and farm families sought ways to organize themselves. Unlike before the war, confidence, not desperation, fueled this wave of cooperative fervor. Farm leaders called meetings throughout North Carolina and the other bright tobacco producing states. Finally, in 1921, they formed the Tri-State Tobacco Growers' Association through which they hoped to follow the model of California's Sun-Maid raisin cooperative. Hoping to control the supply of tobacco on the market—to recreate the conditions of the war years in other words—the Tri-State's organizers strived to get all bright tobacco growers to agree to pool their crops. Aided by county Extension Service agents, organizers set off across Virginia and the Carolinas to sign up bright tobacco growers. They held barbecues; spoke at fairs and churches; and endured the insults of buyers and warehousemen, who would be bypassed if farmers pooled their crops and sold directly to the companies.

They met some success, especially in North Carolina's Old Bright Belt counties, where the idea of cooperation had long been popular. But in the New Bright Belt, where landless farmers who had little say over the disposition of their crops were larger in number, returns were not nearly as good. Prices rose some in the first year, partly because buyers agreed to pay more to undermine the crop's popularity, but by the second year, the Tri-State's weaknesses began to show. Unable to sell its stocks fast enough, the association lost money on carrying costs and failed to deliver on its promised payouts. The cooperative struggled on until 1926.

Pooling the crop was an ambitious plan, but it was doomed from the start. The region was simply too large, the growers too disparate in tenure and power, and the opposition too great to win. But the effort to organize growers nevertheless represented the new spirit of North Carolina tobacco farmers coming out of the Great War. Emboldened by the booming war years, they knew their crops were valuable, and they believed they might have the power to wrest control of them back from the tobacco companies. It was hard to hold on to that faith through the end of the 1920s. The nation as a whole suffered through an agricultural depression, and tobacco was not immune. By 1929 prices were back where they were in 1914, as if the wartime boom had never happened. Many despaired, but others held out hope that the good times could be had again. They continued organizing and agitating, confident that they could make tobacco pay. And in 1933, when New Dealers decided that they had to take on the knotty problem of tobacco, these faithful were still there, eager to support the program.

The Great War is rightly seen as a boom time for American agriculture, but one overshadowed by the Depression that followed. It is tempting, then, to see it as a "blip," an outlier in a long history of agricultural decline. Looking at North Carolina's tobacco farms in the years before and after, though, should lead us to see the war years as a watershed moment that turned history.

Notes

1. "Urges Uncle Sam to Help Farmers," *The Review* (High Point, NC), August 20, 1914; Nannie May Tilley, *The Bright-Tobacco Industry, 1860–1929* (Chapel Hill: University of North Carolina Press, 1948), 354–356, 387.

2. "Conditions in the South," *New York Times*, April 25, 1915; President's Report, June 12, 1916, Danville Tobacco Association Records, Reel 2, Library of Virginia, Richmond, VA.

3. President's Report, June 12, 1916, Danville Tobacco Association Records, Reel 2, Library of Virginia, Richmond, VA.

4. US Department of Commerce, Bureau of Foreign and Domestic Commerce, *Statistical Abstract of the United States: 1920* (Washington DC: Government Printing Office, 1921), 160.

5. For the history of bright tobacco, see Barbara Hahn, *Making Tobacco Bright: Creating an American Commodity, 1617–1937* (Baltimore: Johns Hopkins University Press, 2011); Tilley, *The Bright-Tobacco Industry, 1860–1929*.

6. Pete Daniel, *Breaking the Land: The Transformation of Cotton, Tobacco, and Rice Cultures since 1880* (Urbana: University of Illinois Press, 1985), 23–38.

7. Evan P. Bennett, *When Tobacco Was King: Families, Farm Labor, and Federal Policy in the Piedmont* (Gainesville: University Press of Florida, 2014), 3.

8. Bennett, *When Tobacco Was King*, 37–43.

9. Bennett, *When Tobacco Was King*, 45–47.

10. Bennett, *When Tobacco Was King*, 48–62.

11. Allan M. Brandt, *The Cigarette Century: The Rise, Fall, and Deadly Persistence of the Product that Defined America* (New York: Basic Books, 2007), 53, 45.

12. US Department of Commerce, Bureau of the Census, *Abstract of the Census of Manufactures, 1919* (Washington DC: Government Printing Office, 1923), 228.

13. American Lung Association, "Trends in Tobacco Use," July 2011, Table 2, accessed June 15, 2016, http://www.lung.org/assets/documents/research/tobacco-trend-report.pdf.

14. Tilley, *The Bright-Tobacco Industry*, 613; US Department of Commerce, Bureau of the Census, *Fourteenth Census of the United States, vol. 1, Population: 1920* (Washington DC: Government Printing Office, 1921), 269.

15. US Department of Commerce, Bureau of Foreign and Domestic Commerce, *Statistical Abstract of the United States: 1920* (Washington DC: Government Printing Office, 1921), 160; US Department of Commerce, Bureau of the Census, *Fourteenth Census of the United States, vol. 5, Agriculture* (Washington DC: Government Printing Office, 1922), 833.

16. US Department of Commerce, Bureau of the Census, *Fourteenth Census of the United States, vol. 1, Population: 1920* (Washington DC: Government Printing Office, 1921), 546.

17. "Report of the County Agent, 1918: Surry County, North Carolina," Extension Service Annual Reports, North Carolina, Reel 6, Record Group 33, US National Archives and Records Administration, College Park, MD.

18. "Report of the County Agent, 1919: Davidson County, North Carolina," Extension Service Annual Reports, North Carolina, Reel 7, Record Group 33, US National Archives and Records Administration, College Park, MD.

19. Evan P. Bennett, "Of the Quest of the Golden Leaf: Black Farmers and Bright Tobacco in the Piedmont South," in ed. Debra A. Reid and Evan P. Bennett, *Beyond Forty Acres and a Mule: African American Landowning Families since Reconstruction* (Gainesville: University Press of Florida, 2012), 186.

20. "Report of the County Agent, 1919: Wake County, North Carolina," Extension Service Annual Reports, North Carolina, Reel 8, Record Group 33, US National Archives and Records Administration, College Park, MD.

21. John M. Abner, "Up and Down," Life History of Walter Corbett, December 2, 1938, Folder 282, Federal Writers Project Papers, Collection 3709, Southern Historical Collection, University of North Carolina, Chapel Hill.

22. Bennett, *When Tobacco Was King*, 28–30.

23. "Report of the County Agent, 1917: Granville County, North Carolina," Extension Service Annual Reports, North Carolina, Reel 8, Record Group 33, US National Archives and Records Administration, College Park, MD.

24. *Thirty-first Report of the Department of Labor and Printing of the State of North Carolina, 1917–1918* (Raleigh: State Printers, 1919), 16–19; *Thirty-second Report of the Department of Labor and Printing of the State of North Carolina, 1919–1920* (Raleigh: State Printers, 1921), 23–25.

25. Evan P. Bennett, "Manning the Fields: Remaking Women's Work in the Tobacco South in the Twentieth Century," *Journal of Peasant Studies* 35 (October 2008): 720–741.

26. This account of organization following the war years comes from Bennett, *When Tobacco Was King*, 63–74.

17

Towels, Socks, and Denim

World War I and North Carolina's Cotton Mills

Annette Cox

The North Carolina cotton textile industry saw phenomenal growth during World War I as both the number of spindles and wage earners rose by 25%. Its advance contrasted sharply with that of South Carolina, the other major southern textile state, where spindles increased only by 9% and workers by 3.5% (see Table17.1).[1] Several factors drove North Carolina's exceptional wartime expansion. Its textile production was more diversified than South Carolina's, which primarily produced undyed, unfinished cloth. In contrast, its northern neighbor made towels, socks, and denim, all items needed immediately in Europe. Mills in Gaston County, North Carolina, added more than a quarter of a million spindles during the war to manufacture fine, combed yarn, a product that rose in importance once fighting in the Atlantic cut off German imports. Good fortune in cigarettes brought two families, the Dukes and the Carrs, the luxury of excess capital to invest in cotton cloth. Finally, many of the North Carolina mills, instead of relying on independent selling agents, maintained their own New York sales offices, making it easier to navigate the complexities of war. By December 1915, the war had brought so much profit to the state's cotton mills that a *Washington Post* headline shouted, "Great Wave of Prosperity Now Sweeping Across North Carolina."[2]

However, it was this surge in profits and capacity that eventually caused a serious downturn in cotton textiles during the 1920s and then a collapse during the Great Depression. Once wartime demand disappeared and companies began cutbacks, workers accustomed to the abnormally high earnings of war stubbornly resisted, leading to labor unrest during the interwar period. Exports failed to absorb any surplus goods. Some of the slowdown could be blamed on the war's end, but new developments in retailing and fashion also made times tough for the cotton industry. A state where expansion and profits had been the norm found itself struggling for the next two decades from overcapacity and overproduction.

In 1914, when World War I began, cotton mill owners may have anticipated making profits, but the first months of fighting created only fear and confusion. In the ensuing years, these businessmen continued to find themselves tested again and again by the disruptive forces of war. After Austria-Hungary declared war on Serbia in July 1914, raw cotton traders panicked, creating shock waves that reached North Carolina. At the New York Cotton Exchange, the prospect of a widespread European conflict drove prices so low that several brokerages collapsed. Shortly thereafter, officials closed the market, a shutdown that spread to Chicago and New Orleans. The Charlotte market stopped trading on July 31. Textile magnate Julius Cone of Greensboro described the war as "a commercial and financial cataclysm." The cotton exchanges did not reopen until November 16. Uncertainty continued to plague the cotton industry. The British curtailed US trade with European ports, ending the export of raw cotton and the importation of European dyes, fine goods, and hosiery. At home, a major flood, congested rail lines, coal shortages, and labor scarcity created more problems.[3]

Volatile raw cotton prices, in particular, introduced considerable uncertainty throughout the war. During the 1913–1914 growing season, cotton's average price per pound was 13 cents, a level that fell the next year to 9 cents. Prices rebounded after that and soared from 1917 through 1920, peaking in the 1919–1920 growing season at 38 cents. The next year, the average price per pound tumbled to 18 cents. These gyrations had a significant effect on cloth and yarn prices because the raw material constituted 40% to 50% of the total cost of production. This instability would continue into the 1920s and 1930s undermining the prosperity of the industry.[4]

Initially, the major textile manufacturers in North Carolina took a cautious approach. The manager of the Duke family mills, William A. Erwin, reassured Benjamin Duke on August 4, 1914, that "we are running our mills with all the prudence and economy that conditions enable us to do in these war times. We can but feel very greatly concerned when practically all the great powers of Europe are involved in war." Erwin reported that his mills had cotton on hand to last until October and that raw cotton markets prices were "hardening" at around 8½ cents. Mill owners like the Dukes soon discovered that their interests would diverge from those of the cotton farmers. On September 15, an associate wrote Erwin that the cotton business "is completely blocked by the almost hysterical holding movement. The farmers have forgotten apparently that cotton sold a few years ago at seven and eight cents." Erwin's problems were serious because he had considerable warehouse inventory woven with higher-priced cotton.[5]

The threat to exports forced cotton belt politicians to intensify their lobbying for government assistance. By October 1914, they were so frantic that they offered a bill for $250 million in bonds to buy cotton from farmers. Senator Hoke Smith of Georgia and his allies also lobbied the State Department to pressure the British to open the cotton trade. In October 1914, the British agreed to stop seizing US cotton on its way to Europe. That promise only lasted six months before they announced another blockade. Then in May 1915, the Germans sank the *Lusitania*, forcing the British to institute a complete ban on the cotton trade to continental ports. The specter of submarine warfare led cotton towel producer James Cannon to warn a business associate that "if the Germans are able to go ahead with this kind of warfare and control the shipping—this would eliminate any cotton going out, and if this should be the case, I do not know what the result would be—but think that cotton would be materially lower as it would be impossible for the American mills to consume over 7½ million bales, and this would leave quite a large surplus." Cannon cautioned his associates and managers to buy cotton slowly and methodically, believing that at any point its price might change dramatically.[6]

Later in the war, when cotton prices were higher, the cotton interests stopped agitating for government intervention and instead tried to protect raw cotton from federal regulation. To keep cotton out of war legislation, Senator Smith and his allies threatened to campaign for price controls on all commodities. Late in the summer of 1918, the head of the War Industries Board, Bernard Baruch, recommended controls on raw cotton prices. In response, congressmen in cotton-growing states started a vigorous lobbying effort and forced the Board to reverse its course. In contrast, there was little effort to control prices for cotton cloth. The mills signed contracts with the military and foreign governments that fixed the prices for those orders and left only a small portion of production to consumers, output that had little shipping priority.[7]

North Carolina's denim industry was particularly hard hit by the loss of German synthetic indigo dyes used for overalls and jeans. Erwin warned Benjamin N. Duke of a crisis in early August 1914, when he informed him that nearly all his dyes were German. Executives at Cone Mills, also specialists in denim, became obsessed with their indigo supply. One of its top New York agents, Saul Dribben, spent most of the war seeking out imported indigo dyes or their substitutes. In February 1916, he expressed his determination to Julius Cone: "I am going to try to get hold of every single ounce of color." He warned that "we are going to have the greatest difficulty getting dyes and that there will be the greatest kind of a famine in all colors and that this spring and summer we are going to see worse conditions in this respect than ever before."[8]

North Carolina's textile leaders also found wartime shipping conditions hectic and disorganized. Cannon wrote an associate in May 1917 that "we have to fight all the time without any let up to get cars and material." Railroads were central to the functioning of the state's textile industry, as they brought raw cotton into the state and then sent yarn, cloth, and hosiery north to urban markets. During World War I, the rail infrastructure proved to have inadequate equipment, poorly maintained tracks, and faulty system management. To resolve these problems, President Woodrow Wilson put the railroads under federal control in December 1917, what David Kennedy calls "the most drastic mobilization measure of the war." Once the United States entered the war, mills making consumer products had to give way to trains loaded with military goods. In June 1918, Gastonia's Separk-Gray chain bought advertisements to reassure its customers that it was doing all it could to speed goods north.[9]

Unusually dangerous weather added to the wartime chaos. In July 1916, floods along the Catawba, Broad, and Yadkin Rivers caused widespread devastation. During that summer, two category-four hurricanes converged over western North Carolina bringing more than three days of rain. At one point, the Catawba River, the waterway at the heart of the Piedmont textile belt, rose to 47 feet above flood level and destroyed all nearby rail, telephone, and telegraph lines. One mill in Gaston County was completely washed away along with its warehouse, company store, and 1000 bales of cotton. In another incident, at least ten people died when a crucial bridge between Charlotte and Gastonia collapsed. The storm also disabled hydroelectric plants. The railroads and the Southern Power Company responded quickly and hired repair crews. *Textile World Journal* described the effort as one where "great armies of laborers are being mobilized, and the work of rebuilding is going on at a rate that is nothing short of miraculous."[10]

Despite the urgent repair campaign, problems persisted. Because electricity was scarce, some mills switched back to steam power and increased their purchases of coal. In August 1916, *Textile World Journal* reported that since the storm, "all coal produced has been consumed as fast as mined and hauled away. It is this state of affairs which makes the freight car shortage the governing factor of the coal situation." A coal strike in Tennessee in September 1917 caused another shortage when mills without military contracts could not buy fuel. As a result, the Skyland Hosiery Mill in East Flat Rock announced that it was almost entirely out of coal and had none for employees to burn in their homes. The strike particularly affected nearby Asheville, where there were "desperate circumstances" and "no relief in sight until the strike is settled."[11]

In the winter of 1917–1918, freezing weather further disrupted textile production. One observer concluded that North Carolina was experiencing "the coldest temperatures felt in this section in a generation—in some sections, the coldest and worst snow storms and high-velocity winds on record." The weather had turned bad on December 27 and was so cold that some mills did not reopen after the customary Christmas break. By January 5, some mills were so short of fuel that they were "surrendering coal on hand to meet the needs of their communities." Near the end of the war in October

1918, drought brought stoppages to electric power production. *Textile World Journal* reported that "the hydro-electric power situation in the Southeast has reached such a critical stage on account of the long-continuing drought extending throughout the two Carolinas, Georgia, and Tennessee." Again, some factories switched to coal, and federal administrators ordered those not on war work to make drastic cuts in their use of electricity. [12]

As war orders mounted, North Carolina's mill men began to worry about their labor supply. At first, during the panic, mill owners were quick to cut factory hours. Erwin reported to James B. Duke in October 1914 that "trade is exceedingly dull, and we are running all but our No. 4 Mill on short time, about four days per week."[13] After the initial panic subsided, a serious labor shortage lasted for the rest of the war. David Clark's *Southern Textile Bulletin* began printing pages of employment opportunities. One advertisement came from a new Cherryville mill that sought night spinners, doffers, and a section hand whose wages would range from $1 to $1.80 per night. Labor was so scarce that some mills resorted to bragging about their facilities, citing amenities such as electric lights in every room and "splendid" city water. When the United States entered the war in April 1917, Clark predicted that labor shortages would be "getting worse and may become very severe." He worried that workers would be going home for spring planting, that the new child labor law would eliminate the hiring of teenagers, and that the draft would take men away. He recommended turning again to the one region that had furnished workers before: "Our logical point for securing labor is the mountain district of North Carolina and Tennessee and we believe that a publicity campaign should be run in all the mountain papers for the purpose of showing the mountain people the advantages of cotton mill life." The next month, Clark warned that the draft could take 9,000 men from the factories.[14]

By May 1918, the labor situation was so tight that one Cone Mills executive stopped to reminisce about the low wages the firm had once paid: "when I came to Greensboro in 1904, [unskilled labor] was getting 85 cents a day, and [that rate] had been gradually raised until when the war began we were paying about $1.15 a day, [and that worker] is today getting anywhere from $2.75 to $3.15 a day." Other mills competed for Cone's workers. The Dan River Mills in Danville, Virginia, and the Marshall Field operations distributed handbills in Greensboro boasting of their high wages.[15] One North Carolina mill man resorted to denouncing labor poaching as unpatriotic, a familiar wartime tactic. In a speech to a textile conference, Caroleen mill superintendent W. M. Sherard recommended that "something ought to be done to check the evil of soliciting labor for labor's sake. . . . The habit of moving from one mill to another breeds discontent. A laborer dissatisfied and disappointed infects other people with his spirit of unrest. He is a living example of the old fable of the rotten apple that spoiled the whole barrel." He recommended that the mills start a campaign to educate workers on how much it costs to change jobs because that "represents just so much waste, pure and simple—a waste, which at this critical time in the affairs of the nation, is almost criminal because it could be prevented."[16]

In the fall of 1918, influenza caused further labor supply problems and brought some mills to a standstill. In Concord, all the mills, schools, and theatres were closed for one week in October, but local authorities were not worried because "the disease not being of virulent form in this section." However, in Gaston County, conditions were so much worse that the local Board of Health ordered the closing of all mills, churches, and schools for one month. The textile press reported that "gruesome details are given in certain communications that indicate a particularly gloomy frame of mind."[17]

In a startling development, the wartime labor shortage led a few North Carolina hosiery manufacturers to hire African American labor. For decades, white supremacy had dictated that southern industrial work be reserved for whites. Mill owners did not view this step so much as a challenge to prevailing customs but as just another way of holding down labor costs. Whites were leaving hosiery mills where they earned 80 cents per day for more lucrative positions in spinning where they could command $1.50. In keeping with the segregationist code of the time, these new black workers, mostly women and girls, were put in separate buildings. When the war brought more labor shortages, mills in Halifax and Rocky Mount also found "colored" help satisfactory and capable of producing "good results." *Textile World Journal* found one mill man who lavishly praised young female African American workers: "In their experience, they had found many of the colored girls make as much progress in learning and actual efficiency in four days, as some of the white employees had made in four weeks. They are used on knitting and transfer work, with the looping and dyeing and finishing performed by the white help." In June 1918, the Durham Hosiery Company announced that it was building a new mill in Goldsboro, "which . . . will employ negro labor exclusively." This break with southern hiring practices was temporary and did nothing to open the mills to more African American labor after the war.[18]

On November 11, 1918, the warring nations signed the Armistice, and the next day the government began cancelling orders. That left mills with yarn, cloth, and hosiery made with cotton purchased at high wartime prices. Cannon warned one of his selling agents that the abrupt move was dangerous: "The Government cancelling all contracts I am afraid is going to create textile semi-panic. I do not know how they can expect to do this, unless they are going to pay the losses sustained by the mills. . . . However, I presume there will be some readjustment in some way." Cannon's reaction to the cancellations again showed that mill owners were quick to turn to the government for assistance when circumstances warranted it. The government did settle some contracts by offering 13 cents on the dollar, but mills suffered only temporarily because of the backlog of civilian orders.[19]

Even though there was considerable turmoil during the war years, North Carolina's cotton mills overcame the confusion to make substantial profits. The owners saw cotton cloth purchases boom right away. In October 1914, the British government ordered twelve million towels from mills in the Carolinas. Clark's *Southern Textile Bulletin* reported that the British also wanted to buy one million cotton undershirts. In September 1915, the Navy Department awarded Durham Hosiery Mills a contract for 300,000 pairs of socks. That same month, the J. P. Morgan Bank notified Greensboro's Cone Mills that Great Britain wanted to purchase a half-million yards of denim.[20]

This wave of war orders for towels, socks, and denim, went to mills that on average employed fewer than two hundred workers. However, among North Carolina's factories in 1914 were six large, prosperous firms whose strong financial performance drove the expansion of the industry during the war. Of the 3.7 million spindles in the state in 1914, over 36% were controlled by five of those six. For example, in 1914, the Cannons of Concord directed the production of over 480,000 spindles, 13% of the state's total, while the Cones of Greensboro held 6%. Other firms with substantial holdings included the Dukes, the Holt family, and the combed yarns factories of Gaston County. The sixth major firm, the Durham Hosiery Company, made cheap cotton hosiery on knitting machines.[21]

The families controlling these six groups of mills knew each other well. For example, over the years the Dukes had invested in mills across the state. During the 1890s, the Cones marketed the cloth of many of the state's mills, some of them owned by the Holts. Their social circles frequently overlapped. For example, one of James W. Cannon's daughters was married to Julian S. Carr Jr., the son of the founder of Durham Hosiery. Duke's textile manager, William A. Erwin, was the great-nephew of antebellum textile pioneer Edwin Holt and early in his career, he worked for that family. Except for the Holts, these families also shared a progressive attitude toward business and a willingness to experiment with new strategies.[22]

These progressive families recognized the advantages of careful product selection. Unlike most of the mills in South Carolina, they diversified their output and, at the same time, identified themselves with one particular line. The Cannons focused on towels, the Cones and Dukes on denim, and the Carrs on hosiery. In Gaston County, most mills chose to make combed yarns for the Philadelphia hosiery and fine goods market. With strong backgrounds in merchandising, these men were able to choose products wisely. In addition, the Dukes and the Carrs had accumulated enough wealth from cigarettes to seek out other investments. This access to capital from the tobacco industry also set North Carolina apart from other southern states. No other textile state was home to families with the wealth and connections the Dukes and Carrs enjoyed. In addition, tobacco men knew all about marketing. What made these firms especially influential was their control of their own distribution and selling strategies. Well before World War I, the Cannons, the Cones, and Durham Hosiery established their own selling operations in New York City, no longer relying on independent agents. Unlike most other southern textile manufactures, they had extensive contacts in the northern financial world and could easily access credit and capital. The Dukes needed little help from banks, while combed yarn manufacturers worked closely with a handful of Philadelphia selling agents and with their equipment manufacturer.[23]

Cannon Mills, North Carolina's largest textile firm in 1914, operated fifteen mills, eight of them in Cabarrus County just northeast of Charlotte. Its founder, James W. Cannon, was a native of the state who as a young man sold bolts of cloth in country stores. In 1906, Cannon bought enough land near Concord to establish his own town, a place he named Kannapolis.[24] The state's second largest textile manufacturing company was Cone Mills. Its roots differed from the others because its founders were new to the state; before coming to North Carolina, they sold southern-made cloth out of Baltimore. Moses and Caesar Cone set up their first mills, the White Oak and the Proximity, in Greensboro to diversify backward into weaving. By 1914, Cone had established a significant foothold in denim, selling most of it to Wrangler, then the best-known manufacturer of jeans and overalls.[25]

The tobacco titans, Benjamin N. and James B. Duke, financed the third largest group of cotton mills, managed for them by Erwin, weaving denims, ginghams, and plain cloth. With their cigarette wealth, the Dukes could have undertaken a massive consolidation in the southern textile industry, but they remained satisfied with much less. After hiring Erwin in 1892, they expanded capacity to include mills in Durham and one each in Cabarrus, Davie, Harnett, and Granville Counties. Although the Dukes possessed a legendary marketing expertise, they turned to an outside agency, Joshua Baily of Philadelphia, to market their cotton goods. It was a firm they believed would help them export cloth to China. They did not depend on Baily alone, for Erwin was well known for his marketing skills and frequently traveled to New York.[26]

In contrast, the Holts retained traditional southern marketing customs. They built a series of small mills, a total of 23 by 1914, almost all in Alamance County, with a total of about 173,000 spindles; only one of their mills had over 20,000 spindles. The family patriarch, Edwin Holt, spread out control of his mills among sons, sons-in-law, and grandsons. After Edwin, no one Holt coordinated the management of these mills. Using seven New York selling agents during the war, the Holts pursued a much more fragmented distribution strategy.[27]

Gaston County's combed yarn production rested on the invention of a simplified and mechanized cotton comber by Whitin Machine Works of Massachusetts. Using its credit with northern banks, Whitin chose Gaston as the site for new factories to install that equipment, starting in 1906. The mills were unusually small even for North Carolina, but among them were four chains—Separk-Gray, Armstrong, Rankin, and Lineberger-Stowe—that operated as a single entity when making raw cotton purchases, selecting equipment, and marketing goods. This was the only one of North Carolina mill groups that did not have major government contracts during the war because the military had no need for fine cotton products. Instead, they thrived by selling to domestic customers who had previously bought German products. They all used selling agents in Philadelphia. From 1914 to 1918, the county's spindles grew dramatically from just over 100,000 to 350,000.[28]

Another North Carolina industry up and coming at the start of the war was seamless cotton hosiery, a sector where the state would eventually lead the nation. One of the first and most successful of the state's hosiery manufacturers was Durham's Julian S. Carr and his sons. Carr had been a success in the tobacco business, sold his interests to the Dukes, and then reinvested part of that fortune in hosiery. Knitting machines were new to the South so Carr had to rely on northern equipment manufacturers to install and maintain his equipment. However, he did have plenty of experience in the highly competitive cigarette business and understood that controlling your own marketing was essential. By 1914, Durham Hosiery had a selling office in New York; two mills in Durham; and one each in Chapel Hill, Goldsboro, High Point, Mebane, and Raleigh.[29]

By 1919 these six firms had expanded their capacity from 36% to 55% of the state's spindles, had purchased even more spindles and knitting machines, and, in the case of the Cannons and Cones, had expanded their representation of independent mills. From 1914 to 1919, the state's total number of spindles had increased 25%, and the estimated value of output rose by about 2½ times from about $90 million to an astounding $318 million. Despite labor shortages during these years, the number of workers also increased 25% from 53,703 to 67,297. For hosiery mills, the value of output increased 240%, from $9 million to over $28 million. The number of knitting machines in their possession rose from 10,959 to 14,234. Cannon remained at the top of the heap. By 1918 the company's selling agents marketed the output of a total of 23 mills with 550,000 spindles, up 15% since 1914, and three hosiery mills with 572 knitting machines. Cannon's sales rose from about $5 million in 1915 to just over $16 million in 1918.[30]

Correspondence between Cannon and the owners of these independent mills demonstrates that these businessmen depended on him for more than selling goods. He solved problems brought on by the war, finding dyes, capital, and electric power for his clients. For example, in 1916 Cannon requested credit lines for his mills from the Central National Bank of Philadelphia. In 1916, he advised the treasurer of a mill in Statesville to build more village housing and promised that the Southern Power Company would furnish electricity.

Caesar Cone also maintained close relationships with his seven client mills. For example, in August 1914, Cone offered a loan to R. R. Haynes, the president of Cliffside Mills, as well as extra supplies of dye. In many important ways, these independent firms were well integrated into the larger operations of Cannon and Cone. The war made them even more valuable to their clients.[31]

This wartime growth led by Cannon and Cone also accelerated the transfer of cotton manufacturing from New England to the South (see Table 17.1), a fundamental transformation of the United States textile industry. At the beginning of the war, the leading textile state, Massachusetts, owned over 10.5 million spindles while the South's premier cotton mill state was South Carolina with only 4.5 million. In 1914 North Carolina trailed behind with 3.7 million. However, during the war, South Carolina's mill men installed only 8.7% more equipment, while North Carolina's capacity grew from 3.7 million in 1914 to 4.6 million in 1919. During the war, the number of spindles in Massachusetts grew by only 6.2% and in Rhode Island by 7.4%, while the number of spindles in New Hampshire, Connecticut, and Maine actually declined. By 1927 the number of spindles in Massachusetts had plummeted to 8.8 million, while North Carolina continued to add spindles, reaching over 6 million in 1927, with South Carolina behind at 5.4 million. The emergence of large cotton mills with their own sophisticated marketing operations put North Carolina at the forefront of the migration of spindles to the South.[32]

This wartime expansion and prosperity, however, did not extend into the postwar period. When demand disappeared, production had to be curtailed, and the war's high wages had to be cut. The state's workers resisted and embarked on two decades of intense labor militancy, a new development in southern history. In February 1919, when owners decreased wages, strikes erupted in Charlotte and then spread to Belmont, Concord, and Kannapolis. As labor activism rose during the summer of 1919, unions bragged that they had signed up 40,000 workers. The unrest appeared again in the fall of 1920 after another round of wage and hour cuts. In June 1921, strikes led by the United Textile Workers again began in Charlotte and extended to the Cannon mills in Concord and Kannapolis. Although mill owners defeated these strikes, worker militancy continued to serve as a restraint on them when they sought to impose deeper wage cuts. Real wages for southern textile workers during the 1920s remained "sticky" at levels significantly above those before 1914. Unable to cut labor costs during the late 1920s, owners turned to scientific management techniques, only to cause more strikes.[33]

One possible option for textiles after the war was exports. However, southern mill owners, even progressive ones like Cone, failed to develop the overseas market. At the turn of the century, exports seemed promising to the southern textile industry, as merchants in some Chinese ports bought quite a bit of southern cloth. However, once the Russo-Japanese War ended in 1906, the Japanese began to dominate Asian textiles. Only when World War I began did US sales overseas increase again. From exports of 445 million square yards in 1913, sales rose to 690 million in 1917, an increase of over 55%. Since it took time for European mills to resume operations after the war, US cloth exports peaked in 1920 at 819 million square yards.[34]

During the war, the United States textile industry developed especially lofty expectations for exports to Latin America, a region whose cloth trade had been dominated by Great Britain, Germany, and Italy—three nations that had spent decades catering to the region's preference for cheap colored cloth and generous credit terms.[35] To expand in that market, New York's *American Wool and Cotton Reporter* in the fall of 1914 published three special issues in Spanish and Portuguese. Its editorial page trumpeted a call for the US textile industry "to go after Latin American business" and promised to furnish "all we know of Latin American needs and business methods to any interested textile manufacturer."[36] North Carolina's mills also had hopes for expanding exports. One advertisement in Spanish and Portuguese featured Gastonia's notorious Loray Mill, a factory that had specialized in export cloth since its founding in 1900. In January 1915, a steamship company invited Benjamin Duke on a voyage for "the purpose of enabling bankers, manufacturers, exporters, and importers to become acquainted with the economic resources of Latin America, and to obtain a comprehensive knowledge of the possibilities of that market."[37]

When Cone Mills received orders from Latin America in 1915, Caesar Cone and his sales staff initially took a cautious approach, but they were so intrigued that in 1916 Cone himself visited Havana. After his trip, he recommended that the firm hire a Cuban salesman who could "work up a good business" perhaps selling a million dollars of cloth a year. He even speculated that Havana would be a good place to "dump" unsold goods. He also recognized that US producers faced significant hurdles. He warned that Cuban cloth brokers would "talk different when they can again get what they want in England and other European countries." Cone proved to be right about Cuba. After the peak year of 1920 when the US exported over 160 million square yards to that county, cloth sales leveled off to an average of around 60 million for the rest of the decade.[38]

The campaign to capture more of the Latin American market failed. Textile manufacturers did very little to attract more Latin customers because goods sold so easily at home. There was also a shortage of popular dyes because the British had choked off that trade. After the war, the Japanese moved more aggressively into the region, leading the Latin nations to raise tariffs, a measure that also hurt US goods. The British also recaptured a share of the Latin American market, especially in Argentina. Exporting was one path that North Carolina mill men found closed to them during the 1920s and 1930s.[39]

After the war, the inability of North Carolina's textile industry to expand overseas was but one setback among many. Despite its profits during the war, it found itself in a textile market of growing complexity. In addition to heightened worker militancy, cotton prices proved to be volatile. Shocked by the initial decline and then the stupendous rise of raw cotton during the last years of the war, mill owners could not rely on a reliable cotton supply. After the war, the spread of the boll weevil and weather conditions kept the raw material price unstable and continually threatened the value of inventories. As the decade wore on, there were an increasing number of alternatives to cotton. Fashion turned away from cotton as women chose first silk and then rayon for dresses and hosiery. The decline of immigration took the edge off what had been a booming domestic population. Any profits during the 1920s often went into the hands of the increasingly powerful converters, garment manufacturers, and retailers, rather than to the cloth manufacturers.[40] Both the war and the new, disturbing circumstances of the post-war period turned the 1920s and 1930s into what historian Jack Blicksilver calls, "the long textile depression," a period that lasted until another war brought back prosperity.[41]

Table 17.1. Spindle Comparisons across Northern and Southern Textile Industries.

	United States	NC	SC	GA	AL	Total in 4 Southern States
1909	27,395,800	2,908,383	3,754,251	1,747,483	885,803	9,295,920
1914	30,815,731	3,703,482	4,552,048	2,043,386	998,836	11,297,752
1919	33,718,953	4,622,714	4,949,225	2,459,143	1,106,933	13,138,015
1927	33,607,939	6,073,027	5,422,526	2,921,349	1,447,441	15,864,343
	MA	RI	NH	CT	ME	Total in 5 New England States
1909	9,372,364	2,338,689	1,318,932	1,241,524	1,020,688	15,292,197
1914	10,556,867	2,339,844	1,340,753	1,276,148	1,098,142	16,611,754
1919	11,206,855	2,512,283	1,336,797	1,256,776	1,091,991	17,404,702
1927	8,818,981	2,209,116	1,297,205	1,072,872	1,021,607	14,419,781

Source: Bureau of the Census, Department of Commerce, Biennial Census of Manufactures, 1927 (Washington, 1930), p. 258.

Notes

1. For the number of wage earners, see Bureau of the Census, Department of Commerce, *Fourteenth Census of the United States Taken in the Year 1920, vol. X, Manufactures 1919, Reports for Selected Industries* (Washington, DC: Government Printing Office, 1921), 162.

2. "Great Wave of Prosperity Now Sweeping Across North Carolina," *Washington Post*, December 1, 1915, 5.

3. "Markets Close All Over World," *Daily Record* (Greensboro, NC), July 31, 1914, 1; "War News Force Four Firms to Quit," *New York Times*, August 1, 1914, 3; "Cotton Market Stops," *Daily News* (Greensboro, NC), August 1, 1914, 9; "Charlotte Without Her Cotton Market," *Daily News*, August 2, 1914, 7; "Optimism Shown by Julius Cone About Business Prospect," *Daily News*, August 9, 1914, 1, 3. Studies of US business during World War I include David Kennedy, *Over Here: The First World War*

and *American Society* (Oxford: Oxford University Press, 1980); Robert D. Cuff, *The War Industries Board: Business-Government Relations During World War I* (Baltimore: Johns Hopkins Press, 1973); Paul Koistinen, "The 'Industrial-Military Complex' in Historical Perspective: World War I," *Business History Review* 41 (1967): 378–403; Paul Koistinen, *Mobilizing for Modern War: The Political Economy of American Warfare, 1865–1919* (Lawrence: University of Kansas Press, 1997); Austin Kerr, *American Railroad Politics, 1914–1920: Rates, Wages, and Efficiency* (Pittsburgh: University of Pittsburgh, 1969); Robert Zieger, *America's Great War: World War I and the American Experience* (Lanham, MD: Rowman & Littlefield Publishers, 2000), 57–84.

4. For detailed listing of raw cotton prices from 1910 to 1935, see H. E. Michl, *The Textile Industries: An Economic Analysis* (Washington, DC: Textile Foundation, 1938), 113; Jack Blicksilver, *Cotton Manufacturing in the Southeast: An Historical Analysis* (Atlanta: Georgia State College of Business Administration, 1959), 101. In real terms, a price for raw cotton of $.38 in 1919 was worth $.21 in 1913 dollars." See Measuring Worth, www.measuringworth .com/uscompare/.

5. Correspondence, William A. Erwin to Benjamin N. Duke, August 4, 1914, Folder "August 1–17, 1914"; Erwin to Frederick Baily, September 15, 1914, Folder "September 15–30"; Erwin to Benjamin Duke, September 12, 1914, Folder "September 4–14, 1914"; Alex Sprunt to Erwin, September 15, 1914, Folder "September 15–30, 1914"; all in Box 55, Benjamin N. Duke Papers, David Rubenstein Rare Book & Manuscript Library, Duke University; hereafter cited as B. N. Duke Papers.

6. Gilbert C. Fite, *Cotton Fields No More: Southern Agriculture, 1865–1980* (Lexington: University of Kentucky Press, 1984), 91–95; Correspondence, James W. Cannon to N. B. Mills, October 10, 1916, and November 4, 1916, Folder "M," Box 3; Cannon Mill Records, David M. Rubenstein Rare Book and Manuscripts Library, Duke University, hereafter cited as Cannon Papers. Also see "War's Grave Effect on Cotton Industry," *Daily News*, September 15, 1914, 9; "Reassurance Comes from Senator Smith," *Daily News*, August 26, 1915, 2; Dewey Grantham, Jr., *Hoke Smith and the Politics of the New South* (Baton Rouge: Louisiana State University Press, 1958), 277–291.

7. "War's Grave Effect," 9; Grantham, *Hoke Smith*, 277–291.

8. William A. Erwin to Benjamin N. Duke, August 4, 1914, Folder "August 1–17," Box 55, B. N. Duke Papers; and Saul Dribben to Julius Cone, February 11, 1916, Folder 52, Box 5, Cone Mills Corporation Records, 5247, Southern Historical Association, Louis Round Wilson Special Collections Library, University of North Carolina at Chapel Hill; hereafter cited as Cone Papers.

9. James W. Cannon to T. C. Thompson, May 25, 1917, quoted in Timothy W. Vanderburg, *Cannon Mills and Kannapolis: Persistent Paternalism in a Textile Town* (Knoxville: University of Tennessee Press, 2013),43; Kennedy, *Over Here*, 252, 253; Advertisement, *Textile World Journal* 53 (June 22, 1918): 102.

10. *The Floods of July 1916: How the Southern Railway Organization Met an Emergency* (Washington, DC: Southern Railway Company, 1917), 7–16; *The North Carolina Flood: July 14, 15, 16, 1916* (Charlotte: W. M Bell, 1916); "Southern Floods Will Raise Prices," *New York Times*, July 21, 1916, 10; "Actively Rehabilitating Flooded Mills," *Textile World Journal* 51 (July 29, 1916): 11, 16.

11. *Textile World Journal* 51 (August 26, 1916): 57; "Little Encouragement for Towns That Are Out of Coal," *Daily News*, September 27, 1917, 1.

12. "Mills Hit by Bad Weather," and "Textile Plants Shut Down by Unprecedented Condition" *Textile World Journal* 53 (January 5, 1918): 27, 49; "Power Restrictions," *Textile World Journal* 54 (October 19, 1918): 43.

13. William A. Erwin to James B. Duke, October 5, 1914, Folder "October 1–6, 1914," Box 55, B. N. Duke Papers.

14. "Help Wanted," *Southern Textile Bulletin* 10 (January 27, 1916): 17; Classified advertisement, *Southern Textile Bulletin* 13 (June 7, 1917): 17; David Clark, "Labor Supply," *Southern Textile Bulletin* 13 (April 26, 1917): 12; "Note on North Carolina Draft," *Southern Textile Bulletin* 13 (June 28,1917): 12.

15. J. E. Hardin to Saul Dribben, May 1, 1918, Folder 53, Box 6; Dribben to Julius Cone, April 26, 1918, Folder 53, Box 6, both in Cone Papers.

16. "Problem of Labor Shortage Discussed," *Textile World Journal* 53 (June 29, 1918): 41, 43.

17. "Closes Textile Mills," *Textile World Journal* 54 (October 12, 1918): 69; "Spinners Hard Hit; So. Mills Stopped," *Textile World Journal* 54 (October 26, 1918): 82, 256; "Churches, Schools, and Picture Shows Closed," *Daily Gazette (Gastonia, NC)*, October 9, 1918, 1; "Gastonia Still in Grip of Influenza," *Daily Gazette*, October 16, 1918, 1; "Quarantine Ends Tomorrow Night," *Daily Gazette*, November 1, 1918, 1.

18. "Southern Negro Help," T*extile World Journal* 51 (August 26, 1916): 57. Other articles on African American labor in North Carolina hosiery mills include "Employing Negroes," *Textile World Journal* 53 (January 5, 1918) 49, and "New Mill to Hire Negroes," *Textile World Journal* 53 (June 1, 1918): 83.

19. James W. Cannon to J. C. Leslie, November 20, 1918, Folder "New York Office Correspondence, May–December, 1918," Box 9, Cannon Papers; "The Difficult Process of Demobilizing Industry," *Textile World Journal* 54 (November 23, 1918): 36–37.

20. "Boom Times Confronting Charlotte Cotton Mills," *Washington Post* (October 22, 1914): 5; "Southern Export Orders," *Wall Street Journal* (October 7, 1914): 5; and Correspondence, L. H. Sellars to Caesar Cone, September 1, 1915, Folder 34, Box 4, Cone Papers.

21. For data on the North Carolina textile industry during World War I, see Bureau of the Census, Department of Commerce, *Census of Manufactures, 1914*, vol. 1 (Washington, DC: Government Printing Office, 1921), 1110; *Fourteenth Census of the United States Taken in the Year 1920, State Compendium, North Carolina* (Washington, DC: Government Printing Office, 1925), 6. For data on companies, see *Davison's Textile "Blue Book," Office Edition, 1913–1914* (New York: Davison Publishing Company, 1913), 141–172, 472–478; *Davison's Textile "Blue Book," Office Edition, July 1918 to July 1919* (New York: Davison Publishing Company, 1918), 257–292, 644–655. For southern textile industry history, see Melvin T. Copeland, *The Cotton Manufacturing Industry of the United States* (Cambridge: Harvard University Press, 1912); Broadus Mitchell, *The Rise of Cotton Mills in the South* (Baltimore: Johns Hopkins Press, 1921); Blicksilver, *Cotton Manufacturing in the Southeast*; Brent Glass, *The Textile Industry of North Carolina: A History* (Raleigh: State Department of Archives and History, 1992); David Carlton, *Mills and Town in South Carolina, 1880–1920* (Baton Rouge: Louisiana State University Press, 1982); Mary B. Rose, *Firms Networks, and Business Values: The British and American Cotton Industries Since 1750* (Cambridge: Cambridge University Press, 2000); David L. Carlton, "The Revolution from Above: The National Market and the Beginnings of Industrialization in North Carolina," *Journal of American History* 77 (September 1990): 445–475; Phillip J. Wood, *Southern Capitalism: The Political Economy of North Carolina, 1880*–1980 (Durham: Duke University Press, 1986); Bess Beatty, *Alamance: The Holt Family and Industrialization in a North Carolina County, 1837–1900* (Baton Rouge: Louisiana State University Press, 1999); Jacquelyn Hall *et al.*, *Like a Family: The Making of a Southern Cotton Mill World* (Chapel Hill: University of North Carolina Press, 1987); Gavin Wright, *Old South, New South: Revolutions in the Southern Economy Since the Civil War* (New York: Basic Books, 1986).

22. Beatty, *Alamance*, 126–27, 135, 147, 209; Mena Webb, *Jule Carr: General Without an Army* (Chapel Hill: University of North Carolina Press, 1987), 183.

23. Carlton, "The Revolution from Above," 445–475.

24. Vanderburg, *Cannon Mills and Kannapolis*, 3–46.

25. Bryant Simon, "Choosing Between the Ham and the Union: Paternalism in the Cone Mills of Greensboro," in *Hanging by a Thread: Social Change in Southern Textile*, ed. Jeffrey Leiter, Michael D. Schulman, and Rhonda Zingraff (Ithaca: Cornell University Press, 1991), 83–89; Cone Corporation, *The Story of Cone Denim* (Greensboro: The Cone Corporation, 1950), 4–6.

26. Robert Durden, *The Dukes of Durham, 1865–1929* (Durham: Duke University Press, 1987*)*, 122–151.

27. Beatty, *Alamance*, 123–149.

28. Robert A. Ragan, *The Textile Heritage of Gaston County, North Carolina, 1848–2000: One Hundred Mills and the Men Who Built Them* (Charlotte: R. A. Ragan and Company, 2001), 88–91, 190–194; Thomas R. Navin, *The Whitin Machine Works Since 1831: A Textile Machinery Company in an Industrial Village* (Cambridge: Harvard University Press, 1950), 223–235; *Davison's Textile*

"Blue Book," Office Edition, 1913–1914, 141–172, 472–478; *Davison's Textile "Blue Book," Office Edition, July 1918 to July 1919*, 257–292, 644–655.

29. Copeland, *The Cotton Manufacturing Industry of the United States*, 104–111, 255–259; Webb, *Jule Carr*, 176–190; Pamela C. Edwards, "Entrepreneurial Networks and the Textile Industry: Technology, Innovation, and Labor in the American Southeast, 1980–1925," in *Technology, Innovation, and Southern Industrialization: From the Antebellum Era to the Computer Age*, ed. by Susanna Delfino and Michele Gillespie (Columbia: University of Missouri Press, 2008), 151–160.

30. For data on companies, see *Davison's Textile "Blue Book," Office Edition, 1913–1914*, 141–172, 472–478; *Davison's Textile "Blue Book," Office Edition, July 1918 to July 1919*, 257–292, 644–655. For data on knitting machines, see Bureau of the Census, Department of Commerce, "Knit Goods," *Fourteenth Census of the United States Taken in the Year 1920, vol. X, Manufactures, 1919, Reports for Selected Industries* (Washington, DC: Government Printing Office, 1921), 200, 207. For value of production, Bureau of the Census, *Census of Manufactures, 1914*, vol. 1, 1110; *Fourteenth Census of the United States Taken in the Year 1920, State Compendium, North Carolina*, 6. For Cannon figures, see Vanderburg, *Cannon Mills and Kannapolis*, 41, 43. In real terms, $318 million of goods sold in 1919, amounted to $178 million in 1914 dollars. In hosiery production, $28 million of goods sold in 1919 was $15.7 million in 1914 dollars. In goods sold by Cannon, sales of $16 million in 1918 was $10.3 million in 1915 dollars." Measuring Worth, www.measuringworth.com/uscompare/.

31. William Y. Conrad to James W. Cannon, May 29, 1916, Folder "C," 1916, Box 3; James W. Cannon to N. B. Mills, June 26, 1916, Folder "M," 1916, Box 3, Cannon Papers; Caesar Cone to R. R. Haynes, August 16, 1914, Folder 26, Box 3; R. R. Haynes to Caesar Cone, August 9, 1914, Folder 26, Box 3; Caesar Cone to Charles H. Haynes, February 17, 1916, Folder 26, Box 3, Cone Papers.

32. Bureau of the Census, Department of Commerce, *Census of Manufactures, 1927* (Washington, DC: Government Printing Office, 1930), 258.

33. Hall *et al.*, *Like a Family*, 183–195; Wright, *Old South, New South*, 147–155; Vanderburg, *Cannon Mills and Kannapolis*, 47–57.

34. Annette Cox, "Imperial Illusions: The New South's Campaign for Cotton Cloth Exports," *Journal of Southern History* 80 (August 2014): 613–614.

35. Lars G. Sandberg, *Lancashire in Decline: A Study in Entrepreneurship, Technology, and International Trade* (Columbus: Ohio State University Press, 1974), 197–199; D. A. Farnie, *The English Cotton Industry and the World Market, 1815–1896* (Oxford: Oxford University Press, 1979), 93–96. Also, see "Wartime Exports of Cotton," *Textile World Journal* 54 (August 24, 1918): 86, 202.

36. *American Wool and Cotton Reporter* 28 (September 10, 1914): 14, 15.

37. Loray Advertisement, *American Wool and Cotton Reporter* 28 (October 22, 1914): 3; Travel Department, Fidelity Trust Company of Baltimore to Benjamin Duke, November 3, 1914, Folder "November 1–9, 1914," Box 56, B. N. Duke Papers.

38. Caesar Cone, "Report on Havana," February 19, 1916, Folder 33, Box 3, Cone Papers; W. A. Graham Clark, *Cotton Goods In Latin America, Part I, Cuba, Mexico, and Central America*, Special Agents Series, #31, Department of Commerce and Labor (Washington, DC: Government Printing Office, 1909), 6–14; "Opportunity to Expand As Export Call Broadens," *Textile World Record*, 51 (January 22, 1916): 39; A. J. Marrison, "Great Britain and Her Rivals in the Latin American Cotton Piece-Goods Market, 1880–1940," in *Great Britain and Her World, 1750–1914: Essays in Honour of W. O. Henderson*, ed. Barrie M. Ratcliffe (Manchester: Manchester University Press, 1975), 309.

39. "War-Time Exports and Imports," *Textile World Journal*, 55 (March 8, 1919): 20; Rose, *Firms, Networks and Business Values*, 239–240; Sandberg, *Lancashire in Decline*, 197–199; Marrison, "Great Britain and Her Rivals," 309–348; *Textile World Journal* 53 (June 22, 1918): 23.

40. Blicksilver, *Cotton Manufacturing in the Southeast*, 89–118; Philip Scranton, *Figured Tapestry: Production, Markets, and Power in Philadelphia Textiles, 1885–1914* (Cambridge: Cambridge University Press, 1989), 323–453; Susan Benson, *Counter Cultures: Saleswomen, Managers, and Customers in American Department Stores, 1890–1940* (Urbana: University of Illinois Press, 1987); Michl, *The Textile Industries*, 96–110, 129–161; Rose, *Firms, Networks and Business Values*, 198–241.

41. Blicksilver, *Cotton Manufacturing in the Southeast*, 89.

18

"Let Me Have One of My Boys Back"

Class-based Mobilization of Labor on the Tar Heel Homefront

Pamela C. Edwards

While national and international labor historians identify World War I as a turning point, when labor activists and political progressives compromised to secure the rights of unionization, collective bargaining, and national social services for the laboring classes of the industrialized world, in North Carolina and the American South, more generally, it seems more an era of missed opportunities. William A. Link's *The Paradox of Southern Progressivism* explains exceptionalism in southern labor relations, concluding that white supremacist ideology prevented progressive reformers from compromising with labor activists and undermined any substantial changes in the existing social or industrial order.[1] Expanding on Link's thesis, Janet Hudson meticulously documents the actions and motivations of South Carolina progressives during World War I and concludes that not only were reformers' beliefs about class and labor entangled with—if not inseparable from—white supremacist ideology, but that racism trumped all other considerations.[2] Following the scholarly example of Link, Hudson, and others, this chapter utilizes Council of Defense and other state records to contextualize the labor history of World War I North Carolina within the broader processes of industrialization, progressive reform, and working class activism. Correspondence between state and local council members and other citizens documents social attitudes, revealing views held by middle class office holders, appointed and voluntary officials, managers, owners, and employers on the entangled issues of class, race, and gender. Ultimately, their attitudes shaped wartime policies and determined the success or failure of proposed reforms in labor relations and anticipated new opportunities for North Carolina's working classes both during and after World War I.

Before the Great War, American labor experienced decades of conflict over and progress toward workers' rights to unionize and to live and work in a safe and healthy environment. Between 1875 and 1917, labor conflicts sparked violent encounters when company thugs and state and federal troops sought to repress strikes and other efforts of working people to achieve economic opportunity and civil equality.[3] In these pre-war years, palpable class alignments divided American society; an expanding class of educated professionals identified with values and cultural expressions they believed set them apart from the increasingly class-conscious industrial and agricultural laboring classes.[4] Americans expressed class distinctions through alternative political affiliations. Farmers joined the Populist Party, while some industrial workers supported a viable Socialist alternative, and the middle classes brought diverse reform efforts into both the Democrat and Republican political machines before forming the Progressive "Bull Moose" Party. Culturally constructed ideologies of race and gender complicated all these class and political identities, especially in southern states like North Carolina.[5] The Tar Heel state entered the First World War in the midst of five decades of manufacturing development that provided multiple generations of industrial laborers with job opportunities in new and expanding industries. As Hudson notes in her study of South Carolina, the Great War enhanced this industrializing trend, and the resulting prosperity fostered possibilities for progressive reform in politics, working and living conditions, and labor and race relations in both the Tar Heel and Palmetto states.[6]

North Carolinians moving from family farms into factories between 1880 and 1917 proved an unruly lot. Accustomed to independent, close-knit communities, many rejected factory discipline and challenged the authority of mill owners, joining the International Workers of the World while their agrarian counterparts supported the Populist Party. Facing interracial movements with revolutionary potential, legislators sustained the agricultural and business elites by amending the state constitution and passing Jim Crow laws that discouraged the political participation of less affluent citizens from both races, making it all but impossible for African Americans to vote or the Populist opposition to survive.[7] As the Populists disintegrated and voting roles diminished, Progressive reformers took up the banner of reform within the state's Democratic Party, struggling to improve highways and secure stricter anti-trust laws; they also sought to promote employee welfare through child labor restrictions, employer liability for worker safety, and greater opportunities for public school education. While generally enamored by industrial development, North Carolina's Progressive governors—particularly Locke Craig and Thomas W. Bickett—challenged manufacturers who believed government regulation undermined their control over workers and decreased profits. As war broke out in Europe, North Carolina congressmen Claude Kitchin and E. Y. Webb worked with the American Federation of Labor to ensure the legal status of unions under the Clayton Anti-Trust Act and to finance enforcement of this pro-labor reform with more progressive tax policies.[8] As these middle class reformers sought change from above, North Carolina workers with restricted access to unions and political power embraced mobility as the most effective form of labor protest. If they were unhappy with wages or circumstances, they moved to another mill in search of better pay, sturdier housing, and shorter shifts.[9]

As younger men enlisted and older employees moved from traditional manufacturing jobs into more lucrative war industry positions, America's involvement in the First World War created a fierce competition to retain laborers.[10] A new generation of professional managers offered creative employee and family services, including educational, health, and recreational opportunities, as well as company-controlled labor organizations, which provided the illusion of shared governance while preventing traditional unions.[11] In some ways, the First World War tempered political battles over new protective legislation and regulation of working conditions. Once the United States entered the war, President Wilson established the National War Labor Board (NWLB) to mediate between employers and employees. Under the chairmanship of Frank Walsh, the NWLB defended, however tentatively, the right of southern workers to form unions and engage in collective bargaining with their employers. Many textile workers took full advantage, and between 1914 and 1920, the United Textile Workers (UTW) grew into an industrial union with almost 70,000 members.[12] While only some joined unions, most North Carolina industrial laborers benefited from the higher wages, bonus pay, shorter hours, and company-sponsored services fostered by wartime competition for labor.[13] These advantages, however, were short lived. The armistice brought a rapid rollback of government contracts, leaving textile manufacturers in particular with bloated capacity and stockpiles of unsold goods. As the post-war slump settled across many industries, a rapid decline in wages and working and living conditions radicalized workers throughout the country. In North Carolina, the first textile walkout came in February 1919 after management at the Highland Park Manufacturing Company in Charlotte eliminated wartime bonuses and cut hours of operation. Sympathy strikes followed in Belmont, Concord, and Kannapolis, and workers turned to the UTW for assistance. Between 1919 and 1921, union membership expanded exponentially, and struggles for union recognition and higher wages spread to industrial communities throughout the state.[14]

Post-war economic conditions worked against strikers, as mill managers gladly shut down production, letting labor unrest wear itself out while corporations marketed warehoused backlogs. The UTW lacked resources and could not sustain strikers, and so, despite minimal success in setting wages and limiting hours, most workers returned to jobs without union contracts, while activist leaders were blackballed and unable to find work in North

Carolina. The cotton textile industry did not recover from post-war demo-bilization, becoming one of many older industries that remained depressed throughout the inter-war years. For textile workers in North Carolina who could not transition into a different industry, living and working conditions worsened, and the bright horizons of the First World War gave way to despair. Momentarily silenced, labor frustrations smoldered only to explode again in 1927, when textile workers in Henderson walked off the job and ignited two years of strikes throughout the Carolina Piedmont. Violent clashes between workers and local police, often joined by National Guard soldiers activated by the governor, left martyrs to the cause of economic justice.[15] Before and after the First World War, North Carolina workers launched valiant efforts to break the control of capital and conservative public officials over their lives, but they had little success until the regionwide strikes of 1934, when corporations responded to walkouts and unionization by abandoning the rem-nants of paternalism, breaking up mill villages, and raising wages, effectively destroying the community setting that originally fostered worker activism.[16]

The agricultural and industrial workers of the Tar Heel state developed an activist class consciousness between the 1870s and 1917, putting them in a good position to take advantage of the opportunities World War I offered in terms of progressive legislation that protected workers' rights to unionization, collective bargaining, reasonable hours, and safer working conditions. The fact that many progressive reforms failed in the post-war economic down-turn, despite the mass organization and resistance of workers from diverse industrial, transportation, and agricultural sectors, raises questions about the presence and actions of middle class administrators in North Carolina's businesses and government offices. The next few paragraphs explore issues of labor shortages and recruitment, job creation, and employment through the correspondence of North Carolina's state and local councils of defense. These letters capture the experiences and beliefs of diverse classes of work-ers, reformers, politicians, and employers and speak to the entangled ideol-ogies of race, class, and gender in Progressive era reform, as well as wartime mobilization of labor.

During the First World War, politicians and Council of Defense volunteers often held class-based views of what constituted full-time employment and patriotic labor, views that tended to differ from those of the working peoples they sought to mobilize. Three letters exemplify these divergent perspectives. The all-volunteer membership of North Carolina's state and local councils of defense tended to be male, professional, and from the upper middle classes. Charged with pushing workers and industrialists into wartime production, council members defined full employment and determined who should be fully employed. D. H. Hill, state chairman of the North Carolina Council of Defense, noted in a letter to Spray's Chief of Police: "If these men about whom you write are in the draft ages, they will either have to work forty hours a week or go into the army. . . .[W]arn these people first that they must go to work, and then if they do not heed the warning . . . proceed against them. I hope we can arrest under the vagrancy law any men who are not working."[17] Accompanying Hill's letter, a printed flyer, "Resolutions Adopted by Labor Conference in Raleigh," demanded a mandatory draft of all men ages 18 to 50 and "vigorous suppression of the professional exploiter of labor who is doing so much now to demoralize and disorganize . . . industries." At a time when courts throughout the South provided conscript labor, the resolutions requested that "adequate machinery" be put in place by the state "to enforce the vagrancy laws and to . . . bring the worker and the job quickly in contact."[18] Taken together, the letter and flyer conveyed the council's distrust of North Carolina's working classes. The repeated use of "them" and "these" in reference to workers, who were the subject of "reports" and "warnings" and "arrested as vagrants," set them apart from those in charge. Because of the coercive tone and language used, it is tempting to interpret both as expressions of white supremacist ideals, which is most likely the case, but neither document mentions the race of the laborers to be conscripted, suggesting that all potential laborers were considered fair game.[19]

In October 1918, a middle-aged mother working for the Roanoke Cotton Mills wrote to Governor Bickett describing how difficult it became to provide for her family after her two oldest sons were drafted. Mrs. J. T. Garris claimed that mill management had not only dismissed her youngest son without cause but had also evicted her family from their house in the mill village. She could not find another home large enough for her remaining son, crippled daughter, and herself, and the company refused to let her work in the mill closest to the small house they rented, forcing Garris and her daughter to walk a long distance to work, despite her age and her daughter's infirmity. She implored the governor, "let me have one of my boys back," or at the very least, she hoped he would ask Roanoke Mills to let her work closer to home.[20] To his credit, Bickett followed up on the letter and asked a subordinate to find out what he could about Garris, her sons, and their circumstances. His subordinates passed the governor's request on, and it eventually landed on the desk of James L. Patterson, a manager for the Rosemary Manufacturing Company also in Roanoke Rapids. Patterson made some inquiries, and within a month the Governor received his report. While conceding that the recently widowed mother had made a long-term commitment to Roanoke Mills and that her youngest son, having just lost his father and older brothers, was having difficulty and acting out, Patterson concluded that she was underserving and supported her employer's decision to make life more difficult for Garris and her family. Patterson didn't like Garris, it seems, for several reasons—

she had raised "two families," not one; she had "squandered" life insurance money; and her son was a "degenerate." For Patterson, she was "a type" not a person, and her complaints and concerns could never be justified.[21] These three letters—one from the leader of North Carolina's Council of Defense indicating the need for labor mobilization in the state, the second from an aging working class mother facing serious challenges due in part to wartime circumstances, and the third from a middle class administrator in a North Carolina factory town—serve to highlight class distinctions that operated in the state during the Great War.

Though middle class professionals dominated the government offices and committees tasked with bringing war preparedness to North Carolina, as Link concludes, they seldom demonstrated a clear understanding of the working classes they sought to mobilize, preferring force and intimidation over communication and compassion.[22] For instance, working class recruits complained that the military did not pay soldiers enough to support their families, and so recruitment in North Carolina moved slowly.[23] The discharge files from the 113th Field Artillery Squadron based at Camp Sevier near Greenville, South Carolina, document the financial constraints faced by military families. Colonel Albert Cox received letters from soldiers' friends, wives, and family members asking that they be discharged so that they could come home to earn higher wages. J. R. Winecoff wrote from the town of Glass asking the colonel to assist a soldier's discharge: "He has a wife and 4 little children. The youngest 1 yr old & the oldest 8 and his wife is not strong and they cannot live on the salary Will gets. If you can do anything for him please do it for his family's sake."[24] From Kannapolis, Phylectus Willett complained that she was "physically and financially unable to support herself and 3 children and . . . in need of the support of her husband at home."[25] Similarly, just before enlisting, Corporal George T. Featherston married a woman whose mother, sister, and grandmother lived with them. The mother and grandmother were not physically able to work, and his wife's sister earned only $9.25 per week working for the telephone company. His wife worked as a stenographer for the American Tobacco Company making $60.00 per month but had to resign when their baby was born.[26] The military refused Featherston's discharge application, concluding that the "employer of this soldier's wife should willingly advance sufficient funds to take care of her during her confinement and will undoubtedly do so, if proper request is made."[27] Alternatively, when the vice president of the Wachovia Bank and Trust Company wrote only a month earlier asking that three soldiers formerly in their employ be discharged so that they could rejoin the firm, Colonel Cox issued a quick approval.[28] Discharge files convey a pattern of distrust on the part of military officers for working class soldiers claiming financial hardship but a courteous respect for similar requests made on behalf of white collar enlistees, suggesting that the educated middle classes set themselves apart culturally, politically, and socially from the working classes, both white and black.

Classification of "essential" and "nonessential" jobs, "work or fight" ordinances, and other labor recruitment tactics help weigh the impact of class consciousness on labor relations during the war. Working with local officials, federal and state administrators created a registry of labor so that they could assign workers from the government-maintained pool to employers. The registry discouraged worker mobility as well as intentional competition for laborers between employers.[29] Despite inclusion of representatives of labor on employment boards, reports and recommendations favored employers and management, focusing on punishment and coercion of workers and potential employees. Officials deemed those not doing their part "slackers," a term used in all the correspondence and literature of the day to shame individuals into the fullest level of work deemed appropriate. Indicating the fervent commitment to full employment, a letter addressed to mayors and governing boards throughout the state warned, "If boys over sixteen are not employed, they are in danger of ruin."[30] Lawmakers passed legislation to identify all "slackers" and assign them to employment focused on war production. However, even full employment might not be good enough for government administrators; they classified some jobs as "nonproductive" or "nonessential" and sought to reassign those employed in such positions.[31] North Carolina towns and cities, like Charlotte and New Bern, drafted "work or fight" ordinances, and in some cases, city councils passed them into law. Even as they adopted this course, local and state members of councils of defense recognized that the laws might not be enforceable and were most likely unconstitutional.[32] D. H. Ramsey, Commissioner of Public Safety in Asheville, confided to D.H. Hill, "I am a little fearful that it may not stand the test of the Courts if it is ever seriously attacked; at the same time we are hoping to be able to accomplish the results desired by its enforcement."[33] On August 9, 1918, chairman Hill responded to Ramsey's concerns, agreeing the ordinances were "perhaps of doubtful constitutionality," but noting that before they could "be thrown out by the Supreme Court" the "war will be over and we will not need them so badly."[34] While North Carolina "work or fight" ordinances were similar to the Jim Crow laws that underpinned racial segregation in terms of the demeaning language used and blatant disregard of constitutionally guaranteed rights, neither official correspondence nor the ordinances themselves mention the race of prospective employees, laborer registrants, or slackers, suggesting officials intended they would be applied to all adult males deemed able bodied.[35]

Despite the rhetoric of middle class government officials, many North Carolinians resisted both the labels and the policies associated with labor mobilization efforts. Some factory laborers, for instance, clung to preindustrial and rural values, continuing to move between positions and factories in search of the best employment opportunities. Some resisted bonuses and other incentives offered by manufacturers to encourage them to work longer hours. When employers raised wages, these employees worked fewer hours, taking time off after they earned their typical wage. In other words, maximizing earnings was not the overriding goal for many employees; instead, they valued the ability to keep their own hours, enjoy additional leisure, and control the pace of their workday.[36] Even some employers expressed concern over government definitions of essential and nonessential work. If employees left mills without war-related contracts because they were deemed nonessential, employers overseeing "nonessential" activities might not attract enough workers to maintain production.[37]

As more working age men joined the armed forces and production contracts and employment opportunities expanded, the need for both general and more highly skilled labor burgeoned. When the labor registry and force proved inadequate, government officials worked with employers to identify previously untapped sources of labor, including youth, African Americans, the elderly or retired, and anyone in nonessential positions. For example, officials designated chauffeurs and drivers of any sort, positions often held by African American men, as nonessential, and reassigned them to jobs in war-related production.[38] The First World War extended multiple and new economic opportunities to African American men and women, not only in the military but also in southern and national industrial labor markets, creating another wave in the mass exodus of black people from the South known as the Great Migration.[39] As African American men entered the military in large numbers and black men and women sought opportunities in the North, labor shortages in North Carolina grew more acute, making it easier for black people who did not enlist or relocate to move from agriculture into manufacturing positions.[40] Large numbers of African American women worked in North Carolina's tobacco processing and cigarette factories, employment designated a "patriotic necessity" during the war.[41] Other untapped groups included young people who had not previously worked and older individuals who had already retired. In New Hanover County, the Council of Defense coordinated with the YMCA's Boys' Working Reserve in Wilmington to provide laborers for farms in the surrounding countryside, and many retired physicians and nurses returned to clinics and hospitals to fill the void created when their younger colleagues volunteered for the military.[42]

Though close to twenty percent of North Carolina's industrial labor force was female in 1914, many middle class white women did not work outside the home, and as labor shortages worsened, councils of defense targeted them as a new source of potential employees. During the First World War, North Carolina women worked as unpaid volunteers and as wage earners in the military, private business, and industry.[43] Once the Red Cross set up a home services section, they hired female social workers to assist soldiers' families. Some had just graduated from state colleges, but those without degrees trained for the positions in educational institutes provided by the Red Cross.[44] Many women worked alongside men on committees, in board rooms and hospitals, and in other capacities previously closed to them.[45] Miss F. C. Abbott chaired a Subcommittee on Women in Industry within the Woman's Committee of the Council of Defense. Tasked with moving women into nonessential positions so that men could be released to fill the estimated 1.5 million vacancies in essential wartime jobs, the subcommittee drew middle class white women into the labor force.[46] Men who failed to either enlist or take on essential jobs were "looked upon as slackers" under the broader "work or fight" ordinances, and community labor boards insisted "that no man shall occupy a position which a woman can fill." The definition of nonessential positions was flexible and evolved as the war progressed, but it began with "clerks and office help, ticket-sellers of all kinds, and attendants."[47] In the name of wartime demands for labor, officials redefined or regendered some formerly male jobs for women, and many of those jobs never returned to the male domain. Wartime administrators tended to define jobs typically held by African American men or by women as nonessential, slighting black masculinity as well as women's contributions.[48]

Because racial segregation hampered communication between the largely white members of the state Council of Defense and North Carolina's African American communities, local council members contacted black community leaders, typically ministers, principals, or teachers, in an effort to work across racial barriers. In Wilmington, Dr. A. J. Wilson, Presiding Elder of the Colored Methodist Church, and George F. King, "a writer of superior merit," helped to organize the African American community in support of the Council of Defense. Similar to Janet Hudson's findings in South Carolina, white administrators praised leading blacks in Wilmington and other North Carolina towns who contributed time and money to the war effort.[49] African Americans volunteered in large numbers to assist young men in registering for the armed services and to provide welcome stations, aid for military families, bandages, food, and more. Not only did African American men volunteer for the military in record numbers, black recruits were approved for service at substantially higher rates than white recruits, and they received less training before boarding ships bound for Europe. Additionally, most African American soldiers from North Carolina and all states served as manual laborers, most prominently as stevedores, unloading multiple tons of arms, rations, and supplies in record time.[50] African American women in North Carolina volunteered and worked as nurses, Red Cross nurse's aides, and in all relief programs.[51] At the same time, African American community leaders, such as Nathaniel S. Hargrave of Parmele, took the opportunity created by wartime preparedness and outreach to draw attention to educational needs in black communities: "I sat in the room where men registered . . . and I tell you Sir it was a sad thing to see strong looking young men shake their heads no; when asked to sign their names." He went on to argue that literacy in the African American community would provide more skilled labor for both military and nonmilitary employers, but this required better funding for schools: "$200.00 will pay the salary of seven teachers each month," he noted.[52]

The state Councils of Defense made constant demands on local council members and other community leaders, black and white, to organize volunteers, enforce regulations, and encourage efficient use of labor and resources. At times their demands became intrusive, if not disruptive, and some citizens refused to cooperate. In one instance, Chairman D. H. Hill expressed his frustration: "North Carolina people are so slow to report that I often am at a loss to know what has been done."[53] As the war progressed, those who had repeatedly responded with energy and initiative to calls for volunteer labor and committee service increasingly refused, noting their own overtaxed schedules and the inefficiency of overlapping organizations at the local level. In one case, James Sprunt, president of the Wilmington cotton dealership of Alexander Sprunt and Son, expressed his exasperation with the Council of Defense's ongoing solicitations for more volunteers and more committees: "With deference to the patriotic purposes of these additional organizations, do you not think it is about time to call a halt and concentrate upon those already established?"[54] While clearly irritated with the local council, African American Thomas Knight sought to reassure them of his patriotism: "I am glad to be of such service as my feeble capacity will permit, and whatever you or the local committee shall command I shall take pleasure in obeying . . . [and] will make use of my best endeavors to prove myself worthy of the same, and to show my countrymen that I am no 'slacker.' I hate the word."[55] Lynn Williamson, chairman of the Alamance County Council of Defense, complained that a government building project in Burlington would engage "all surplus . . . carpenters, brick masons, laborers, plumbers, and electric linemen," most of whom were to be diverted from the city's textile manufacturers, "to put up this building . . .which is most unnecessary work." The textile manufacturers of Alamance County, he noted, "engaged in necessary work. The erection of this building is opposed by the best citizens all over the County. . . . [H]eads of Government are urging the people to stop all unnecessary work while they themselves are engaging in the most unnecessary work."[56] Expressions of frustration and noncooperation with government officials came from all classes and races, suggesting a lack of consensus on how best to achieve wartime labor preparedness.

While restrictions reduced employment in some sectors, government contracts for war production created new jobs in others. In May 1917, the

Durham Hosiery Mills won a $55,000 contract to supply 550,000 pairs of cotton socks for the Navy, securing employment for hundreds of hosiery operatives.[57] More exciting for many North Carolinians, federal officials selected Wilmington for the construction of shipyards expected to create thousands of jobs, increasing the city's population by some ten to fifteen thousand.[58] As labor shortages deepened and the need for ships became urgent, attracting workers became a priority task assigned to the shipyards' chief engineers.[59] In a letter marked "Skilled Workmen," the local council chairman in Graham received orders to register applicants interested in moving to Wilmington, and officials asked George F. Newman, president of the Newman Machine Company in Greensboro, to supply laborers for the shipyard out of his own workforce.[60] Newman replied to the Council of Defense in Raleigh somewhat heatedly, suggesting that the government tone down its rhetoric and provide more factual information: "From some of the speeches that have been made . . . a large number of our men have gotten the impression that the Government ship yards are going to draft all skilled mechanics regardless of what class they have been put in by the exemption boards. . . . We know that this is not the intention of the Government, but it has created unrest among our men, and we ask that you kindly give us information."[61] Other industries had similar problems. One of the largest wartime projects in North Carolina was the construction of Fort Bragg, a U.S. Army training facility located near Fayetteville, which the War Industries Board classified as an "A-1 Priority." It was to be the "the largest artillery camp in the East" and would require some 7000 skilled carpenters and an additional 7000 laborers to construct. There was not enough labor in North Carolina to cover requirements, so agents worked through the US Employment Service to recruit workers from other states, circumventing restrictions on labor competition approved for only the most urgent projects.[62] Clearly, wartime production needs offered multiple opportunities for skilled and general workers in North Carolina, be they black, white, male, or female.

Agriculture was among the most essential labor sectors for the war effort, and state officials publicized the farm products required for war preparedness and encouraged those with arable land to cultivate them. For instance, a shortage of lubricating oil for military airplane engines meant that North Carolina farmers needed to commit acreage to the production of castor oil beans.[63] There was also a spike in the demand for food, as troops, imprisoned draft dodgers, and workers congregated in previously unknown numbers increased dependence on the food surplus produced by agricultural laborers. Vegetables, meats, and fruits had to be cultivated, harvested, slaughtered, processed, and packaged in canneries before being shipped to military installations in the states and abroad to war zones. Likewise, increased demand on the food supply fostered concomitant domestic shortages.[64] Home and farm extension workers attempted to convey information on what needed to be produced to farming families throughout North Carolina, but communication across racial and gender barriers proved more difficult in rural communities than in urban and industrial settings. In a letter to James Sprunt of Wilmington addressing agricultural labor, Chairman Hill indicated that outreach to African Americans was not going well: "The work among the negroes needs to be pressed. . . . I wish we could pay the expenses of several negro workers to give their whole time to service among their race."[65] Volunteer labor loomed large in food processing, as officials urged women throughout the state to plant garden plots in backyards, in flower pots, on urban rooftops, or wherever they could find the space. Home economists expanded efforts to teach rural and urban women alike the art of canning produce to stock pantries for the winter months. In some cases, they set up community canneries where women gathered to process and preserve the harvest. Many women donated food to Red Cross Soldiers' Aid Committees to stock hospitality counters at train depots and other points of departure where soldiers waited before being transported to training camps or boarding ships for Europe.[66]

Most of North Carolina's soldiers and sailors came from farms; some owned their own farms, while others were sharecroppers, tenants, day laborers, or sons of farming families. Whatever their position in the agricultural economy, removal to military service created labor shortages, particularly during planting and harvest seasons. One task of the Red Cross Soldiers' Aid Committees was to recruit workers to gather "the crops of absent soldiers."[67] Labor shortages continued throughout America's involvement in the war, and in 1919, as the ceasefire took hold, many farmers waited anxiously for sons and laborers to muster out and return to help with the planting and harvest. If they arrived in the spring, veteran sons and employees could assist with putting in the crop, and if they mustered out in July or August, they would be home in time for the fall harvest. An attorney from Yanceyville wrote on behalf of farmers: "Is there any provision made . . . whether men who have their places waiting for them will be mustered out sooner than the others[?] . . . [T]his is an agricultural county and all the boys who left the county can return and take their same positions."[68] The wartime agricultural labor shortage proved particularly detrimental for smaller farms and farming families.

The Tuttle family owned a small farm just outside Elizabeth City where they were raising five children when their oldest son joined the service. He assisted his father in planting just before shipping out, but the family could not find laborers for the harvest. They relied on their son's labor, so much so that he requested a percentage of his military wages be sent home, but the Army refused to comply with his request. Mrs. Tuttle wrote to Governor Bickett early in 1919, "Dear Governer [sic] just think what $15 pr month means for a man of the farm with labor $2.00 pr day and scarce at that the Government had to take the boys . . . but we do need a living." She noted that her husband "could have taken his saw and hatchet and gone to Norfolk and have gotten $8 or $10 pr [*sic*] day as many did but no he stuck to his crop." They relied on neighbor girls to collect their guano but did not know how they were going to manage at harvest time, "if there isn't something done to get the farm boys home to work the crop this year or some allowance made so farmers can get help." Like many others, Tuttle challenged the wisdom of officials who did not seem to comprehend the urgent need for agricultural laborers: "People who are educated say rent your land out but little farms like ours wouldn't rent out and near support our family besides we have to stay somewhere." She went on to predict scarcity in agricultural products and to describe how the tenancy system was collapsing: "At wages farmers can afford to pay cotton stayed in the fields this fall lots of it there now." Even if the farmer could rent out land to a tenant or sharecropper, the tenant might plant the crop but soon abandon it to take a job that paid wages, leaving little or no profit for the landowner. She underlined the labor shortage by recalling her youth and her father's truck farming practices: "I have known my father to go out after supper and hire 10 or 12 hands for next day." With direct references to the racial hierarchy in southern agriculture, she noted the departure of black sharecroppers, tenants, and day laborers from the available labor pool: "Last year you could have looked all day and until bedtime and couldn't" find anyone willing to help in the fields. Representative of a petit, white, agricultural bourgeoisie, Tuttle understood the labor shortage in agriculture from the perspective of race and class: "what are the farmers that his help has been taken. . . . [P]eople with education that are making good money can live but what will we do if our boys stay and we cant [*sic*] get our support off the farm."[69] Letters like Tuttle's capture unheard voices and complicate explanations of class distinctions in the changing labor conditions fostered by the First World War.

In the post-war years, neither the supply of farm labor nor farm profitability returned to the pre-war status quo. Many farm workers moved permanently into the industrial labor force, and small-scale farming declined as the century progressed. In particular, thousands of African American tenant farmers and sharecroppers left the land and found employment in the service and industrial sectors of northern and southern cities. Likewise, the North Carolina cotton textile industry did not fully recover from the post-war collapse, though other industries—such as cigarettes, paper, meat processing, furniture, and even particular textile sectors, including woolens, worsteds, and rayon—fared better in the interwar years. Fort Bragg survived budget cuts and became one of the largest employers in the state, and communication, transportation, and power generation facilities developed during the war grew to employ thousands of North Carolinians. While textile workers organized to achieve higher wages, improved living and working conditions, as well as union representation in the 1930s, right-to-work legislation passed in the 1940s institutionalized the ongoing collaborative resistance of politicians and industrialists to collective bargaining rights for both blue and white collar laborers. Similar efforts on the part of the Sharecroppers and Tenant Farmers Union, the Tobacco Workers International Union, and the Amalgamated Association of Street and Electric Railway Employees met with some success during the Great Depression, though as in textiles, these victories were often of limited duration.[70]

The correspondence of North Carolina's state and local councils of defense indicates that the Great War nurtured divergent expectations among North Carolina's laboring and professional classes. Most workers made willing sacrifices for the war effort, though a healthy skepticism informed their evaluation of soldiers' wages and both military and nonmilitary demands on their families, labor, and time. White collar managers and administrators embraced progressive ideals of efficiency and measured individual contributions on the homefront by the number of hours worked and the significance of the jobs performed. Their determination of what constituted significant or essential labor, however, was corrupted by constructions of race and gender, as well as institutional momentum. Terms such as "slacker," "nonessential," "idler," and "degenerate" peppered the correspondence of council members and other officials, but they were careful not to associate these words with a particular "race" in writing. Other primary sources, such as arrest records and court transcripts, might reveal a more overt white supremacy in the enforcement of North Carolina's labor policies during World War I, but in councils of defense communications that language was avoided.[71] The language they did use conveyed a distrust and disrespect of workers who did not respond as officials believed they should to government and administrative conceptions of wartime labor demands. Secondary texts based on meticulous primary research document racial discrimination in the recruitment, training, housing, and treatment of African American soldiers in World War I, as well as of African Americans in early twentieth-century southern society more generally, but North Carolina's councils of defense correspondence reveals a class-based pattern of coercion.[72] The goal of the politically and economically empowered classes in both cases was to control laboring peoples and to undermine their unification across race and gender barriers. Caught in both an American and southern paradox, those who orchestrated North Carolina's World War I labor policies spoke the language of progressive reform while simultaneously encouraging the repression of laboring peoples, their activism, and their unions.

Notes

1. William A. Link, *The Paradox of Southern Progressivism, 1880–1930* (Chapel Hill: The University of North Carolina Press, 1992), kindle location [kl] 858—1293.

2. Janet G. Hudson, *Entangled by White Supremacy: Reform in World War I-era South Carolina* (Lexington: The University of Kentucky Press, 2009), 7, 78–82, 164–175.

3. Philip S. Foner, *History of the Labor Movement in the United States, vol. 2, From the Founding of The A.F. of L. to the Emergence of American Imperialism* (New York: International Publishers, 1977), 47–234, 261–278; Philip S. Foner, *History of the Labor Movement in the United States, vol. 4, The Industrial Workers of the World 1905–1917* (New York: International Publishers, 1980), 40–113, 214–390, 473–548; Philip S. Foner, *History of the Labor Movement in the United States, vol. 6, On the Eve of America's Entrance into World War I, 1915–1916* (New York: International Publishers, 1982), 13–122, 143–188.

4. David Montgomery, *The Fall of the House of Labor: The Workplace, the State, and American Labor Activism, 1865–1925* (New York: Cambridge University Press, 1989), 214–329.

5. Foner, *History of the Labor Movement in the United States, vol. 2,* 279–344, 388–403; Link, *The Paradox of Southern Progressivism,* kl 858–1293; Hudson, *Entangled by White Supremacy,* 185–205.

6. Hudson, *Entangled by White Supremacy,* 1–2; Gavin Wright, *Old South New South: Revolutions in the Southern Economy since the Civil War* (New York: Basic Books, 1986), 124–197.

7. Jacquelyn Dowd Hall, Robert Korstad, and James Leloudis, "Cotton Mill People: Work, Community, and Protest in the Textile South, 1880–1940," *American Historical Review* 91, no. 2 (April 1986): 259; Wright, *Old South New South,* 64–70, 116.

8. George B. Tindall, *The Emergence of the New South, 1913–1945* (Baton Rouge: Louisiana State University, 1967), 4–16, 30–31, 43–44.

9. Jacquelyn Dowd Hall et al., *Like a Family: The Making of a Southern Cotton Mill World* (New York: W.W. Norton & Company, 1987), 105–109.

10. Hall, *Like a Family,* 183–184.

11. Pamela C. Edwards, "In Good Faith': Labor Policies in the Durham Hosiery Mills, 1895–1925," *North Carolina Historical Review* 81, no. 4 (October 2004): 370–376; Tindall, *The Emergence of the New South,* 325–326.

12. Hall, *Like a Family,* 185–187; Peter S. Foner, *History of the Labor Movement in the United States Vol. 7: Labor and World War I, 1914–1918* (New York: International Publishers, 1987), 174–176.

13. Edwards, "In Good Faith," 378–391; Hall, *Like a Family,* 183–187; Tindall, *The Emergence of the New South,* 321–329.

14. Hall, *Like a Family,* 183–195; Edwards, "In Good Faith," 379–392; Tindall, *The Emergence of the New South,* 318–341; Philip S. Foner, *History of the Labor Movement in the United States Vol. 8: Postwar Struggles, 1918–1920* (New York: International Publishers, 1988), 63–169.

15. Hall, *Like a Family,* 195–236; Tindall, *The Emergence of the New South,* 339–353: Philip S. Foner, *History of the Labor Movement in the United States, vol. 10, The T.U.E.L., 1925–1929* (New York: International Publishers, 1994), 271–291.

16. Hall, *Like a Family,* 353–357; Tindall, *The Emergence of the New South,* 505–539.

17. D. H. Hill, Chairman, to H. Eanes, Chief of Police, Spray, NC (July 1, 1918), Labor, North Carolina Council of Defense Records, WWI 1, World War I Papers (WWI), Military Collection (MC), State Archives of North Carolina (SANC), Raleigh, NC.

18. "Resolutions Adopted by Labor Conference in Raleigh" (June 4, 1918), Labor, North Carolina Council of Defense Records, WWI 1, WWI, MC, SANC.

19. While Council of Defense correspondence does not document white supremacist enforcement of work or fight ordinances, secondary scholarship supports my conclusion that wartime labor policies "most likely" singled out and unfairly targeted black North Carolinians. See Glenda Elizabeth Gilmore, *Gender and Jim Crow: Women and the Politics of White Supremacy in North Carolina, 1896–1920* (University of North Carolina Press, 1996); J. Timothy Cole, *The Forest City Lynching of 1900: Populism, Racism, and White Supremacy in Rutherford County, North Carolina* (McFarland, 2003); David Cunningham, *Klansville, U.S.A.: The Rise and Fall of the Civil Rights-Era Ku Klux Klan* (Oxford Reprint Edition, 2014); Amy Louise Wood, *Lynching and Spectacle: Witnessing Racial Violence in America, 1890–1940* (University of North Carolina Press, 2011). The masking of white supremacy with progressive and patriotic phrases and the exclusion of

racist terminology represents part of Link's analysis in *The Paradox of Southern Progressivism*. In other words, language mattered, and at least some of the Progressives knew this and used terms as well as omissions to disguise the inherent racism embedded in policies and practiced through implementation of those policies. Link also indicates a class-based language, which disguised negative stereotypes of poor whites and the working classes, particularly those living in Appalachia, with the rhetoric of the Social Gospel, a Christian interpretation of progressive reform.

20. Mrs. J. T. Garris, Roanoke Rapids, to Goverent [*sic*] Bickett (October 7, 1918), Soldiers' Families, North Carolina Council of Defense Records, WWI 1, WWI, MC, SANC.

21. James L. Patterson, Rosemary Manufacturing Company, Roanoke Rapids, to W. E. Daniel, Chairman, Committee on Home Relief, American Red Cross (November 22, 1918), Soldiers' Families, North Carolina Council of Defense Records, WWI 1, WWI, MC, SANC.

22. Link, *The Paradox of Southern Progressivism*, kl 43–52, 1294–3522; Hudson, *Entangled by White Supremacy*, 101–147.

23. S. R. Winters, "Debate Plans to Help Recruiting. . . ," *News & Observer* (Raleigh, NC) (May 10, 1917), Durham, News Clippings cover and pages 3–30, *Everywoman's Magazine*, WWI 1, WWI, MC, SANC; John R. Finger, "Conscription, Citizenship, and 'Civilization': World War I and the Eastern Band of Cherokee," *The North Carolina Historical Review* 63, no. 3 (July 1986): 283–308; Jeanette Keith, "The Politics of Southern Draft Resistance, 1917–1918: Class, Race, and Conscription in the Rural South," *The Journal of American History* 87, no. 4 (March 2001): 1335–1361; Roger William Riis, "Combing the Draft for Slackers. . . ," *The American Legion Weekly* (January 30, 1920): 1–2, accessed August 12, 2014, http://www.oldmagazinearticles.com /-wwl_draft_dodgers_pdf.

24. J. A. Winecoff, Glass, NC, to Colonel Albert Cox, Greenville, SC (October 20, 1919), Discharges (general), Military Organizations, WWI 7, WWI, MC, SANC.

25. Harold G. Cauble, Kannapolis, NC, to Colonel Cox, Greenville, SC (October 23, 1917); Eulalia P. Nantz, Affidavit Sworn before C. E. Sour, Notary Public, Cabarrus County, NC (October 30, 1917) along with multiple related letters, Discharges (general), Military Organizations, WWI 7, WWI, MC, SANC.

26. Corporal George F. Featherston, Battery "C" 113th F. A., to Commanding General, A. E. F. (July 6, 1918), Discharges (general), Military Organizations, WWI 7, WWI, MC, SANC.

27. E. E. Boyce, Captain 113th F. A., Adjutant, orders (July 6, 1918); Nollie W. Blount "b" 113th F. F., A. E. F. to C. O. Battery "E", 113th F. A., A. E. F. (January 6, 1919); Alfred W. Horton, Captain 113th F. A. to Wiley C. Rodman, Captain 113th F. A. (January 2, 1919 and January 6, 1919), Discharges (general), Military Organizations, WWI 7, WWI, MC, SANC.

28. Vice President, Wachovia Bank & Trust, Winston Salem, NC, to Colonel Albert L. Cox, Greenville, SC (December 24, 1918); Albert L. Cox, Colonel, 113th F. A. Commanding, memo (December 26, 1918), Discharges (general), Military Organizations, WWI 7, WWI, MC, SANC.

29. William Browne Hall, Assistant Chief, to W. S. Wilson, Secretary, NC Council of Defense, Raleigh (July 27, 1917); J. B. Densmore, Director General, Department of Labor, to J. B. Ramsey, President, First National Bank, Rocky Mount, NC (July 23, 1918); Henry P. Kendall, Chairman, Committee on Industrial Relations, "Organization of Local Labor Administrations," Chamber of Commerce of the United States (July 18, 1918), Labor, North Carolina Council of Defense Records, WWI 1, WWI, MC, SANC.

30. D. H. Hill, Chairman, to the Mayors and Governing Boards (August 6, 1918), Labor, North Carolina Council of Defense Records, WWI 1, WWI, MC, SANC.

31. J. A. Roland, West Jefferson, NC, to North Carolina Council of Defense (July 19, 1918); D. H. Hill to Mayor F. I. Sutton, Kinston, NC (August 26, 1918); D. H. Hill to H.F. Robinson, Lincolnton, NC (August 26, 1918), Labor, North Carolina Council of Defense Records, WWI 1, WWI, MC, SANC.

32. Thomas Griffith to D. H. Hill, Chairman, Raleigh, NC (August 2, 1918); J. G. McCormick, Chair, New Hanover County Council of Defense, to D. H. Hill (August 8, 1918); Mandel Sener,

Secretary-Manager, Chamber of Commerce, New Bern, NC, to D. H. Hill, Chairman (August 9, 1918); D. H. Hill, Chairman, to D. H. Ramsey, Commissioner of Public Safety, Asheville, NC (August 9, 1918), Labor, North Carolina Council of Defense Records, WWI 1, WWI, MC, SANC.

33. D. H. Ramsey, Commissioner of Public Safety, Asheville, to D.H. Hill, Chairman, (August 7, 1918), Labor, North Carolina Council of Defense Records, WWI 1, WWI, MC, SANC.

34. D. H. Hill, Chairman, to D. H. Ramsey, Commissioner of Public Safety, Asheville, NC (August 9, 1918), Labor, North Carolina Council of Defense Records, WWI 1, WWI, MC, SANC.'

35. Please see endnote 19 above for secondary sources documenting the history of white supremacy in North Carolina.

36. Hall, *Like a Family*, 184; Tindall, *The Emergence of the New South*, 324–333.

37. E. S. Parker Jr., Graham, NC, to D. H. Hill, Chairman (August 31, 1918), Labor, North Carolina Council of Defense Records, WWI 1, WWI, MC, SANC.

38. J. A. Roland, Ashe Supply & Hardware Co., West Jefferson to Council of Defense, West Jefferson, NC (July 19, 1918), Labor, North Carolina Council of Defense Records, WWI 1, WWI, MC, SANC.

39. Wright, *Old South New South*, 52, 64–70.

40. Michael Sistrom, "North Carolinians and the Great War: The Impact of World War I on the Tar Heel State—Introduction to the Home Front," Documenting the American South, (University Library. The University of North Carolina at Chapel Hill, 2004; hereafter cited as DocSouth), accessed August 12, 2014, http://docsouth.unc.edu/wwi/-homeintro.html; Chad Williams, "African Americans and World War I," *Africana Age: African & African Diasporan Transformations in the 20th Century*, accessed August 12, 2014, http://exhibitions.nypl.org /africanaage/essay-world-war-i.html; Leslie Brown, *Upbuilding Black Durham: Gender, Class, and Black Community Development in the Jim Crow South* (Chapel Hill: The University of North Carolina Press, 2008), kl 4573–4734.

41. Tindall, *The Emergence of the New South*, 58–59; Leslie Brown and Anne Valk, "Black Durham Behind the Veil: A Case Study," *OAH Magazine of History* (January 2004): 23–27; Brown, *Upbuilding Black Durham*, kl 477–483, 4378–4573.

42. C. Walton Johnson, Boys' Work Secretary, YMCA, Wilmington, NC, to J. G. McCormick, Chairman, New Hanover Co., North Carolina Council of Defense (July 31, 1917), Boys' Working Reserve; J. G. McCormick, Chairman, to Maj. J. W. Long, Greensboro, NC (July 17, 1917); J. G. McCormick, Chairman, to Jackson Greer, Esq., Chairman, Whiteville, NC (July 26, 1917); J .L. Long, Major MRC, United States, to J. G. McCormick, Chairman, Wilmington, NC (July 25, 1917); Chairman to C. F. Harvey, Kinston, NC (August 2, 1918); "Excerpts from Report of Committee on Nursing of the General Medical Board of the Council of National Defense," (October 21, 1917), Committee on Health & Sanitation, North Carolina Council of Defense Records, WWI 1, WWI, MC, SANC; D. H. Hill, Chairman, to County Chairman (October 15, 1918), Warren – Correspondence of Walter G. Rogers; "All of the ten medical men in Warren, according to Dr. W.P. Perry, in a statement" (September 3, 1918) [newspaper clipping p. 89], Warren County War Activities, North Carolina County War Records, WWI 2, WWI, MC, SANC.

43. Archibald Henderson, "North Carolina Women in the World War: An Address," North Carolina Literary and Historical Collection (1920) DocSouth, accessed August 12, 2014, http:// docsouth.unc.edu/wwi/henderson/menu.html; Soldiers' Business Aid Committee, Organization of; Correspondence of Laura Holmes Reilley, Chair, Woman's Committee, North Carolina Council of Defense Records, WWI 1, WWI, MC, SANC; Correspondence and other records, Sistrom, "North Carolinians and the Great War," DocSouth.

44. Joseph C. Logan, Director of Civilian Relief, The American Red Cross, to All Red Cross Chapters in the South Division, (n.d.) ARC Correspondence and other records, Soldiers' Business Aid Committee, North Carolina Council of Defense Records, WWI 1, WWI, MC, NCSA; Sistrom, "North Carolinians and the Great War"; Henderson, "North Carolina Women in the World War," DocSouth.

45. William J. Breen, "Southern Women in the War: The North Carolina Woman's Committee, 1917–1919," *The North Carolina Historical Review* 55, no. 3 (July 1978): 251–283; William J. Breen, "Black Women and the Great War: Mobilization and Reform in the South," *The Journal of Southern History* 44, no. 3 (August 1978): 421–440.

46. William Browne Hall, Assistant Chief, Section on Cooperation with States, to W. S. Wilson, Secretary, North Carolina Council of Defense, Raleigh (July 27, 1917), Labor; Correspondence of Laura Holmes Reilley, Chair, Woman's Committee, North Carolina Council of Defense Records, WWI 1, WWI, MC, SANC.

47. "Non-Essentials' to be Listed by Labor Boards," North Carolina Council of Defense (n.d.), Labor, North Carolina Council of Defense Records, WWI 1, WWI, MC, SANC.

48. Breen, "Black Women," 421–440; Valarie J. Conner, "The Mothers of the Race in World War I: The National War Labor Board and Women in Industry," *Labor History* 21, no. 1 (Winter 1979/1980): 31–54; William Graebner et al., "Notes and Documents: Uncle Sam Just Loves the Ladies: Sex Discrimination in the Federal Government, 1917," *Labor History* 21, no. 1 (Winter 1979/1980): 75–85; Maurine Weiner Greenwald, "Women Workers and World War I: The American Railroad Industry, A Case Study," *The Journal of Social History* 9, no. 2 (Winter 1975): 154–177.

49. James Sprunt, Wilmington, NC, to D. H. Hill, Chairman (December 14, 1917), Negroes, North Carolina Council of Defense Records, WWI 1, WWI, MC, SANC; Hudson, *Entangled by White Supremacy*, 103–108.

50. Arthur E. Barbeau and Florette Henri, *The Unknown Soldiers: Black American Troops in World War I* (Philadelphia: Temple University Press, 1974),34–55, 89–110.

51. Thomas H. Knight to D. H. Hill, Chairman (December 21, 1917), Negroes, North Carolina Council of Defense Records, WWI 1, WWI, MC, SANC.

52. Correspondence, Nathaniel S. Hargrave to D. H. Hill, Chairman (September 25, 1918), Negroes, North Carolina Council of Defense Records, WWI 1, WWI, MC, SANC.

53. D. H. Hill, Chairman, to Fred W. Dick, Wilmington, NC (August 15, 1918), Soldier's Business Aid Committee – New Hanover, North Carolina Council of Defense Records, WWI 1, WWI, MC, SANC.

54. James Sprunt, Wilmington, NC, to D. H. Hill, Raleigh (September 18, 1917), Soldier's Business Aid Committee – New Hanover, North Carolina Council of Defense Records, WWI 1, WWI, MC, SANC.

55. Thomas H. Knight to D. H. Hill, Chairman (December 21, 1917), Negroes, North Carolina Council of Defense Records, WWI 1, WWI, MC, SANC.

56. Lynn Williamson, Chairman, Alamance County, to D. H. Hill, Chairman (February 19, 1918), Public Service Reserve, United States; From unknown to Lynn Williamson (February 20, 1918), Skilled Labor, North Carolina Council of Defense Records, WWI 1, WWI, MC, SANC.

57. "Durham Hosiery Mills Awarded Big Contract," *Greensboro Daily News* (May 15, 1917); *Everywoman's Magazine, 3, nos. 6–7,* [clippings] Durham, North Carolina County War Records, WWI 2, WWI, MC, SANC.

58. J. G. McCormick, Chairman, New Hanover County, to Dr. D. H. Hill, Chairman, Raleigh (April 25, 1918), Committee on Health & Sanitation, North Carolina Council of Defense Records, WWI 1, WWI, MC, SANC.

59. James Sprunt, Alexander Sprunt and Son Cotton, Wilmington, NC, to Hon. D. H. Hill, State Council of Defense, Raleigh (February 11, 1918); DHH [D.H. Hill], Chairman, Raleigh, to James Sprunt, Wilmington, NC (February 12, 1918), Shipbuilding, North Carolina Council of Defense Records, WWI 1, WWI, MC, SANC.

60. D. H. Hill [illegible] to Lynn B. Williamson, Graham, NC (February 20, 1918); George F. Newman, President, Newman Machine Co., Greensboro, NC, to W. S. Wilson, Secretary, Raleigh (February 12, 1918), Skilled Labor, North Carolina Council of Defense Records, WWI 1, WWI, MC, SANC.

61. George F. Newman, President, Newman Machine Co., Greensboro, NC, to W. S. Wilson, Secretary, Raleigh (February 12, 1918), Skilled Labor, North Carolina Council of Defense Records, WWI 1, WWI, MC, SANC.

62. H. W. Baum, Manager, James Stewart & Co., Inc., Camp Bragg, Fayetteville, NC, to Hon. T. W. Bickett, Governor, Marshall, NC (September 14, 1918), Labor, North Carolina Council of Defense Records, WWI 1, WWI, MC, SANC.

63. James Sprunt, Alexander Sprunt and Son Cotton, Wilmington, NC, to D. H. Hill, Chairman, Raleigh (February 11, 1918), Shipbuilding, North Carolina Council of Defense Records, WWI 1, WWI, MC, SANC.

64. James W. Sullivan, Assistant to Samuel Gompers, Advisory Commission of the Council of National Defense, Washington, DC, to Joseph Hyde, Geological and Economic Survey, Chapel Hill, NC (June 22, 1917), Labor, North Carolina Council of Defense Records, WWI 1, WWI, MC, SANC.

65. D. H. Hill, Chairman, Raleigh, NC, to James Sprunt, Wilmington, NC (February 12, 1918), Shipbuilding, North Carolina Council of Defense Records, WWI 1, WWI, MC, SANC.

66. and other records, Soldiers' Business Aid Committee; Correspondence of Laura Holmes Reilley, Chair, Woman's Committee, North Carolina Council of Defense Records, WWI 1, WWI, MC, SANC; Sistrom, "North Carolinians and the Great War," DocSouth.

67. T. L. Caudle, Robinson, Caudle & Pruette, Wadesboro, NC, to D. H. Hill, Chairman, Raleigh (September 7, 1918), Soldier's Bus Aid – Anson, North Carolina Council of Defense Records, WWI 1, WWI, MC, SANC.

68. Robert T. Wilson, Attorney-at-Law, Yanceyville, NC, to D. H. Hill, Raleigh (December 14, 1918), Soldier's Business Aid Committee – Caswell, North Carolina Council of Defense Records, WWI 1, WWI, MC, SANC.

69. Mrs. J. F. Tuttle, Elizabeth City, NC, to the Governor of NC (January 20, 1919), Soldiers' Families, North Carolina Council of Defense Records, WWI 1, WWI, MC, SANC.

70. Beverly Jones and Claudia Egelhoff, eds., *Working in Tobacco: An Oral History of Durham's Tobacco Factory Workers* (Chapel Hill: Internet Archive, University of North Carolina, 2012), 4–11; John N. Schacht, "Toward Industrial Unionism: Bell Telephone Workers and Company Unions, 1919–1937," *Labor History* 16, no. 1 (Winter 1975): 5–36; Russell Allen review of John N. Schacht, *The Making of Telephone Unionism, 1920–1947,* in *Industrial and Labor Relations Review* 41, no. 1 (October 1987), 166–168; Jeffrey M. Leatherwood, " 'Battle of the Barn': Charlotte's 1919 Streetcar Strike in Rhetoric and Reality" *Journal of North Carolina Association of Historians* 19 (April 2011): 52–82; Jeffrey M. Leatherwood, " 'Grant Us a Contract': Spartanburg as Prelude to the Carolina Regional Transit Strike," *Proceedings of the South Carolina Historical Association* (2009), 41–57; Wiley J. Williams, "Right to Work Law," in ed. William S. Powell, *Dictionary of North Carolina Biography*, NCPedia, http://www.ncpedia.org/right-work-law.

71. Please see endnote 19 above for secondary sources documenting the history of white supremacy in North Carolina.

72. Barbeau and Henri, *The Unknown Soldiers*, 34–55, 89–110; Williams, *Torchbearers of Democracy*, 95–98, 195–196.

CONTRIBUTORS

A recent graduate of the Public Policy Ph.D. Program at the University of North Carolina at Charlotte, **LAUREN A. AUSTIN** completed her dissertation on the 1918–1919 influenza epidemic in North Carolina. She also graduated from the University of North Carolina at Chapel Hill and earned an MA in history at UNC Charlotte.

EVAN P. BENNETT is an associate professor of history at Florida Atlantic University. He is the author of *When Tobacco Was King: Families, Farm Labor, and Federal Policy in the Piedmont* (2014) and co-editor of *Beyond Forty Acres and a Mule: African American Landowning Families since Reconstruction* (2012).

JIM BISSETT is professor of history at Elon University. He is the author of *Agrarian Socialism in America: Marx, Jefferson, and Jesus in the Oklahoma Countryside, 1904–1920*, which received the Oklahoma Historical Society's award for best book on Oklahoma history in 2000. He has a PhD from Duke University.

SHANNON BONTRAGER is an associate professor at Georgia Highlands College. He has published articles in *Church History* and the *Journal of the Early Republic*. His manuscript on American cultural memory from the Civil War to the Great War is under contract with the University of Nebraska Press. He holds history degrees from Central Michigan University and Georgia State University where he earned his PhD.

WILLIAM P. BRANDON, PhD, MPH, CPH, Emeritus MMF Distinguished Professor of Health Policy at UNC Charlotte, graduated Phi Beta Kappa from Johns Hopkins and earned degrees from London School of Economics (MSc, Government), Duke (PhD, Political Science), UNC Chapel Hill School of Public Health (MPH) and professional public health certification. Before UNCC he taught at University of Rochester Medical School, Seton Hall, and Baruch (CUNY). His scholarship includes many publications, faculty fellowships at

JHU's SPH (Robert Wood Johnson Foundation), Oman Medical College (Fulbright), NC State (GSK), Hasting Center (NEH), Georgetown (NEH), Columbia (NEH), and considerable extramural research funding.

KARL CAMPBELL is associate professor of history at Appalachian State University where he teaches courses in recent United States and North Carolina history. A graduate of Warren Wilson College (BA) and the University of North Carolina at Chapel Hill (MA, PhD), he is the author of *Senator Sam Ervin, Last of the Founding Fathers* and is writing a biography of former North Carolina Governor Luther Hodges.

An independent scholar, **ANNETTE COX** received degrees in history from UNC-Greensboro and UNC-Chapel Hill. A specialist in textile history, she has published in *Business History Review*, the *Journal of Southern History*, and the *North Carolina Historical Review*.

LEE CRAIG is Alumni Distinguished Professor of Economics at North Carolina State University. He has published six books, including *Josephus Daniels: His Life and Times,* and more than one hundred scholarly articles, chapters, and reviews. He was a chapter editor of *Historical Statistics of the United States* and is currently on the editorial boards of *Cliometrica* and *Historical Methods*. He received his PhD from Indiana University.

JEFFREY J. CROW is the former director of the Office of Archives and History and deputy secretary of the North Carolina Department of Cultural Resources. He received his PhD from Duke University where he was elected to Phi Beta Kappa. He is the author or editor of numerous publications on North Carolina and southern history. His most recent publication, coedited with Larry E. Tise, is *New Voyages to Carolina: Reinterpreting North Carolina History* (2017).

MELISSA EDMUNDSON earned her PhD from the University of South Carolina and is a lecturer of English at Clemson University. She is author of *Women's Ghost Literature in Nineteenth-Century Britain* (2013) and *Women's Colonial Gothic Writing, 1850–1930: Haunted Empire* (2018). In addition to women's writing, she also specializes in WWI literature and has published essays on Wilfred Owen, Rebecca West, H. D. Everett, and Rose Macaulay.

Independent Scholar and Adjunct Instructor **PAMELA EDWARDS** has authored numerous articles, including "Nurturing Birth and Death in Our Southern Appalachian Homes," *Anthology of Appalachian Writers* (2013), "West Virginia Women in World War II" *West Virginia History* (2008), and "Entrepreneurial Networks and the Textile Industry" *Technology, Innovation, and*

Southern Industrialization (2008). She holds degrees from Appalachian State University and a PhD from the University of Delaware.

GARY R. FREEZE is the William R. Weaver Professor of Humanities at Catawba College. He is the author of a local history trilogy, *The Catawbans: Crafters of a North Carolina County* (1995), *Pioneers in Progress* (2003), and *Boomers and Bypasses* (2016), and of a textbook, *North Carolina: People and Progress* (2016). He holds a BA, MA, and PhD from the University of North Carolina at Chapel Hill.

KURT GESKE is a retired trial lawyer and retired Army Reserve officer with the rank of Major. He currently serves as the director of the Gaston County (NC) Department of Veterans Services. He has BA and JD degrees from Santa Clara University, and an MA (History) from UNC Charlotte.

JANET G. HUDSON is author of *Entangled by White Supremacy: Reform in World War I Era South Carolina* (2009) (2010 George C. Rogers Jr. Award). Her project on African American soldiers from North Carolina who served in World War I can be found at www.blacksoldiersmattered.com. She earned an MA and PhD from the University of South Carolina.

A professor of history at Edinboro University, **JERRA JENRETTE** has published in the *Historical Journal of Massachusetts*, the *Journal of Popular Culture*, the *Journal of Erie Studies*, and *West Virginia History*. Most recently, she published a brief article on "Salem and Religion" in the *Encyclopedia of Religion and Popular Culture* (2016). She has degrees from Mars Hill College, Appalachian State University, and a PhD from West Virginia University.

VINCE LOWERY is an associate professor of humanities and history at the University of Wisconsin, Green Bay. Lowery's article, "The Transatlantic Dreams of the Port City Prophet: The Rural Reform Campaign of Hugh MacRae," received the 2013 R. D. W. Connor Award from the Historical Society of North Carolina. He is also the co-editor of *The Dunning School: Historians, Race, and the Meaning of Reconstruction* (2013) with John David Smith. He earned degrees in history from James Madison University and the University of North Carolina, Wilmington, and a PhD from the University of Mississippi.

A Senior Lecturer at the University of North Carolina at Charlotte, **SHEPHERD W. MCKINLEY** is the author of *North Carolina: New Directions for an Old Land* (2006) and *Stinking Stones and Rocks of Gold: Phosphate, Fertilizer, and Industrialization in Postbellum South Carolina* (2014 George C. Rogers Jr. Award). He has degrees from Duke University and UNC Charlotte, and a PhD from the University of Delaware.

JONATHAN F. PHILLIPS, Dean of Academics, United States Marine Corps Command and Staff College, joined the faculty at the United States Marine Corps Command and Staff College in January 2010 and served as a security studies department head from 2012–2016. His scholarly interests include: American military affairs, civil-military relations, private military contractors, and humanitarian assistance/disaster relief missions. He earned a PhD at the University of North Carolina at Chapel Hill.

An assistant professor of history at Meredith College, **ANGELA P. ROBBINS** is the author of "Alice Morgan Person," in volume one of *North Carolina Women: Their Lives and Times* (2014.) She received her PhD in history in 2010 from UNC-Greensboro, where she specialized in women's history.

STEVEN SABOL is a professor of history at UNC Charlotte. He earned his PhD from Georgia State University. His most recent book, *"The Touch of Civilization": Comparing American and Russian Internal Colonization,* appeared in 2017. He is the former editor of First World War Studies and Nationalities Papers. His current research includes projects ranging from the first Red Scare in the US, Russia in the First World War, to Swedish immigration to the US.

INDEX